INVITATION TO
CRITICAL THINKING

INVITATION TO CRITICAL THINKING

Second Edition

Vincent E. Barry
Bakersfield College

Joel Rudinow
Sonoma State University

Holt, Rinehart and Winston, Inc.

Fort Worth   Chicago   San Francisco   Philadelphia
Montreal   Toronto   London   Sydney   Tokyo

Publisher: Ted Buchholz
Acquisitions Editor: Jo-Anne Weaver
Senior Project Editor: Dawn Youngblood
Production Manager: Tad Gaither
Manager of Art & Design: Guy Jacobs
Text Design: Tom Dawson/DUO Design Group
Cover Design: Guy Jacobs

LIBRARY OF CONGRESS CATALOGING-IN-PUBLICATION DATA

Barry, Vincent E.
    Invitation to critical thinking/by Vincent E. Barry and Joel Rudinow
    —2nd ed.
          P. cm.
    Bibliography: p.
    Includes index.
    1. Critical Thinking. 2. Logic. I. Rudinow, Joel. II. Title
BC177.B35   1989   89-11059
160—dc20   CIP

ISBN: 0-03-014213-X

Address Editorial Correspondence To: 301 Commerce Street, Suite 3700,
                                        Fort Worth, TX 76102

Address Orders To: 6277 Sea Harbor Drive, Orlando, FL 32887
                       1-800-782-4479, or 1-800-433-0001 (in Florida)

Printed in the United States of America

0 1 2 3   039   9 8 7 6 5 4 3 2 1

Drawing by David Suter. Reprinted by permission. (Page 65.)

Holt, Rinehart and Winston, Inc.
The Dryden Press
Saunders College Publishing

One of the most exciting developments in education in recent years has been the emergence of courses in informal logic and critical thinking designed to help students develop skills and dispositions for reasoning effectively and independently in real-life practical situations. The goal of such instruction is to equip students with the skills they need to assess ordinary, everyday arguments logically and to use these assessments in solving problems, in making decisions about what to do and what to believe, and in expressing themselves orally and in writing. We share these goals and have written the second edition of *Invitation to Critical Thinking,* with such courses in mind. Specifically, we intend the book to (1) help students understand and evaluate arguments of some substance, depth, and complexity—tasks that many students find troublesome; (2) help students learn to deal intelligently and autonomously with the mass media, through which so much of the information confronting each of us is presented; and (3) help students develop critical standards of assessment and judgment to apply to their own thinking and writing, for success in college as well as their intellectual development in general, depend on intellectual autonomy, which in turn requires the ability and the willingness to "be one's own best critic".

Like the first edition of *Invitation to Critical Thinking,* the second edition is organized into four main sections: "Awareness", "Analysis", "Evaluation", and "Generation". Part One (*Awareness*) consists of Chapters 1–3, which are intended to effect a kind of consciousness raising. Before confronting arguments, we want students to be aware of some common blocks to effective thinking, of the centrality of language in thinking, and of the impact of mass media on thinking.

Part Two (*Analysis*), consisting of Chapters 4–6, systematically introduces the notion of an argument and specific strategies and procedures for identifying arguments, breaking them down into their structural elements, diagramming the structural relationships among these elements, and discovering and filling in their missing elements.

Part Three (*Evaluation*) consists of Chapters 7–12 and presents a comprehensive overview of, and an integrated approach to, the evaluation of arguments, and places argument evaluation ultimately in the overall context of reading comprehension.

Part Four (*Generation*), consisting of Chapters 13 and 14, helps students to integrate the entire range of sensitivities, strategies and skills presented in the book into their own thinking projects and activities, particularly their own problem solving and argumentative essay composition.

The organization of the book hints at some of the topics covered. The following is a more detailed list of topics, including those that are new (√√) and those that are substantially revised (√) in this edition.

        What critical thinking is and is not (Chapter 1)

√   Some common obstacles to critical thinking, including self-deception, egocentricity and ethnocentricity (Chapter 1)

√   Functions of language (Chapter 2)

√√   Meaning and linguistic conventions (Chapter 2)

√   Persuasive advertising techniques (Chapter 2)

        Television's impact on thought and behavior (Chapter 3)

        News media and the forces that shape judgments of newsworthiness (Chapter 3)

        Arguments: what they are, and how to recognize them (Chapter 4)

        A method for diagramming ("casting") argument structure (Chapter 5)

√   Methodology and guidelines for filling in missing premises (Chapter 6)

√√   Deductive validity and argument forms (Chapter 7)

√   Methodology and guidelines for verifying assertions (Chapter 7)

√   Fifty-five common informal fallacies of language, relevance, and evidence (Chapters 8–10)

        A comprehensive seven-step format for evaluating both short arguments and longer argumentative essays (Chapters 11–12)

        Methodology and guidelines for writing argumentative essays (Chapter 13)

√√   Methodology, guidelines, and strategies for problem-solving (Chapter 14)

Pedagogically, the text is designed to encourage, guide, and reinforce the student's grasp of the material, and at the same time to foster independence. Each part begins with an overview of the material to be covered in its chapters, and each chapter opens with the highlights of the chapter in the sequence of coverage. Periodic "Quick Check" exercises are provided in almost all the chapters for immediate reinforcement. Answers and comments for most of these are collected in Appendix 1. Each chapter is briefly summarized and reviewed, and supplied with "Applications" exercises for further study and analysis. New to this edition are a recommended supplementary reading list (Appendix 2) and a glossary of basic critical thinking terminology (Appendix 3).

The authors wish to acknowledge the support, guidance, and encouragement of the many individuals who have contributed to the writing of this book. In addition to Philip A. Pecorino of Queensboro Community College, Peter Angeles of Santa Barbara City College, Phyllis Woloshin of Oakton Community College and Anita Silvers of San Francisco State University, who contributed especially constructive reviews of the manuscript of the first edition, the present edition owes much to a great many valued colleagues and students.

The new member of this writing team would like to thank Jo-Anne Weaver and Dawn Youngblood of Holt, Rinehart and Winston, who shepherded the project smoothly through editorial and production phases.

Working with Vincent Barry as co-author has also been a great pleasure. He gave free reign, along with encouraging support and constructive suggestions, which made writing much easier than it would otherwise have been. George Freund of Santa Rosa Junior College and Philip Pecorino each gave detailed and helpful recommendations for revision of the text. The collegiality, support, and encouragement of the members of the Department of Philosophy at both Sonoma State University and Santa Rosa Junior College have been invaluable throughout this project. Special thanks are also due to Richard Paul and the staff of the Center for Critical Thinking and Moral Critique at Sonoma State University for the opportunity to work in a deep and concentrated way in the area of critical thinking and critical thinking instruction. Richard Abrahams gave access to and instruction on the computer and software, without which this project couldn't have been accomplished. Penny Caudle has been a tireless teaching assistant and shared, along with Ian McCarthy, in the work of producing an instructor's manual. Finally, and most important, thanks and a big hug to my wife, Dawn, for helping me stick with it and for putting up with me while I did.

Joel Rudinow
Sonoma, California

CONTENTS

Preface   v

PART 1: AWARENESS

Chapter 1: Blocks to Critical Thinking   1

Critical Thinking: What it is and What it is not   2
Blocks to Critical Thinking   8
     Frame of Reference   9
     Egocentricity and Resistance to Change   10
     Wishful Thinking and Self-Deception   11
     Ethnocentricity and Cultural Conditioning   12
     Hasty Moral Judgment   12
     Reliance on Authority   13
     Labels   15
Summary   16
Applications   17

Chapter 2: Communication I: Language and Advertising   21

Functions of Language   22
     Multiple Functions   24
     Quick Check on the Functions of Language*   25
Meaning in Language: Language as Convention   25
Dimensions of Meaning: Denotation and Connotation   28
Definition   29
     Denotative Definition   30
     Logical Definition   30
     Quick Check on Logical Definition*   33
     Stipulative Definition   33
     Persuasive Definition   34
     Quick Check on Stipulative and Persuasive
        Definitions*   35
     Ambiguity and Vagueness   35
Issues and Disputes   36
     Factual Issues and Disputes   37
     Evaluative Issues and Disputes   38
     Interpretive Issues and Disputes   38
     Quick Check on Disputes*   39
The Information Environment   40
Advertising   42
     False Implication   43
     Quick Check on False Implication*   44

Contents

Ambiguity and Vagueness in Advertising   44
    Quick Check on Ambiguity and Vagueness
      in Advertising*   47
    Exaggeration   47
      Quick Check on Exaggeration*   50
    Psychological Appeals   50
    Hidden Facts   52
Summary   54
Applications   57

Chapter 3: Communication II: Television and the News   63

Television's Impact on Thought and Behavior   63
    Television's Reality Warp   65
      Quick Check on Television's Reality Warp   69
News   70
    Newsworthiness   72
      Quick Check on Newsworthiness   76
    Values   77
    Objectivity   77
    The Dramatic and the Visual   79
    Efficiency and Economy   80
      Quick Check on News Values   82
    News Sources   82
Summary   87
Applications   90

PART 2: ANALYSIS

Chapter 4: The Anatomy of Arguments   93

Argument   93
Argument Identification   95
      Quick Check on Argument Identification*   96
Argument Analysis   97
    Premises and Conclusions   97
    Signal Words   98
      Conclusion Signals   98
      General Area Premise Signals   99
      A Caution Concerning Ambiguity   100
      Specific Premise Signals   101
      Arguments Without Signals   102
      Quick Check on Argument Analysis*   103
    Incompletely Stated Arguments   104
    Unexpressed Conclusions   105
    Unexpressed Premises   105
      Quick Check on Incompletely Stated
       Arguments*   107
    Premise Support   107
      Quick Check on Premise Support   109
Summary   110
Applications   111

Chapter 5: Casting Arguments   117

Argument Organization: Series and Chain   119
    *Quick Check on Argument Organization**   120
A Casting Method   121
    *Quick Check on Casting**   125
Casting Support Premises   126
    *Quick Check on Casting Premise Support**   131
Casting Unexpressed Premises and Conclusions   133
    *Quick Check on Casting Unexpressed
    Premises and Conclusions**   134
Guidelines for Casting Rhetorical Features   135
    *Quick Check on Casting Rhetorical
    Features**   141
Summary   142
Applications   144

Chapter 6: Missing Premises   149

The Importance of Filling in Premises   149
The Difficulties of Filling in Premises   152
When to Fill in Premises   154
    The "What-if" Strategy   154
    *Quick Check on the "What-if" Strategy**   155
Guidelines for Reconstructing Premises   155
    Plausibility   156
    *Quick Check on Plausibility**   157
    Relevance   157
    Topic Coverage Strategy   158
    *Quick Check on Relevance and the Topic
    Coverage Strategy**   158
    Fidelity to the Arguer's Position   159
    *Quick Check on Filling in Missing
    Premises**   161
Longer Arguments   163
Summary   168
Applications   170

PART 3: EVALUATION

Chapter 7: Criticizing Arguments   175

Cogency   176
Argument Form   176
    Deductive Validity   179
    *Quick Check on the Concept of Deductive
    Validity**   179
    Formal Fallacies   179
    A Fool-Proof Test for Deductive Validity   180
    *Quick Check on Testing for Deductive
    Validity**   182

Contents

Some Additional Deductive Argument Forms — 182
   Four Forms With Hypothetical Premises — 182
   A Deductive Form Involving Disjunction — 185
   Quick Check on Valid Deductive Arguments — 186
Inductive Arguments — 187
   Deductive and Inductive Signal Words — 188
   Quick Check on Valid Inductive Arguments — 188
   Strength in Inductive Arguments — 189
   Assessing Inductive Strength — 190
   Quick Check on Inductive Strength* — 191
Truth — 192
   Verification — 193
   Quick Check on Verification and Cogency* — 194
   Necessary Truths — 194
   Verifying Factual Assertions — 195
   Observations — 195
   Hypotheses — 196
   Quick Check on Verifying Factual Assertions — 197
   Evaluative Disputes and Value Judgments — 197
   Quick Check on Value Judgments* — 198
   Verifying Value Judgments — 199
   Quick Check on Clarifying Language* — 202
   Weighing Reasons and Arguments — 203
Summary — 205
Applications — 206

Chapter 8: Criticizing Arguments II: Informal Fallacies of Language — 209

Informal Fallacies — 209
   Organization of the Informal Fallacies — 211
Fallacies of Ambiguity — 212
   Equivocation — 212
   Amphiboly — 213
   Accent — 214
   Composition — 214
   Division — 215
   Quick Check on Fallacies of Ambiguity* — 215
Rhetorical Fallacies — 216
   Abuse of Vagueness — 216
   Assumption-Loaded Labels — 217
   Euphemism — 217
   Extreme Quantifiers and Intensifiers — 219
   Minimizers — 219
   Rhetorical Questions — 220
   Innuendo — 220
   Complex Question — 221
   The Phantom Distinction — 222
Summary — 222
Applications — 223

Chapter 9: Criticizing Arguments III:
Informal Fallacies of Relevance   227

Irrelevant Appeals   228
    Ad Hominem   228
      Abusive Ad Hominem   229
      Circumstantial Ad Hominem   230
      Guilt by Association   230
      Genetic Appeal   231
      Poisoning the Well   231
      Quick Check on Ad Hominem Appeals*   232
    Appeal to Authority   233
      Invincible Authority   233
      Irrelevant Expertise   234
      Testimonials   234
      Unidentified Experts   235
      Experts With Axes to Grind   235
      Division of Expert Opinion   235
      Popularity   236
      Positioning   236
      Tradition   237
      Novelty   237
      Provincialism   238
      Quick Check on Appeals to Authority*   238
    Emotional Appeals   239
      Mob Appeal   239
      Appeal to Pity   240
      Appeal to Fear or Force   240
      Quick Check on Emotional Appeals*   241
    Diversion   242
      Humor or Ridicule   242
      Two Wrongs   242
      Tu Quoque   243
      Common Practice   243
      Straw Person   243
      Red Herring   244
    Summary   244
    Applications   246

Chapter 10: Criticizing Arguments IV:
Informal Fallacies of Evidence   251

Fallacies of Statistical Inference   252
    Small Sample   252
    Unrepresentative Sample   253
      Slanted Study   254
      Bad Base Line   254
    Suppressed Evidence   255
    Gamblers' Fallacies   256
      Quick Check on Fallacies of Statistical
      Inference*   257

Contents

Fallacies of Comparison   258
   Questionable Analogy   258
   Questionable Classification   260
     Quick Check on Fallacies of Comparison*   261
Fallacies of Questionable Cause   261
   Confusing Correlations With Causes   262
   Overlooking a Common Cause   262
   Post Hoc   262
   Causal Oversimplification   262
   Slippery Slope   263
     Quick Check on Fallacies of Questionable Cause*   264
Unwarranted Assumptions   265
   False Dilemma   265
   Begging the Question   266
   Invincible Ignorance   266
   Arguing From Ignorance   266
     Quick Check on Unwarranted Assumptions*   267
Some Additional Informal Strategies for Critizing Arguments   268
   Checking for Consistency   268
   Tracing Implications   269
A Final Word of Caution   269
Summary   270
Applications   272

Chapter 11: Applying a Format   277

Format for Analysis and Evaluation   277
   Step 1: Clarify Meaning   278
   Step 2: Identify Conclusion and Premises   278
   Step 3: Cast the Argument   278
   Step 4: Fill in Missing Premises   279
   Step 5: Examine the Main Premises and Support for Justification   280
   Step 6: Examine the Arguments for Fallacies   280
   Step 7: Give an Overall Evaluation   281
Applying the Seven Steps   282
   Argument 1   282
   Argument 2   284
   Argument 3   287
Summary   290
Applications   291

Chapter 12: The Extended Argument   297

Organization   297
   Thesis   298
     Quick Check on Thesis Identification*   300
   Macro and Micro Analysis   302
An Essay Critiqued   302

Contents

A Second Essay Critiqued 311
An Alternative Casting Method: The Outline 320
Summary 321
Applications 322

PART 4: GENERATION

Chapter 13: Writing the Argumentative Essay 331

Argument and Persuasion 332
The Thesis 332
Step 1: Selecting Subjects 333
Step 2: Focusing: Identifying Possible Topics 334
Step 3: Focusing: Selecting and Limiting the Topic 335
Step 4: Determining Your Attitude Toward the Topic 336
Step 5: Writing the Thesis Statement 337
Step 6: Testing the Thesis Statement 338
Quick Check on Thesis Formulation 338
Main Points 339
Audience Awareness 340
Persona 342
Quick Check on Audience and Persona 342
Appreciating Your Opponent's Position 344
Anticipating Objections 345
Organizational Approaches 345
Inductive Approach 346
Pro-and-Con Approach 346
Cause-and-Effect Approach 347
Analysis-of-Alternatives Approach 348
*Quick Check on Organization** 349
Testing the Logic of the Essay 350
Step 1: Construct an Outline 351
Step 2: Indicate Relationships Between Main Points and Thesis and Between Support Material and Main Points 352
Step 3: Fill in Missing Premises 352
Step 4: Examine the Outline for Possible Informal Fallacies 353
Writing the Essay 355
Beginning 355
Developing 357
Ending 358
Summary 359
Applications 361

Chapter 14: Solving Problems 363

An Everyday Problem 364
Core Skills 364

Contents

Awareness   365
    Sharpening Observation Skills   365
    Problem Finding   366
Analysis   367
    Defining the Problem   367
    Clarifying the Problem   368
    Clarifying Available Information   368
    Recognizing Patterns and Relationships   368
Evaluation and Generation   370
    Evaluating Options   370
    Evaluating Consequences   370
    Evaluating the Analysis   371
    Challenging Assumptions   371
    Redefining the Problem   372
    Evaluating Strategies   373
    Evaluating and Generating Information   373
    Quick Check on Core Skills   374
More Problem Solving Strategies   376
    Breaking a Problem Down Into Sub-Problems   376
    Working Backward   377
    Analogous Problems   377
    Quick Check on Problem Solving Strategies   378
Myths About Problem Solving   378
    Problem Solving is Ineffable   379
    All Problems are Soluble   379
Summary   380
Applications   382

Appendix 1: Answers to Starred * Quick Checks   385

Appendix 2: Suggestions for Further Reading   409

Appendix 3: Glossary   415

Index   417

INVITATION TO
CRITICAL THINKING

PART ONE

AWARENESS

BLOCKS TO CRITICAL THINKING

1

In 1988 voters in the state of California were presented with not one, but SIX separate ballot initiative measures, sponsored by a diverse array of interest groups each claiming to provide the definitive answer to the question of insurance reform and regulation in the state. A consumer interest group proposed a measure providing for an elected officer to regulate insurance rates and also calling for rate rollbacks, among other changes. The insurance industry countered with a barrage of measures, including a "no-fault" proposal and a measure to limit lawyer contingency fees. The lawyers countered with measures of their own, including, with the collaboration of Mothers Against Drunk Driving, a "good driver" initiative.

During the heat of the campaign we asked our students for their views on insurance reform. After all, they were of voting age; most of them drove, so the question of how insurance rate structures are regulated affected their lives directly; and there was no shortage of information in circulation at the time. The response oscillated between cynical indifference to the entire issue and frustration bordering on rage. The proposed measures were not circulated generally until the Voter's Manual was sent to all registered voters just prior to the election, and they were written in complicated and, for most voters, impenetrable legalese. Yet voters were besieged for months prior to the election with appeals for support from all sides. Some $75 million was spent on saturation television advertising, and literally tons of paper were circulated throughout the state in the form of direct-mail campaign literature extolling the virtues of this measure and (more typically) decrying the deficiencies of that one. "What do you want from me?" a typical student said. "One group says what the other denies. I don't know what to make of any of it!"

This is not only a typical, but an understandable response when we are faced with an avalanche of contentious and conflicting claims. And since that is so frequently what we are faced with, we often read or hear something and simply don't know what to make of it. Put another way, we are often unable to react critically to the information or claims we encounter. As a result we react emotionally—with fear, anger, outrage, even despair. The other side of the coin is that, unable to formulate intelligent viewpoints of our own, we rely on the same kinds of emotional, even irrelevant, appeals to back up what we assert.

It should be encouraging to learn that with some basic critical thinking skills a great deal of this sort of confusion and frustration can be avoided. Perhaps, like our students, you don't know what to make of much of what you read and hear. Or perhaps you don't know how to go about formulating rational positions on personal and social issues. If so, you can benefit immensely from developing some basic critical thinking skills.

This book should help you do just that. It is meant to assist you in developing a rational basis for your beliefs by providing procedures for analyzing, testing, and evaluating your opinions and those of others.

This book is divided into four main parts: "Awareness," "Analysis," "Evaluation," and "Generation." Part One ("Awareness") is devoted to consciousness raising. It aims to make you aware of (1) the nature of critical thinking and blocks to exercising it, (2) the centrality of language in thinking and in expressing what is thought, and (3) the impact of the information environment on how we see and think about the world and ourselves.

Part Two ("Analysis") introduces you to some basic skills you need for understanding communication designed to convince you of something. Specifically, it shows you how to identify arguments, portray their structures, and fill in their missing assumptions.

Part Three ("Evaluation") teaches you how to respond intelligently to arguments by systematically criticizing and testing them. It includes a seven-step procedure for argument evaluation and gives special attention to argumentative essays.

Finally, Part Four ("Generation") helps you apply what you've learned in the preceding parts to constructing your own arguments and solving problems. It shows you how to use your critical thinking skills in writing argumentative essays, such as those you are typically asked to compose in college, and gives you strategies for reasoning your way out of problems and toward their solutions.

This opening chapter attempts to make you aware of what critical thinking is and why most of us don't, can't, or won't think critically. Its underlying assumption is that the first step toward becoming an effective thinker is to become aware of and start cultivating habits of mind that allow a calm, rational examination of statements and issues.

CRITICAL THINKING: WHAT IT IS AND WHAT IT IS NOT

Before proceeding, indicate which of the following five statements you think are true and which you think are false:

1. Critical thinking is the same as disagreement.

2

2. Critical thinking aims to embarrass or humiliate, allowing you to dominate somebody else.
3. Critical thinking entails nitpicking.
4. Critical thinking requires no imagination or creativity.
5. Critical thinking can be applied only to the beliefs and positions of others.

If you think any of these statements is true, you are misinformed about critical thinking. But don't feel bad. There's widespread ignorance among the well- and not-so-well-educated about the nature and function of critical thinking. And the number of people who don't, can't, or won't think critically is even greater.

Just what is critical thinking? We can begin to answer this question by considering the five preceding statements.

1. Critical thinking is *not* the same as disagreement. There is a considerable difference between disagreement and critical thinking. A disagreement is a clash of views. When you assert an opinion and someone else denies it or states an opposing opinion, you are disagreeing but not yet thinking critically. For example:

> *HE:* Handguns should be outlawed.
> *SHE:* There should be no gun-control legislation.
> *HE:* There's far too much violence on television. Why just the other night . . .
> *SHE:* Compared with movies, there isn't much violence on television.
> *HE:* Premarital sex increases the chances of a successful marriage. Why look at my wife and me . . .
> *SHE:* I don't see how having sex before marriage could improve the marriage's chances of succeeding.

Obviously, disputes like this are commonplace. When the parties to the dispute feel strongly about their positions, they are likely to reassert them, as if stating them again and again, perhaps in other words, will establish them as true. Although such disagreements call for critical thinking if the parties to them are to reach agreement or enlightenment, they are not themselves examples of critical thinking.

Critical thinking involves determining and assessing the reasons for an opposing view. It aims to find out whether a position is worth holding, thereby serving as a basis for further discussion and inquiry that, ideally, will lead the disputants to a better understanding of an issue. You believe handguns should be outlawed; someone else doesn't. If you're thinking critically, you'll closely inspect the reasons for and against each position. You don't merely keep reasserting your positions. Rather, you look at the reasons for each other's position. Just as important, each of us should be willing to have our positions subjected to this kind of scrutiny.

2. Critical thinking *does not* aim to embarrass or humiliate, and it *does not* allow you to dominate somebody else. Thinking critically *does* give one a kind of power. After all, if you can determine and assess the reasons for a belief, if you can make a discussion more enlightening, you stand a good chance of getting to the nub of an issue, of solving problems, of gaining greater control over your life, of attaining truth. In short, critical thinking does help you gain knowledge, and knowledge, as commonly observed, is a kind of power.

But notice that the power critical thinking gives you is the power that comes from knowing, from attaining truth and justified belief. It is not the tyranny of imposing one's will on another, of inflicting humiliation, or even of trying to persuade another of your viewpoint. The goal of critical thinking is the justification of belief. A belief is justified when better reasons count for it than against it. Critical thinking helps you take measure of your beliefs. When they are justified, you know you have a solid basis for believing what you do, that you can defend your beliefs if necessary, and that you have legitimate grounds for action. But you can never *justify* your beliefs by dominating or humiliating others, or even by persuading others to believe as you do. Those who think they can are tyrants, not critical thinkers.

3. Critical thinking *does not* entail nitpicking. A nitpicker is one who is unduly preoccupied with minutiae, with trivial details. The critical thinker, by contrast, is concerned with substance, not trivia. Yes, thinking critically requires analysis, which in turn calls for attention to detail. But the details the critical thinker attends to are both relevant to a position and significant to its support. They are not side or trivial issues.

Suppose you claim, "Many children enjoy watching Saturday-morning television. So they aren't being exploited." Upon hearing this assertion, someone replies, "Just what do you mean by 'enjoy watching'?" And you then spend the rest of the afternoon wrestling over the meaning of "enjoy watching."

Language clarification certainly is an important part of thinking critically. If we don't have the same understanding of the meaning of words, we lack a common basis for thinking critically about a subject. But that doesn't mean that every term always needs to be defined before we can proceed to think critically.

In the following episode of Peanuts, Linus gets some advice from Charlie Brown about paying critical attention to detail in an argument. But Linus has trouble applying it in a relevant and substantive way.

The use of some terms simply is not problematic. What Lucy and Linus both mean and understand by "stomach" is probably the same. Even more important, it's not what's at issue. Similarly, if someone asks you what you mean by "enjoy watching," they are very likely nitpicking. Worse, they're probably steering you down the path of some semantic dead end while illumination of the real issue lies in another direction.

Incidentally, nitpickers like to introduce irrelevancies. For example, suppose someone said to you, "But I know a kid who doesn't enjoy watching Saturday-morning television," or "Saturday-morning television is full of commercials," or "Saturday-morning television is replacing outdoor recreation." Maybe so, but these observations are irrelevant to the issue at hand: whether or not kids who enjoy watching Saturday-morning television are being exploited. So far, nothing has been offered which shows that the person is thinking critically about what you asserted. What has been offered is a mix of hairsplitting and irrelevancy.

4

"Peanuts," by Charles M. Schulz, 1969. Reprinted by permission of UFS, Inc.

In contrast, suppose someone said to you, "But is it necessarily true that when kids are enjoying themselves they are not being exploited?" Now we're getting to the heart of your position, of what you're assuming. It is the assumption that allows you to claim that because many kids enjoy watching Saturday-morning television they are not being exploited. The person has zeroed in on something both relevant and significant to your position, something you must toss around if you're interested in thinking critically about this important matter. If at this point you accuse the person of nitpicking, then you simply don't know the difference between thinking critically and nitpicking. And if you say that the person is dragging in side issues, you simply can't distinguish between the relevant and the irrelevant, the significant and the trivial.

Of course, focusing on what is both relevant and significant to a position isn't always an easy matter. In fact, in complex discourse it can be a formidable challenge. Most of us need training to distinguish the relevant from the irrelevant, the significant from the trivial. In part, the study of critical thinking is designed to provide this training.

4. Critical thinking *does* require imagination and creativity. Some view critical thinking as a dry-as-dust exercise in analysis. Although it's true that critical thinking requires painstaking analysis, it also can call for creative thinking, for it sometimes requires the formulation of examples to discredit a position. Here's a very simple example. Suppose a couple spends $62 in twenty minutes while shopping at a supermarket. Upon leaving the store, the husband mumbles, "Sixty-two bucks in twenty minutes! Why, this inflation is out of control!"

His wife demurs. "Not necessarily," she says. "Just yesterday I was in there for over an hour and spent only twelve dollars. And the Warbucks next door just spent over thirty thousand dollars in ten minutes."

"Yes, but that was on a Mercedes."

"That's my point," says the wife. "Inflation isn't measured by how fast we spend our money but by how much our money can buy compared with some previous time."

This woman is thinking critically; she is examining what her husband asserted. But notice how she does it. Through an imaginative use of examples, she makes the point that inflation isn't measured by how fast we spend our money, as her husband implied, but by what our money can buy relative to some past time. When critical thinking calls for such imaginative use of examples, it is creative.

Critical thinkers are also being creative when they formulate possible solutions to a problem or explanations for a phenomenon. Think of a detective, and you'll see what we mean. Yes, good detectives must test and evaluate solutions or explanations; that is, they must think critically. But they must first be able to devise possible solutions or explanations, what in science are called "hypotheses." Failing that, they can't solve the crime. Coming up with hypotheses requires a fertile imagination, a creative mind.

The relation between critical and creative thinking is perhaps best seen in the laboratory. Consider, for example, how medical researcher Ignaz Semmelweis discovered *and* demonstrated the importance of physician hygiene in patient care.

Between 1844 and 1846, the death rate from a mysterious disease termed "childbed fever" in the First Maternity Division of the Vienna General Hospital averaged an alarming 10 percent. Curiously the rate in the Second Division, where midwives rather than doctors attended the mothers, was only about 2 percent. How could this difference be explained? More important, did the explanation account for the disease itself?

Despite heroic efforts for two years to account for the higher rate of childbed fever in the doctor-supervised division, Semmelweis remained thwarted. Then one day a colleague accidentally cut himself on the finger with a student's scalpel while performing an autopsy. Although the cut seemed harmless enough, the man died shortly thereafter, exhibiting symptoms identical to those of childbed fever. A thought struck Semmelweis. Perhaps doctors and medical students, who spent their mornings doing autopsies before making their divisional rounds, were unwittingly transmitting to the women something they picked up from the cadavers.

By drawing on a vast repertoire of knowledge and experience but also on imagination and intuition, Semmelweis had devised a possible solution to the mystery of childbed fever. Now he had to criticize his explanation, that is, subject it to tests. If Semmelweis was right, then the disease could be checked by requiring the doctors and students to clean their hands before examining patients.

Semmelweis insisted that they do just that. Doctors and students were forbidden to examine patients without first washing their hands in a solution of chlorinated lime. *Voilà!* In 1848 the death rate in the First Division fell to less than 2 percent.

The point is that, although the critical and creative aspects of thinking can be distinguished, they cannot be easily separated. The effective critical thinker inevitably is creative. Sometimes, as in the example involving the husband and wife, creativity yields imaginative examples that point up the weakness of a position. Other times, as with Semmelweis, it yields solutions to a problem or explanations for a phenomenon that then must be tested and evaluated, that is, criticized. Still other times it yields imaginative leaps from assertions to their implications, thereby raising a discussion to a more illuminating level. In such cases a solution, explanation, or proposal has already been made. Upon hearing it the listener makes an imaginative inferential jump that typically is a test of verification. Consider, for example, this exchange:

SUE: People who attempt suicide are looking for sympathy.
SAM: You mean suicide attempts can be explained as appeals for sympathy?
SUE: Exactly.
SAM: If that's the case, then *we could at least expect suicide attempts to be rare in a society that's indifferent or hostile to its individual members.*

You'll probably agree that Sam's inference (which is italicized) shows considerable resourcefulness. For one thing, Sue never quite said what Sam inferred. In fact, she may not have even considered the implication of her position. Furthermore, because no society like the one Sam envisions now exists, Sam probably has never lived in such a society. He may not even be aware of any. Nevertheless, he's able to *imagine* one. And his hypothetical society is most germane, for if the suicide rate in such a society were low, then Sue's position would be supported. Thus, in thinking critically about what Sue said, Sam has devised an imaginative test for it.

5. Critical thinking can be applied *not only* to the beliefs and positions of others *but also to our own.* Although it's true that you can apply critical thinking scalpel-like to dissect the claims you encounter, its application is by no means confined to the views of others. How many times have you pondered a personal problem? Perhaps you agonized about whether to go to college, or what to major in, or whether to marry. Furthermore, as an intelligent, responsible citizen you probably want to clarify your position on important social issues: capital punishment, abortion, gun control, violence on television, nuclear arms control, and the like. The resolution of personal problems and the formulation of viewpoints on social issues call for critical thinking. Indeed, individuals who cannot think critically are like rudderless boats, destined to flounder through life at the mercy of every eddy and crosscurrent that touches them.

The preceding observations suggest that *critical thinking is a process that emphasizes a rational basis for beliefs and provides a set of standards and procedures for analyzing, testing, and evaluating them.* Critical thinking helps you understand and deal with the positions of others and to clarify your own. It aims to give you a basis for justifying beliefs and for directing further investigation and inquiry.

With these preliminary remarks behind us, let's now turn to another issue: the rarity of critical thinking. Although critical thinking may not be as rare as a dog without fleas, it is uncommon enough for us to wonder why. Why don't most people think critically? Why do people find thinking critically so difficult? Why is it that people can so often be taken in by hucksters and confidence artists when just a little critical thinking would protect them from exploitation? Answering these questions calls for a look at some blocks to critical thinking. And this involves taking a look at human nature.

BLOCKS TO CRITICAL THINKING

Let's try a little thought experiment. Try saying the following sentence about yourself:

Some of my beliefs are false.[1]

Some of you are probably having trouble with this. "After all," someone might say, "part of believing something is believing that it's true. So if I were to do an inventory of my beliefs, they'd all seem true to me." Or, to put it another way, "If I knew something was false, I wouldn't believe it. So it doesn't really make sense for me to say that some of my own beliefs are false."

Others of you probably found this a perfectly natural idea. "After all," someone might equally well say, "I've been mistaken in the past. I've learned on numerous occasions, and pretty much throughout my life, that things that I believed to be true were really false. Why should it be any different now? So if I were to do an inventory of my beliefs, I probably wouldn't notice the false ones, but I'd still bet there are some in there somewhere."

Both reactions make a great deal of sense. And together they tell us something important about what critical thinking is and why people find it difficult. The second reaction expresses a kind of intellectual maturity and humility, a recognition of human liability to error. This attitude of intellectual humility, which amounts really to a recognition of one's own human fallibility, is a fundamental characteristic of the critical thinker.

But as the first reaction shows, there are some equally deep-seated obstacles in each of us which stand in the way of development of this attitude. Belief, for example, is a kind of investment of trust or confidence. And once we've made an investment, we're committed. We feel tied in. Like any investment, a belief is inherently difficult to walk away from, even when the evidence begins to mount up that it was a bad investment. The natural inclination is to try one's best to salvage the investment, even to the point of denying the evidence. As we shall see presently, this small point about the nature of belief explains quite a bit about blocks to critical thinking.

Frame of Reference

Let's try another little thought experiment. A moment ago the idea came up of doing an inventory of your own beliefs. Try now to describe what this would actually be like. How long would it take? How would you start? What kind of procedure would you use? How would you keep track?. . . After you've struggled with this for a while, go ahead and start an inventory of your beliefs. Give yourself a measured five minutes and see what you come up with. Try this with somebody else and compare notes.

See if you don't notice that you've got more beliefs to keep track of than you might have thought at first—and beliefs of more different kinds than you might have thought at first. Maybe you began to notice that you have beliefs about what beliefs are and about how many of them you have, and so on.

And consequently you may have begun to wonder about an "inventory control" problem. Have these beliefs that you've just noticed been there all along? Or are they new ones that have now arisen as a result of the fact that you're paying a new and peculiar kind of attention to your beliefs? Five minutes into your inventory, can you be sure that you still have all the beliefs you had when you started?

This too tells us something about blocks to critical thinking. Each of us has a belief structure into which we have incorporated an indefinitely large number of beliefs—so many that trying to count them seems crazy. Most of these beliefs we routinely just assume without any conscious deliberation. So, if you're like most people, the vast bulk of your belief structure is probably "subterranean" and functioning in a largely unexamined way below the threshold of your awareness. The sheer volume of a normal person's belief structure, especially coupled with the largely unexamined status of most of its specific contents, greatly increases the likelihood of mistaken beliefs among them.

Second, your belief structure is not static or permanent. Rather, it undergoes almost constant change and revision as you deal with incoming information. Let's consider how this process normally works.

We live in what has come to be known as the "information age," a label which derives from the awesome volume of information bombarding us on a daily basis. Just think of the amount of material contained in the average metropolitan daily newspaper. Now multiply that by seven days a week, and then again by the number of metropolitan population centers you can think of in a few short minutes. That should be enough to make the point that there's far too much information to pay attention to, let alone absorb. And that's just daily newspapers. Then there are weekly, monthly, quarterly, and annual publications, and books, not to mention radio and television, which together add up to literally hundreds of separate stations, channels, and cable services, many of them broadcasting round the clock. Again, it's obvious that there's just no way to pay attention to it all, let alone absorb it.

Consequently, each of us has to be very selective about where we direct our attention in this overwhelming flow of information. Actually, this is nothing new or peculiar to our age. In fact, it's part of the human condition. There's always more to pay attention to than any of us has attention. And if you're like most people, even within the narrow range of information you become aware of, you continue to be selective. Some incoming information will be actively incorporated into your belief structure, some will be rejected. What do you suppose are the main factors that govern this process? What do you suppose determines these selections?

Among the most important and influential of these factors are the existing contents of your belief structure. The way we deal with incoming information is determined in large part by what we already believe. This is what we mean by a person's "frame of reference" or "world view." *We each have a tendency to view the world, including ourselves, according to our own frame of reference; that is, according to the organized body of accumulated beliefs that we rely on to interpret new experiences and guide our behavior.* So it seems that one's belief structure influences the course of its own ongoing management and development.

Don't forget, large portions of your belief structure normally function unexamined below the threshold of your awareness, which makes it more likely that it contains mistaken beliefs. And beliefs are inherently difficult to give up. So the fact that this same belief structure functions also as a frame of reference against which new information is evaluated and revisions to the belief structure are considered explains quite a bit about human fallibility. Such an arrangement, unavoidable and natural though it may be, makes it much more likely that mistaken beliefs will perpetuate themselves within our belief structures if we don't make a special effort to guard against it.

Egocentricity and Resistance to Change

Let's explore further how difficult it can be to make such a special effort. Not many people regularly read political journals that present views contrary to the ones they hold. Probably even fewer have ever seriously investigated religious views incompatible with their own. And precious few ever consider alternatives to their views of what's right and wrong, good and bad. Indeed, many of us react to beliefs, values, and attitudes that challenge our own with self-righteous contempt.

The fact is that most of us not only avoid views contrary to our own, we systematically expel them from our experience. We resist change. Why?

We resist change partly because we perceive it as a threat to who and what we are and partly because we believe in the superiority of our own culture, in the view that "mine is better—my ideas, my values, my race, my country, my religion." *In a word, we are naturally "egocentric." We are naturally inclined to favor and defend ourselves and the positions, values, traditions, and groups with which we identify ourselves.*

Even the history of science is rife with examples of this kind of resistance to change. For example, Galileo's astronomical treatise, the *Dialogue on the Two Chief Systems of the World* (1632), was a thoughtful and devastating attack on the traditional geocentric view of the universe proposed by the ancient Greek Ptolemy (second century A.D.) and accepted by most scholars and scientists of Galileo's time. Galileo's treatise was therefore an attack not only on the views of those authorities but also on their self-concepts. Predictably enough, they reacted violently. Pope Urban was persuaded that Simplicio, the butt of the whole dialogue, was intended to represent himself. His vanity seriously wounded, the pope ordered Galileo to appear before the Inquisition. Although never formally imprisoned, Galileo was threatened with torture and forced to renounce what he had written. In 1633 he was banished to his country estate. His *Dialogue,* together with the works of Kepler and Copernicus, was placed on the Index of Forbidden Books, from which they were not withdrawn until 1835.

Wishful Thinking and Self-Deception

Not only is our belief structure so constituted as to harbor self-perpetuating falsehoods, but we frequently engage in wishful thinking and even self-deception. No doubt you know people who have on occasion talked themselves into believing things that they knew weren't true, for example, that they were ready for the midterm exam when in fact they weren't really prepared, and knew at some level that they weren't really prepared.

How can this be? you might wonder. How can a person know that something is false and continue to believe it? How can a person be both the successful deceiver and the victim of the deception at the same time? These are very good questions. There is something deeply puzzling about self-deception. If we were perfectly rational creatures, we would no doubt recognize the inconsistency involved in self-deception, and so self-deception probably would never occur. But there is little doubt that it does occur. We are rational creatures, but not perfectly so. We are also (in some ways and at some times) irrational creatures, and our wishes and desires often overwhelm our good sense. So we often persist in believing what we want to believe or what we wish were true in spite of what we know or have every reason to believe. And we do this sometimes at great peril to others and even ourselves.

Why would we do something as irrational as deceive ourselves? someone might ask. But this is not quite as good a question. It seems to be based on the assumption that self-deception is necessarily and always completely irrational. To be more fair, we should be prepared to admit that sometimes the truth is just too painful for people to watch or look at. Some Americans, for example, still find it too painful to confront the ugly reality of the Reagan presidency, which outdid—in scandal and corruption and outright contempt for the American people and the Constitution—all previous presidencies, including the self-described "cancerous" Nixon administration. Some Jews find it too painful to confront the ugly reality of the state of Israel supplying armaments to a white racist government in South Africa. Some people find it too painful to confront the ugly reality of a world poised constantly on the brink of nuclear holocaust. So people go into what some psychologists call "denial." They just refuse to believe it. They just say No. The world contains such monstrous ugliness sometimes that you can't simply say that this kind of self-deception is always *completely* irrational. It *is* always irrational, just not completely so. Of course, self-deception of any sort stands directly in the way of thinking critically.

Ethnocentricity and Cultural Conditioning

So far we have been exploring blocks to critical thinking from the point of view of individual human psychology. We should not overlook the social dimension of human nature. Humans are naturally social beings. We do not survive well or prosper in isolation. Rather, we collect together in groups: families, communities, nations, cultures. Our welfare as individuals is largely determined by how well we do within our groups and how well our groups do. Being a successful member of a successful family in a successful community, nation, or culture is what human welfare is about.

And this has an inevitable impact on our individual psychological lives and belief structures, on how and what we think. Cooperation among the individual group members and group loyalty are both essential to the organization of the group, to the coordination of any group project, to the maintenance of the group as a stable entity. Thus, there is a natural tendency in any group toward conformity and orthodoxy. We tend to incorporate into our belief structure the ideas, attitudes, and values of those in our group. And there arises within any group a hierarchy of authority through which orthodoxy is established and conformity to it is reinforced.

All of this is perfectly natural and understandable in terms of its survival value for the individual, for the group, and for the species. However, it also contributes greatly to our human fallibility, because obviously nothing guarantees that the orthodox views within a given group will always be the correct ones or even the most advantageous ones for the group and its individual members. History provides a steady stream of examples of entire populations getting swept up and misled en masse. Both orthodoxy and conformism constitute blocks to critical thinking.

Hasty Moral Judgment

A moral judgment is an evaluation of someone or something as good or bad, right or wrong. We make moral judgments all the time, and these are largely influenced by cultural conditioning. We term the child abuser an "evil person," and child abuse "wrong," "heinous," or "reprehensible." We denounce naked aggression and welcome efforts to rebuff it. We deplore the liar and admire the truth teller. We take positions on issues such as abortion, capital punishment, and pornography that reflect approval or disapproval. "Abortion should [or should not] be legalized"; "Capital punishment is [or is not] justifiable as the most effective way of deterring certain serious crimes"; "Pornography should [or should not] be carefully controlled." Moral judgments all.

Often we make such judgments hastily. For example, we judge people on the basis of their looks, background, or associations. We base such judgments not on careful consideration of factual evidence but on emotion, prejudice, preconception, intolerance, or self-righteousness. Because hasty moral judgments are essentially nonrational—that is, unreasoned—they blunt the goals of critical thinking: insight and understanding.

This doesn't at all mean that you shouldn't have strong moral beliefs. But there's a big difference between moral convictions that arise out of careful deliberation and those that precede and preclude it.

Reliance on Authority

An authority is an expert source of information outside ourselves. The source can be a single individual (a parent, a teacher, a celebrity, a clergy member, the president), a group of individuals (doctors, educators, a peer group, a national consensus), or even an institution (a religion, a government agency, an educational establishment). Whatever its form, authority exerts considerable influence on our belief structures.

Just think about everything you claim to know that is based on authority. Facts and opinions about world history, the state of your health, the direction of the economy, the events of the day, the existence of God and an afterlife—the list seems endless, the topics unbounded. In fact, without relying on authority, we would know very little of what we take for granted.

But there's a danger. We can so rely on authority that we stop thinking for ourselves. Puzzled about something, we might invoke some authority to decide the answer for us. When dealing with a controversial issue, we might find out what the majority thinks and, looking no further, adopt the same position. Following authority blindly blocks critical thinking and undermines intellectual autonomy.

To get some idea how influential authority can be, consider a series of experiments conducted by psychologist Stanley Milgram in the 1960s.[2] You may know that Milgram's experiment consisted of asking subjects to administer strong electrical shocks to people whom the subjects couldn't see. The subjects supposedly could control the shock's intensity by means of a shock generator with thirty clearly marked voltages, ranging from 15 to 450 volts and labeled from "Slight Shock (15)" to "XXX—Danger! Severe Shock (450)."

Before you think that psychologist Milgram was sadistic, we should point out that the entire experiment was a setup: No one was actually administering or receiving shocks. The subjects were led to believe that the "victims" were being shocked as part of an experiment to determine the effects of punishment on memory. The "victims," who were in fact confederates of the experimenters, were strapped in their seats with electrodes attached to their wrists "to avoid blistering and burning." They were told to make no noise until a "300-volt shock" was administered, at which point they were to make noise loud enough for the subjects to hear (for example, pounding on the walls as if in pain). The subjects were reassured that the shocks, though extremely painful, would cause no permanent tissue injury.

When asked, a number of psychologists said that no more than 10 percent would heed the request to administer a 450-volt shock. In fact, well over half did—twenty-six out of forty. Even after hearing the "victims" pounding, 87.5 percent of the subjects (thirty-five out of forty) applied more voltage. The conclusion seems unmistakable: A significant number of people, when asked by an authority, will hurt others.

Authority not only influences the behavior of people, it also affects their judgment, perhaps even more so. For example, consider these three lines:

A_____ _

B_____ __

C_____ _

Which of the three matches the one below?

_____

Undoubtedly, *B*. Do you think you could ever be persuaded to choose *A* or *C*? Maybe not, but experiments indicate that some individuals can be persuaded to alter their judgments, even when their judgments are obviously correct. These experiments involved several hundred individuals who were asked to match lines just as you did. In each group, however, only one subject was naive, that is, unaware of the nature of the experiment. The others were confederates of the experimenter, who had instructed them to make incorrect judgments in about two-thirds of the cases and to pressure the dissenting naive subjects to alter his or her correct judgment.

The results: When subjects were not exposed to pressure, they inevitably judged correctly. But when the confederates pressured them, the naive subjects generally changed their responses to conform with the unanimous majority judgments. When one confederate always gave the correct answers, naive subjects maintained their positions three-fourths of the time. But when the honest confederate switched to the majority view in later trials, the errors made by naive subjects rose to about the same level as that of subjects who stood alone against a unanimous majority.[3]

Make no mistake about it: Authority cows us. We are impressed, influenced, and intimidated by authority, so much so that, under the right conditions, we abandon our own values, beliefs, and judgments.

Certainly none of this is intended to undermine the legitimacy of authority entirely as a source of information and guidance in developing and managing one's belief structure. When (1) the authority asserting a given view is indeed an expert in the field, (2) authorities are generally agreed on that view, and (3) we can, at least in theory, find out for ourselves whether the view is correct, then we have solid grounds for relying on authority. But even then we must realize that the authority derives its credibility and force ultimately from the weight of evidence supporting the views it asserts.

Authority plays such a influential role in our thinking that we will say more about it later in our study. Here it's enough to note that a slavish reliance on authority blocks critical thinking.

Labels

Labels are essential for communication. They make it possible for us to communicate a complex situation a piece at a time. The use of labels helps us react specifically to some part of the environment and to deal with new and unfamiliar environments by picking out familiar features. For example, there are about four billion entities in the world today corresponding to our label "the human race." We can't possibly deal individually with so many human beings. We can't even individuate the dozens we encounter daily. Instead we must group them, drawing the many into a single unit by means of a label.

But as useful as labels are, they can be blocks to thinking. First, by lumping things into categories, labels ignore individual differences. For example, to call Gloria Steinem a "feminist" is to ignore other aspects of her identity, for Steinem is also a "voter," "licensed driver," "taxpayer," "consumer," "author," and so on. Labeling her a "feminist" encourages us to see her exclusively in terms of that label. The result can be a distortion.

Linguist Irvin Lee gives a graphic example of how the very act of labeling causes us to overlook all other features of an entity, many of which might offer a more accurate representation than the label we choose.

> I knew a man who had lost the use of both eyes. He was called a "blind man." He could also be called an expert typist, a conscientious worker, a good student, a careful listener, a man who wanted a job. But he couldn't get a job in the department store order room where employees sat and typed orders which came over the telephone. The personnel man was impatient to get the interview over. "But you're a blind man," he kept saying, and one could almost feel his silent assumption that somehow the incapacity in one aspect made the man incapable in every other. So blinded by the label was the interviewer that he could not be persuaded to look beyond it.[4]

Besides causing us to overlook individual differences, labels tend to encourage polarization and oversimplification. That is, they encourage us to view things in stark black-and-white terms, for example: "democracy/totalitarianism," "Democrat/Republican," "pro-life/pro-choice," "capitalist/communist," "people who love America/people who do not," "people who pull their own weight/people who do not," and so on.

There is a natural human tendency in this direction anyway. There is, after all, an inherently understandable value in simplicity. We look for simplicity in the answers and solutions we seek, and even more in the questions and problems we face. We find the suspense of doubt and uncertainty inherently uncomfortable, and we're generally in a hurry to arrive at resolution and equilibrium. We often think that if we can manage to see things in simple terms, we stand a far better chance of escaping doubt quickly than if we consider the complexities of an issue.

The danger in this is that we get trapped thinking in terms of mutually exclusive categories and ignore other alternatives, such as compromise positions. The fixed patterns of thought are not altered by incoming information but instead alter it. Rather than allowing us to think critically, they inhibit analysis by obscuring, eliciting knee-jerk reactions, and forcing one to take sides.

Becoming aware of and overcoming the obstacles we've been discussing—developing the skills and dispositions of the critical thinker—are essential to success in a fulfilling career and to success in the wide variety of social roles each of us is destined to play. This can safely be said because the skills and dispositions of critical thinking are essential to something even more fundamental and basic: personal autonomy. Each of us needs to know how to act freely as a human being and how to learn for ourselves. Lacking this knowledge, you remain a slave to the ideas of others and the machines programmed by them. A person who cannot think for herself can never go beyond what others have learned or thought and remains enslaved to the ideas of others. Frankly, we can think of no better way to understand the study of critical thinking than as a set of tools and procedures of self-guidance essential to thinking and learning for oneself.

Summary

This chapter was designed to dispel some common misconceptions about critical thinking and to make you aware of some blocks to thinking critically.

1. Critical thinking is not the same as disagreement.
2. Critical thinking does not aim to embarrass or humiliate.
3. Critical thinking does not entail nitpicking.
4. Critical thinking does require imagination and creativity.
5. Critical thinking can be applied to our own beliefs, as well as to others.

In a nutshell, *critical thinking is a process that emphasizes a rational basis for beliefs and provides a set of standards and procedures for analyzing, testing, and evaluating them.*

Many people don't, can't, or won't think critically. The main reason for this inadequacy is that people fall victim to certain blocks, clichéd patterns of viewing things. Each of us has a belief structure into which we have incorporated an indefinitely large number of beliefs—so many that trying to count them seems crazy. Most of these beliefs we routinely just assume without any conscious deliberation. And beliefs are inherently difficult to give up.

In addition, we each have a tendency to view the world, including ourselves, according to our own frame of reference; that is, according to the organized body of accumulated beliefs that we rely on to interpret new experiences and guide our behavior.

Such an arrangement, unavoidable and natural though it may be, makes it much more likely that mistaken beliefs will perpetuate themselves within our belief structures if we don't make a special effort to guard against it.

But this does not come naturally to us. We are naturally inclined to favor and defend ourselves and the positions, values, traditions, and groups with which we identify ourselves. In addition we have natural tendencies toward wishful thinking, self-deception, hasty moral judgment, and oversimplification.

Nevertheless, critical thinking is necessary if we are to make sense of what we hear and read, gain insight into the information and claims that bombard us, make discussions more illuminating, and develop and evaluate our own positions on issues.

Applications

1. Many subjects typically evoke hasty moral judgments that are culturally conditioned. For example, "honesty" generally elicits the judgments "good" or "desirable," whereas "dishonesty" elicits the judgment "bad" or "undesirable." State the moral judgment that the following subjects typically elicit.

   cheating on one's spouse   racially mixed marriages
   equal opportunity   caring for the elderly
   drug abuse   equal pay for equal work
   pornography   free enterprise
   violence   individuality
   cheating on taxes   welfare

2. Many Americans probably would consider the following statements truisms. State your reasons for accepting or questioning them.

   a. A person who tries hard enough will eventually succeed.
   b. Rich people aren't happy.
   c. A college education is necessary to succeed in life.
   d. Honesty is the best policy.
   e. People who can't find a job simply aren't trying.
   f. Every cloud has a silver lining.
   g. The best offense is a good defense.
   h. The business of America is business itself.

    i.   The best government is the one that governs least.

    j.   Might makes right.

3. Specify whether an individual, a group, or an institution is the authority appealed to in the following passages.

   a. **Joe:** You know, I think I'm going to start banking at Great Western.
      Jill: Why's that?
      Joe: Well, I saw Dennis Weaver do a commercial for them the other day. I figure a guy as successful as Dennis must know something about saving money.

   b. **Frank:** You know, I think all political parties should be entitled to TV time, not just the major ones.
      Winnie: I don't agree. The major parties represent the significant viewpoints. The other parties don't.
      Frank: Why do you say that?
      Winnie: Well, by far the vast majority of Americans belong to the Republican or Democratic parties. So what those parties have to say obviously is important.

   c. **Joyce:** No more Tang for me. I'd prefer something more nutritious.
      George: More nutritious? Don't you realize that NASA chose Tang for its astronauts?
      Joyce: No kidding! Hmm, maybe I won't switch after all.

   d. **Bill:** There's no question that humans are inherently aggressive.
      June: I disagree.
      Bill: If you do, you'll have to buck some real heavyweights, like Darwin, Lorenz, and Ardrey. As for me, I think their endorsement of the aggressionist view offers conclusive evidence for it.

   e. **Stan:** There's no question that the Golden Rule is a sound moral principle.
      Stu: Why do you say that?
      Stan: Because it's basic to every religion and society. You can go back thousands of years and find some version of the Golden Rule operating in society.

4. Which of the following statements would you take on authority? Why? Why not?

   a. Hell exists (meaning the preternatural abode of evil and not, as philosopher Jean-Paul Sartre once suggested, other people).

   b. Sugar contributes to tooth decay.

  c. The earth was once visited by astronaut gods.

  d. $E = mc^2$

  e. The Declaration of Independence was adopted on July 4, 1776.

  f. Mercy killing is immoral.

  g. The Mona Lisa is an outstanding painting.

  h. Democracy is the best form of government.

  i. The Vietnam War was necessary.

  j. Laetrile is not an effective way to treat cancer.

5. State one political, one scientific, one medical, and one religious belief that you take on authority.

6. It's no secret that in our culture women traditionally have been expected to please men and to depend on them, while men play an active role. But the part that labels play in both reflecting and reinforcing this cultural assumption sometimes goes overlooked. For example, women are much more identified with something to eat (e.g., "sugar"), compared with pets (e.g., "chick"), and associated with plants (e.g., "clinging vine") than men are. How many food, pet, and plant labels for women can you list? How many similar labels for men can you list? How do such labels condition people to assume certain social roles?

7. Some labels communicate both a fact and a judgment of that fact. This makes discussions involving religious, racial, and political groups especially complex. For example, to many Americans the word "communist" means simultaneously "one who believes in communism" (fact) and "one whose ideals and purposes are godless and repellent" (judgment). As a result, sometimes it's necessary to speak and write in roundabout terms if you wish to avoid arousing traditional prejudices that hinder clear thinking. Identify three such words and give a substitute for each that is less loaded.

8. Sometimes people assume that the label attached to a person or thing is a sufficient reason for drawing conclusions about the entities to which such labels are attached. Advertisers expect the typical consumer to make such inferences. For example, the manufacturers of Superflite Golf Balls presumably want golfers to infer from the label alone that using these balls will lengthen their drives. Similarly, owners of "discount" stores presumably want shoppers to believe that everything in their stores has been discounted. Give three examples of labels that presumably are intended as sufficient reasons for drawing

conclusions about the objects to which the labels are attached.

9. Which of the following statements would you strongly support or oppose? Try to account for your reaction in terms of the blocks discussed.

   a. Polygamy and polyandry should be legalized.
   b. "America the Beautiful" or some other song should replace "The Star-Spangled Banner" as our national anthem.
   c. The U.S. Constitution should be amended to prohibit burning of the flag.
   d. College students should be allowed to determine curricula and take whatever courses they want toward graduation.
   e. High school students should be allowed to smoke on campus.
   f. Sex education should be introduced in junior high schools and continue right on through high school.
   g. Parents should make birth control devices available to their adolescent offspring.
   h. The draft should apply as equally to females as to males.
   i. There should be tax penalties for people having more than two children.
   j. A person convicted of drunk driving should receive a mandatory jail sentence.
   k. A pregnant woman, in consultation with her physician, should be allowed to have an abortion on demand.
   l. Prayer should be mandatory in all public schools.
   m. Television networks (CBS, NBC, ABC) should be allowed to televise pornographic programs after 11 P.M.
   n. Homosexuals should not be allowed to teach in elementary schools.
   o. All religious institutions should be required to pay taxes.

[1]This exercise is derived from Jonathan Bennett's unpublished lectures on Descartes, given at the University of British Columbia, 1970–1972.
[2]Stanley Milgram, *Obedience to Authority: An Experimental View* (New York: Harper & Row, 1974).
[3]See S. E. Asch, "Effects of Group Pressure Upon the Modification and Distortion of Judgment," in M. H. Guetskow (ed.), *Groups, Leadership and Men* (Pittsburgh: Carnegie Press, 1951); S. E. Asch, "Opinions and Social Pressure," *Scientific American* (September 1955): 31–35; S. E. Asch, "Studies of Individual and Conformity: A Minority of One Against a Unanimous Majority," *Psychological Monographs* 70 (1956): 9.
[4]Gordon Allport, *The Nature of Prejudice* (Reading, Mass.: Addison-Wesley, 1954).

COMMUNICATION I: LANGUAGE AND ADVERTISING

2

*"Some people have a way with words.
Some no have way."*
—Steve Martin

Try to imagine what thinking would be like without language. Hard to imagine, isn't it? In fact, the harder you try, the more you notice language creeping into the effort, the more you notice yourself trying to "put the ideas into words," so to speak, the more it becomes apparent that what we think, even how we think, can't be separated from language.

Language is the fundamental medium of our thinking, the fundamental medium within which our thoughts take form and gain expression. Two important consequences flow from this for our purposes in this text: (1) paying close attention to language is essential to finding out what and how people think, and (2) perhaps even more important, language itself exerts a powerful influence on what and how we think.

Language (narrowly conceived, as words) is, of course, not the only thing one pays close attention to in finding out what and how people think. Posture, gesture, vocal inflection, timing, context, and so on, all are meaningful dimensions of human communication, and they frequently guide our interpretations of people's words. But it is language that is central and basic. Indeed, to say that posture, gesture, vocal inflection, timing, context, and so on, are meaningful dimensions of human communication is as good as saying that they are linguistic dimensions of human communication—either part of language (more broadly conceived) or language-like.

Even more important, profound, and surprising is the influence language exerts on what and how we think. A living language is, of course, an immensely flexible medium, and a medium which is still evolving. So we are understandably only dimly aware, if we are aware at all, of the limitations language sets on what we can meaningfully say, and indeed on what we think. But consider the fact that in Arabic there are more than 5000 terms that pinpoint differences of age, sex, and bodily structure among camels, whereas we have only "camel." Consider how much more it must be possible to think and to say about camels in Arabic than in English.

Then, too, language embodies features like rhythm and rhyme, alliteration and onomatopoeia, emotional appeal, and so on. These are features that have subtle but deep and powerful psychological influence on what we believe, what we agree and disagree with, what we remember or forget; in short, on what and how we think. For these reasons too, then, close attention to language is essential to deepening our awareness of what and how we think.

FUNCTIONS OF LANGUAGE

So subtle and complicated an instrument is language that we often overlook its many uses. As a result we can get caught in the snares laid by language in the way of the thinker: We can fail to understand, or can even misinterpret, communication. A basic part of thinking effectively, then, is grasping how language functions.

We can impose some order on the rich variety of language usage by dividing it into five broad categories. Although this division is a simplification, it does pinpoint the main kinds of language usage essential to critical thinking.

1. Informative. A main use of language is to communicate information. This is typically accomplished by formulating and then affirming (or denying) statements. *Language used to affirm or deny statements is said to perform an informative function.*

The following statements are typical examples of the informative use of language:

> Washington is the nation's capital.
> Laetrile is not an effective treatment for cancer.
> U.S. presidential elections are held quadrennially.
> Business administration is currently the most popular college major.
> One out of ten Americans has herpes.
> The Democrats have never controlled the U.S. House of Representatives.

Notice that the last statement is false. "Information" as used here is taken to include *misinformation;* that is, false statements as well as true. Furthermore, statements whose truth is in doubt, such as "Extraterrestrial life exists" and "The next president will be a Republican," are still functionally informative.

2. Expressive. Besides conveying information about the world, language also serves to express feelings. *Whenever language is used to vent or arouse feelings, it is said to perform an expressive function.*

Poetry furnishes the best examples of the expressive function of language:

So fair, so sweet, withal so sensitive,

Would that the Little Flowers were to live,

Conscious of half the pleasures which they give . . .

—William Wordsworth

The poet did not compose these lines to report any information but to express certain emotions he felt and to evoke a similar response in the reader.

But expressive language need not be confined to poetry. We express sorrow by saying "What a pity" or "That's too bad" and enthusiasm by shouting "Wow!" or "Right on!" And we express feelings of affection, passion, and love by murmuring "Darling" or "Honey" or like terms of endearment. None of these uses is intended to communicate information, but rather feelings.

3. Directive. *Language serves a directive function when it is used in an attempt to direct the behavior of another.* The clearest examples of directive discourse are commands and requests. When a teacher tells a class to "study for tomorrow's test," he doesn't intend to communicate information or express emotion but to bring about a specific action: studying. This sort of directive utterance depends on the teacher's having some measure of authority and perhaps also power over those to whom the command is issued. Commands are not always appropriate as a means of getting people to do what we want. When the same teacher asks the audiovisual technician to set up a projector in his classroom, he is again using language directively, that is, to produce action. But here the directive is in the form of a request, rather than a command. The effectiveness of requests to elicit behavior depends on the willingness of the other party to cooperate. If the teacher first asks the technician if she has a projector available, he is also using language directively, for questions typically are requests for answers.

4. Persuasive. *Language serves a persuasive function when it is used in an attempt to influence the beliefs or motivations of another.* The persuasive function of language is close to the directive function. However, we recognize that other people, just like us, are free agents, and that we are rarely in a position of such authority that we can effectively *command* their behavior, much less their beliefs. Furthermore, we cannot always presume a willingness on the part of others to cooperate with our agenda. What do we do when we can neither command nor presuppose willingness to cooperate? We try to be persuasive. We try to influence the beliefs and motivations of people. For example, a parent might try to "reason with" a child: "If you don't finish your chores, we won't have time to go to the ball game."

5. Performative. Language can also be used in the performance of an action, for expressing certain words in a specific context can bring something about. For example, suppose that during a marriage ceremony the bride says, "I do." Or, in bumping into you, someone says, "I apologize." Or in christening a ship, a person says, "I name this ship the *Nautilus*" and breaks a bottle of champagne across its hull. Or, after a heated discussion about the relative merits of baseball teams, a friend says to you, "I bet you five bucks that the Dodgers make it to the World Series." Although all these utterances have the form of informative utterances, they certainly are not reporting the performance of some action that undoubtedly is done—the action of promising, apologizing, christening, betting. Rather, in saying what they do, the speakers are actually performing the action. When the bride says, "I do," she is not describing or reporting the marriage ceremony, she is actually carrying it out; when a person says, "I apologize," she is not describing or reporting an apology, but actually performing it. Utterances of this kind, which include verdicts and promises, are called "performative utterances." *Language serves the performative function, then, when it is used in certain contexts to make something so.*

Multiple Functions

You don't have to be a linguist to realize that a given communication need not employ just a single language use. Indeed, most ordinary communication likely will exhibit multiple uses of language.
Consider, for example, this poem:

My heart leaps up when I behold

  A rainbow in the sky;

So was it when my life began;

So is it now I am a man;

So be it when I should grow old;

  Or let me die!

The Child is father of the Man;

And I could wish my days to be

Bound each to each by natural piety.

—*William Wordsworth*

Although this poem, like most, is primarily expressive discourse, it can be said to be informative in the sense that the poet is stating that the adult can learn from the child and directive in the sense that the poet is urging us to get in touch with the feelings and intuitions of childhood. On the other hand, a classroom lecture, essentially informative, may express something of the professor's own enthusiasm, thus serving the expressive function. By implication, it may also serve some directive function, perhaps bidding the class to verify independently the lecture's conclusions.
The fact is that most ordinary language usage has mixed functions. This is an important point to remember when thinking critically about some discourse, for buried amid the rhetorical flourishes may lie the contentions that are the

object of our critical inspection. We will say considerably more about this in later chapters when we discuss argument analysis and portrayal.

***Quick Check on the Functions of Language
(Answers on Page 385)**

What language functions are exhibited by each of the following passages? Explain.

1. Baseball umpire: "You're out!"
2. A flat tax rate is outrageous because it favors the rich and penalizes the poor. This is why you must urge your legislators to vote against it.
3. Although we tend to look on our presidents as great men, some of them were indecisive, petty, unintelligent, and unscrupulous.
4. I wouldn't vote Democratic if I were you. Don't you realize the Democrats are the "war party"?
5. Thomas "Tip" O'Neill, the former cantankerous Speaker of the House, was a crafty legislator whose political roots can be traced to the leftist-leaning philosophy of Franklin Delano Roosevelt.
6. "A civil war is like the heat of a fever; but a foreign war is like the heat of exercise, and serveth to keep the body in health." (Francis Bacon, *Essays*)
7. "War is the greatest plague that can afflict humanity; it destroys religion, it destroys states, it destroys families. Any scourge is preferable to it." (Martin Luther, *Table-Talk*)
8. "We must all hang together or assuredly we shall all hang separately." (Benjamin Franklin, to the other signers of the Declaration of Independence)

MEANING IN LANGUAGE:
LANGUAGE AS CONVENTION

How do words get to mean what they mean? For example, how does the word "cat" come to stand for the creature? This is the sort of question that could easily lead to a lengthy and inconclusive debate, because it raises very deep and fundamental questions about what language and meaning are *in essence.* And these are by no means easy questions to answer.

A primitive theory of meaning in language might answer such questions by supposing first that the relationship between the word "cat" and the creatures that the word refers to is *the* basic and essential meaning relation in language: that words are essentially labels for things; and second that the relationship between the word "cat" and the creature is somehow rooted in "the nature of things." Neither of these ideas, however plausible they might seem at first glance, goes very far or helps us very much to understand meaning in language. For one thing, it is not at all easy to see what kind of a "thing" the word "the" could be a label for. Then too, though some words, like "hiccup" and "splash," do seem to have some sort of identifiable natural connection to the things they stand for, most do not. For example, look at the last fifteen or so words in the last sentence. A more subtle and sophisticated account of meaning in language seems called for.

Let's try looking at things this way: Words are noises to which human beings have assigned meaning. Speakers of English use "cat" to refer to feline creatures, whereas speakers of French use "chat," speakers of Spanish use "gato," and speakers of German use "katze." There is nothing "required" or "natural" about such assignments of meaning to noises. Any other sound could have been made to stand for what "cat" stands for in English, and likewise in the other language communities. These assignments of meaning are merely "conventional"; they are based on human conventions.

Other words, like "the," and "and," and "so," and "on," and so on, have meanings in accordance with their conventional uses, with the roles they conventionally play in putting words together into meaningful sentences.

Much the same can be said of syntax as of word meaning. *"Syntax" refers to the structural regularities in the ways words are put together to communicate thoughts and ideas.* In English we put adjectives before nouns, as in "white house." In Spanish the adjective typically follows the noun: "casa blanca." The difference is a matter of convention.

Let's take a moment to explain more deeply what we mean by a "convention." *A convention is simply a behavioral regularity that humans maintain and follow in order to solve problems of coordination.* For example, suppose that you and your friend are cut off in the middle of a telephone conversation. You have what we might call a "coordination problem." What each of you should do depends on what the other person does. If you both pick up the phone and dial, you both get a busy signal. If you both hang up and wait, well, . . . you wait. You get back in contact if, and only if, one of you dials while the other hangs up and waits. What should you do? Well, suppose that in the past when this sort of thing has happened, you have always been the one to dial, and that has worked, and you know it has worked, and your friend knows it has worked, and you know that your friend knows it has worked, and you know that your friend knows that you know this. So, if you now pick up the phone and dial while your friend hangs up and waits, and you do these things because you are both thinking that this will solve the coordination problem, because both of you know that it has worked in the past, you are following a "convention."[1]

The basic problems of communication, understanding others and making oneself understood, are coordination problems. Language can usefully be understood as a vast system of conventions that we learn to follow in order to solve the problems of communication.

A number of interesting and important consequences follow from this way of viewing language. First of all, linguistic conventions are, in one sense, arbitrary. This means that they could have been other than they are. And, indeed, linguistic conventions evolve, sometimes quite rapidly and dramatically. But although linguistic conventions could have been other than they are and may well change, they nevertheless do regulate meaningful discourse. Linguistic conventions are thus a lot like the rules in a game.

Think of the rules governing organized sports like American football or basketball and you'll see what we mean. One rule in American football states that the dimensions of the playing field between the end zones is 100 yards; another prescribes exactly eleven participants per team. These rules are arbitrary; they could be other than what they are. For example, Canadian football is played on a 110-yard field with twelve participants on a side. And the rules of a game can be changed by common consent. For example, the three-point field goal was recently instituted in professional and collegiate basketball. But the rules, whatever they are, do regulate the game. If you choose to play American football, then you must play by its rules. If you play Canadian football, you must observe its rules.

Similarly, in playing the language game we must generally abide by the conventions of the particular language in which we are attempting to communicate. And we can rightly expect others to do the same. Conventions in language are somewhat more flexible and informal than rules are in games. For one thing, you don't get thrown out of the game for committing five unconventional speech acts. Furthermore, sometimes violating a linguistic convention can be a very creative and effective way of communicating something unique and special. Nevertheless, meaningful departures from the conventions of our language presuppose those conventions as generally binding. If this were not the case, departing from our language's conventions would lead to hopeless confusion.

The Rule of Common Usage

In *Through the Looking Glass,* Alice and Humpty Dumpty have the following conversation:

> ". . . there are 364 days when you might get un-birthday presents."
> "Certainly," said Alice.
> "And only *one* for birthday presents, you know. There's glory for you!"
> "I don't know what you mean by 'glory'," Alice said.
> Humpty Dumpty smiled contemptuously. "Of course you don't—till I tell you. I meant, 'there's a nice knock-down argument for you!' "
> "But 'glory' doesn't mean 'a nice knock-down argument'," Alice objected.
> "When I use a word," Humpty Dumpty said, in a rather scornful tone, "it means just what I choose it to mean—neither more nor less."[2]

Just imagine the confusion that would reign if, like Humpty Dumpty, each of us used words to mean exactly what we wanted them to mean, "neither more nor less." To avoid such chaos and inconvenience, we generally presuppose a conventional interpretation of what someone says. If a writer or speaker doesn't indicate a departure from common usage, you are right in taking for granted that the person is following common usage. Of course, this works both ways. Generally speaking, it's best to *follow common usage.* When you do use a word in an unconventional way, you will need to give your audience extra guidance to your meaning. If you don't, they will be justified in assuming that you are using the word in a conventional sense. It should be obvious what happens if you and your audience are not coordinated regarding what you mean: Communication breaks down.

DIMENSIONS OF MEANING: DENOTATION AND CONNOTATION

Critical thinking is concerned largely with informative statements. These statements are both the product and object of critical inspection. They of course consist of words in certain arrangements. Unless we know the meanings of these words, we cannot think critically about the statements that contain them, nor can we respond intelligently to the statements. Let's now look more closely at word meaning and develop an important distinction between two of its dimensions: denotation and connotation. Although these dimensions of meaning apply to various parts of speech—nouns, verbs, adjectives, adverbs, pronouns, and so on—for the sake of simplicity we will confine our remarks to the meaning of general nouns that can apply to numerous particular items around us, for example, "bridge," "building," "school," "politician," "book."

Consider the word "bridge." What does the word "bridge" mean? In one sense, the word means what it serves to refer or point to. It points to a group of objects: bridges. This pointing-to relationship between the word and its objects is called *denotation.* The group of objects denoted by a term is called the term's *extension.*

The denotative meaning of a word is the word's extension, or the group of objects denoted by that word. For example, the denotative meaning of "bridge" is that group of objects we commonly identify as bridges; the denotative meaning of "building" is that group of objects to which the term "building" commonly applies.

It is not by chance, however, that the terms "bridge" and "building" refer to the objects they refer to, for these objects share some common features or properties. Bridges and buildings have characteristics that make them bridges or buildings and not, say, tunnels or silos. These characteristics, which define the extension of the term, are called the term's *intension.* The intension of a term is an important part of the term's connotations. *The connotative meaning of a word includes the word's intension, or the set of characteristics that define the term's extension.*

The denotative meaning of a word, plus that portion of the word's connotation that corresponds to its intension, add up to the word's *literal* meaning. But many words have additional dimensions of meaning, which are included among its connotations. Quite often a word has special meaning for an individual or group of individuals because it evokes an emotional response. *The emotional conno-*

tation of a word refers to its emotional impact. For example, the literal intension of "prima donna" is "the principal female singer in an opera company." But, because the term has come by convention to carry the added connotation of "a vain, temperamental person," no woman or man would want to be called a "prima donna." Consequently, using the term "prima donna," especially outside of the specialized context of opera, is an effective way of putting someone down.

Similarly, the word "tabloid" literally means a newspaper whose format is about half the size of a standard-size newspaper page. But most tabloid newspapers tend toward sensationalism. As a result "tabloid" conventionally carries an additional negative or pejorative connotation. And so, similarly, to call a newspaper a tabloid is to put it down.

Of course, emotional connotations need not be derogatory. Many are complimentary. Terms such as "statesperson" (as opposed to the negative "politician"), "moderate" (as opposed to the negative "wishy-washy"), and "professor" (as opposed to the negative "pedagogue") all carry a positive emotional charge.

The nonliteral connotations of words are particularly important to the persuasive function of language. They make it possible, by the careful selection of terminology, to color a statement emotionally and to communicate a bias.

So far we have learned about the various ways that language functions, the conventional basis of meaning in language, different dimensions of meaning in language, and how some of these dimensions of meaning can be used to communicate bias. Nothing is more essential to thinking effectively about what you read, hear, and write than sensitivity to a word's nonliteral connotations. Only with such sensitivity can you understand both what someone literally means, which may be obvious, and what that person wants to suggest, which may be far more important than the superficial meaning. This doesn't mean that in thinking about a passage you must consider every single word for implications and sub-surface meanings. Many words—articles, conjunctions, prepositions, and some adverbs—carry no emotional impact, because they are being used simply as connectives or relational devices. Other words, such as scientific or technical terms, are often free of any emotional connotations and are not intended to evoke any vivid pictures or emotional responses. But the fact remains that many words and expressions do carry additional positive or negative connotations, and it's important to be sensitive to these if you are to think effectively about the passages in which they are contained.

DEFINITION

A definition is an explanation of the meaning of a term. So much depends on meaning in language that a discussion of language would be incomplete without a discussion of definition. Definition can take a number of forms, depending chiefly on the purposes of the writer or speaker. We will focus on four kinds of definition: denotative, logical, stipulative, and persuasive.

Denotative Definition

We can define denotative definition as we defined denotative meaning: *A denotative definition of a term explains its meaning by giving or indicating its extension.* For example, if someone didn't know what "reptile" meant, you could help that person by giving a denotative definition like this one: "Snakes, lizards, turtles, and crocodiles are reptiles." Here you are explaining the meaning of the general term by indicating the kinds of things included in its extension. A special case of denotative definition is called *ostensive definition,* which consists of pointing out examples of the term being defined; for instance, pointing to an actual lizard in order to help someone understand the meaning of "lizard." Notice that for most terms it would be difficult, if not absolutely impossible, to give a complete ostensive or denotative definition.

Logical Definition

Understanding what a term means involves knowing how to use it correctly. But to know how to use a term doesn't require you to know everything that it can be applied to—that is the complete extension. But remember that the extension of a term is determined by the term's intension. Thus, an alternative to denotative definition would be to explain the meaning of the term by giving its intension. This is sometimes called "logical definition."

A logical definition of a term explains its meaning by giving its intension, or the set of characteristics that define the term's extension. Accordingly, the logical definition of "spoon" is "a utensil consisting of a small, shallow bowl with a handle, used in eating or stirring." And the logical definition of "square" is "equilateral rectangle."

Notice that these definitions can be understood as consisting of a simple two-step procedure: (1) locating the term being defined within a larger class, and (2) showing how its extension differs from those of the other terms in the class. Thus:

Term	*Class*	*Distinguishing Characteristics*
A spoon	is a utensil	consisting of a small, shallow bowl with a handle, used in eating or stirring
square	rectangle	equilateral

Similarly:

Term	Class	Distinguishing Characteristics
A watch	is a mechanical device	for telling time and is usually carried or worn
Ethics	is a branch of philosophy	concerned with whether an action is good or bad, right or wrong

A logical definition, which gives the intension of a term, is a precise, economical way of identifying something. Writers have many occasions to use logical definitions. For example, if they are using an obscure term such as "tsunami," they might briefly define it as "an unusually large sea wave produced by an undersea earthquake or volcanic eruption." Leaving unusual or obscure terms undefined impedes communication and blocks thinking.

Over the years a number of rules have been developed for formulating logical definitions. There is nothing sacred or immutable about these rules. In fact, blind reliance on them may occasionally hamper the defining process. But if they are viewed as guidelines and not imperatives, these rules can help you move toward clarity and precision in your writing and thinking.

Rule 1. *A logical definition states both the necessary conditions and the sufficient conditions for being in the term's extension.* As we saw earlier in our discussion of intension, there are certain "essential characteristics" that define a term's extension. These "essential characteristics" are of two kinds. *A necessary condition is a characteristic or set of characteristics <u>required</u> for membership in the extension of a term.* For instance, in the logical definition of square as an equilateral rectangle, both "equilateral" and "rectangle" indicate necessary conditions. In other words, both equilaterality and rectangularity are required for membership in the extension of the term "square." If you find out that something is not rectangular, or is not equilateral, you don't need to know anything more about it. You already know that it isn't square. *A sufficient condition is a characteristic or set of characteristics that are <u>by themselves adequate</u> for membership in the extension of a term.* Again, in the logical definition of square as an equilateral rectangle, the set of characteristics, equilateral and rectangle, together constitute a sufficient condition. In other words, if you find out that something is both equilateral and rectangular, you don't need to know anything more about it. You don't have to know its size, its age, its color, its value, or molecular structure. You already know that it is square.

Notice that with a term like "square," providing a logical definition is relatively simple and straightforward. Providing the essential characteristics of concepts such as "justice," "liberty," and "equality" is considerably more difficult. Indeed, whole treatises have been penned by philosophers and others in an attempt to nail down the defining characteristics of these concepts.

Rule 2. *A good logical definition is not circular.* A definition is circular if it defines a word in terms of itself. To define "inertial" as "of or pertaining to inertia" is a circular definition. A better definition is "pertaining to the property of matter by which it retains its state of rest or its velocity along a straight line so long as it is not acted upon by an external force." Again, to say that a bequest is something that is bequeathed is to offer a circular definition. A better rendering would be "a disposition by will of property."

Rule 3. *A good logical definition is neither too broad nor too narrow.* This rule means that a logical definition should not denote more or fewer things than are denoted by the term itself. On the one hand, to define "pungent" as "pertaining to any taste or smell" is far too broad. Some tastes or smells are mild, whereas "pungent" means "sharp or biting tastes or smells." On the other hand, to define "shoes" as "a leather covering for the human foot" is too narrow, for a shoe can be made of wood or canvas, or even of iron and for the foot of a horse.

Rule 4. *A good logical definition does not use obscure or figurative language.* Obscure language, as in "a lie is an intentional terminological inexactitude," does nothing to illuminate the meaning of the term. Remember that a definition is an explanation of the meaning of a term. As such, it presumably is an attempt to help someone understand something. If the terminology in which the definition is formulated is even less familiar than what is being defined, or more difficult to grasp and understand, then the definition backfires. Of course, "familiarity," "obscurity," and so on, are themselves relative terms. What is obscure to one person may be quite clear and familiar to another. A legal definition may be obscure to those not trained in the law but perfectly understandable to lawyers. In the last analysis, obscurity must be judged according to the background of the audience for whom the definition is intended.

The same cautions apply to figurative language, that is, language that is expressive or highly descriptive. To define "bread" as "the staff of life" does little to explain what bread is. Defining "discretion" as "something that comes to people after they are too old for it to do them any good" is amusing but unenlightening. Indeed, such a statement assumes that you already have some idea of what "discretion" means. Statements such as these have their uses, to be sure. For example, they may be insightful. But they do not make good candidates for the work of definition.

Rule 5. *A good logical definition is not negative when it can be affirmative.* A definition should explain what a term means, not what it doesn't mean. There are countless things that "spoon," "skyscraper," and "triangle" do *not* mean. Listing all these things, even if it were possible, would not indicate the meaning of these terms. Of course, some words defy affirmative definition. "Orphan" means a child whose parents are *not* living; "bald" means the state of *not* having hair on one's head. Barring such terms that *must* be defined negatively, definitions should be stated in the affirmative.

---

*Quick Check on Logical Definition
(Answers on Page 386)

Criticize the following definitions in terms of the criteria for a good logical definition.

1. A dinosaur is a prehistoric animal.
2. Rape is forcing a woman to have sex against her will.
3. Philosophy is the study of the classical Greek works of Plato and Aristotle.
4. Hate is an emotion.
5. A circle is a closed plane curve.
6. A bad person is a person who does bad things.
7. Hell is other people.
8. Democracy is a government in which everybody may vote.
9. A cat is a domesticated animal with four legs.
10. Alimony means when two people make a mistake and one of them continues to pay for it. In contrast, palimony means when two people *knew* they would make a mistake and one of them continues to pay for it.
11. A star is a stellar body visible in the heavens at night.
12. "A cynic is one who knows the price of everything and the value of nothing." (Oscar Wilde)
13. Ornament means something not necessary for practical use.
14. "Faith is the substance of things hoped for, the evidence of things not seen." (Hebrews 11:1)
15. "Faith may be defined briefly as an illogical belief in the occurrence of the improbable." (H. L. Mencken)
16. "Economics is the science which treats of the phenomena arising out of the economic activities of men in society." (J. M. Keynes)
17. "Justice is doing one's own business, and not being a busybody." (Plato)

Stipulative Definition

Both denotative and logical definitions attempt to explain the conventional meaning of a term. But suppose a writer wants to communicate an idea for which no conventionally understood term is exactly right. Earlier we alluded to the fact that writers often depart from the standard use of a word and employ it in an unconventional way. In specialized or technical disciplines, it frequently becomes necessary to set up terminology with specialized technical meanings. In geometry, for example, the words "point," "line," and "plane" are given quite specific meanings that are quite a bit more precise than they have conventionally. *A stipulative definition is one that attaches an unconventional, perhaps unique meaning to a term for use in a particular context.* Ordinarily, writers stipulate definitions when (1) they believe that a word is ambiguous and they want to give it a more precise meaning; or (2) finding that no word exists for some meaning they have in mind, they invent one, as with "glitch" for "a brief unwanted surge of electrical power."

Persuasive Definition

When a word has acquired a complimentary meaning, people sometimes try to use it to carry a literal meaning different from its ordinary one in order to exploit the word's favorable meaning. For example, assume that the word "sophisticated" has a logical meaning equivalent to "having or showing worldly knowledge and experience." A clever writer may now try to redefine "sophisticated" in order to take advantage of its favorable meaning. Thus, "*true* sophistication is doing what's in one's self-interest." Of course, there is no such thing as the "true" or "real" meaning of a word, only common or uncommon and exact or inexact meanings. But audiences seldom make these distinctions. As a result, writers and speakers can use the favorable meaning of a word such as "sophisticated" to convince the audience that to be sophisticated is to look out for "number one."

A *persuasive definition, then, is a definition that attaches a different literal meaning to a word while preserving its original emotional impact.* Persuasive definitions are sleight-of-hand tricks: Writers and speakers change the literal meaning but keep the emotive one. With luck the audience will never spot the switches and will accept the author's assertion.

Words with high emotional charges, positive or negative, are the ones most subject to persuasive definition. These words are most likely to appear in discussions of controversial issues. Often dead giveaways for a persuasive definition are intensifiers such as "real" (as in "A *real* American would never avoid the draft"), "true" ("A *true* Democrat would never support policies that result in unemployment"), "genuine" ("War is never a *genuine* option in resolving international conflict"), and "good" ("*Good* citizens always vote"). But persuasive definitions need not be so verbally telegraphed. They can come larded with emotive language, as in "Democracy is the freedom to be self-governed" or "Democracy is the tyrannical oppression of the individual by the unenlightened majority."

Don't misunderstand. Sometimes writers do clarify the meaning and legitimately advance a claim. So long as they don't insist on the old positive or negative overtones of a term after they have indicated a new meaning they are, in effect, using a stipulative definition. But when they change a word's meaning while preserving its old emotive force, they're trying to pull a fast one. Don't let them.

1. How many stipulative definitions can you find so far in this chapter?
2. Which of the following definitions are persuasive and which are stipulative?

   a. The only true criminal is the one who commits crimes not in the heat of passion but calculatingly, cold-bloodedly.
   b. Any good American would stand up and support the president's energy program.
   c. Patriots stand by their country, right or wrong.
   d. A trial by jury is the right that guarantees justice to all citizens by allowing them to be judged by their peers.
   e. "We hear about constitutional rights, free speech and the free press. Every time I hear these words I say to myself, 'That man is a Red, that man is a Communist.' You never heard a real American talk in that manner." (Jersey City Mayor Frank Hague, speech before the Jersey City Chamber of Commerce, January 12, 1938)
   f. "The superstar celebrity—F. Lee Bailey, Andy Warhol, Rod Stewart—is the fast-food throwaway version of the hero. To be a good goalie or dance a broken-field run with nimble abandon is really a matter of youth, coordination and television coverage. A sterling character might help, but good knees are essential. The true hero is the man or woman who changes a place or a world, makes it fitter for others." (Herbert Gold, "The Hostages Are Special, But No Heroes—Let's Not Be Cruel," *Los Angeles Times*, January 20, 1981)

AMBIGUITY AND VAGUENESS

With the background of the preceding discussion of meaning and definition we may now distinguish and define two important concepts having to do with the clarification of meaning and which will prove increasingly useful as we proceed: ambiguity and vagueness. Each corresponds to a source of confusion in communication (which may help explain why they so often are confused with each other).

An ambiguous term or expression is one with more than one conventional interpretation. In other words, it can be understood and defined in more than one way. For example, the word "bank" can mean:

1. any piled-up mass, such as snow or clouds
2. the slope of land adjoining a body of water

3. the cushion of a billiard or pool table
4. to strike a billiard shot off the cushion
5. to tilt an aircraft in flight
6. a business establishment authorized to receive and safeguard money, lend money at interest, and so on.

A vague term or expression is one that has an indefinite extension. In other words, it is not entirely clear what it does and does not apply to. For example, the term "bald" clearly applies to Don Rickles and Herschel Bernardi. It clearly does not apply to Michael J. Fox. But there is an indefinite area in between where it isn't clear whether a person is bald or not. Vagueness admits of degrees, according to how clearly cases fall within and without its extension and how large the indefinite area is. Thus "bald" is less vague than "happy."

ISSUES AND DISPUTES

Should there be a law against abortion? Should animals be used in medical experimentation? Will the stock market stay above the 2000 mark through the fiscal year? Will a black man or a woman be elected president in this century? Is there intelligent life in outer space? Do single-income households still out-number two-income households? Do the changes in Soviet leadership and in-ternal policy indicate a fundamental shift in philosophy and direction? These are all questions to which a number of significant and conflicting alternative re-sponses are both genuinely open and defensible. They are good examples of what we call an "issue." *An issue is a genuinely disputable topic. And a dispute is a disagreement or controversy over an issue.* It is what happens when one of several opposed positions on a particular issue gets challenged from the point of view of another.

There are some interesting and important differences among the types of issues illustrated in the above list, and accordingly among the kind of dispute we commonly encounter in actual discourse. Before turning to discuss these differences, let us explain more deeply what we mean by "genuinely disputable," by pointing out and setting aside another kind of thing that frequently *passes for* an issue: verbal disputes.

Philosopher William James tells the story about how on a camping trip every-one got into a dispute over the following puzzle:

> The corpus of the dispute was a squirrel—a live squirrel supposed to be clinging to one side of a tree-trunk; while over against the tree's opposite side a human being was imagined to stand. This human witness tries to get sight of the squirrel by moving rapidly round the tree, but no matter how fast he goes, the squirrel moves just as fast in the opposite direction, and always keeps the tree between himself and the man, so that never a glimpse of him is caught. The resultant problem now is this: *Does the man go round the squirrel or not?* He goes round the tree, sure enough, and the squirrel is on the tree; but does he go round the squirrel?[3]

James's idea was that although you can easily imagine people going round and round in an endless dispute over such a puzzle, you can just as easily dissolve the puzzle by drawing a simple terminological distinction: It all depends on what you mean by 'going round' the squirrel.

> If you mean passing from the north of him to the east, then to the south, then to the west, then to the north again, obviously the man does go round him, for he occupies these successive positions. But if on the contrary you mean being first in front of him, then on the right of him, then behind him, then on the left, and finally in front again, it is quite as obvious that the man fails to go round him, for by the compensating movements the squirrel makes, he keeps his belly turned towards the man all the time, and his back turned away.[4]

Because it hardly matters which meaning of 'going round' the squirrel applies, this could be called a "purely verbal" dispute.

Another example is the old dispute "If a tree falls in the forest and nobody is there to hear it, is there a sound?" Clarifying the meaning of 'sound' will settle the dispute. Accordingly, if you're talking about sound waves, then certainly there are sounds whether or not anyone is there to hear the tree fall. But if you mean sound sensations—the experience of sound—then the falling tree makes no sound, for no one is there to experience the sound sensations. In this instance, then, clarification of a term is sufficient to resolve the dispute.

Wouldn't it be nice if all disputes were as trivial and easy to dissolve as these. Wouldn't it be nice if disputes arose simply because of trivial disagreements about the meanings of words and could be dismissed as mere "matters of semantics."

In fact, most of the disputes that concern us are genuine, and genuinely challenge our reasoning capacities. They and the issues they concern generally fall into one of the following common categories.

Factual Issues and Disputes

Consider again the following examples:

> Will the stock market stay above the 2000 mark through the fiscal year?
> Will a black man or a woman be elected president in this century?
> Is there intelligent life in outer space?
> Do single-income households still outnumber two-income households?

Each of these is a question to which a number of significant and conflicting alternative responses are both genuinely open and defensible. We can imagine people taking sides in response to each of these questions, and disputing the matter at length. But settling issues like these can't be easily accomplished by clarifying terminology. Presumably such issues are settled, if they are settled at all, by appeal to evidence of certain kinds. In the case of the first three questions, the available evidence isn't yet sufficient to settle the issue. But at least we have a pretty clear idea about what sort of evidence we're looking for: *empirical evi-*

dence—that is, *experience,* either direct observational experience or indirect (for example, experimental) experience. And in the case of at least the first two questions, we have a pretty clear idea of when we may expect conclusive evidence to become available. *Factual issues are ones for which empirical verification procedures are appropriate.* In Chapter 7 we will be discussing factual issues and empirical verification procedures in greater detail. Suffice for the moment to say that when people disagree about how many planets there are in the solar system, or whether capital punishment is a deterrent, they are engaged in factual disputes concerning factual issues. There is no way to settle these issues except by investigating the facts of the case.

Evaluative Issues and Disputes

Evaluative disputes are differences of opinion about matters of value and concern, what we call "value judgments." For example, the questions

> Should there be a law against abortion?
> Should animals be used in medical experimentation?

indicate evaluative issues. Each is a question to which a number of significant and conflicting alternative responses (which presumably would reflect differences of opinion about value judgments) are both genuinely open and defensible. Accordingly, if a dispute were to arise about either of these questions, it would be an evaluative dispute. Evaluative issues and disputes raise some special problems for the critical thinker, which we will say more about in Chapter 7.

Interpretive Issues and Disputes

Suppose that in her first speech before the United Nations General Assembly the newly appointed U.S. ambassador makes three explicitly unfavorable references to apartheid. Is the United States "sending a message" to Pretoria? And if so, what is the message?

Or suppose we've just watched the feature film *Wall Street.* At what point in the plot does the character Bud Fox realize that Gordon Gecko has been manipulating him? Is it at the moment when he realizes that a board of directors meeting of the company Gecko has named him president of has been called without his knowledge? Is it at the moment during the meeting when it comes out that Gecko plans to liquidate the company?

Or take this example again:

> Do the changes in Soviet leadership and internal policy indicate a fundamental shift in philosophy and direction?

Each of these questions indicates an issue concerning how things should be interpreted or understood. Such issues frequently arise in our attempts to understand things whose meaning may be flexible, complicated, multilayered, obscure, or even deliberately veiled. Issues of this sort are probably the most complex and difficult issues procedurally that we are likely to encounter in every-day discourse. Yet, they are also absolutely fundamental to the process of communication, for they have to do with the discernment of meaning. Indeed, many, perhaps most, of the activities you will be performing throughout this book involve interpretation. Deciding whether a particular passage is an argument or not involves interpretation. Deciding whether a passage is intended to serve an expressive or persuasive or informative function involves interpretation.

There is no single simple procedure for resolving interpretive issues or settling interpretive disputes. Rather, there are a number of kinds of information relevant to interpretation, some of which have already been mentioned, and some of which we will be discussing further in Chapter 7.

For example, the conventions governing the use of a term or expression are relevant to its interpretation. Similarly, there are "diplomatic conventions," which would be relevant to the interpretation of communications between one government (for example, through its U.N. ambassador) and another.

In addition to conventions, information about the context surrounding a passage is relevant to its interpretation. Knowing that a particular speech was delivered before the U.N. General Assembly rather than, for example, by confidential communiqué to the South African ambassador is an important piece of information that can guide us closer to an accurate understanding of what was meant. Contextual information in the case of oral communication, as well as in film and video, includes facial expression, vocal inflection, bodily posture, timing, and so on.

It should be apparent already that gathering and sifting evidence of such a wide variety, especially in living contexts, where time is of the essence, is a process of considerable complexity and subtlety. And there is a good deal of disagreement among theorists about what the proper procedures are for doing interpretive work and how they should be applied in different sorts of interpretive controversy.

Nevertheless, interpretation is something you are probably pretty good at by now. So you no doubt already recognize that some interpretive issues can be resolved relatively firmly and easily, whereas others are more difficult and may in fact remain "up for grabs." In disputed cases, perhaps the most useful procedural strategy is the use of hypothetical reasoning. This involves formulating and testing interpretive hypotheses. *A hypothesis is an idea that we suppose to be true, although we do not yet know it to be true.* This is a procedure that also has important applications in dealing with factual issues. We will be discussing it in greater detail in Chapter 7.

*Quick Check on Disputes (Answers on Page 386)

Of the following disputes, which are genuine and which are merely "verbal"? Of the genuine disputes, which are factual, which are evaluative, and which are interpretive? Explain how you arrive at your answers.

1. **John:** The Gilsons served a delightful little brunch.
   Joan: The Gilsons served a magnificent banquet.
2. Brad has an old car. One day he replaces one of its defective parts. The next day he replaces another. Before the year is out, Brad has replaced every part in the entire car. Is Brad's car the same car he had before he began the replacements?
3. A bad peace is even worse than war. (Tacitus) The most disadvantageous peace is better than the most just war. (Erasmus)
4. Phil told his brother Fred, "When I die I'll leave you all my money." A week later he thought better of his promise and decided to leave all his money to his estranged wife instead. So Phil wrote in his will, "I leave all my money to my next of kin" (his wife). Unknown to Phil, his wife had died in a car accident. The day after he made out his will Phil himself died, and his money went to his next of kin—his brother Fred. Did Phil keep his promise to his brother Fred or didn't he?
5. Our country: in her intercourse with foreign nations may she always be right; but our country, right or wrong! (Stephen Decatur) Our country, right or wrong. When right, to be kept right; when wrong, to be put right. (Carl Schurz)
6. **James:** Take a look at this new study. The majority of people in the United States now favor gun control.
   Jane: Take a closer look at that study. It's based on interviews with college students. It hardly represents the views of the majority of Americans.
7. **Gene:** That example where Tacitus and Erasmus seem to be disagreeing about peace is just a verbal dispute. They just mean different things by the word "peace."
   Jean: No, I think they have a factual dispute. They really disagree about history.

THE INFORMATION ENVIRONMENT

So far our study has aimed to heighten awareness of (1) the blocks to critical thinking and (2) the centrality of language in thinking and expressing thoughts. Our awareness-raising excursion now turns to the information environment—the countless bits and pieces of data that we are regularly exposed to and that help shape how we see ourselves, others, and the world.

In our discussion of language we confined our attention to verbal meaning: to words and expressions made up of words. But words and sentences are not the only meaningful things we encounter in the information environment. There are all sorts of meaningful items all around. Graphic material, too, is meaningful. Think for a minute of logos:

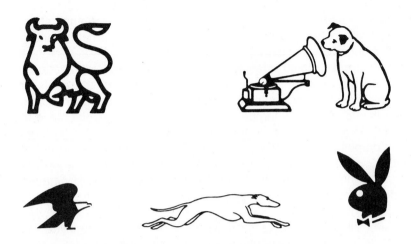

or the logo-like international symbols used in airports and so on to indicate where the baggage claim area and the telephones and the rest rooms are located:

Then there is nonverbal audio material: foghorns, car horns, sirens, dial tones, the doorbell, music.

And all of these forms of meaningful material—words, graphics, and sound—are to be found in all sorts of complicated meaningful combinations, both static and in motion, throughout the information environment. Photographs, billboards, bumper stickers, t-shirt designs, the Yellow Pages, radio jingles, the Top Forty, Muzak, music videos, television ads, movies, the half-time show at the Super Bowl, and on and on—obviously there are far too many sources of information for this single chapter to cover.

But to round out our awareness-raising excursion, we do intend to look more closely at three important and related source areas in which meaningful combinations are found—advertising, television, and the news—and which, taken together, form a wellspring of information that shapes our views of reality, our values, our judgments, and even our actions.

Each of these areas is in its own right a giant that can be viewed from a number of perspectives: not just as a category of information, but as an industry, as a system, as an institution, and so on, with its own inner complexity in many dimensions and its own far-reaching implications in many directions. Consequently, this chapter cannot begin to exhaust all that can be said about these three areas. At best we might hope to flush out a few of the subsurface messages that are transmitted through these media and prime you with questioning strategies that will help you become a more critical receiver of information and a more sophisticated observer of society.

One very powerful questioning strategy is to seek functional explanations, or try to understand the peculiar features of things in terms of the goals or purposes the things serve.[5] For example, if we are trying to understand or explain what a telephone is and why it has the peculiar features it has, a good place to begin would be to ask what a telephone is for and what its peculiar features contribute to that purpose or goal. Thus, for example, it has a handset with that distinctive peculiar shape so that you can easily hold it in one hand while you both talk and listen. And so the handset constitutes a very useful combination of features in a device designed to enable people to converse outside each other's physical presence.

We will be using this strategy extensively in what follows. And we invite you to do the same. It is important to remember that things generally serve a multiplicity of purposes, and that frequently some of the purposes a thing serves can be identified as more basic, central, or essential than others. For example, a telephone may have a particular color scheme in order to fit into the interior decor, or to be visible at a certain distance along a sidewalk. Yet these functional characteristics are less essential to it as a telephone than the handset feature.

ADVERTISING

Let us apply this strategy to advertising. What goals or purposes can you identify as served by advertising? We can see right away that advertising performs at least two functions: Looked at from the point of view of the consumer, advertising provides information about available goods and services relevant to making choices in the marketplace. Looked at from the point of view of the advertiser, advertising is designed to persuade consumers to purchase one product rather than another, in other words, to motivate and direct consumer behavior.

Perhaps you can identify other functions that advertising performs. If so, can you see ways in which the functions relate to each other? Which functions seem basic? Of the two mentioned so far, the second is arguably the most basic, since it is the function for which advertising is *produced* and *paid for.*

Moreover, notice that the two functions mentioned so far are not always compatible. The goal of motivating consumer behavior is not always best served by providing the information the consumer needs to make an informed choice in his own best interests. Awareness of this fact is extremely useful in coming to understand perhaps the most remarkable peculiarity about advertising as a category of information: namely, the prevalence in advertising of deceptive techniques, practices, and devices. In their attempts to persuade, advertisers often obfuscate, misrepresent, and even lie. This is not, of course, to say that *all* advertising is essentially misleading or dishonest. But, to put the matter tactfully, neither is the widespread use of deception and con artistry in advertising accidental. In addition to its efforts to baffle and confuse the consumer's reasoning, advertising also frequently attempts to override reasoning by appealing to emotion.

The vast array of deceptive and manipulative advertising devices is a subject in itself worthy of an entire book. We would recommend Jeffrey Schrank's *Snap, Crackle and Popular Taste* (New York: Delacorte, 1977) to anyone interested in pursuing this subject in greater depth. Here we can only scratch the surface with a small sample of common devices. They are false implication, the use of ambiguity and vagueness, exaggeration, psychological appeals, and hidden facts.

False Implication

Among the devices used regularly to sell products, false implication is potentially the most dangerous. *False implication consists of stating something that usually is true while implying something else that is false.* Usually the implied falsehood is more relevant to motivating the purchase than the stated truth.

Here's an example. In promoting to physicians a powerful tranquilizer called Haldol, McNeil Laboratories described the drug as a means of controlling "disruptive behavior in nursing home patients with minimal risk of sedation and hypotension." In a three-page ad headlined I MADE A FLOWER TODAY that ran in many health journals in 1978, McNeil pictured a smiling, alert, and wrinkle-free woman holding a cloth flower. On the facing page, it boasted of Haldol's effectiveness in keeping nursing home patients under control. The implication was clear: Not only could a nursing home keep patients under control with Haldol, it could also *make them cheerful and creative and able to perform delicate tasks.* However, as McNeil admitted in small print in the corner, the woman pictured had made the flower as part of a vocational group therapy project and was not a patient receiving Haldol.

Or consider this recently encountered candy bar wrapper imprinted in bold type with the words BIGGEST EVER! The implication is clearly that the candy bar used to be smaller than it is now, that it has been *increased in size.* The truth of the matter is that the candy bar is as big as it's ever been—and also as small as it's ever been—because it's the same size as it's always been.

A particularly common variety of false implication is the peculiar use of superlative adjectives in the promotion of parity products. Parity products are products that are identical regardless of brand name. Aspirin is a good example of a parity product. Aspirin is aspirin is aspirin. It doesn't matter whether you put it in the bottle that says "Bayer" on it or in the bottle with the regional brand name or the bottle with the generic label. You get the same number of milligrams of the same chemical formula per tablet. Understandably, producers of parity products work very hard in their ads to promote name recognition and brand loyalty and frequently use superlatives such as "best," "strongest," "most powerful," and so on to describe their products. "How can this be!" you may ask. "If all of the products are identical, they must all be equally good, equally strong, equally powerful, and so on." Quite right. If you have this doubt, it's probably because you recognize that normally a superlative implies a comparison. For example, consider the following sets of adjectives:

Superlative:	best	strongest
Comparative:	better	stronger
Descriptive:	good	strong

Normally, as you read down the list, each adjective implies the one below. If something is better than something else, this implies that it is good. If something is best, this implies it is better than the rest. Not so in parity ads. In parity ads you almost never encounter explicit comparisons between one parity product and another, because to say that one parity product is better than another would be false. Yet, they almost all describe themselves in superlative terms. In the context of this sort of employment the superlative "best" is taken to mean "there are none better"; the superlative "strongest" is taken to mean "there are none stronger"; and so on. Thus, if an over-the-counter pain reliever is described as "the strongest pain reliever you can buy without a prescription," this should *not* be interpreted to mean "stronger than the other over-the-counter pain relievers," although that is what the advertiser expects you to think because that is what would normally be implied by such a claim. The truth of the matter is that the pain reliever is "as strong as any of the other over-the-counter pain relievers"; in other words, you are simply getting the maximum dosage that may legally be dispensed without a doctor's prescription, the same as with all of the other over-the-counter pain pills.

*Quick Check on False Implication (Answers on Page 387)

What's the implication in each of the following?

1. London Fog commercials that are set in London.
2. A package photo for McDonald's cherry pie that shows more than 100 luscious-looking cherries.
3. A Bayer aspirin commercial that shows an announcer holding a bottle of Bayer while stating that doctors recommend aspirin for pain relief (more recently, as a means to reduce risk of heart attack).
4. "Dial—the most effective deodorant soap you can buy."

Ambiguity and Vagueness in Advertising

An ambiguous word or expression is one that has more than one meaning. *Ads frequently exploit ambiguity as a means of suggesting something that they cannot truthfully say more explicitly.*

Suppose, for example, a government study found that Grit filter cigarettes were lower in tar and nicotine than its filter-tip competitors. As part of its advertising, Grit claims: "The Government Supports Grit Filters." "Support" here is ambiguous. It could mean that government research supports Grit's claim that it is lower in tar and nicotine than its competitors, but it could also mean that the government endorses the use of Grit.

The danger of the ambiguous ad is that it is open to interpretation. We consumers are left to draw our own conclusions, and it is likely to be the incorrect one from our viewpoint but the desired one from the advertiser's. For example, for years consumers inferred from Listerine's ads that its mouthwash effectively fought bacteria and sore throats. In 1978 the FTC concluded that Listerine ads were extremely misleading and ordered the company to run a multimillion-dollar disclaimer. Similarly, the makers of Coricidin like to advertise: "At the first sign of a cold or flu—Coricidin." Although it is never explicitly stated that Coricidin can cure the common cold, that implication is rather strong. When pressed, the product's manufacturers concede that the medicine can at best provide only temporary relief from symptoms. Then why not say that, rather than couching the ad in such ambiguous language that a stronger and ultimately misleading conclusion can be inferred? Answer: because ambiguous ads work. They effectively motivate consumer behavior.

Ambiguous Comparisons   Advertisers frequently make comparisons that can be interpreted in more than one way, again, in order to effectively suggest what cannot truthfully be said explicitly. The most common device is simply to leave the comparison unfinished.

For example, in one famous ad we are told, "Anacin: Twice as much of the pain reliever doctors recommend most." Compared to what? And what exactly *is* the pain reliever doctors recommend most? Well, as you might guess, the pain reliever doctors recommend most is aspirin. Can it be then that what the ad is really saying is that one tablet of Anacin contains twice as much aspirin as one aspirin tablet?

In unfinished comparisons some advertisers think they have found the greatest thing since sliced bread. The Continental Baking Company, in promoting Profile Bread as a weight loss product, said that a slice of Profile contained seven fewer calories than other breads. When challenged by the Federal Trade Commission (FTC), Continental was forced to reveal that this was merely because Profile was sliced thinner than most other breads.

Here's one from Detroit. "Ford LTD—700% quieter!" Compared to what? Viewers of this ad are understandably prone to fill out the comparison for themselves in one of several ways relevant to selecting a new car. So, for example, many viewers naturally assume that the ad means that this year's model is 700 percent quieter than last year's model, or that the Ford LTD is 700 percent quieter than the competitors in its price category. When the FTC challenged the claim, Ford admitted that the real basis of the comparison was exterior noise. The inside of the car was 700 percent quieter than the outside.

Positive Emotional Charge   Certain vague words have become particular favorites of advertisers, apparently because they carry a positive emotional charge.

"Homemade," "country taste," "down-home flavor," "quality," "nutritious," "fun," "pleasure," and "good times" immediately come to mind. In recent times, "natural" has surfaced as a special favorite of advertisers, as in

> "It's natural for fresh breath." (Ad for Wrigley's Doublemint gum)
> "It's only natural." (Ad for Winston cigarettes)

and

> "Welcome to the pure and natural world of feminine care." (Ad for a feminine deodorant spray)

Although the word "natural" has extremely positive connotations today, it is hopelessly vague as it is most frequently used in advertising. What does it mean in these ads? That the use of the product has become rather commonplace? That using the product is as natural as, say, eating or sleeping? In what sense are gum chewing, smoking, and using feminine deodorant sprays "natural"?

In contrast with these vague uses, notice that the word "natural" has also a quite specific meaning in some advertising contexts. As applied to a product's ingredients, "natural" means "not artificial," whereas "artificial" means "human-made." This is the sense in which, for example, Tree Sweet Products Company was challenged to defend its claim that its grape drink contained only "natural color." When the company was unable to defend this claim, it was forced to pay a consumer-plaintiff $250,000 in punitive damages and an estimated seventy-five-cent refund to everybody who purchased the grape drink between 1973 and 1976.

Weasel Words Already we have seen a number of devices and strategies whose function is to enable the advertiser to suggest what cannot truthfully be said in an explicit and straightforward way. Another such device is known as the "weasel word." This expression is derived from the egg-eating habits of weasels. A weasel will bite into the eggshell and suck out the contents, leaving what appears to the casual observer to be an intact egg. Similarly, *a weasel word or phrase is a device whose function is to evacuate the substance from what appears on the surface to be a substantial claim.* In effect, what the weasel word does is to make the claim in which it is used a vague claim, while, at the same time, at least partially concealing the vagueness.

"Help" functions in advertising as a weasel. "Help" means "aid" or "assist" and nothing more. Yet as one author has observed, "'Help' is the one single word which, in all the annals of advertising, has done the most to say something that couldn't be said."[6] Once "help" is used to qualify a claim, almost anything can be said after it.

Accordingly, we are exposed to ads for products that "help keep us young," "help prevent cavities," and "help keep our houses germ free." Just think of how many times a day you hear or read pitches that say "helps stop," "helps prevent," "helps fight," "helps overcome," "helps you feel," and "helps you look." But don't think "help" is the only weasel in the advertiser's arsenal.

"Like" (as in "makes your floor look like new"), "virtual" or "virtually" (as in "virtually no cavities"), "up to" (as in "provides relief up to eight hours"), "as much as" (as in "saves as much as one gallon of gas"), and other weasels say what cannot be said. Studies indicate that on hearing or reading a weasel-containing claim, we tend to screen out the weasel and take the assertion as an unqualified statement. Thus, on hearing that a medicine "can provide up to eight hours' relief," we screen out the "can" and the "up to" and infer that the product will give us eight hours' relief. In fact, according to a strict reading of the wording of the ad, the product may give no relief at all; and if it does give relief, the relief could vary in length from a moment to just under eight hours.

*Quick Check on Ambiguity and Vagueness in Advertising (Answers on Page 387)

Comment on the ambiguity in the following ads:

1. "Fleischmann's—made from 100% corn oil"
2. "Coffee-mate gives you more body, more flavor"
3. "Free gifts with every new deposit"
4. "With Real Blueberry Buds and Other Natural Flavors" (front of the package of Aunt Jemima frozen Jumbo Blueberry Waffles)
5. "Most Colgate kids got fewer cavities"
6. "In today's Army, you can earn good money, while learning a skill to make even more money. . . . If you qualify [for a number of jobs], you can enlist for one of hundreds of exciting Army skills. Or you can choose the initial area of unit you'd like to serve in, near home in the continental United States or someplace new. Your choice will be guaranteed in writing before you enlist."
7. "We try harder" (Avis)
8. "Pleasure is where you find it" (Viceroy cigarettes)
9. "When you can't take five, take three! Anacin Three"

Exaggeration

Let's remind ourselves once again that the primary goal of advertising is to motivate the purchase. It is therefore in the advertiser's interest to convey whatever information he may have that would incline the consumer toward making the purchase. The advertiser naturally wants to maximize the consumer's inclination regardless of the actual weight of evidence he may have to bring to bear on the consumer's rational deliberations. Therefore, advertisers frequently resort to the use of hyperbolic language, or "hype."

This terminology derives from "hyperbole," which refers to an exaggeration or extravagant language used as a figure of speech. For example, someone may say, "I could sleep for a week!" an extravagant way of saying "I'm very tired"; or "I could eat a horse!" an exaggerated way of saying "I'm very hungry."

In advertising, such extravagance is intended not to inform but to *excite* the consumer. Here are just a few of literally hundreds of exaggerations you come across daily in reading and watching television.

"Spectacular Two-day Fur Sale"
"Waterford: The Ultimate Gift!"
"Diamonds are forever!"
"She was the 1st and the goddess of the moon. The Mystery and the Danger . . . a closeup tribute to a beautiful and immortal legend." (ad for *The Last Sitting,* a photo essay of Marilyn Monroe)
"Whirlpool at sizzling low prices!"
"The amazing 'Face-Lift-in-a-Jar'—Used by Hollywood Stars who didn't want plastic surgery"
"Stand without help or pain" (ad for the Cushion-Lift chair)
"You won't believe your eyes!" (ad for Medical Curiosities)
"Incredible! $3.25 worth of E-A-D cream FREE!"
"Wipe away stretch marks instantly!" (ad for Fade-Out)
"Shampoo, Wave & Curls! No Permanent! No Nitely Curlers! No Teasing! No Blow Driers! Chic Salon look for pennies!" (ad for Wave & Curl)
"A most incredible achievement in cosmetic science! Remove skin discolorations forever!" (ad for Dermacure)
"Amazing new 'computerized' forehead thermometer makes oral, rectal thermometers obsolete!' (ad for Tel-A-Fever)

It is true that the FTC and the Food and Drug Administration (FDA) sometimes make advertisers defend their boasts. If they can't they are censured, as in the Profile and Listerine cases. In the tire industry, the FTC has questioned Goodyear's claim that its Double-Eagle polysteel tires can be driven over ax blades without suffering damage. It has also asked Sears Roebuck and Company to prove its claim that its steel-belted radial tires can give 60,000 to 101,000 miles of service. In the auto industry, the FTC has questioned Volkswagen's claim that its squareback sedan gets about 25 miles per gallon and that it saves drivers 200 gallons of gas more a year than the average domestic compact. In addition, the FTC has asked General Motors to verify its boast that its Vega's ground beams provide more side-impact collision protection than those of any other comparable compact. And it has questioned Chrysler's claim that its electronic system never needs tuning.

But before you conclude that the government regulators are protecting you from the onslaught of exaggeration in advertising, remember that the vast majority of claims are never questioned. More important, the law permits what in the trade is termed "puffery."

Puffery   Puffery is defined in law as advertising or other sales representations that praise an item with vague subjective opinions, superlatives, or exaggerations. In his book *The Great American Blowup,* Ivan L. Preston gives a long list of examples, including:

> "When you say Budweiser, you've said it all."
> "When you're out of Schlitz, you're out of beer."
> "You can be sure if it's Westinghouse."
> "Toshiba—in touch with tomorrow."
> "With a name like Smucker's, it's got to be good."
> "Come to where the flavor is." (Marlboro)
> "Prudential is the strength of Gibraltar."
> "The rock of Prudential—Above and Beyond!"
> "You'll love it at Levits.' "

Lawmakers permit puffery because they have decided, on the basis of actual cases, that most puffery is not deceptive. Certainly, in some cases puffery is not deceptive. When an oil company says that you'll have a tiger in your tank when you use its gasoline, no one expects a tiger. But are most puffs so outlandish that no one takes them seriously?

If puffery were not deceptive, it wouldn't sell products. But advertising experts agree that puffs sell. What's more, a survey conducted in 1971 by R. H. Bruskin Associates supports the view that puffery deceives. In that survey a sample of citizens was asked whether they felt that various advertising claims were "completely true," "partly true," or "not true at all." Although puffery was not identified by name, a number of claims fell into that category and were rated as follows:

> "State Farm is all you need to know about life insurance." (22% said completely true, 36% said partly true)
> "The world's most experienced airline." (PAN AM) (23% said completely true, 47% said partly true)
> "Ford has a better idea." (26% completely true, 42% partly true)
> "You can trust your car to the man who wears the star." (Texaco) (21% said completely true, 47% partly true)
> "It's the real thing." (Coca-Cola) (35% said completely true, 29% said partly true)
> "Perfect rice every time." (Minute Rice) (43% said completely true, 30% partly true)
> "Today aluminum is something else." (Alcoa) (47% said completely true, 36% partly true)[7]

The conclusion seems unmistakable: Puffery does work. Evidently, it does deceive at least some people, even though our lawmakers think otherwise. And, even where it doesn't actually deceive, it excites, and this probably accounts even more deeply for its effectiveness as an advertising strategy. Because the law doesn't restrict the use of puffery, we must guard against being victimized by it.

*Quick Check on Exaggeration (Answers on Page 388)

Comment on the use of exaggeration and puffery in the following ads and names:

1. Top-Flite Golf Balls
2. Super Shell
3. True cigarettes
4. Wonder Bread
5. "Take the road to flavor in a low-tar cigarette." (Raleigh Lights)
6. "Ahhhhhh! Anusol."
7. "The pleasure is back. Barclay."
8. "Bud—the King of beers!"

Psychological Appeals

Since the advertiser naturally wants to maximize the consumer's inclination toward the purchase, regardless of the evidence he may have to bring to bear on the consumer's rational deliberations, advertisers frequently resort to psychological appeals, just as they do to the use of hype. *A psychological appeal is one that aims to persuade by engaging human emotions and emotional needs, rather than reason.*

An automobile ad that presents the product in an elitist environment peopled by members of the "in" set appeals to our desire for status. A life insurance ad that portrays a destitute family woefully struggling in the aftermath of a provider's death aims to persuade through pity and fear.

Ads that rely primarily on pitches to wealth, status, power, prestige, security, sex, masculinity, femininity, acceptance, approval, and so on, are offering to sell more than just the product. We wish to be more powerful than we are, to have more prestige than we do, to be more masculine or more feminine, to get more and better sex, and so on. And if we do not in fact wish for these things, the ads are designed and function to encourage us to. Such ads, in short, are calculated to appeal to, and in many cases to engender, a sense of psychological dissatisfaction.

Sexual Pitches   Perhaps the best example of such appeals is the increasingly explicit and pervasive use of sexual pitches in ads. Consider the sexual innuendo pulsating in this ad for men's cologne:

SCENE: *An artist's skylit studio. A young man lies nude, the bedsheets in disarray. He awakens to find a tender note on his pillow. The phone rings and he gets up to answer it.*
WOMAN'S VOICE: You snore.
ARTIST [SMILING]: And you steal the covers.
More cozy patter between the two.
THEN A HUSKY-VOICED ANNOUNCER INTONES: Paco Rabanne. A cologne for men. What is remembered is up to you.

While sex has always been used to sell products, it has never before been used as explicitly in advertising as it is today. And the sexual pitches are by no means confined to products like cologne. The California Avocado Commission supplements its "Love Food from California" recipe ads with a campaign featuring leggy actress Angie Dickinson, who is sprawled across two pages of some eighteen national magazines to promote the avocado's nutritional value. The copy line reads, "Would this body lie to you?"

Not to be outdone, Dannon Yogurt recently ran an ad featuring a bikini-clad beauty and the message "More nonsense is written on dieting than any other subject—except possibly sex."

Subliminal Advertising   Some students of marketing claim that ads like these appeal to the subconscious of both marketer and consumer. Purdue psychologist and marketing consultant Jacob Jacoby contends that marketers, like everyone else, carry around sexual symbols in their subconscious that, intentionally or not, they use in ads. A case in point: the widely circulated Newport cigarette "Alive with Pleasure" campaign. One campaigning ad featured a woman riding the handlebars of a bicycle driven by a man. The main strut of the bike wheel stands vertically beneath her body. In Jacoby's view such symbolism needs no interpretation. In short, Newport is hawking more than a cigarette: It's selling sexual gratification.

Author Bryan Wilson Key, who has extensively researched the topic of subconscious marketing appeals, claims that many ads take a subliminal form. *Subliminal advertising is advertising that communicates at a level beneath our conscious awareness,* where some psychologists claim the vast reservoir of human motivation primarily resides. Most marketing people would deny that such advertising occurs. Key demurs. In fact, he claims, "It is virtually impossible to pick up a newspaper or magazine, turn on a radio or television set, read a promotional pamphlet or the telephone book, shop through a supermarket without having your subconscious purposely massaged by some monstrously clever artist, photographer, writer or technician."[8]

See what you think about the following example. Can you find a hidden message in the picture?

Hint #1: Not all subliminal advertising is sexual. Look closely at the upper portion of the Round Table logo—the part that looks like a set of medieval heraldic banners. Do you wonder why the middle one is rounded on the bottom?

Hint #2: Suppose the middle banner is in the shape of a letter of the alphabet.

Hidden Facts

If the primary goal of advertising is to motivate the purchase, it is hardly to be expected that advertisers would feature the weaknesses and shortcomings of their products. And in fact advertisers do regularly conceal unfavorable information about their products. As a result consumers who rely heavily on advertising for product information rarely have the complete information they need to make a fully informed choice about product price and quality. The facts hidden from them are hard to detect because background information is required to do so—an observation that also applies to false implications. This is why it's so important to keep informed by reading as much independent consumer literature as possible.

As an example of a hidden fact, recall the old Colgate-Palmolive ad for its Rapid Shave cream. It showed Rapid Shave being used to shave "sandpaper." We were told, "Apply, soak, and off in a stroke." Certainly this was an impressive ad for any man who had ever scraped his way awake. But Colgate failed to mention that the "sandpaper" in the demonstration was actually Plexiglas and that actual sandpaper had to be soaked in Rapid Shave for about eighty minutes before it came off in a stroke.[9]

More recently, Campbell's vegetable soup ads showed pictures of a thick, rich brew calculated to whet even a gourmet's appetite. What Campbell's didn't mention was that clear glass marbles had been deposited in the bowl to give the appearance of solidity.

Then there's the whole area of feminine deodorant sprays, currently an industry in excess of $55 million, whose ads are rife with hidden facts. Typical ads for these products not only fail to mention how unnecessary they are, but even more important, they omit to mention that they often produce negative side effects: itching, burning, blistering, and urinary infections. Now the Food and Drug Administration (FDA) requires a caution to accompany these products.

Certainly among the most dramatic cases of hidden facts is the one involving Pertussin Medicated Vaporizer, which the FDA ordered removed from market shelves on July 2, 1973, because the product was suspected to have caused the deaths of eighteen people. In the ten years the Pertussin Medicated Vaporizer had been available, shoppers who read the can's label had found nothing to make them wary of the product's contents. On the contrary, the product's manufacturers claimed it could "build a roomful of relief" from colds and hay fever. The spray's directions encouraged the spraying of the product on handkerchiefs, in rooms, and even on pillows and sheets. "Repeat as often as necessary" and "safe even in the nursery" seemed to reassure even the most skeptical of consumers. As for its ingredients, Pertussin listed the harmless menthol and oil of eucalyptus, stock ingredients in these products.

How could eighteen people possibly die after using such an innocuous substance? They apparently ingested the propellants and solvents the product contained. Evidently, Pertussin's manufacturers failed to indicate that menthol and oil of eucalyptus made up only 12 percent of the total ingredients of their product. The remaining 88 percent consisted of propellants and solvents. Moreover, these chemicals break down about equally between fluorocarbons and trichloroethane, which tend to upset the heartbeat and depress other vital activities such as breathing. Again, no mention was made of these facts.

The conclusion we can draw from this brief discussion of hidden facts in ads is that each of us must not only be scrupulous about examining the information imparted in ads but also must read more widely, especially in independent consumer literature. We must educate ourselves to all the facts, not just those a manufacturer gives us in order to sell a product.

In beginning to think critically about the messages imparted in advertising, then, keep in mind the advertiser's use of false implication, ambiguity and vagueness, exaggeration, psychological appeals, and hidden facts. Truth is rarely foremost in the minds of advertisers. For the advertising agency, the first consideration in concocting a campaign is how it can be said effectively and got away with so that (1) people who buy won't feel let down by too big a promise that doesn't come true and (2) the ads will avoid quick and certain censure by the FTC.

Summary

Language is the fundamental medium of our thinking: the fundamental medium within which our thoughts take form and gain expression. Two important consequences flow from this for our purposes in this text: Paying close attention to language is essential to finding out what and how people think; perhaps even more important, language itself exerts a powerful influence on what and how we think.

Language has several functions:

1. Informative: language used to affirm or deny statements. Example: "Washington, D.C., is the nation's capital."
2. Expressive: language used to vent or arouse feelings. Examples: "Right on!" expresses enthusiasm; "That's too bad" expresses disappointment or sorrow.
3. Directive: language used to cause or prevent overt action. Examples: "Study for the test," "Is the overhead projector available?" "Please deliver an overhead projector to my classroom."
4. Persuasive: language used in an attempt to influence the beliefs or motivations of another when we can neither command nor presuppose willingness to cooperate. Example: If you don't finish your chores we won't have time to go to the ball game."
5. Performative: language used in certain contexts to make something so. Example: assertion by a bride during a wedding ceremony that "I do."

Meaning in language is conventional. A convention is simply a behavioral regularity that humans maintain and follow in order to solve problems of coordination. Although the conventions of a language are arbitrary (that is, they could be other than what they are), how we use and order them is not. We must generally follow our language's conventions if we are to communicate with other users of the language. In general, you should follow common usage, and unless otherwise indicated you can correctly assume that a speaker or writer is doing so.

Two of the important dimensions of word meaning are the denotative and the connotative. The denotative meaning of a word is the word's extension, or the group of objects denoted by that word. For example, the denotative meaning of "bridge" is that group of objects we commonly identify as bridges; "building" denotes the Pan American building, the Empire State building, and so forth.

The connotative meaning of a word includes the word's intension, or the set of characteristics that define the term's extension. For example, the extension of the word "square" is defined by the characteristics "equilateral" and "rectangular."

The denotative meaning of a word, plus that portion of the word's connotation that corresponds to its intension, add up to the word's *literal* meaning. But many words have additional dimensions of meaning, which are included among its connotations. Quite often a word has special meaning for an individual or group of individuals because it evokes an emotional response. The emotional connotation of a word refers to its emotional impact.

The definition of a word is an explanation of its meaning. Four kinds of definition, or techniques for defining, can be distinguished:

1. Denotative: giving the collection or class of objects to which the term may be correctly applied. Example: "Snakes, lizards, turtles, and crocodiles are reptiles."
2. Logical: giving the collection of properties shared by all those, and only those, objects in a term's extension. Example: "A spoon (term) is a utensil (class) consisting of a small, shallow bowl with a handle, used in eating and stirring (distinguishing characteristics)." A good logical definition (1) states the essential characteristics of the term being defined, (2) is not circular, (3) is neither too broad nor too narrow, (4) does not use obscure or figurative language, and (5) is not negative when it can be affirmative.
3. Stipulative: attaching unconventional, perhaps unique, meaning to a term. Ordinarily, writers stipulate definitions when (1) they believe that a word is ambiguous and they want to give it a more precise meaning; or (2) finding that no word exists for some meaning they have in mind, they invent one, as with "glitch" for "a brief unwanted surge of electrical power."
4. Persuasive: attaching a different literal meaning to a word while preserving its old emotional impact. Example: "A real American would never avoid the draft." Words like "real," "true," "genuine," and "good" often telegraph persuasive definition.

An ambiguous term or expression is one with more than one conventional interpretation. In other words, it can be understood and defined in more than one way. For example, the word "bank" can mean any piled-up mass, such as snow or clouds; the slope of land adjoining a body of water, the cushion of a billiard or pool table; a business establishment authorized to receive and safeguard money, lend money at interest, etc.

A vague term or expression is one that has an indefinite extension. In other words, it is not entirely clear what it does and does not apply to, for example, the term "bald."

An issue is a genuinely disputable topic. And a dispute is a disagreement or controversy over an issue. Some disputes are "purely verbal," for example, the old dispute "If a tree falls in the forest and nobody is there to hear it, is there a sound?" Clarifying the meaning of "sound" is sufficient to resolve the dispute. But most of the issues that concern us are genuine and fall into one of three categories: factual, evaluative, or interpretive.

Factual issues are ones for which empirical verification procedures are appropriate, for example, when people disagree about how many planets there are in the solar system or whether capital punishment is a deterrent.

Evaluative issues involve differences of opinion about matters of value and concern, what we call "value judgments"; for example, should there be a law against abortion, or should animals be used in medical experimentation?

Interpretive issues concern how things should be interpreted or understood. Such issues frequently arise in our attempts to understand things whose meanings may be flexible, complicated, multilayered, obscure, or even deliberately veiled; for example, do the changes in Soviet leadership and internal policy indicate a fundamental shift in philosophy and direction?

Central to learning how to think critically is an awareness of the information environment. Three key forces shape how and what we think: advertising, television, and news. One very powerful strategy for exploring and understanding such large and powerful institutions is to seek functional explanations, or try to understand the peculiar features of things in terms of the goals or purposes the things serve.

Advertising does more than inform. The primary function of advertising is to persuade consumers to purchase one product rather than another, in other words, to motivate and direct consumer behavior. The goal of motivating consumer behavior is not always best served by providing the information the consumer needs to make an informed choice in his own best interests. Awareness of this fact is extremely useful in coming to understand the prevalence in advertising of deceptive techniques, practices, and devices, such as, for example,

1. False implication, which consists of stating something that usually is true while implying something else that is false. Usually the implied falsehood is more relevant to motivating the purchase than the stated truth.
2. The use and abuse of ambiguity and vagueness as means of suggesting something that cannot truthfully be said more explicitly. Examples include unfinished comparisons and weasel words.
3. The use of hype or exaggeration not to inform but to *excite* the consumer. This includes puffery, a legal form of advertising.
4. Psychological appeals that aim to persuade by engaging human emotions and emotional needs, rather than

reason. This approach sometimes involves the use of subliminals, which are designed to communicate below the threshold of conscious awareness.

5. The concealment of relevant, usually unfavorable, facts about a product.

Applications

1. Explain why the italicized word in each of the following sentences reflects the writer's insensitivity to emotional connotations. Supply a more appropriate word.

   a. Fortunately, the president has made *drastic* changes in our economic policies; otherwise inflation would be out of control.
   b. Teachers don't assign homework to make students' lives miserable but *merely* to help students learn.
   c. Attractive as the vice presidency of a large U.S. corporation was, Alice decided to *spurn* the offer and seek a presidency elsewhere.
   d. The French painter Paul Gauguin found in Tahiti a *sensual* quality that really appealed to him as a painter.

2. Give the present emotional connotations of the following terms: "New Right," "liberal," "social worker," "censorship," "CIA," "gay" (as opposed to "homosexual"), "United Nations," "big business," "judges," "open marriage," "virginity."

3. Assume that you have been asked to write slogans for placards to be used by the groups listed below for the causes listed in the right-hand column. Write a slogan for each, then explain why you chose the words or phrases you did and precisely what emotional effects you wanted.

Group	Cause
Mothers Against Drunk Driving	demanding tougher penalties for drunk driving
The Nuclear Freeze	nuclear disarmament
feminists	pressing for the passage of ERA (Equal Rights Amendment)
moral majority	demanding prayer in public schools

crime victims   demanding that they
                                       qualify for public
                                       assistance

Vietnam veterans   pressing for "store-front"
                                       services and other
                                       assistance

4. The same thing can be called by different names,
   depending on whether one is for it or against it. For
   example, if you're for a proposal to outlaw retail
   discounts on certain merchandise, you might call it the
   "fair trade practices act"; if you're against it you might
   call it a "price-fixing law." Take a specific topic, an
   issue, or current piece of legislation and give it a
   favorable and an unfavorable name by which it could be
   designated.

5. This exercise will help you see how we sometimes
   confuse the kinds or classes of things a term includes
   with the term's emotional connotations. For each of the
   following persons, give three descriptive adjectives
   (neutral, positive, and negative) that you would
   associate with that person. (You might think in terms of
   appearance, manner, ideas, and so on). Then ask
   yourself to what extent your responses are derived from
   your experience with actual persons included under the
   terms, and to what extent your responses derive from
   how other people respond.

   a. a Texan, a Russian, a Mexican, a Californian, a New
      Yorker
   b. A physician, a construction worker, a secretary, a
      stewardess, a prostitute
   c. A Jew, a Roman Catholic, a Mormon, a Jehovah's
      Witness
   d. A member of the Rotary Club, the American Legion,
      the John Birch Society, the National Organization of
      Women, the American Civil Liberties Union, the
      National Association for the Advancement of Colored
      People (NAACP)

6. Tell a group of friends that you are going to read them a
   short list of words and ask them to indicate the feelings
   that each word evokes: C (complimentary), D
   (derogatory), N (neutral). Then read this sequence of
   words: (a) opera singer, (b) Shakespearean actor, (c)
   Communist, (d) lawyer, (e) star football player, (f) a

black. Now check the responses. In fact, each of these words can be applied to one particular individual, the late Paul Robeson. Does this exercise tell you anything about how words can affect one's feelings about a given person or object?

7. Pretend that you have just attended some function or witnessed some event. Write a paragraph that contains a strictly factual account of the affair and then write one that, besides being informational, also carries a distinct bias.

8. For the following passages, show how the writer (1) has taken a word with a highly emotional charge (identify the word and its charge), (2) formulated a new meaning for it (indicate the meaning), and (3) then preserved a context that encourages the word's old emotive force (in other words, changes the word's literal meaning but preserved its emotional impact.)

   a. I don't know why some people get so mad about companies that deceive, even jeopardize, consumers. Such practices are part of the meaning of free enterprise, which everyone knows is the foundation of our political, social, and economic institutions. Free enterprise means that all of us should do what we think is best for ourselves. That's all business is doing—looking out for itself. If consumers are deceived or damaged, then that's their fault. Let them take a page from the book of free enterprise and look out for themselves. Rather than condemning business for being ambitious, aggressive, shrewd, and resourceful, we should praise it for acting in accordance with the doctrine of free enterprise, which is the American way.
   b. Murder is whatever prevents a life from coming into existence. By this account, abortion is murder. All societies have proscriptions against murder, and rightly so. There is no more heinous act than to take the innocent life of another. A society that does not stand up to murderers cannot call itself truly civilized. It's obvious, then, that if the United States is worthy of the term "civilized," it must prohibit abortion and deal harshly with those who have committed or commit abortions, since these people are murderers.

9. Keeping in mind the devices advertisers use to sell products, comment on the following pitches:

   a. Four bars of Ivory cost about the same as three bars of most other soaps. So buy four bars of Ivory and "it's like getting one bar free."

   b. "Alka Seltzer: the best antacid you can buy without a prescription."

   c. **Reluctant Auto Buyer:** I don't know. The sticker price doesn't seem like such a deal to me.

   Salesperson: Okay, tell you what I'm going to do. I'm going to slash three hundred bucks off the sticker price.

   R.A.B.: Now you're talking!

   d. Congratulations!! Your name has been selected by our computers as an eligible participant in our $10 Million Giveaway. You may already have won this Cadillac Seville! Or this Dream Vacation for two! Or this Dream House! Or $1 Million in CASH!

   e. "Incredible. Almost 50% of America's children don't get their recommended daily allowance of Vitamin C. That's why I'm glad my whole family loves the fresh taste of Tang Instant Breakfast Drink. It gives us a full day's supply of Vitamin C." (Florence Henderson for Tang)

   f. "Fact: Ready-to-eat cereals do not increase tooth decay in children.

   Fact: Ready-sweetened cereals are highly nutritious.

   Fact: There is no more sugar in a one-ounce serving of a ready-sweetened cereal than in an apple or banana or in a serving of orange juice.

   Fact: The per capita sugar consumption in the United States has remained practically unchanged for the last 50 years."

   (Excerpt from a two-page ad entitled "A statement from Kellogg Company on the Nutritional Value of Ready-Sweetened Cereals")

   g. "At Phillips 66, it's performance that counts."

   h. "Wisk puts its strength where the dirt is."

   i. "At Bird's Eye, we've got quality in our corner."

   j. "Of America's best tasting gums, Trident is sugar-free."

   k. "Here's 7 cents to try a cereal that's big with kids. Save 7 cents when you buy Post Honeycomb cereal. It's a big, nutritious cereal kids love to eat. . . . Fortified with 8 essential vitamins." (Ad for Post Honeycomb)

10. Report to the class on five ads that make use of psychological appeals.

11. Identify and document three ads that hide facts.

[1] This account of linguistic convention is derived from Jonathan Bennett, *Linguistic Behavior* (London: Cambridge University Press, 1976) and David Lewis, *Convention* (Cambridge: Harvard University Press, 1969).

[2] Lewis Carroll, *Through the Looking Glass,* in *The Complete Works of Lewis Carroll* (New York: Random House, 1936), p. 214.

[3] William James, *Pragmatism,* Lecture II (Cambridge: Harvard University Press, 1975).

[4] Ibid.

[5] For a detailed discussion of this strategy, see David N. Perkins, *Knowledge as Design* (Hillsdale, N.J.: Erlbaum, 1986).

[6] Paul Stevens, "Weasel Words: God's Little Helpers," in Paul A. Eschol, Alfred A. Rosa, and Virginia P. Clark (eds.), *Language Awareness* (New York: St. Martin's Press, 1974).

[7] From Ivan L. Preston, *The Great American Blowup* (Madison: University of Wisconsin Press, 1975) reported in Howard Kahane, *Logic and Contemporary Rhetoric* (Belmont, Calif.: Wadsworth, 1980), p. 186.

[8] Wilson Bryan Key, *Subliminal Seduction* (New York: New American Library, 1972), p. 11.

[9] Samm Sinclair Baker, *The Permissible Lie* (New York: World, 1968), p. 16.

COMMUNICATION II: TELEVISION AND THE NEWS

3

Understanding television and its impact on our society is a formidable undertaking that has already become a significant and specialized area of research and generated a vast literature. Again, at best what we can hope to accomplish in the short amount of space we can give the subject here is to begin an exploration of this important medium and to suggest directions for further exploration. Just as with advertising, we recommend and will be using a questioning strategy that seeks to understand television in terms of its functions.

Viewed as a technology and information medium, television has immense functional potential for human society. Now with the enhancement of satellite transmission technology, television makes possible the instantaneous transmission of audiovisual information on a worldwide basis. Now an international audience of almost any size can witness a significant event, say, an international summit meeting or the Olympic Games, as it is occurring. All of this makes possible a degree of social organization and coordination, on a planetary level, never before possible.

TELEVISION'S IMPACT ON THOUGHT AND BEHAVIOR

Television's educational potential is likewise immense. The flexibility of the medium is such that almost any subject whatever can be televised in some fashion and conveniently made available to an audience virtually anywhere. And it will accommodate virtually any audio or visual mode of presentation, from typographic, to didactic, to dramatic, to musical, with facility and in virtually any imaginable combination. This makes television probably *the* most flexible and powerful vehicle yet devised for the presentation and reinforcement of instruction at almost any level of sophistication and development, from preschool preliteracy to the most advanced. No one questions television's capacity to attract and hold the attention of human observers. And now with the enhancement of widely available videotape technology, television program material, like literature, is open to quite detailed study and analysis, not only by the producer, which was always the case, but also by the viewer.

Empirical studies confirm the highly plausible idea of a connection between television and the formation of patterns of human thought and behavior. For example, research conducted by James Bryan at Northwestern University has demonstrated that children who watched a five-minute videotape in which the characters donate their prize-winning certificates to charity were influenced by the segment to later do the same. Other researchers have replicated Bryan's work. They have found that children who watch videotapes of people sharing money and candy are also influenced to share. Similarly, in one of a series of studies using "Mr. Rogers' Neighborhood"—a children's television program stressing cooperation, sharing, and friendship—a group of researchers under directors Aletha Huston and Lynette Friedrich-Cofer found that the show, in conjunction with role-playing techniques, succeeded in producing more instances of empathy and helpfulness among children who watched the show than among those who watched shows unrelated to positive social behavior. Programs such as "Lassie," "I Love Lucy," "The Brady Bunch," and "Father Knows Best" have been studied in Australia. Segments were designated as either "high" or "neutral" in positive social values. Children who watched "high" segments—which stressed concern for others, sympathy, and task persistence—were found to be more helpful and cooperative after four weeks of such viewing than children who watched the "neutral" segments of these programs.

But all of this raises a very puzzling question: Why is it, then, that television does, on the whole and with only a few notable exceptions, such a lousy job in the service of society's pressing educational needs? Consider this brief letter to the writer of an advice column:

> A woman writes that her niece's three-year-old saw a dog lying in the street after it had been hit by a car. When the niece used the incident to warn her children about the dangers of running out into the street, the child replied "Oh, no! Momma, Wonder Woman would fly down and stop the car."[1]

The fact that the episode recounted involves the impressionable mind of a pre-schooler speaks volumes about the actual impact of television on how we think and see the world. It is true that as we mature we realize that there is no Wonder Woman to rescue us from life's perils; we grow out of that television fantasy, at least as a literal representation of real life. But television remains a central and deeply influential part of the education process that makes adults out of children. How and what we think, what we value, what role models we follow, what we aspire to, how we view ourselves, other people, and the world—all are influenced by the messages that television programs transmit to viewers. And the portrait of the world television ultimately supplies us is only somewhat less obvious in its distortions and in the inappropriateness of the values it embodies than the world of Wonder Woman.

The results of studies like those mentioned above are consistent with the report issued by the National Institute for Mental Health in May 1982. The institute reported that there exists a consensus among most of the research community that violence on television does lead to aggressive behavior by children and teenagers who watch the programs.

Fewer studies have been conducted to discover what, if any, effect television has on the adult viewer. One conducted by Dr. Rod Gurney at UCLA studied 183 married couples to see what would happen if husbands were assigned certain shows to watch. After only seven consecutive evenings, the wives (who were the observer-reporters, and who, of course, didn't know what programs the husbands were watching) found that the husbands viewing highly "helpful" programs showed less "harmful" behavior toward family members.

The question remains how to reconcile television's powerful potential as a teaching tool with the abysmal social lessons it generally teaches. In order to understand television and its role and impact in our culture more deeply we need to view television not only as a technology and an information medium but also as an industry and an institution.

Viewed in these terms, television's primary function in our culture has been to assemble audiences and sell them to advertisers. A corollary is that the primary function of television programming and its production is to hold the television audience in place and to maintain a favorable audience attitude for the receipt of the advertiser's message, to maintain what is known in the industry as "buying mood."

This explains first of all why television programming is almost 100 percent entertainment. Even television news and public affairs programming is presented as entertainment, a topic to which we will return shortly. Entertainment provides the audience a form of immediate gratification requiring minimal activity. Thus it perfectly suits the purpose of holding the audience at tranquil attention. The question remains, however, why does television entertainment embody such an unrealistic portrait of society and inappropriate set of values?

Television's Reality Warp

George Gerbner, Dean of the University of Pennsylvania's Annenberg School of Communications, is perhaps the nation's leading authority on the social impact of television. Since 1967, he and his assistants have videotaped and thoroughly analyzed some 4000 prime-time programs involving more than 16,000 characters. They then drew up multiple-choice questionnaires that offered correct answers about the world at large along with answers that represented what Gerbner saw as misrepresentations and biases of the world according to television. These questions were posed to a wide sampling of citizens of all ages, educational backgrounds, and socioeconomic strata. In every survey the Annenberg team found that heavy viewers of television (those watching more than four hours a day), who make up about one-third of the population, typically chose the television-influenced answers, whereas light viewers (those watching fewer than two hours a day) selected the answers corresponding more closely to actual life. Here's a summary of some of the dimensions of reality warp.[2]

Sex:
1. Male prime-time characters outnumber females by three to one.
2. Women are usually depicted as weak, passive satellites to powerful, effective men.
3. TV males generally play a variety of roles, whereas females are portrayed as lovers or mothers.
4. Less than 20 percent of TV's married women with children work outside the home. In real life more than 50 percent do.

Conclusions: Television's distortions reinforce stereotypical attitudes and increase sexism. An Annenberg survey showed that heavy viewers are far more likely than light ones to feel that women should stay at home and leave the running of the country to men.

Age:
1. People over sixty-five are generally underrepresented on TV.
2. Old people are typically portrayed as silly, stubborn, sexually inactive, and eccentric.

Conclusions: Again stereotypes are reinforced. Heavy viewers believe that the elderly make up a smaller portion of the population today than two decades ago. In fact, old people are the fastest-growing age group. Heavy viewers also believe that old people are less healthy today than twenty years ago. The opposite is true: Old people as a group are healthier than they were before.

Race:
1. The overwhelming number of television blacks are portrayed as employed in subservient, supporting roles.
2. Blacks rarely are portrayed as doing interesting and important things.
3. Blacks are typically presented as accepting minority status as inevitable and even deserved.

Conclusions: TV's distortion of blacks reinforces stereotypes and encourages racism. This conclusion is supported by Annenberg surveys that included questions like "Should white people have the right to keep blacks out of their neighborhoods?" and "Should there be laws against marriages between blacks and whites?" Heavy viewers answered "Yes" to these questions far more frequently than light viewers.

Work:
1. Only 6 to 10 percent of television characters hold blue-collar or service jobs, whereas 60 percent of the real work force are employed in such jobs.
2. TV overrepresents and glamorizes the elite occupations (for example, law, medicine, entertainment, and athletics)
3. TV neglects to portray the occupations that most young people will end up in (for example, small business and factory work)

Conclusions: Heavy viewers generally overstate the proportions of American workers who are physicians, lawyers, entertainers, or athletes. By glamorizing elite occupations, TV sets up unrealistic expectations. Doctors and lawyers often find they can't measure up to the idealized image TV projects of them, and young people's occupational aspirations are channeled in unrealistic directions. The problem is especially frustrating for adolescent girls, who are given two conflicting views: the woman as homebody versus the woman as glamorous professional.

Health:
1. TV characters exist almost entirely on junk food and quaff alcohol fifteen times more often than water.
2. Despite such a punishing diet, video characters remain slim, healthy, and beautiful.
3. Health professionals typically are portrayed as infallible.
4. TV may be the single most pervasive source of health information.

Conclusions: The Annenberg investigators found that heavy TV watchers eat more, drink more, and exercise less than light viewers and have unflinching faith in the curative powers of medical science. TV's idealized image of medical people coupled with its complacency about unhealthy life-styles leaves both patients and doctors vulnerable to disappointment, frustration, and even litigation.

Crime:
1. On TV, crime rages about ten times more often than in real life.
2. Fifty-five percent of TV's prime-time characters are involved in violent incidents at least once a week versus less than 1 percent in real life.
3. Video violence imparts lessons in social power. It shows who can do what to whom and get away with it. Usually those at the bottom of the power ladder are portrayed as not getting away with what a white, middle-class American male can.

Conclusions: Television breeds fear of victimization. In all demographic groups in every class of neighborhood, heavy viewers overestimated the statistical chances of violence in their own lives. They also harbored an exaggerated distrust of strangers—what Gerbner calls the "mean world syndrome." Forty-six percent of heavy viewers living in cities rated their fear of crime "very serious" as opposed to 26 percent of light viewers. The fear is especially acute among TV's most common victims: women, the elderly, nonwhites, foreigners, and poor citizens. In short, TV gets people to think of themselves as victims.

Among other things, this study belies the glib idea that TV is simply a reflection of the way things are. In many important respects, it is not. Why, then, does Hollywood offer what it does?

Remember that television's primary institutional function has been to assemble audiences for sale to advertisers. Given the astronomical cost of television advertising time, literally hundreds of thousands of dollars for thirty seconds of network prime time, it makes very good sense now to ask what sort of audiences advertisers want to reach with their messages. Indeed, the television and advertising industries are jointly obsessed with demographics, or various ways of measuring audiences. Prime-time sponsors want to reach the audience that buys most of the consumer products advertised on the tube. This audience happens to be white, middle class, mostly female, and between the ages of eighteen and forty-nine. These are the family-formation and career-building years during which household disposable income and consumer activity reach their peak. Like Gerbner, many observers believe that TV's scenes and fictional characters are tailored to what programmers perceive to be either this audience's expectations or what advertisers would like this audience's expectations to be. In short, TV creates a world for its best consumers.

Television does more than distort reality; it goes a long way to determine it. If social arrangements are portrayed repetitively in a certain way, and these portrayals are transmitted on a massive scale to the public at large, who come to accept them as realistic and begin to follow them as patterns and expect others to follow them as patterns, then social reality comes more and more into line with the televised portrait in certain areas and respects. Life begins to imitate art. In this way television becomes a powerful transmitter of ideology.

"Ideology" refers to the shared assumptions, doctrines, and ways of thinking in terms of which society defines itself. It is often conveyed through symbolic imagery. Such imagery is visible not only throughout television programming but even more prominently in the carefully composed ads interspersed throughout it. Consider, for example, the images of domestic family life in terms of which all sorts of household products are promoted, or the image Ford used in a recent television commercial of a committed and enthusiastic multiracial work force in an automobile assembly plant—where "Quality is Job One!"

Ideology is also spread by means of myths, which are stories that teach, explain, and justify the practices and institutions of a given society to people in that society. The "rags to riches" myth, for example, teaches that even the poorest of us can become wealthy and powerful. Myths deal with what is most important to us: love, death, violence, sex, work, success, failure, and so on; and they have a profound impact on consciousness, often influencing our thoughts and actions in subtle and unperceived ways. They manifest themselves most prominently in the plots, the story lines of television programming, and in the themes and patterns that one finds repeated again and again in plot after plot and story after story.

TV sitcoms, for example, invariably present problems that are resolved within an allotted time, usually thirty minutes. Crime dramas also present situations involving conflict that arrives at resolution at the end of the hour. These generally use a plot formula in which good is pitted against evil. The regular characters are the "good guys" and are associated with conventional morality and law and order. Intruders are evil, thus mirroring and promoting fear of outsiders and fostering group cohesion. The resolution is always in favor of the "good guys," which reinforces a commitment to conventional morality and faith in the system.

We're accustomed to thinking that ideology is transmitted by an elaborate apparatus or set of rituals, for example, military pomp and parades, religious rites, political speeches, heady lectures given in university classes, and so on. It is true that ideology is passed on to the masses in these ways. But the centrality of the electronic media in our society has endowed them with the traditional functions of ritual and myth in the transmission of ideology. Watching television is itself a ritual, governed chiefly by the rhythm of television programming, which together with the content of that programming is determined for the immense mass of the viewing audience by an exceedingly tight little group. About 100 people in Hollywood produce more than 95 percent of all network programming and thereby essentially determine what most Americans will see. Even more important, they thereby effectively determine what most Americans have available as nationally shared experience and vocabulary. In the words of Dean Gerbner,

Television is a hidden curriculum for all people. . . . You can turn the set off, but you still live in a world in which vast numbers of people don't turn it off. If you don't get it through the "box" you get it through them.[3]

Quick Check on Television's Reality Warp

1. What characters, programs, or depictions could you point to on TV to support or controvert Gerbner's observations?
2. In view of Gerbner's account of television's reality warp and its connection to television's institutional function, how would you account for the themes and the success of "The Cosby Show"?
3. In recent years a number of highly successful television series ("Hill Street Blues," "L.A. Law," and "Wiseguy") have abandoned the conflict/resolution plot formula in favor of one in which conflict remains unresolved and carries over from one program to the next. How would you account for this in terms of television's institutional structure and function? What ideological lessons do such "ongoing" stories convey?

69

NEWS

Perhaps the most disturbing of the detectable effects of television is the impact it has apparently had on journalism, on the news as it is gathered, reported, and interpreted in our society. Neil Postman, professor of communications at New York University and a media analyst who has taken considerable interest in critical thinking, notes in his most recent book, *Amusing Ourselves to Death: Public Discourse in the Age of Show Business*, that news and public affairs programming on television has degenerated almost entirely into entertainment, and that more traditional print journalism is being dragged along in the same direction. We have already discussed the centrality of entertainment as a dominant value in television programming generally. One look at a typical national or local newscast will quickly confirm Postman's observations that television news consists almost entirely of discontinuous fragments presented in an essentially entertaining format and that it effectively trivializes everything it touches. In case this assessment sounds uninformed or too harsh, Postman goes on to quote from Robert MacNeil, executive editor and co-anchor of the "MacNeil-Lehrer News Hour," who writes that the essential idea in television news production is

> . . . to keep everything brief, not to strain the attention of anyone but instead to provide constant stimulation through variety, novelty, action, and movement. You are required to pay attention to no concept, no character, and no problem for more than a few seconds at a time. [The assumptions controlling the production are] that bite-sized is best, that complexity must be avoided, that nuances are dispensible, that qualifications impede the simple message, that visual stimulation is a substitute for thought, and that verbal precision is an anachronism.

There are, to be sure, some notable exceptions to this general rule: Ted Koppel's "Nightline" program, particularly the week-long series of programs he produced in 1988 in the Holy Land; and the occasional "MacNeil-Lehrer Report." But such exceptions tend to prove the rule.

If we assume Postman's account to be a fair assessment of the general trend in television journalism, what evidence is there of a similar tendency in journalism as a whole? Postman notes the emergence of *USA Today* and its rapid rise in the first two years of publication to the position of the nation's third-largest daily newspaper. Its stories are uncommonly short, frequently no longer than a single paragraph, approximating the level of demand on reader attention typical of television. Its design is colorful and emphasizes graphics over verbal text. It is even sold on the streets through dispensers that resemble television sets. The successful *USA Today* format has begun to penetrate the approach of more traditional dailies, chiefly local and regional dailies, particularly as they have become absorbed into larger organizations like the New York Times chain and undergone editorial and management changes. Here is some even more interesting evidence of the deterioration of journalism.

Since 1976 Sonoma State University Professor of Communications Studies Carl Jensen has conducted an annual national research project, called Project Censored, to explore and publicize significant and underreported news stories.

Each year researchers in a seminar on mass media select twenty-five stories from a list of several hundred stories nominated by journalists, educators, librarians, and the general public as stories of national significance that failed to get due coverage in the mainstream of both print and broadcast journalism. These stories are then reviewed by a panel of professional journalists and media analysts to determine the ten best censored stories of the year.

In 1985 the top ten included the massive secret aerial war being waged under U.S. Defense Department supervision against the civilian population of El Salvador, officially a U.S. ally in Central America. This siege involved the heaviest aerial bombardment ever seen in the Western Hemisphere: well-documented studies of more than one-half million tons of hazardous waste, including radioactive waste and nerve gas, produced by the American military establishment and thus exempt from Environmental Protection Agency regulation; and something the news media must certainly have been aware of, a virtual explosion of media mergers, paving the way for an international information monopoly.

In 1986 the top ten included stories on high-level efforts to restrict the flow of information by eliminating, classifying, and privatizing government documents; a new official government "disinformation" program permitting the government to release deliberately false, incomplete, and misleading information; organized official harassment of political opponents of Reagan administration policies in Central America; and a story that eventually, about a year later, did hit the big time: Contragate.

In 1987 the top ten included further information on the growing media monopoly, indicating that the number of corporations controlling more than half the media business in the United States had dropped from fifty (in 1983) to twenty-nine; the CIA/contra/drug connection; and the role of George Bush in the Iranian arms deal.

All these stories were, of course, reported in American media sources. Jensen's point is that they received nowhere near the attention they each inherently deserved in mainstream media coverage. They were essentially marginalized, a fact that can hardly be accounted for in terms of the unavailability of information. Nor can the marginalization of coverage of such stories be accounted for in terms of the traditional understanding of the journalist's "watchdog" function, for these are precisely the kind of story that watchdog journalism would be expected to seize upon. Nor can the media's silence on these issues be accounted for in terms of limitations on mainstream time and space. Jensen demonstrates this last point by compiling a parallel list of the top ten Junk Food News stories of the year.

Junk food journalism, according to Jensen, creates "news" out of sensationalized, personalized, homogenized, inconsequential trivia. In 1984 the biggest junk food news story of the year was literally a junk food item: Clara Peller's "where's the beef?" ad campaign, to which the mainstream media devoted the equivalent of over $100 million worth of free publicity. In 1985 top honors went to another junk food item: the introduction of a new soft-drink formula, the "new, old, classic, and cherry Coke" story. Just how big was that story? It was so big that a year later Coca-Cola took out full-page ads commemorating the media event, which read in part:

On April 22, 1985, the American public witnessed an event so important, it was covered in every newspaper, and on every TV newscast from Bangor to Big Sur!

In 1986, precious hours and pages of mainstream media attention were devoted to such crucial items as the seventy-fifth anniversary of the Oreo cookie, the fifteenth anniversary of Walt Disney World and Imelda Marcos's 3000 pairs of shoes. In 1987, with the nation's economy, administration, and foreign policy all in ruinous disarray, the mainstream media spent months focused on the saga of Jim and Tammy Bakker, on the basis of a seven-year-old fifteen-minute tryst.

Newsworthiness

All of this raises the important question: What determines the newsworthiness of a story? What eventually gets reported as news reflects the judgments of newsworthiness made by those who report and edit it. But these judgments are in turn influenced by a number of factors that consumers of news rarely glimpse. We might expect these factors to flow more or less directly from an account of the social functions of the news media and the profession of journalism. The primary functions of news media and the professional standards of journalism are most frequently spelled out in our society in terms of democratic theory and ideals. Thus columnist Anthony Lewis writes in response to charges that the press has become "too adversarial" in its relations with government officials and too powerful and independent for its own good:

> The press is protected by the 1st Amendment not for its own sake but to enable a free political system to operate. In the end the concern is not for the reporter or the editor but for the citizen. . . . What's at stake when we speak of Freedom of the Press is the freedom to perform a function on behalf of the polity. . . . By enabling the public to assert meaningful control over the political process the press performs a crucial function in effecting the societal purpose of the 1st Amendment. Therefore a cantankerous press, an obstinate press, a ubiquitous press must be suffered by those in authority in order to preserve the even greater values of freedom of expression, and the right of the people to know.

But some of the factors that influence judgments of newsworthiness are quite plainly irrelevant to and even at odds with this traditional and idealistic conception of journalism's function as protector of the public against official lies and abuses of power. In addition to the subversion of these lofty concerns by the drift in the direction of trivial entertainment, the traditional values embodied in Lewis's account are influenced by a complex set of forces operating both in and around the media.

Students of journalism have observed that, like sociology, journalism is an empirical discipline. This means that the news consists of findings based on an investigation of the world and the people in it. But it also means that the news reflects the concepts and methods that underlie this investigation. These in turn are shaped by a set of assumptions about the nature of reality. What, then, is journalism's view of reality?

For ten years sociologist Herbert Gans spent considerable time in four television and magazine newsrooms, observing and talking to the journalists who choose most of the news stories that inform us about ourselves and our world. Gans was interested in their values, professional standards, and the external pressures that shaped their judgments. His study of the unwritten rules of American journalism helps clarify how our society works and how our perceptions of it are formed.[4] Gans's findings about journalism's view of reality can be conveniently ordered according to the following categories: people in the news, activities, race, class, sex, age, political ideologies, and foreign news.

People in the News   Journalists like to say that news should be about individuals rather than groups or social issues. And they achieve this aim: Most news is indeed about individuals. But not all individuals, or even most individuals, or even the most influential individuals are covered in the news.

About three-quarters of domestic news deals with individuals who are well known: the incumbent president, presidential candidates, members of the House and Senate, state and local officials, alleged lawbreakers, and flouters of social convention. Of these, probably fewer than fifty are repeatedly covered. Overlooked are those figures who are often thought to play important roles: military leaders, political party officials, large campaign contributors, heads of local and state political organizations, business lobbyists, and so on. About one-fifth of all news time and space is devoted to individuals who are not known: protesters, rioters, strikers, lawbreakers, voters, survey respondents, and participants in unusual activities.

Activities   The activities covered in the news are largely determined by the dominant well-known figures. Thus, coverage concentrates on government conflicts and disagreements (about 15 percent of the coverage); government decisions, proposals, and ceremonies (about 14 percent); government personnel changes (about 22 percent); violent and nonviolent protests (about 10 percent); crimes, scandals, and investigations (about 25 percent); and actual and averted disasters (14 percent).

Race   Over the past decade or so, the primary societal division in the news has been racial, although this was largely an outgrowth of the ghetto disorders of the 1960s. In general, the national news features middle- and upper-middle-class blacks who have overcome racial, economic, and political obstacles. Less affluent blacks more often are noteworthy as protesters, criminals, or victims. Blacks who already have been integrated into national institutions and those who make no attempt to enter them tend to be ignored, as do poor blacks, simply because they are poor and unknown.

Class   Rarely does domestic news deal with income difference among people or with people as earners of income. This stands in sharp contrast to foreign news coverage (and of course to television's general fascination with personal wealth). For example, stories over the past ten years about Chile, Nicaragua, and El Salvador regularly described demonstrations and conflicts, among upper-, middle-, and working-class groups. Domestic events rarely are couched in such class-conscious terms. To the degree that the news has a conception of the stratification system, it recognizes four strata: poor, lower-middle class, middle class, and rich. What journalists see and refer to as "lower-middle class," sociologists would call "working class," a term journalists eschew, perhaps because of its Marxist overtones. Moreover, journalists disregard the sociologists' "lower-middle class," that is, skilled and semiskilled white-collar workers, who, next to blue-collar workers ("working class"), are the largest economic stratification in the country. In effect, then, the news lumps the working class and upper-middle class together into "middle class." Not only does this stratification blur significant economic and cultural differences between the classes within this category, it also makes the so-called middle-class group appear to be more numerous than it would be by the more exacting sociological stratification. In any event, most news is about the minority affluent class (the top 1 to 5 percent of the nation's income distribution), because these people tend to be the "knowns" in society. Most important, the news rarely discusses a possible connection between lack of property and powerlessness.

Sex　In the 1970s the primary national division in the news was that between the sexes. Although most people featured in the news continue to be men, both print and electronic journalism have regularly reported on the women's liberation and feminist movements, as well as on male-female relations and related issues. But a large proportion of the stories has concerned the successful entry of women into traditionally all-male occupations and institutions (such as banking). As a result of the emphasis on politics and professions, the activities of organized women's movements and the advances of professional women have been covered in the news far more than either the feminist activities of unorganized women or the concerns of working-class feminists. Thus, comparatively little attention has been given to the wage disparity between women and their male counterparts, on-the-job sexual harassment, the way prostitution is reported, and the depiction of violence directed against women.

Age　Because most news is about politics, in which age divisions are relatively unimportant, the news takes little notice of age groups. Most people over sixty-five and under twenty-five are nearly invisible. When the elderly do get coverage, typically it's in the context of need (health care) or disaster (victims of crime), both of which fall under the rubric "the problems of the elderly." The general impression given, then, is that the elderly are nonproductive, out of touch, sick, lonely, poor, and victimized. Curiously, a study conducted in 1975 by the American Council on Aging turns up quite a different portrait of the elderly in America. Only 21 percent of those interviewed who were at least sixty-five actually found themselves with health problems; only 12 percent in that age category actually felt lonely; only 15 percent felt their income was too low to live on; and only 23 percent considered themselves threatened by crime.

When "middle-class" young people are given coverage, it is typically in the context of violations of social standards. Thus, over the past ten years, adolescents have appeared on the news variously as protesters, criminals, hippies, pot smokers, mystics, and lovers of music that is viewed by the general public as at best cacophonous, at worst downright inimical to morality and social stability.

Political Ideologies   The news spectrum embraces several ideological positions, ranging from "far left" to "far right." Both television and newspapers approve the moderate core, which would include both liberals and conservatives. To the degree that political groups deviate from the acceptable center, they are handled less seriously and kindly. Thus, radicals on the left are portrayed as socialists or communists, radicals on the right as neo-nazis. Moreover, journalism makes no distinction between democratic and revolutionary socialists, nor between those who preach revolution and those who practice or condone violence. It applies the "ultraconservative" label without distinction to those who favor aid to private enterprise and to libertarians, who advocate complete free-market enterprise and the assumption of many public services by private industry. It uses "liberal" as a catchall for those who favor the New Deal or its latter-day versions as well as for those like former California Governor Jerry Brown and former New York Governor Hugh Carey, who favored cutbacks in welfare expenditures.

Foreign News   Whatever occurs on the international scene that is relevant to America's interests is generally reported; what is not immediately perceived as connected to our interests is ignored until its relevance emerges. But this observation about the media's ethnocentrism must be quickly qualified by another: Because foreign news is given less coverage than domestic, only the most dramatic foreign events receive coverage.

Sometimes the concern for drama eclipses newsworthiness. Television is particularly susceptible to this concern, as evidenced by the crash of a Russian commercial jet in Luxembourg in September 1982. Each of the networks focused on this event, replete with film.

Other times the sensational qualities of an event crowd out its significance. For example, in the winter of 1981, a popular circus performer known as "Boris the Gypsy" was arrested in Moscow for dealing in the black market. NBC covered the incident, mentioning Boris's rumored friendship with Soviet President Leonid Brezhnev's daughter and the previously reported death of Brezhnev's longtime confidant Mikhail Suslov. NBC concluded that Brezhnev's political power was waning. ABC went further, quoting unconfirmed reports that Brezhnev's son was also being questioned for an unspecified wrongdoing and that a power struggle might be brewing within the Kremlin. Overlooked in the reports on these tales of high intrigue were questions of profound relevancy to the United States: Who were the major leaders contending for Brezhnev's position? In what ways would their ascendancy affect U.S.-USSR relations?

So journalists clearly make judgments about reality that help determine what they consider newsworthy. Since these judgments carry bias, they slant the news, for better or worse. But like all other empirical disciplines—and for that matter all other purposeful endeavors in general—journalism does not limit itself to reality judgments. News gathering and news making are also conducted within a framework of values. The daily news that you see, hear, and read originates with values (and the biases they carry) common to (1) the daily press as a whole, (2) the individual medium, (3) the key figures determining news content, and (4) society generally. While not exhaustive, these four categories do account for the chief sources of news values, a subject to which we now turn.

Quick Check on Newsworthiness

Suppose that you're the producer of a typical thirty-minute local newscast. You are in charge of story assignments and other editorial matters. It has been a pretty routine day: lots of stories have been breaking and developing (see list below). How would you compose the newscast? Which of these stories would you cover? Which order would you put them in? Which would you "lead" with? Which would you "feature" and promote with "news teases"? How much time would you devote to each? Which would you leave out?

1. A U.S. boxer is late to his Olympic event and thus is required to forfeit the match according to the "walkover" rule.
2. An inner-city tenement house burns to the ground, leaving all its residents homeless, without any possessions except those which they were wearing or carrying. No one dies or is injured and there are no heroic rescues.
3. Following the state board of education's decision to distribute extra funding to those school districts whose standardized test scores show improvement over last year's scores, students in one district announce that unless they are allowed to decide how that extra money will be spent, they will purposely do poorly on the test. The district refuses the students' demand and so the students carry out their threat.
4. A group of octogenarians from the United States meet with a similar group from the People's Republic of China to discuss history's impact on, and their hopes for, the two countries' future relations.
5. The state legislature votes down a bill that would have provided significant funding for childcare for the preschool-aged children of lower-income families.
6. A U.S. senator introduces a bill that would provide all legal U.S. residents with government-subsidized medical care, to be funded by an increase in individual income tax.
7. While on vacation at the family ranch, the First Lady is seen hanging out laundry in the morning.

8. While on tour with her orchestra, a Soviet tuba player defects to the United States. She is a distant relative of the Soviet premier.
9. An Ohio salesclerk wins the fifth-largest lottery jackpot in history, totaling $12 million.
10. Non-union construction workers complain that although the major U.S. corporation for which they work maintains high safety standards, their supervisors are forcing them to work in unsafe conditions.
11. A large group of Virgin Island nationals are demanding that the United States allow their country to become a self-governing nation. This group also proposes to establish a socialist economy.
12. Federal officials arrest five Puerto Rican citizens for undisclosed reasons.
13. A local sixth grade class has established a year-long pen pal project with a similar group of Iranian students.
14. A national women's convention is held to discuss progress, or lack thereof, on issues related to the Equal Rights Amendment.
15. The governor's nephew is arrested for alleged possession of one-quarter ounce of marijuana.
16. The local National League baseball team wins its third game in a row, thereby taking sole possession of second place in its division.

Values

Numerous professional values influence what is judged to be newsworthy. Three of them warrant special attention: objectivity, the dramatic and visual, and efficiency and economy.

Objectivity

Objectivity entails impartiality. In being objective, reporters, at least in theory, are supposed to "let the facts speak for themselves." They are not supposed to comment on or to interpret what they report but, in the role of disinterested party, simply to inform the public. Presumably, opinions are relegated to editorials and commentaries. Objectivity has been honored as a news value by American journalists ever since Adolph S. Ochs took on the languishing *New York Times* in 1896 and sought to rid it of any signs of bias on the part of his reporters, his editors, or himself. This value endures to this day. All reporters like to consider themselves objective; to be objective is to be thought unbiased.

But things are not quite this simple. In fact, the ideal of objectivity arguably carries with it a number of built-in biases.

For instance, objectivity arguably favors acquaintance with something, a type of knowledge philosopher William James, for one, distinguished from knowledge about that thing. Thus, you may be acquainted with the parliamentary system of government; that is, you've heard of it and know it functions in Britain and Canada. At the same time, you may have little or no knowledge about how a parliamentary system of government operates: what makes it different from a democratic republic; how, when, and where it originated; and so on. Thus, you have acquaintance with the parliamentary system but not knowledge about it.

Whatever we are acquainted with is likely to be concrete and descriptive; what we know about tends to be abstract and analytic. We typically become acquainted with things through personal experience or some other type of immediate apprehension. In contrast, we usually acquire knowledge about them through formal education or systematic investigation. Acquaintance emphasizes fact; knowledge stresses concepts. A newspaper announcement of a new drug to fight cancer provides acquaintance with the fact that a new cancer therapy is available rather than knowledge about how it works. The announcement of still another skirmish in the Middle East provides acquaintance with the fact rather than knowledge about why it happened and about the likely short- and long-term effects. Although acquaintance with and knowledge about something can be located on a continuum, and we can develop knowledge about matters that we earlier only were acquainted with, each kind of knowing is used for different purposes.[5]

In the view of most students of journalism, news is largely a matter of timely acquaintance with the world. But if news is not enhanced by "knowledge about," it can provide only a superficial understanding of what is being reported; for it is then a report of events, not of their significance, their connection with other events, or relevant hidden facts. Accordingly, for most reporters the truthful reporting of, say, a speech lies in its being accurate regarding the spelling of the speaker's name, what the speaker said, the size of the audience and its responses, and other descriptive details. But the reporter is not usually expected to assess the validity of the speaker's assertions if they have not been publicly contradicted. In fact, the norms of their profession usually prevent reporters from providing what knowledge they possess about something, for this would not be "objective."[6] For example, suppose the reporter knew for certain that the speaker was lying through his teeth. To comment on this would require knowledge about the issue, which if introduced would violate the ideal of objectivity.

Thus objectivity, as understood by most reporters, carries a built-in bias favoring acquaintance with, rather than knowledge about, the world, the superficial rather than the in-depth, the signalizing of events rather than the analysis of their significance. The preeminent journalist Walter Lippman said it best several decades ago:

> News and truth are not the same thing. . . . The function of news is to signalize an event, the function of truth is to bring to light the hidden facts, to set them into relations with each other, and make a picture of reality on which a man can act.[7]

Readers and viewers who forget this are apt to think erroneously that in the news they have the whole picture, a sufficient knowledge about people, events, and issues.

Still, it's difficult in most areas of inquiry to prevent our likes, dislikes, hopes, and fears from influencing our judgments. Journalism is no exception. And reporters will be as biased by their perceptions of their news organization's and editors' preferences as by their own life histories. Don't forget that the print and electronic press are commercial enterprises whose very existence depends on a financial profit. They are competitive enterprises that are and must be concerned with ratings, sales, and growth. They are large-scale enterprises interlocked with other industries. Finally, they are enterprises whose owners obviously have influence over the occupational status of their employees. These realities necessarily influence what is considered newsworthy. Recall the masthead of the *New York Times.* Emblazoned across it is the motto "All the news that's fit to print." Implied is the editor's prerogative to exercise personal judgment about what is appropriate for publication.

The Dramatic and the Visual

It's no secret that in the United States many more people are killed each year in auto accidents than in airplane accidents. In fact, about four times as many deaths can be attributed to auto smashups. Yet, the intensity of media attention accorded a plane crash by far outpaces that given the cumulatively greater numbers of deaths in automobile accidents. Why? Because perceptions seem affected by what we are better able to describe than explain. The dramatic quality of a singular event typically evokes popular interest. Both television and newspapers feed this popular interest by focusing on the dramatic and, in the case of television, the visual.

For example, on March 2, 1982, CBS ran two news items on the Soviet Union: one on the outcome of Poland's General Wojciech Jaruzelski's visit to Moscow, the other on a young Soviet couple who crashed their car into the U.S. embassy compound in Moscow. The Jaruzelski spot was given twenty seconds; the more dramatic and visual crash, two minutes and twenty seconds.

Advances in technology have made possible, and hence imperative, reliance on the dramatic and visual in television news coverage, especially in local news. The "action-cam" or minicam is a perfect example. Since its appearance as a regular tool of TV news coverage around 1975, this portable, hand-held camera has been hailed by many news directors as the device that freed journalism from the dreary "talking heads" era. But the short history of the action-cam doesn't bear out such pronouncements. Because no one can predict when a story will actually break, much of the so-called on-the-scene coverage consists of prearranged clichés (such as pickets, protests, press conferences) or of reporters standing at the place (such as a bank) where something significant has happened (such as robbery) some time ago.

But more important, it is the action-cam and not the intrinsic value of the day's stories that influences the nightly news agenda. If you disagree, consider the opinion of Walter Jacobson, coanchor of WBBM-TV's successful newscast in Chicago:

> The whole newscast is dictated by what the action-cam can do. We put stories on the air that are not worth anything. . . . Examples? All right. A 22-year-old man and his girl friend are in a boat on Lake Michigan near the shore. It's a windy day and their boat capsizes. They're all right, but the Coast Guard tows the boat in. We pick up the Coast Guard call on our squawk box. We send an action-cam crew racing out to the lake. And we do a live shot: "Patrol boat bringing in sunken boat at this moment!"
>
> My feeling is, what the hell does the story mean? It doesn't help the viewer get through the city's system. It doesn't help him exercise his franchise as a voter. It doesn't really tell him anything he needs to know. It drives me nuts.[8]

Don't be too hasty to write off this episode as nothing but a waste of time and resources. What we perceive as our community's or nation's pressing problems reflect the issues featured in the press. If the issues to be covered are determined largely by appeal to dramatic and visual content rather than intrinsic news worth, we can be left thinking that the riveting events presented are more important than they really are. A classic example of such misperception was the sudden concern about a seeming "crime wave" in New York City shortly after famed muckraker Lincoln Steffens and his fellow reporters at police headquarters engaged in some competitive sensationalizing in the 1910s. Nearly a half-century later, a study of crime news published in four Colorado newspapers showed that the amount of coverage varied independent of the actual crime rate. But—and here's the point—the public's perception of the level of criminality reflected not how much crime actually was committed but the amount of crime news reported.[9]

The other side of the coin is that, no matter how significant, what is not dramatic and visual goes ignored, at least until it becomes highly visible. Festering social, sexual, racial, environmental, and economic problems can go unreported, not to say unexamined, until some dramatic event catches media attention: a demonstration, a strike, a march on Washington, a riot. For example, throughout the year one rarely sees or hears any reports about educational issues. Yet, come September, the cameras are rolling and microphones waiting to record the drama of the latest teachers' walkout or strike, the reasons for which inevitably get lost in sensationalized reports on how many thousands of students are being hurt. One of the more subtle social implications of this kind of approach to news coverage is that, feeling they lack the coverage needed to inform public opinion, groups that see themselves as victims have little recourse but to attempt to manage the news through dramatic, symbolic protests that often produce serious, if temporary, social dislocations.

Efficiency and Economy

The media operate under the economic and technological constraints that typify other mass-production processes. As a result, efficiency of operations emerges as a key value in news judgment. To see why, you need only consider how the mountain of material made available to a news medium (primarily by its wire services) is reduced to usable size.

Working constantly under pressure of deadlines, editors often make split-second decisions regarding comparative newsworthiness, whether of facts to be included in a story that might be too long or of stories competing for limited space or time. (Of course, other judgments precede these, including the editor's deciding who to send on a story and the reporter's deciding which facts to include, stress, downplay, or omit.) Decisions about which stories to run and how much coverage to give them occur in rapid succession, and rarely is there time for reflection.

Besides working under the pressure of deadlines and having to process reams of potential news, editors work within structural constraints. For example, the reason that most newspapers exist is to provide what's called "straight news." But straight news fills hardly more than a quarter of most dailies.[10] So a basic constraint on news judgment is the "news hole." Whoever decides how large a newspaper will be effectively determines how much straight news it will contain. Who decides? Usually the advertising department. The editor's job, then, is not one of making the newspaper conform to the stories of the day but of fitting the stories of the day into the space allotted them by personnel whose primary function is to make money for publishers.

What about the prominence given stories? Will they go on the front page or in a less important place? Will they be given a couple of paragraphs or several columns? In fact, editors never see all the stories of the day before they make their decisions. Efficiency of operations dictates an editorial decision-making process that begins well before editors know what all the news reports will look like. This means that the later news typically has the least chance of inclusion. More important, editors usually scan five times more words in five times more individual stories than they can use. On large metropolitan dailies (over 350,000 circulation) they may see ten times more words and seven times more stories than we will ever see. What is discarded is never knowable to the reader or viewer. In short, the vast majority of stories that arrive in newsrooms, in a sense, never happen.[11] This is just as true of television news.

In making their news judgments, then, editors work within severe constraints of time and space. These constraints finally emerge as institutional values associated with profit. The order of the day is efficiency of operations, which means that the allotted space must be filled up in the time available. The good editor succeeds; the bad one doesn't. The result: instantaneous editorial judgments. Snap judgments are by definition unreflective, and they are profoundly influenced by the press's reality judgments. Judgment made with little or no reflection usually carries a bias and runs a high risk of inaccuracy or misrepresentation. This is especially true of television news, for which the economic and technological constraints are even greater than for print news. Thus, during the television coverage of the attempted assassination of President Reagan, viewers were told by two networks that Press Secretary James Brady had died. Indeed, they were exposed to the understandable frustration and irritation of one anchor, the late Frank Reynolds of ABC, who at one point in the coverage wondered aloud if it were known for a fact that Brady had died.

The values that we've just discussed are embedded in the news profession as it functions in this society. But beyond them are a whole cluster of sociocultural norms that the news parrots. Various sociologists have compiled lists of these values, and you should consult them to deepen your awareness of how the news media function. Journalist Jack Neufield, for example, speaks of "organic" values, among which he includes "beliefs in welfare capitalism, God, the West, Puritanism, the Law, the family, property, the two-party system, and perhaps most crucially . . . that violence is only defensible when employed by the state."[12] Similarly, journalist Herbert J. Gans writes of "enduring" values, under which he lists ethnocentrism, altruistic democracy, responsible capitalism, small-town pastoralism, individualism, moderatism, social order, and national leadership. Value judgments in these areas influence news content and presentation as much as the professional values we have focused on.

Quick Check on News Values

Evaluate the coverage of a specific event of national importance (like the July 3, 1988, shooting down of the Iran Air Airbus by the U.S. missile cruiser *Vincennes*) with respect to objectivity. Look for bias in word choice, headlines, and amount of copy. Determine whether readers are acquainted with or given knowledge about the issue.

News Sources

News sources, together with reality judgments and professional values, are responsible for shaping the news. Although sources alone don't determine the news, they go far toward focusing the journalist's attention and shaping news content. Powerful, authoritative people are a primary source of news. This explains in part why the media reflect the opinions and interests of the rich and powerful. Such figures can always supply information and are both authoritative and productive, as sources need to be. As a result, journalists develop a kind of institutionalized relationship with the most regular sources—high public officials and those associated with them—and at times even are assigned to them. Beat reporters in effect become almost allies of these sources, either because they develop a mutually beneficial relationship with them or because they identify with them.[13] Even when general reporters cover an especially important story, they typically consult the same sources and are effectively managed by them.

To get some idea of the predominance of high public officials as news sources, consider a decade-old analysis conducted of the origin of 2850 domestic and foreign stories that appeared in the *New York Times* and the *Washington Post*. Seventy-eight percent of the stories had public officials as their sources.[14] To a large degree, this reliance on public officials both reflects and accounts for journalists' reality judgments. More important for those of us who are trying to learn how to think critically about the information we get, it means that most of the information parallels the values and viewpoints of the public officials who are its primary sources, a point we'll return to shortly.

By far the single most valuable public official news source is the president. As George E. Reedy, press secretary to President Lyndon Johnson, pointed out:

There is no other official of the government who can make a headline story merely by releasing a routine list of his daily activities. There is no other official of the government who can be certain of universal newspaper play by merely releasing a picture of a quiet dinner with boyhood friends. There is no other official who can attract public attention merely by granting an interview consisting of reflections, no matter how banal or mundane, on social trends in fields where he has no expertise and in which his concepts are totally irrelevant to his function as a public servant.[15]

While support for Reedy's claim is not hard to find, one of the most dramatic examples in recent times involves President Richard Nixon's trip to China in 1972. Although the visit promised little hard news and few members of the press knew enough about China to provide interpretive reporting, all the networks and every major daily sent reports to cover that event: Forty-three commentators, cameramen, and technicians from the television networks, and forty-four reporters and photographers from the print media made the trip.[16] Commenting on the press entourage accompanying Nixon to Peking, the *New York Times*'s Russell Baker observed:

When President Nixon goes to China he will take most of the American television industry with him. Harry Reasoner, Walter Cronkite, John Chancellor, Barbara Walters, Dan Rather, Herb Kaplan, Bernard Kalb, Eric Sevareid and many more. . . . We already know that the President could make it very difficult for anyone else to get attention on television, but until the Peking trip we did not realize that he had the power to pack the entire television industry into an airplane and transport it lock, stock and Sevareid out of the country. This is not entirely due to Presidential power, let it hurriedly be said, but rather a disclosure of how thoroughly absorbed television has become with the Presidency. . . . Television is exceedingly Presidential. It is at its best with the bold, simple stories about strong men in familiar situations and this is the kind of story the White House, of all America's institutions, is most likely to provide consistently.[17]

As Baker intimates, through its automatic coverage of the words and deeds of the president, public officials, and other high-ranking sources, the news often gives coverage that is disproportionate to the significance of what is being reported. Further evidence of this appeared in the *Washington Post* after the 1970 congressional elections. *Post* writer Robert Harwood called our attention to a study of the front page of the *Washington Post* in the seventeen days preceding the November elections, and specifically to coverage that seemed to indicate a decided Republican bias. During that period the *Post* printed thirty page-one stories about the GOP campaign, which took up 268 inches of front-page space. In contrast, only six front-page stories about the Democrats were printed, and those stories took up 35 inches of space. Along with the stories, the *Post* printed fifteen front-page pictures of Republican campaigners, which took up 306 inches of space and only one picture of a Democrat, which took up 10 inches. In short, the Republicans received twelve times more space on the front page of the *Washington Post* during those seventeen days than the Democrats did. It's almost irresistible to conclude that the *Post* favors Republicans, that it's a one-party paper. The inaccuracy of this inference would stem from ignorance about the degree to which high-ranking sources can influence, even determine, news media. As Harwood put it:

> Like most American newspapers, we [i.e., the *Post*] are vulnerable to a syndrome that might be called Pavlovian journalism after the Russian who taught dogs to salivate when bells ring.
>
> We salivated over the Republicans last fall for one reason only—the President was out campaigning for them. No matter that he had very little to say that was significant or unpredictable at the whistlestops along the way. No matter that he did very little beyond waving at crowds. No matter that there was very little or no evidence that what he said or did affected a single voter. The mere fact that he was out there was Page One news in the *Washington Post*. What he was doing was "important," we told ourselves, because Presidents are "important" men.
>
> That kind of circular reasoning frequently affects our news judgment and results in statistical imbalances. . . . It says something about our sense of values and about our perspectives on the world.[18]

Presidents and other people and events are covered, then, not necessarily because they are newsworthy but because they could be. As a result, sources with a track record for newsworthiness—typically because they hold high stations in the social structure—are covered routinely. What they or others associated with them say and do dominates the news, even when the specific events in which they're involved aren't very important. Over-reliance on such sources can give credence to rumors, hearsay, speculation, and all manner of stories for which there is no hard evidence.

A good example of this occurred in the winter of 1981 when Libyan leader Muammar Kaddafi supposedly sent a "hit team" to the United States to assassinate President Reagan and other high officials in the U.S. government. Even though there was no hard evidence for the suspected plot, the press ran it as a working story, primarily because administration officials, including the president himself, gave it importance and credibility. Running with the story, television and newspapers variously relied on "informed" and "reliable"—although rarely identified—sources at home and abroad to keep this dramatic and sensational story on the front burner of news coverage for at least a month. As a result, between November 25 and Christmas Day, 1981, viewers were told that

1. The number of hit men being searched for was three (ABC), five (CBS), six (ABC), ten (ABC, CBS), twelve (CBS) and thirteen (NBC).
2. The would-be assassins had entered the United States from Canada (ABC, CBS), were in Mexico (NBC).
3. Carlos "the Jackal" was a possible hit team member (CBS, NBC).
4. The personal habits of various hit team members involved wearing cowboy boots and Adidas jogging shoes and smoking English cigarettes.
5. The hit team was composed of (a) three Libyans (ABC, NBC), (b) three Iranians (CBS, NBC), (c) two Iranians (ABC), (d) one East German (NBC, CBS, ABC), (e) one Palestinian (ABC, CBS, NBC), and (f) one Lebanese (ABC, CBS, NBC).
6. One hit team member visited Phoenix, Arizona (ABC).

All this information came from off-camera interviews with sources—"officials," "security officials," "Capitol Hill sources"—unwilling to be identified and thus as introduced by such phrases as "It's been learned," "ABC has learned," and the like. On the evening news of November 26, ABC anchor Frank Reynolds announced it was known that Libyan agents were in this country to assassinate the highest officials of the U.S. government. Neither Reagan, CIA Director William Casey, nor Secretary of State Alexander Haig had confirmed this. In fact, William Webster, the head of the FBI, told ABC's Sam Donaldson on January 3, 1982, "We've never confirmed any hard evidence about a hit team inside the United States."[19] And ABC Senior Correspondent John Scali, who first broadcast reports about the Libyan plot on ABC, insisted, "No one ever told me there was hard evidence."[20]

In fact, the only thing the press knew for sure was that security around Reagan and his top aides had been increased and that Reagan had been briefed about a possible plot. That the expressed concern of administration officials was well founded was strictly the opinion of the press. It's entirely possible that Muammar Kaddafi exploited the American press's reliance on "official sources" for information and on television's penchant for the sensational to influence events in the United States. At least that's the thesis of *Time* magazine's David Halevy. Halevy was able to check a number of purported hit team names on a Tel Aviv-based computerized system listing 55,000 to 60,000 terrorists and came up empty. His conclusions:

> While the threat was perceived as serious, too few in the American media looked at the possibilities of Kaddafi playing a disinformation game. Send squads to Europe. Send Libyans to the North American continent. Just get the word out. Kaddafi is no madman—he's a shrewd Bedouin who understands the demands of his society, and also how Western society works. Take that supposed voice intercept of Kaddafi threatening Reagan's life. In the Middle East, everybody who ever makes a phone call assumes the call can be intercepted by somebody.[21]

Even more likely, however, is that the episode resulted as part of a disinformation campaign orchestrated by the United States and intended to stir up public sentiment against an "official enemy." What is meant by this odd word "disinformation?" "Disinformation" is a technical term in the "intelligence community" meaning not merely false information, but misleading information—misplaced, irrelevant, fragmentary, and superficial information designed to foster the illusion of understanding while actually leading the recipient astray. Halevy's research is, if anything, even more consistent with the hypothesis of a campaign directed by the United States than with his own arabesque speculations, which amount in the end to more of the usual and predictable mainstream fare of Kaddafi-bashing.

It may be difficult for us to believe, even in these cynical post-Watergate and Contragate times, that the U.S. government would play such dirty tricks on its own people, that it would subvert the free press, and that committed professional journalists would go along with it. But consider this more recent series of developments in U.S.-Libyan affairs: On October 8, 1986, Bernard Kalb, a prominent career journalist (the *New York Times,* CBS, NBC), called a press conference to announce his resignation from the position he then held in the U.S. State Department as the nation's principal foreign policy public relations officer. What were the events that led up to Kalb's resignation? On April 14, 1986, U.S. warplanes bombed Libya in retaliation for what Washington said was Kaddafi's sponsorship of international terrorism. The United States continued to attempt to mobilize world opinion in opposition to Libya and Kaddafi by means of what was later exposed as a disinformation campaign, designed to confuse world public opinion and mislead the media. Word was put out that Kaddafi was still supporting terrorism and that another U.S. military "retaliation" was in the works. On August 25 the *Wall Street Journal* reported that "the U.S. and Libya are on a collision course." The story was picked up by the networks and other major media. As the story gained momentum, numerous official briefing officers passed along information—always attributed to anonymous sources like "senior White House officials"—confirming the *Journal's* story. Then on October 2 the *Washington Post* published excerpts from an earlier White House memo written by President Reagan's national security adviser, Admiral John Poindexter, which advised a strategy that "combines real and illusionary events—through a disinformation program—with the basic goal of making Kaddafi think that there is a high degree of internal opposition to him within Libya, that his key trusted aides are disloyal, and that the U.S. is about to move against him militarily." This revelation put Kalb in a moral bind. We may presume that Kalb was not privy to the memo prior to its publication, and that he, like many other official briefing officers, was passing along what he thought to be authoritative and responsible information in good faith—that is, until he learned of the memo, at which point he promptly resigned.[22]

This episode demonstrates the extent to which reliance on high officials for information results in managed news; that is, news that the sources cut to fit their own purposes. Because more news occurs than a journalist could begin to cover, news people must rely on surrogate observers—on "briefings"—to acquaint themselves with the day's events. But these sources are continually deciding what information to provide; what details to stress, downplay, or suppress; and when the story should be given to the press, if at all. By the account of journalist Richard Borchler, "Scores of American newspapers give their readers no hint that the 'news' they are reading has been 'generated,' 'leaked,' provided not by journalistic legwork and thought but by a government handout which is 'not for attribution.' "[23] When the events being covered happen to be highly technical, the reporter's reliance on canned copy can become total.

Case in point: the press's coverage of the first moonwalk. Here's a snippet from an article describing how the National Aeronautics and Space Administration (NASA) coddled the press during the coverage of that historic event:

> Dr. Wernher von Braun held a microphone in the big golden auditorium of the Manned Spacecraft Center.
> "I would like to thank you for all of the fine support you have already given the program. Because without good public relations and good representations of these programs to the public, we would have been unable to do it. . . ."
> NASA has assembled scores of publicists into one of the most effective and accommodating public relations machines in the history of press agentry. . . .

The press kit . . . 250 pages is forbidding. The NASA press men . . . accept with equanimity the odds that of the 3,700 people who get press credentials for Apollo 11, maybe a couple dozen were intimately conversant with the press kit.

The next superhandout from NASA is the 350-page flight plan. With it, you can make a timetable for your leads and bulletins, and naps and lunches. . . .

There was life on the moon and his name was Armstrong. He said . . .

Get the NASA man. Get the tape. Get the transcript. Get it right. NASA quoted it: "That's one small step for man, one giant leap for mankind."

Okay, that's official. We go with that and stick with that.[24]

In responding to news, then—in using it to understand, think about, and form judgments about the world—remember that news carries a number of built-in biases. These result chiefly from the reality judgments journalists make, the professional and sociocultural values they hold, and the sources they rely on.

Summary

Viewed as a technology and an information medium, television has immense functional potential for human society. For example, it is potentially the most powerful and effective educational tool yet devised. Yet, it evidently falls far short of its potential in terms of its actual social and educational impact.

This can be understood in terms of television's institutional function in society, which has been to assemble audiences for sale to advertisers. A corollary is that the primary function of television programming is to hold the television audience at tranquil attention and in a mood receptive to the advertiser's message. This explains why television programming is almost 100 percent entertainment.

George Gerbner's Annenberg research term has conducted extensive studies of TV's impact on heavy viewers. He has found that television paints a distorted picture of reality that reinforces stereotypes toward sex, race, and age; gives a distorted view of elite occupations; and breeds fear of victimization.

The most plausible explanation for these television distortions is that sponsors want to reach the audience that buys most of the consumer products advertised on the tube: a white, middle-class audience between the ages of eighteen and forty-nine—the family-formation and career-building years during which household disposable income and consumer activity reach their peak. Observers like Gerbner believe that TV's scenes and fictional characters are tailored to what programmers perceive to be either their audience's expectations or what advertisers would like this audience's expectations to be. In short, TV creates a world for its best consumers.

Television does more than distort reality; it goes a long way to determine it. If social arrangements are portrayed repetitively in a certain way, and these portrayals are transmitted on a massive scale to the public at large, who come to accept them as realistic, and begin to follow them and to expect others to follow them as patterns, then social reality comes more and more into line with the televised. Life begins to imitate art. In this way television becomes a powerful transmitter of ideology.

"Ideology" refers to the shared assumptions, doctrines, and ways of thinking in terms of which society defines itself. It is often conveyed through symbolic imagery visible throughout television programming and in carefully composed ads, for example, the images of domestic family life in terms of which all sorts of household products are promoted.

Ideology is also spread by means of myths, which are stories that teach, explain, and justify the practices and institutions of a given society to people in that society. These myths can be seen in the plots or story lines of television programming, and in the themes and patterns which one finds repeated again and again in them.

TV sitcoms, for example, invariably present problems that are resolved within an allotted time, usually thirty minutes. Crime dramas also present situations involving conflict that arrives at resolution at the end of the hour.

Perhaps the most disturbing of the detectable effects of television is the impact it has apparently had on the news as it is gathered, reported, and interpreted in our society. News and public affairs programming on television has degenerated almost entirely into entertainment, and traditional print journalism is moving in the same direction.

What eventually gets reported as news reflects the judgments of newsworthiness made by those who report and edit it. But these judgments are in turn influenced by a number of factors that consumers of news rarely glimpse, including journalists' reality judgments, professional values, and news sources, and by the dictates of time and space as determined by advertisers.

Journalism's view of reality results in the following:

1. People: Usually only well-known figures are regarded as newsworthy; the less well knowns are ignored or infrequently reported.
2. Activities: Usually only activities of the well known are considered newsworthy.
3. Race: Typically the national news considers newsworthy only middle- and upper-class blacks who have overcome racial, economic, and political obstacles.
4. Class: Rarely does domestic news consider as newsworthy the income differences among people and the connection between property and power.
5. Sex: The successful entry of certain women into traditionally all-male occupations and institutions usually is considered newsworthy, as are the efforts of organized

women's movements. The activities of unorganized women and the concerns of working-class women are largely ignored.

6. Age: The elderly are considered newsworthy usually in the context of social problems (as recipients of health care or as victims of crime); young people typically are covered in the context of protest, crime, or the flouting of social convention.

7. Political ideologies: Both television and print news favorably report on the moderate core of the political spectrum and handle critically extremes to the right or left; they also tend to overlook differences among politicians and group them under a single heading (as when they describe both Jerry Brown and Hugh Carey as "liberals").

8. Foreign news: What affects America's interests is considered newsworthy; what doesn't, or what is not immediately perceived as doing so, is usually ignored. Drama sometimes eclipses news significance (reporting the crash of a Soviet jet). Just as often the sensational crowds out stories of news significance (the arrest in Moscow of Boris the Gypsy).

Journalism's professional values of striving for objectivity, the dramatic and visual, and efficiency and economy result in the following:

1. Objectivity carries a built-in bias favoring acquaintance with, rather than knowledge about, things when reporting. Reporters are influenced by their perceptions of their news organizations' and editors' preferences as much as by their own life histories.

2. The dramatic and visual often are given top priority, as for example in giving twenty seconds to a story covering a Polish official's visit to Moscow but two minutes and twenty seconds to a story about a younger Soviet couple's crashing their car into the U.S. embassy compound in Moscow. Advances in technology (the action-cam) encourage news choices that favor the dramatic and visual.

3. The news media operate within institutional constraints of ratings, circulation, and profit. Efficiency of operations is of overriding concern.

News sources are a third force shaping the news. Powerful, authoritative people like the president are a primary source of news. Preoccupation with these sources can make the press susceptible to rumor, hearsay, and speculation, or even willful manipulation and disinformation, as, for example, in coverage of the alleged Kaddafi plot to assassinate President Reagan and other high government officials.

Applications

1. Watch and listen closely to several episodes of some television program. Determine what worldview is illustrated. (For example, the old show "Trapper John" presented a world in which doctors are competent, caring, and successful; have a good sense of humor, and often get intimately involved in the personal lives of their patients.) Then decide whether this worldview corresponds with your own experience.

2. Use the following chart to record the coverage of an entire local newscast with respect to (1) order of stories, (2) subject of story (such as crime or natural disaster), (3) time given to each story, (4) whether the coverage acquaints you with or gives you knowledge about the subject, and (5) the nature of the visuals accompanying each story, if any (such as minicam coverage of the bank where a robbery occurred or on-the-street coverage of a burning building).

Story Order	Subject	Time (in seconds)	Acquaintance with or knowledge about
1. 2. 3. etc.			

Using the information from your log, draw some tentative conclusions about the story priorities of your local newscast. What considerations about television news coverage help explain these priorities?

3. How would you account for these two seeming contradictions to the money/ratings explanation of the TV reality warp? (a) If female viewers are so important to advertisers why are female characters cast in such unflattering light? (b) Because the corporate world

provides network TV with all of its financial support, why are businesspeople on TV portrayed in such a sinister light ("Dallas," "Falcon Crest," "Dynasty," and the like)?

4. Follow one story of international significance, such as the elections in El Salvador, the coup in Paraguay, the withdrawal of Russian forces from Afghanistan, for a period of a week in one or more of the major metropolitan dailies, such as the *New York Times*, the *Washington Post*, the *Los Angeles Times*, the *Wall Street Journal*. Identify the sources of authoritative attribution. Who are the people, in other words, that the reporters quote or refer to in order to establish facts? What significant patterns, if any, do you notice? What significance do you attach to such patterns?

[1] Dorothy Singer and Jerome Singer, "Today's Lesson Will Be Mork and the Fonz," *TV Guide*, June 12, 1982, p. 35.

[2] George Gerbner, "Television: Modern Mythmaker," *Media and Values*, Summer/Fall, 1987.

[3] Ibid.

[4] Herbert J. Gans, *Deciding What's News* (New York: Vintage Books, 1980).

[5] See Bernard Roscho, *Newsmaking* (Chicago: University of Chicago Press, 1975), pp. 13–14.

[6] Ibid.

[7] Walter Lippmann, *Public Opinion* (New York: Free Press, 1965), p. 226.

[8] Ron Powers, "Now! Live on the Action Cam! A Reporter Talking!" *TV Guide*, June 19, 1982, p. 22.

[9] F. James Davis, "Crime News in Colorado Newspapers," *American Journal of Sociology* 57 (June 1952): 325–330.

[10] Roscho, *Newsmaking*, p. 111.

[11] Ben H. Bagdikian, *The Information Machines: Their Impact on Man and the Media* (New York: Harper & Row, 1971), p. 90.

[12] Jack Neufield, "Journalism: Old, New and Corporate," in Ronald Weber (ed.), *The Reporter as Artist: A Look at the New Journalism Controversy* (New York: Hastings House, 1974), p. 56.

[13] Roscho, *Newsmaking*, p. 83.

[14] Leon V. Sigal, *Reporters and Officials: The Organization and Politics of Newsmaking* (Lexington, Mass.: Heath, 1973).

[15] George E. Reedy, *The Twilight of the Presidency* (New York: Mentor Books, 1971), pp. 101–102.

[16] "Made for Television," *Newsweek*, February 21, 1972, p. 100.

[17] Russell Baker, *New York Times*, February 10, 1972, p. 43.

[18] Robert Harwood, "Pavlovian Journalism: Different Standards for Presidents," in *Of the Press, by the Press, for the Press (and Others Too)* (Washington, D.C.: Washington Post Company, 1974), pp. 91–92.

[19] John Weisman, "Why American TV Is Vulnerable to Foreign Propaganda," *TV Guide*, June 12, 1982, p. 12.

[20] Ibid.

[21] Ibid., p. 121.

[22] Conrad Fink, *Media Ethics: In the Newsroom and Beyond* (New York: McGraw-Hill, 1988), pp. 241–243.

[23] Richard Rorchler, "Managing the News," *Commonwealth*, March 22, 1963, p. 659.

[24] Charles K. Siner, Jr., "How the Moonwalk Was Reported from Houston: YOU AND NEIL AND BUZZ—YOU MADE IT," *The Quill* 57 (September 1969): 8–12.

PART TWO

ANALYSIS

THE ANATOMY OF ARGUMENTS | 4

So far our study of critical thinking has been a kind of logical consciousness raising. We have tried to make you aware of (1) the nature of critical thinking and blocks to its exercise, (2) the crucial role of language in thinking, and (3) the impact of mass media on how we view things.

Such awareness is a good beginning on the road to more effective thinking. But to sharpen your awareness and apply it effectively you will need additional analytical skills to recognize, understand, inspect, and assess what you hear, read, and write.

This part of the book deals with the analytical skills you need to improve your thinking. It focuses on argument, which is at once a product of critical thinking and an object to which critical thinking is applied.

ARGUMENT

The study of argument can be divided into four main areas: argument identification, argument analysis, argument evaluation, and argument construction. Argument identification is simply a matter of recognizing arguments and telling them apart from other sorts of material. Argument analysis involves taking arguments apart into their structural elements and seeing how they are intended to work. Argument evaluation involves criticizing them and appraising their strengths and weaknesses. And argument construction is simply the generation of original arguments of our own.

Before we begin with argument identification, let us first isolate the sense of the term "argument" with which we are most concerned here. Consider this portion of the Monty Python's Flying Circus "Argument Clinic" sketch.

CUSTOMER: Is this the right room for an argument?

ATTENDANT: I told you once.

Customer: No you haven't.

Attendant: Yes I have.

Customer: When?

Attendant: Just now.

Customer: No you didn't.

Attendant: I did.

Customer: Didn't!

Attendant: Did!

Customer: Didn't!

Attendant: I'm telling you I did.

Customer: You did not!

Attendant: Oh, I'm sorry. Just one moment. Is this the five-minute argument or the full half hour?

Customer: Oh, just the five minutes.

Attendant: Ah, thank you. Anyway, I did.

Customer: You most certainly did not.

Attendant: Look, let's get this thing clear. I quite definitely told you.

Customer: No, you did not.

Attendant: Yes I did.

Customer: No you didn't.

Attendant: Yes I did!

Customer: No you didn't!

Attendant: Yes I did!

Customer: No you didn't!

Attendant: Yes I DID!

Customer: No you DIDN'T!

Attendant: DID!

Customer: Oh now look. This isn't an argument.

Attendant: Yes it is.

Customer: No it isn't. It's just contradiction.

Attendant: No it isn't.

Customer: It IS!

Attendant: It is NOT!

Customer: Look. You just contradicted me.

Attendant: I did not.

Customer: Oh, you did.

Attendant: No, No, No.

Customer: You did just then!

Attendant: Nonsense.

Customer: Oh, this is futile. . . .

Attendant: No it isn't.

Customer: I came here for a good argument.

Attendant: No, you didn't. No, you came here for an argument.

Customer: Well, an argument isn't just contradiction.

Attendant: Can be.

Customer: No it can't. An argument is a connected series of statements intended to establish a proposition.

Attendant: No it isn't.

Customer: Yes it is. It's not just contradiction.

Attendant: Look, if I'm going to argue with you I must take up a contrary position.

Customer: Yes, but that's not just saying, "No it isn't."

Attendant: Yes it is.

Customer: No it ISN'T![1]

The humor here depends heavily on a commonly understood sense of the term "argument" as a kind of verbal conflict—which often becomes extremely pointless and frustrating. That is not the sense of the term "argument" with which we're most concerned here. Rather, we're interested in the sort of thing the customer described when he said:

> "An argument is a connected series of statements intended to establish a proposition."

In other words, *an argument is a set of assertions one of which is understood or intended to be supported by the other(s).* We will stipulate this as our working definition of what an argument is for our purposes in this text.

Here is a simple example: "Mothers are females. Joan's a mother. Therefore, Joan's a female." "Joan is a female" is the statement that the others are intended to establish. If we wanted we could combine all three statements into a single sentence and still have an argument. "Because (1) mothers are female and (2) Joan is a mother, (3) Joan is a female." So an argument can take the form either of individual assertions or of a single sentence that embodies those assertions.

ARGUMENT IDENTIFICATION

We often assert things without arguing for them: "Baseball is a popular sport in the United States. Football is generally played in the winter. Hockey is a popular sport in Canada. Basketball can be played inside or outside. Soccer is played throughout the world." These statements are nonargumentative. None of them is intended to support or establish any of the others; so, taken as a group, they do not constitute an argument.

We also use statements to explain things: "The class on the history of music has been canceled for lack of enrollment"; "The horse was frightened by a snake in the grass"; "Last night's rain made the streets wet." These are explanatory statements. They help explain something: the cancellation of the class, the fright of the horse, the wet pavement. They are, in other words, presumably intended to help someone understand something more deeply.

The basic difference between such nonargumentative statements and arguments is one of intent or purpose. If people are interested in establishing the truth of a claim and offer evidence intended to do that, then they are arguing, and what they are offering is an argument. But if they regard the truth of a claim as nonproblematic, or as already having been established, and are trying to help us understand *why* it is the case (rather than establish that it is the case), then they are explaining. Thus, when we say, "The streets are wet because it rained last night," we are not trying to establish that the streets are wet. We are taking that as an established truth and are offering an explanation of how they got that way. But if we say, "You should take your umbrella today because the forecast calls for rain," we are trying to persuade you that you should take your umbrella by offering the weather forecast as a reason. We are not taking the statement that you should take your umbrella as an established truth, rather we are trying to show how it follows from the other statement. Thus, we are setting forth an argument.

It is not so difficult to identify cases of pointless and frustrating verbal conflict, especially when one is involved. But identifying arguments, in the sense relevant to our purposes, can be much more difficult, especially when they are embedded in larger contexts. This is in part because (1) recognizing arguments involves recognizing the speaker's or the writer's intentions, (2) speakers and writers can have complex intentions, and (3) they do not always make their intentions perfectly clear in what they say.

Distinguishing arguments from explanations, or jokes, or instructions is a matter of discerning the author's intentions to persuade by appeal to reasons. Sometimes it is clear that what the author is trying to do is to persuade by appeal to reasons. In that case what the author has put forward is clearly an argument. Sometimes it is clear that the author is trying to do something other than persuade by appeal to reasons. In that case what the author has put forward is clearly not an argument. Sometimes an author may be trying to do two or more things at once; say, persuade by appeal to reasons and amuse the reader. Sometimes it's just not clear what the author is trying to do.

***Quick Check on Argument Identification
(Answers on Page 389)**

Determine which of these passages express or contain arguments.

1. Most people I know prefer foods with no preservatives added. So I imagine such foods are good for you.
2. Since the president has expressed a view, the issue is closed.
3. Of course vitamin C helps prevent colds. A Nobel laureate has said so.
4. "Even the most productive writers are expert dawdlers, doers of unnecessary errands, seekers of interruptions—trials to their wives and husbands, associates, and themselves. They sharpen well-pointed pencils and go out to buy more blank paper,

rearrange their office, wander through libraries and bookstores, change words, walk, drive, make unnecessary calls, nap, day dream, and try not 'consciously' to think about what they are going to write so they can think subconsciously about it." (Donald M. Murray, "Write Before Writing," quoted in Morton A. Miller (ed.), *Reading and Writing Short Essays* [New York: Random House, 1980], p. 275.)

5. "It is worth saying something about the social position of beggars, for when one has consorted with them, and found that they are ordinary human beings, one cannot help being struck by the curious attitude that society takes toward them." (George Orwell, *Down and Out in Paris and London* [New York: Berkeley, 1967], p. 125.)

6. "Willy Loman never made a lot of money. His name was never in the paper. He's not the finest character that ever lived. But he's a human being, and a terrible thing is happening to him. So attention must be paid. He's not to be allowed to fall into his grave like an old dog. Attention, attention must be paid to such a person. . . ." (Arthur Miller, *Death of a Salesman*)

7. "While taking my noon walk today, I had more morbid thoughts. What *is* it about death that bothers me so much? Probably the hours. Melnick says the soul is immortal and lives on after the body drops away, but if my soul exists without my body I am convinced all my clothes will be loose fitting." (Woody Allen, "Selections from the Allen Notebooks," *Without Feathers* [New York: Random House, 1972], p. 10.)

8. "Gentlemen of the jury, surely you will not send to his death a decent, hard-working young man, because for one tragic moment he lost his self-control? Is he not sufficiently punished by the lifelong remorse that is to be his lot? I confidently await your verdict, the only verdict possible: that of homicide with extenuating circumstances." (Albert Camus, *The Stranger*)

ARGUMENT ANALYSIS

As we indicated earlier, argument analysis involves taking arguments apart into their structural elements and seeing how they are intended to work. Argument analysis is a natural extension of argument identification, because argument identification already involves recognizing a set of assertions as constructed for a certain intended purpose.

Premises and Conclusions

If an argument is a set of assertions one of which is understood or intended to be supported by the other(s), then we may proceed to define two important basic concepts for both argument identification and argument analysis: the concepts of premise and conclusion. *The premises of arguments are the assertions offered in support of the conclusion. The conclusion is the assertion that the premises are offered to support.*

Thus far we have considered two simple arguments:

1. All mothers are females.
   Jane is a mother.
   _____

   Jane is a female.

2. The weather forecast calls for rain.
   _____

   You should take your umbrella today.

The solid line indicates the transition from supporting material to what the material supports, or from premise(s) to conclusion. Statements above the line are the premises; statements below the line are conclusions.

Signal Words

As we mentioned earlier, identifying arguments can be difficult, especially when they are embedded in larger contexts, because recognizing arguments involves recognizing the author's intentions. Similarly, identifying the premises and conclusion of an argument can be difficult, especially when we find them embedded in longer passages. If you learn to read and listen carefully, however, you can pick up clues to the presence of arguments and to the identity of premises and conclusions in written or spoken discourse. One of the most important clues is the *signal word,* or *signal expression.* Authors frequently use signal words or expressions to signal their intentions.

A signal word or expression is a word or expression that indicates the presence of a premise or conclusion. There are three main kinds of signal words: (1) words or phrases that signal conclusions, (2) words or phrases that help locate the general area where premises are to be found, and (3) words or phrases that help locate particular premises.

Conclusion Signals   The English language has a rich store of clue words and phrases that often indicate conclusions, that is, what is being argued for. They include

so
thus
therefore
consequently
it follows that

as a result
hence
finally
in conclusion
we see, then, that
one can conclude that
shows that

On first reading a passage, it is often useful to underline its conclusion indicators. You will thereby alert yourself to an important part of the argument's structure: the conclusion. Consider, for example, the following passage:

Capital punishment deters crime. It also ensures that a killer can never strike again. It follows that capital punishment should be permitted.

"It follows that" in the last sentence helps locate the argument's conclusion: "Capital punishment should be permitted." The first two assertions are reasons or premises used to support that conclusion.

Here's another example, followed by a comment:

Example: "A teacher who asks a question is tuned to the right answer, ready to hear it, eager to hear it. He will assume that anything that sounds close to the right answer is meant to be the right answer. So, for a student who is not sure of the answer, a mumble may be the best bet." [John Holt, *Why Children Fail* (New York: Delacorte, 1982), p. 82. Underscore added.]

Comment: The word "so" in the last sentence helps locate the conclusion: "for a student who is not sure of the answer, a mumble may be the best bet." The author offers two reasons to support this conclusion: (1) "a teacher who asks a question is tuned to the right answer, ready to hear it, eager to hear it" and (2) the teacher "will assume that anything that sounds close to the right answer is meant to be the right answer."

General Area Premise Signals General area premise signals are words or phrases that indicate the general area of the passage within which you will likely find a premise. Conclusion signals function as general area premise signals, because they indicate not only that conclusions follow but also that premises likely precede. But there are other general area premise signals, and premises typically are found after them. Such expressions include the following:

since
because
for
for the reason that
this follows from
consider the following

after all
the following reasons
inasmuch as
insofar as

Again, in reading a passage, underline such expressions in order to discover another important part of an argument's anatomy: its premises. Consider the following example:

Capital punishment should not be permitted <u>because</u> it allows the possibility of executing an innocent person. Indeed, people have been executed who have been proved innocent later.

In this passage the word "because" indicates that what follows it is the reason for the arguer's opposition to capital punishment. It helps locate the general area in which the premise is to be found.

Here is another example, from an earlier exercise, followed by a comment:

Example: "It is worth saying something about the social position of beggars, <u>for</u> when one has consorted with them, and found that they are ordinary human beings, one cannot help being struck by the curious attitude that society takes toward them." [George Orwell, *Down and Out in Paris and London* (New York: Berkeley, 1967), p. 125. Underscore added.]

Comment: In this passage the word "for" indicates the general area in which the premise can be found. It signals the author's reasons for asserting, "It is worth saying something about the social position of beggars."

A Caution Concerning Ambiguity Before turning to other premise signals, we should caution you to distinguish between argumentative and nonargumentative functions of some premise signals. For example, if we compare

You should take your umbrella <u>because</u> the forecast calls for rain

with

The streets are wet <u>because</u> it rained last night,

we see that the first is an argument in which the word "because" indicates a premise but that the second is not an argument at all. In the second, "because" has an explanatory, not a logical function: It indicates that the assertion is intended merely to explain the wetness of the streets. "Because" and other such terms (like "since" and "for") are ambiguous. That is, they can be understood in more than one way. Sometimes they function to indicate the presence of an argument, and sometimes not.

The point is this: Because some signal words are ambiguous, the presence of signal words cannot be relied on mechanically as an absolutely foolproof indication of the presence of an argument. Like most interpretive tasks, identifying arguments—and even recognizing an expression as an argument signal—is in large measure context dependent.

Specific Premise Signals   Besides expressions that indicate generally where premises or conclusions are likely to be found, there are words and phrases that help point out specific individual premises in a passage. Such expressions may be termed specific premise signals. They include

1. devices for numbering premises, such as "first,. . . second,. . . third,. . .";
   "in the first place,. . . in the second place,. . . finally . . ."
2. devices used for indicating the accumulation of different considerations
   related to the same conclusion, such as "for one thing . . . for
   another . . ."; ". . . furthermore . . ."; ". . . moreover . . ."; ". . . in
   addition . . ."; ". . . also . . ."; "consider this . . . and this . . . and finally
   this . . ."
3. devices used to contrast considerations related to the same conclusion,
   such as "however . . ."; "despite this,. . ."; "nevertheless . . ."; "but . . ."

Underlining such expressions will help you focus on the premises of an argument, as illustrated in this passage:

> Prisons in the United States are an abysmal failure. First, they don't rehabilitate anyone. Second, they don't so much punish as provide free room and board. Third, they further alienate those with well-established antisocial tendencies. Fourth, they bring criminals together, thereby allowing them to swap information and refine their unseemly crafts. Finally, those who do time are far more likely to commit additional crimes than those who have never been in prison.

In this passage the arguer uses "first . . . second . . . third . . . finally . . ." to indicate the accumulation of reasons that support the conclusion that prisons in the United States are an abysmal failure. Here's an additional example followed by a comment.

Example: "There is nothing in the biorhythm theory that contradicts scientific knowledge. Biorhythm theory is totally consistent with the fundamental thesis of biology, which holds that all life consists of discharge and creation of energy, or, in biorhythmic terms, an alternation of positive and negative phases. In addition, given that we are subject to a host of smaller but nonetheless finely regulated biological rhythms, it seems reasonable that larger rhythms will also come into play." [Bernard Gittelson, *Biorhythms: A Personal Science* (New York: Basic Books, 1977), p. 146. Underscore added.]

Comment: In this passage the arguer uses "in addition" to indicate the accumulation of the premises: (1) "biorhythm theory is totally consistent with the fundamental thesis of biology" and (2) "given that we are subject to a host of smaller but nonetheless finely regulated rhythms, it seems reasonable that larger rhythms will come into play." These premises support the conclusion stated in the opening sentence: "There is nothing in the biorhythm theory that contradicts scientific knowledge."

Arguments Without Signals   Although authors who are putting forward arguments frequently do signal their intentions by means of devices such as we've just discussed, frequently they do not. Many of the arguments we encounter and express contain no signals. Rather, the author's intention is left implicit, or "for the reader to figure out." Take this one, for example:

> When we cheat impersonal corporations, we indirectly cheat our friends— and ourselves. Department of Commerce data show that marketplace theft raises the cost of what we buy by more than 2%. Doctors who collect Medicare and Medicaid money for unnecessary treatments cost the average taxpayer several hundred dollars a year. The same applies to veterans who collect education money but who do not attend school.

This passage contains four sentences but no explicit verbal clues to its status as an argument. Yet, evidently the passage is an argument, because one of the claims contained in it is evidently supported by the others. How can we tell this?

The passage opens with the general claim that when we cheat impersonal corporations we are really cheating our friends and ourselves. This claim is what the arguer is advancing; it is the conclusion. How can we tell this?

If we ask the natural next question, "Why should we believe this claim?" or "What reasons support it?", the next three sentences in the passage are evidently responsive to our question. They cite several pieces of evidence: (1) Department of Commerce data which show that marketplace theft raises the cost of what we buy by more than 2 percent; (2) federal estimates which indicate that doctors who collect Medicare and Medicaid money for unnecessary treatments cost the average taxpayer several hundred dollars a year, and (3) veterans who collect education money but who do not attend school further inflate the taxpayer's bill. In effect, the author has anticipated the challenge, the demand for support for a controversial claim, that naturally arises in the reader's mind and has supplied evidence to meet it. These three assertions are therefore the argument's premises.

In dealing with passages that contain no signal words, an effective first question is "What, if anything, is being advocated? What claims is the arguer attempting to establish as true? What is the arguer trying to convince me of or get me to do?" This helps you determine whether the passage expresses or contains an argument, and if so, it helps you locate the argument's conclusion.

Having done that, you can then locate the premises by asking questions like "What reasons, data, or evidence does the arguer offer in support of the conclusion?" Arguments with no signal words require close contextual analysis. Contextual analysis is a set of skills that take considerable time and much exercise and practice to develop and refine. But they are well worth mastering.

Here are some additional arguments without signals to get you started:

Example: "Names are far more than mere identity tags. They are charged with hidden meanings and unspoken overtones that profoundly help or hinder you in your relationships and your life." [Christopher A. Anderson, *The Name Game* (New York: Simon & Schuster, 1977), p. 1.]

Comment: The first claim is the conclusion. The second sentence helps establish the conclusion by anticipating and responding to the predictable challenge "What functions, other than identity tags, do names perform?" Thus, the second claim supports the first.

Example: "An unhappy alternative is before you, Elizabeth. Your mother will never see you again if you do *not* marry Mr. Collins, and I will never see you again if you *do*.'" [Jane Austen, *Pride and Prejudice*]

Comment: The speaker is attempting to show Elizabeth that an unhappy alternative faces her. The alternative is unhappy because should Elizabeth not marry Mr. Collins, her mother will never see her again; if she does marry Mr. Collins, then the speaker, who happens to be her father, will never see her again. Thus, the first sentence is the conclusion, the second the premise.

*Quick Check on Argument Analysis (Answers on Page 389)

Using the tools and concepts outlined above, determine which of the following passages contain arguments, and analyze those that do.

1. TV shows like "Dallas" and "Dynasty" portray marriage in a most unflattering light. First, the partners are always quarreling. Second, they are always lusting after someone they're not married to.
2. Two out of three people interviewed preferred Zest to another soap. Therefore, Zest is the best soap available.
3. In the 1980s more and more people will turn to solar heating to heat their homes because the price of gas and oil will become prohibitive for most consumers and the price of installing solar panels will decline.
4. People who smoke cigarettes should be forced to pay for their own health insurance. They know smoking is bad for their health. They have no right to expect others to pay for their addiction.
5. It's no wonder that government aid to the poor fails. Poor people can't manage their money.
6. Even though spanking has immediate punitive and (for the parent) anger-releasing effects, parents should not spank their children,

for spanking gives children the message that inflicting pain on others is an appropriate means of changing their behavior. Furthermore, spanking trains children to submit to the arbitrary rules of authority figures who have the power to harm them. We ought not give our children those messages. Rather, we should train them to either make appropriate behavioral choices or to expect to deal with the related natural and logical consequences of their behavior.

7. In the Dukakis-Bentsen Bush-Quayle contest, we have the best argument yet in favor of a none-of-the-above category on the ballot. No further justification is necessary.

8. Public schools generally avoid investigation of debatable issues and instead stress rote recall of isolated facts, which teaches students to unquestioningly absorb given information on demand so that they can regurgitate it in its entirety during testing situations. Although students are generally not allowed to question it, much of what is presented as accurate information is indeed controversial. But citizens need to develop decision-making skills regarding debatable issues in order to truly participate in a democracy. It follows then that public schools ought to change their educational priorities in order to better prepare students to become informed, responsible members of our democracy.

9. "In policy debates one party sometimes charges that his or her opponents are embracing a Nazi-like position. . . . Meanwhile, sympathizers nod in agreement with the charge, seeing it as the ultimate blow to their opponents. . . . The problem with using the Nazi analogy in public policy debates is that in the Western world there is a form of anti-Nazi 'bigotry' that sees Nazis as almost mythically evil beings. . . . Firsthand knowledge of our own culture makes it virtually impossible to equate Nazi society with our own. The official racism of Germany, its military mentality, the stresses of war, and the presence of a dictator instead of a democratic system make Nazi Germany in the 1940s obviously different from America in the 1980s. . . ." (Gary E. Crum, "Disputed Territory," *Hastings Center Report,* August/September 1988, p. 31)

Incompletely Stated Arguments

Just as authors sometimes put forward arguments without signals, leaving it up to the listener or reader to recognize their implicit intentions, so they frequently put forward arguments that are not completely stated, leaving it up to the listener or reader to fill in the missing element(s). Sometimes the conclusion of an argument is left implicit. Sometimes a portion of the support in an argument is implied but not stated. But implicit conclusions and premises are nevertheless important elements in the logical structure of arguments and need to be taken into account in their analysis and evaluation.

Unexpressed Conclusions

Suppose that you are standing in line at the polling place on Election Day, waiting to have your registration verified and receive your official ballot, and you overhear the official say to the person in front of you:

> I'm sorry, sir, but only those citizens whose names appear on my roster are eligible to vote, and your name does not appear.

Clearly there is something further implied here. The implied conclusion, which is evidently intended to follow from the two claims expicitly made, is that the person in front of you is not eligible to vote. This example, then, does express an argument. And recognizing it as such depends on recognizing that the two claims that are explicitly stated are intended to support the unstated conclusion.

Here are three more arguments whose conclusions are unexpressed.

Argument: "Yond Cassius has a lean and hungry look. . . . Such men are dangerous." (Wm. Shakespeare, *Julius Caesar*)

Unexpressed conclusion: Cassius is a dangerous man.

Argument: "Only demonstrative proof should be able to make you abandon the theory of Creation; but such a proof does not exist in nature." [Moses Maimonides, *The Guide for the Perplexed*]

Unexpressed conclusion: Nothing in nature should be able to make you abandon the theory of Creation.

Argument: "When we regard a man as morally responsible for an act, we regard him as a legitimate object of moral praise or blame in respect of it. But it seems plain that a man cannot be a legitimate object of moral praise or blame for an act unless in willing the act he is in some important sense a 'free' agent." [C. Arthur Campbell, "Is 'Freewill' a Pseudo-Problem?" *Mind* LX, No. 240 (1951), 447.]

Paraphrased: To regard someone as morally responsible means that we regard the person as morally praiseworthy or blameworthy. But you can't praise or blame a person who does not have free will.

Unexpressed conclusion: Free will is a precondition of moral responsibility.

Unexpressed Premises

Just as conclusions can be implied but unstated, so when we argue we frequently leave premises unexpressed. Yet, unexpressed premises are just as important as the explicit premises to the structure of arguments. Suppose once more that you are standing in line at the polling place on Election Day, and you overhear the official say to the person in front of you,

> I'm sorry sir, but only those citizens whose names appear on my roster are eligible to vote.

Here again the context makes clear that the official is offering support for the claim that the person in front of you is not eligible to vote. But in addition to the unstated conclusion, there is an unstated premise:

> Your name does not appear on my roster.

How can we determine this? Consider the argument from the stated premise to the unstated conclusion:

> Only those citizens whose names appear on my roster are eligible to vote.
> _____
> Therefore, you are not eligible to vote.

The missing premise "Your name does not appear on my roster" is clearly implied here, because only if it is also assumed as a premise does the stated premise count as a reason for the person's ineligibility to vote. Therefore, it is reasonable to suppose that it is intended as a premise in the argument.

Here are three additional examples of arguments with unexpressed premises.

Argument:	Bill must be a poor student, for he spends most of his time watching television.
Unexpressed premise:	Any student who spends most of his time watching television must be a poor student.
Expressed premise:	Bill spends most of his time watching television.
Conclusion:	Bill must be a poor student.
Argument:	It's hard to appreciate Jackson Pollock's painting *Convergence,* for it's a work of modern art.
Unexpressed premise:	It's hard to appreciate modern art.
Expressed premise:	Jackson Pollock's painting *Convergence* is a work of modern art.
Conclusion:	It's hard to appreciate Jackson Pollock's painting *Convergence.*
Argument:	Because Smith married largely for sexual reasons, his marriage won't last long.
Unexpressed premise:	Marriages entered into largely for sexual reasons don't last long.
Expressed premise:	Smith married largely for sexual reasons.
Conclusion:	Smith's marriage won't last long.

We have intentionally kept these examples simple. But filling in the missing premises of an argument can be a very difficult part of the process of argument analysis, and it raises some tricky interpretive problems. We will say more about this subject in Chapter 6. Suffice it here to point out that unexpressed premises are part of the structure of many arguments.

Quick Check on Incompletely Stated Arguments

Identify the missing element(s) in the following incompletely stated arguments:

1. Since Vice President Bush has promised not to raise taxes he should be elected president.
2. Governor Dukakis is a crass political opportunist, just like all candidates who choose running mates with views opposed to their own.
3. It's wise to shop around before buying a car, but Frank didn't.
4. Ads always attempt to persuade. Sometimes they do so by means of an argument. But in many cases the argument is left largely implicit, as in this ad for Coca-Cola. "Coca-Cola is a proud sponsor of the U.S. Olympic team." (Identify the missing conclusion *and* the missing premise.)
5. The exam will probably be difficult because Professor Robbins is composing it.
6. Whether or not creation theory should be taught in public school alongside the theory of biological evolution depends on whether creationism is a scientific viewpoint. According to scientific standards, creationism is not a scientific theory but a religious one. Therefore, creationism should not be taught in public school alongside the theory of evolution.
7. Nuclear power plants are economical and reliable sources of energy. But they're potentially dangerous, and whatever is potentially dangerous shouldn't be built on a widespread basis.

Premise Support

When we set forth an argument, we recognize that people generally require reasons to persuade them to accept an assertion. But because the premises of an argument, like its conclusion, are assertions, people may well require reasons to accept them also. Recognizing this, authors frequently anticipate the need to supply further support for the premises of their arguments—in other words, to build in arguments premises, as it were, for the premises.

Consider the structural features of these two arguments, which deal with censorship.

Argument 1: Censorship is acceptable only if it can be easily enforced. But censorship cannot easily be enforced. Therefore censorship is not acceptable.

Argument 2: Censorship is acceptable only if it can be easily enforced. But censorship cannot be easily enforced. The main problem with enforcement is determining which works will not be censored. Therefore, censorship is not acceptable.

The argument contained in the two examples is identical.

> **Premise:** Censorship is acceptable only if it can be easily enforced.
> **Premise:** Censorship cannot be easily enforced.
> **Conclusion:** Censorship is not acceptable.

However, argument 2 differs from argument 1 in offering some support for the second premise. The argument states that if we consider the problems of identifying which works need not be censored, there is good reason to think that censorship cannot be easily enforced. In effect, there is a third premise expressed in the second argument:

> The main problem of enforcement is determining which works will not be censored.

This premise, like the first two premises, supports the conclusion. But unlike the first two premises, this one supports it indirectly, by supporting the second premise. How do we determine this? Well, consider the natural question that arises in response to the second premise: "What reason is there to suppose that censorship cannot easily be enforced?" (or "What's the problem with enforcing censorship?"). The third premise is responsive to this question. Evidently, the author has anticipated the challenge to the second premise and supplied a reason to meet it. Thus, it is reasonable to interpret the third sentence in the second argument as support for the second premise, which, together with the first premise, is intended to support the conclusion.

Of course, the reason supplied to support the premise can itself be challenged. Recognizing this, authors sometimes provide support for the support for the premises of an argument, and so on, occasionally at considerable length and with considerable complexity.

For example, consider the same argument with more developed support, as represented by the italicized portion of the following passage:

> Censorship is acceptable only if it can be easily enforced. But censorship cannot be easily enforced. The main problem is determining which works will not be censored. *For example, some have said that the "classics" will and should be exempt from censorship. But what is a "classic"? Any traditional definition probably would exclude new works, for a work usually cannot be recognized as a classic until some time after its release. That means that the censor must determine which works will become classics, surely an impossible task. As a result, censors will have little choice but to ban those "nonclassics" that smack of smut. If you think this is an idle fear, recall that plenty of works of art and literature that today are considered classics were once banned. Works by Chaucer, Shakespeare, Swift, and Twain are just a few. More recently, the works of William Faulkner, Ernest Hemingway, and James Joyce were banned. There is no question, then, that determining which works will not be censored is a major, perhaps insurmountable, problem in enforcing censorship.* Therefore, censorship is not acceptable.

There is no simple way to determine how much support is needed to substantiate a premise and, by implication, an argument's conclusion. But surely the more controversial the conclusion, the more support it needs. The same goes for premises. The more controversial a premise, the more likely it is to be challenged. Thus, the more important it becomes to the argument that the premise be supported.

The importance of premise support becomes most apparent in extended argument, that is, in the multiparagraph arguments that we commonly encounter in editorials, reviews, and the like, and in the essays we are called on to write. Because the following chapters deal with refining analytical and evaluative skills, they take up the challenge of determining adequate premise support. It's enough here, therefore, simply to acknowledge premise support as an integral part of the structure of many arguments.

Quick Check on Premise Support

1. Here's an argument in opposition to standardized tests. Identify premises and premise support. Then state any missing premises you find.

   "Multiple-choice questions distort the purposes of education. Picking one answer among four is very different from thinking a question through to an answer on one's own, and far less useful in life. Recognition of vocabulary and isolated facts . . . dominate these tests, rather than questions that test the use of knowledge. Because schools want their children to perform well, they are often tempted to teach the limited sorts of knowledge most useful on the tests. . . ." (Edwin P. Taylor and Mitchell Lazarus, "Standardized Tests: They Don't Measure Learning," *New York Times,* May 1, 1977, sec. 12, p. 1.)

2. Identify all the elements in this argument:

   "Short of some startling event, the prospects are that foreign policy won't be a significant issue in the (1988 presidential) campaign. Major foreign governments, the Soviet Union as well as allies, are unusually relaxed this year as they anticipate a new U.S. administration. . . . The impression is that main policy lines have been set and won't change drastically whoever wins. . . . President Reagan has switched from active commie-bashing to active search for negotiated agreements with Moscow on a long list of issues; NATO has broad support; and attempts continue to relieve rather than inflame regional hot spots. There have already been changes of many top policy makers, achieving a certain consensus likely to continue even with a new set of people. . . ." (Flora Lewis, syndicated columnist for the *New York Times,* writing in the *Santa Barbara News-Press,* September 19, 1988, p. A-14.)

Summary

An argument is a set of assertions one of which is understood or intended to be supported by the other(s), in other words a connected series of statements intended to establish the truth of some statement.

In contrast, explanations take the truth of a statement for granted and give reasons that account for it.

Recognizing arguments involves recognizing the speaker's or the writer's intentions. Speakers and writers can have complex intentions, and they do not always make their intentions perfectly clear in what they say.

Distinguishing arguments from explanations, or jokes, or instructions is a matter of discerning the author's intentions to persuade by appeal to reasons. Sometimes it is clear that what the author is trying to do is to persuade by appeal to reasons. In that case, what the author has put forward is clearly an argument. Sometimes it is clear that the author is trying to do something other than persuade by appeal to reasons. In that case, what the author has put forward is clearly not an argument. It is not always clear whether what the author has put forward is an argument or not.

Example of an argument: You should take your umbrella, because the weather forecast calls for rain.
Example of an explanation: The streets are wet because it rained last night.

Arguments are composed of premises and conclusions. The premises of arguments are the assertions offered in support of the conclusion. The conclusion is the assertion that the premises are offered to support.

Example with conclusion italicized: *You should take your umbrella,* because the weather forecast calls for rain.

Signal words, which are terms and phrases that indicate the presence of premises and conclusions, are often helpful in recognizing arguments. However, some signal words are ambiguous, and not all arguments contain signal words. Therefore, signal words are not to be mechanically relied on as foolproof indicators of the presence of arguments.

Some conclusion signals: so, thus, therefore, consequently, it follows that
Some general area premise signals: since, because, for, insofar as
Some specific premise signals: first,. . . second,. . . third; for one thing,. . . for another; on the one hand,. . . on the other

When faced with a passage that contains no signals, you should first ask, What, if anything, is being advocated? What claim is the arguer attempting to establish as true? Answering questions like these will help you determine whether the passage contains an argument, and if so, to locate the argument's conclusion. Having done that, you can locate the premises by asking questions like these: Why is this conclusion so? What reasons, data, or evidence does the arguer give for advancing the conclusion?

Just as authors sometimes put forward arguments without signals, so they frequently put forward arguments that are not completely stated, leaving it up to the listener or reader to fill in the missing element(s). Sometimes the conclusion of an argument is left implicit:

Example: "Yond Cassius has a lean and hungry look. . . . Such men are dangerous.
Unexpressed conclusion: Cassius is a dangerous man.

Sometimes a portion of the support in an argument is implied but not stated:

Example: Because Smith married largely for sexual reasons, his marriage won't last long.
Unexpressed premise: Marriages entered into largely for sexual reasons don't last long.

An additional feature of the anatomy of many arguments is premise support. There is no simple way to determine how much support a premise needs, but generally the more controversial the claim the more support needed.

Applications

1. Decide which passage are arguments and which are not. Analyze the arguments by (1) underlining all signal words, if any; (2) locating the conclusion; and (3) locating the premises.

   a. The game has been delayed because of rain.
   b. We must maintain a strong defense; otherwise, we will invite war.
   c. Most teachers want better pay. It follows that most teachers are in favor of unions.
   d. Anyone who criticizes and disrupts society is a threat to social stability. That's why civil disobedience should have no place in society.

e. Because students come to school to learn, they should have no say in curriculum decisions.

f. "The shad, perhaps, or any fish that runs upriver [would be ideal for sea ranching]. . . . They range out to sea, using their own energies, grow, and then come back." (John D. Isaacs, "Interview," *Omni*, August 1979, p. 122.)

g. "In bureaucratic logic, bad judgment is any decision that can lead to embarrassing questions, even if the decision was itself right. Therefore . . . no man with an eye on a career can afford to be right when he can manage to be safe." (John Ciardi, "Bureaucracy and Frank Ellis," in *Manner of Speaking* [New Brunswick, N.J.: Rutgers University Press, 1972], p. 250.)

h. "An arctic mirage is caused by a temperature inversion created when the air immediately above the earth's surface is cooler than air at a higher elevation. Under these conditions, light rays are bent around the curvature of the earth. The stronger the inversion, the more bending. With a high degree of bending, the earth's surface looks like a saucer, and the landscape and ship normally out of sight below the horizon are raised into view on the saucer's rim. The effect can last for days and cover thousands of kilometers." (Barbara Ford, "Mirage," *Omni,* August 1979, p. 38.)

i. "And the tragic history of human thought is simply the history of a struggle between reason and life . . . reason bent on rationalizing life and forcing it to submit to the inevitable, to mortality; life bent on vitalizing reason and forcing it to serve as a support for its own vital desires." (Miguel de Unamuno, *The Tragic Sense of Life* [New York: Dover, 1921], p. 63.)

j. "Vitamin E is an essential part of the whole circulation mechanism of the body, since it affects our use of oxygen." (Ruth Adams and Frank Murray, *Vitamin E: Wonder Worker of the 70's* [New York: Larchmont Books, 1972], p. 17.)

k. "Why are youngsters rediscovering booze? One reason is pressure from other kids to be one of the gang. Another is the ever-present urge to act grown up. . . . Perhaps the main reason is that parents don't seem to mind. . . ." (Carl T. Rowan, "Teenagers and Booze," in *Just Between Us Blacks* [New York: Random House, 1974], pp. 95–96.)

2. Identify the unexpressed premises in b, c, d, and e.

3. Identify the conclusions, premises, and premise support in these arguments:

    a. Part of believing something is believing that it's true. So if I were to do an inventory of my beliefs, they'd all seem true to me. Or, to put it another way, if I knew something was false, I wouldn't believe it. So it doesn't really make sense for me to say that some of my own beliefs are false.

    b. I've been mistaken in the past. I've learned on numerous occasions, and pretty much throughout my life, that things that I believed to be true were really false. Why should it be any different now? So if I were to do an inventory of my beliefs, I probably wouldn't notice the false ones, but I'd still bet there are some in there somewhere.

    c. "Nor is there anything smart about smoking. A woman who smokes is far more likely than her nonsmoking counterpart to suffer from a host of disabling conditions, any of which can interfere with her ability to perform at home or on the job. . . . Women who smoke have more spontaneous abortions, stillbirths, and premature babies than do nonsmokers, and their children's later health may be affected." (Jane E. Brody and Richard Engquist, "Women and Smoking," *Public Affairs Pamphlet 475* [New York: Public Affairs Committee, 1972], p. 2.)

    d. "Since the mid '50's, for example, scientists have observed the same characteristics in what they thought were different cancer cells and concluded that these traits must be common to all cancers. All cancer cells had certain nutritional needs, all could grow in soft agar cultures, all could seed new solid tumors when transplanted into experimental animals, and all contained drastically abnormal chromosomes—the 'mark cancer.' " (Michael Gold, "The Cells That Would Not Die," in "This World," *San Francisco Chronicle,* May 17, 1981, p. 9.)

    e. "One woman told me that brown spots, a bugaboo to older women, were twice as numerous on the left side of her face and arm due to daily use of her car. The right, or interior, side of her face and right arm showed far fewer brown spots. Since these unattractive marks seem to be promoted by exposure to the sun, either cover up or use a good sunscreen." (Virginia Castleton, "Bring Out Your Beauty," *Prevention,* September 1981, p. 108.)

f. "It also appears that suicide no longer repels us. The suicide rate is climbing, especially among blacks and young people. What's more, suicide has been appearing in an increasingly favorable light in the nation's press. When Paul Cameron surveyed all articles on suicide indexed over the past 50 years in the *Reader's Guide to Periodical Literature,* he found that voluntary death, once portrayed as a brutal waste, now generally appears in a neutral light. Some recent articles even present suicide as a good thing to do and are written in a manner that might encourage the reader to take his own life under certain circumstances. Last year, a majority of Americans under 30 told Gallup pollsters that incurable disease or continual pain confer on a person the moral right to end his life." (Elizabeth Hall with Paul Cameron, "Our Failing Reverence for Life," *Psychology Today,* April 1976, p. 108.)

g. "If there were clear boundaries between the animals and people, each side having its own territory, friction would be minimized. But that is not the case. Although some of the 5000 square miles of ecosystem that lie outside the park are protected areas—including neighboring Ngorongoro Conservation Unit and Masai Mara Game Reserve in Kenya—sizable sectors have no conservation status. Consequently, the migratory herds spend a good part of their annual cycle competing with humans for food." (Norman Myers, "The Canning of Africa," *Science Digest,* August 1981, p. 74.)

h. President Reagan promised us a balanced budget by 1984. But since taking office, he has multiplied the budget deficit by more than 250 percent. And he refused to address seriously the issue of the budget deficit until after the 1984 reelection campaign. Because such behavior clearly amounts to a betrayal of the public trust, President Reagan was unworthy of reelection.

4. The following statements represent conclusions of arguments. For each conclusion state a premise, one piece of evidence that supports it, and the missing premise. For example:

> **Conclusion:** Drunk drivers should be severely punished.
> **Premise:** Drunk drivers threaten public safety.
> **Support:** Statistics indicate the automobile accidents that result in deaths involve at least one drunk driver.

Missing premise: Whoever threatens the public safety should be severely punished.

a. Conclusion: Children should (should not) be given allowances.
b. Conclusion: The best medical care available should (should not) be provided all Americans regardless of their ability to pay for it.
c. Conclusion: Individuals should (should not) be allowed to grow marijuana for personal use.
d. Conclusion: Unmarried female adolescents should (should not) be allowed to obtain birth control devices without being reported to their parents.

5. Examine the premises, unexpressed premises, and support material you constructed for the preceding conclusions. Can you account for any of them in terms of cultural conditioning, reliance on authority, hasty moral judgment, black-and-white thinking, labels, or frame of reference? For example, in the sample the missing premise—"Whoever threatens the public safety should be severely punished"—stems from several cultural assumptions. One is that any threat to the general welfare is undesirable. A second is that as soon as any aspect of a person's conduct affects prejudicially the interests of others, society has jurisdiction over it. A probable third is that physical punishment deters crime.

[1]Monty Python's Flying Circus, "The "Argument Clinic," *The Second (in Sequence Not Quality) Monty Python's Flying Circus Videocassette* (London: Python (Monty) Pictures Ltd., 1970).

CASTING ARGUMENTS | 5

In the last chapter you learned that an argument consists of one or more premises and a conclusion and that many arguments also contain support for their premises as well as unexpressed premises or conclusions. Before you can critically examine an argument, you must be able to identify its structure: You must pick out the premises and conclusion, see what support is offered for the premises, and determine whether there are any missing premises or conclusions. If the argument is very simple, identification presents little problem, and you may proceed with your critical analysis. But when the argument is a long one (as in an editorial or essay), then you need some method of portraying its structure before you can criticize it.

This chapter teaches you how to cast arguments; that is, how to portray their structure. It gives you a simple three-step procedure for cutting through the verbiage in a passage, detecting the argument, and diagramming it. Casting is a useful skill for several reasons.

First, it helps you zero in on arguments. In longer passages it's not always easy to spot arguments and follow the author's line of thought. Casting reduces the chances that you'll be overwhelmed by a piece of writing or a speech.

Second, casting lets you look beyond the asides, the fluff, and the other rhetorical devices that writers and speakers often use in arguing. Such flourishes, though sometimes enlivening, can distract (indeed, sometimes they are intended to). You must be able to penetrate these rhetorical colorings to reach the arguments they camouflage. Casting helps you do this.

Third, evaluating longer arguments can become unwieldy, for you may have to reproduce or refer to them continuously. Casting, as you will see, greatly reduces, if not eliminates, this tedious task.

One final and important word about casting before we begin. You will soon discover that portraying an argument's structure demands careful judgment. Casting involves interpretation. And you know what that means: Interpretive issues can and will arise. When people are casting an argument, they won't always agree. You might consider a statement to be merely a single assertion, someone else might see two assertions in it; you might consider an example integral to an argument, someone else might not. Although it is possible for people to be mistaken in their interpretations, and in their castings, it is also possible for several conflicting interpretations, or several conflicting castings, each to have some reasonable basis in the text of an argument. So keep in mind that, except for the very simplest arguments, there is almost always room for alternative castings. Don't be unduly concerned or confused by this. Keep in mind that casting is a means to an end, not an end in itself. You are learning to cast an argument so that by better understanding it, by following its line of thought, you are able to assess it critically. Ultimately, casting helps you to offer substantive criticism of an argument, not trivial, irrelevant, or unfair criticism.

"But I see you're having difficulty following my argument."

Drawing by Gahan Wilson; copyright © 1985 The New Yorker Magazine, Inc.

ARGUMENT ORGANIZATION:
SERIES AND CHAIN

As a first step in learning to cast, let's distinguish two ways in which premises may support their conclusions: (1) a set of premises or reasons may each independently support the conclusion; or (2) a set of premises or reasons may function together in an interdependent way as support for the conclusion. Consider, for example, the following argument concerning the legalization of voluntary euthanasia, which as you probably know refers to the practice of allowing terminally ill patients to elect to die.

> Our traditional religious and cultural opposition to euthanasia is a good reason for not liberalizing euthanasia laws. Also, permitting a patient to make a death decision would greatly add to the person's suffering and anguish. Additionally, once a death decision has been carried out, there is no chance of correcting a mistaken diagnosis. Therefore, voluntary euthanasia should not be legalized.

This passage presents a *series* of three *mutually independent* reasons in support of the view that voluntary euthanasia should not be legalized. Although each of these reasons is related to the conclusion, they are not dependent on one another as support. Any of them could be deleted without undermining the status of the others as support, although the argument itself as a whole probably would be weakened. In short, each is a separate reason for opposing the legalization of voluntary euthanasia. In presenting independent reasons such as these, arguers are not concerned with tight linkage between them, because one reason need not logically entail any of the others.

By way of contrast, consider the following argument on the same subject:

> Voluntary decisions about death by definition presuppose freedom of choice. But freedom of choice entails the absence of freedom-limiting constraints. Such constraints almost always are present in cases of the terminally ill. Therefore, terminally ill patients cannot make a voluntary decision about death.

The assertions in this passage are interdependent. The elimination of any one of the supporting reasons not only weakens the argument as a whole but also undermines the status of the others as supporting reasons. For example, the claim that freedom of choice entails the absence of freedom-limiting constraints does not by itself support the conclusion that the terminally ill cannot make a voluntary death decision. Only when it is linked together with the claims that a voluntary decision presupposes freedom of choice and that freedom-limiting constraints are almost always present in cases of terminal illness does it support the conclusion. In this example, then, we have three *interdependent* reasons linked together in a *chain*.

With these preliminary remarks behind us, let's develop a method of casting arguments that, among other things, portrays these organizational patterns.

*Quick Check on Argument Organization (Answers on Page 391)

Identify the organizational structure (series or chain) of the following arguments:

1. "What, after all, is the foundation of the nurse's obligation to follow the physician's orders? Presumably, the nurse's obligation is to act in the medical interest of the patient. The point is that the nurse has an obligation to follow physician's orders because, ordinarily, patient welfare (interest) thereby is ensured. Thus when a nurse's obligation to follow a physician's order comes into *direct* conflict with the nurse's obligation to act in the medical interest of the patient, it would seem to follow that the patient's interests should always take precedence." (E. Joy Kroeger Mappes, "Ethical Dilemmas for Nurses: Physicians' Orders Versus Patients' Rights," in T. A. Mappes and J. S. Zembatty [eds.], *Biomedical Ethics* [New York: McGraw-Hill, 1981], p. 100.)

2. Getting unbiased information about troublesome students may be impossible. Public officials, who owe us detailed and accurate reports, often give in to their fear of incessant questioning and potential lawsuits. They may become experts at covering, rationalizing, minimizing, and denying what is going on. Many clinicians are afraid of losing their jobs, such as they are. Teachers may seek relief from difficult children no matter what the cost. Parents seem to see the whole scene from the sole viewpoint of their particular child. . . .

3. "[Chairman of the Federal Reserve, Alan] Greenspan's own remarks are vaguely reassuring. He told the Senate Banking Committee that he does not foresee a recession this year or next, and he agreed that given the burden of debts that have accumulated, a recession now would have "adverse" consequences for weakened financial institutions, not to mention bankrupt debtors. Furthermore, Greenspan does not buy the argument of the financial markets that the low unemployment rate is about to produce runaway wages. . . ." (William Greider, "The Real Election in America This Year," *Rolling Stone*, August 25, 1988, p. 41.)

4. Even though spanking has immediate punitive and (for the parent) anger-releasing effects, parents should not spank their children, for spanking gives children the message that inflicting pain on others is an appropriate means of changing their behavior. Furthermore, spanking trains children to submit to the arbitrary rules of authority figures who have the power to harm them. We ought not to give our children those messages. Rather, we should train them to either make appropriate behavioral choices or to

expect to deal with the related natural and logical consequences of their behavior.

5. Public schools generally avoid investigation of debatable issues and instead stress rote recall of isolated facts, which teaches students to unquestioningly absorb given information on demand so that they can regurgitate it in its entirety during testing situations. Although students generally are not allowed to question it, much of what is presented as accurate information is indeed controversial. But citizens need to develop decision-making skills regarding debatable issues in order to truly participate in a democracy. It follows then that public schools ought to change their educational priorities in order to better prepare students to become informed, responsible members of our democracy.

A CASTING METHOD

Professor of philosophy Michael S. Scriven has formulated a lucid and concise method of casting arguments that is especially useful for our purposes.[1] It consists of three steps:

1. putting brackets at the beginning and end of each assertion
2. numbering assertions consecutively in the margin or above the line of type
3. setting out the relationships between the relevant assertions in a tree diagram to be read down the page

To see how this method works, we will reconsider the two arguments about euthanasia just presented. Let's try casting the first, which uses a series structure.

Steps 1 & 2: [Our traditional religious and cultural opposition to euthasia is a good reason for not liberalizing euthanasia laws.] Also [permitting a patient to make a death decision would greatly add to the person's suffering and anguish.] Additionally, [once a death decision is carried out, there is no chance of correcting a mistaken diagnosis.] Therefore, [voluntary euthanasia should not be legalized.]

Step 3:

The tree diagram shows (a) the number of assertions in the argument, (b) the order of their appearance, and (c) which are the premises and which the conclusion. It also indicates that each of the premises is an independent reason offered in support of the conclusion.

Now let's apply the procedure to the second argument, which uses a chain structure.

> **Steps 1 & 2:** [Voluntary decisions about death by definition presuppose freedom of choice.][1] But [freedom of choice entails the absence of freedom-limiting constraints.][2] [Such constraints almost always are present in cases of the terminally ill.][3] Therefore, [terminally ill patients cannot make a voluntary decision about death.][4]
>
> **Step 3:**

$$\underbrace{① + ② + ③}_{④}$$

Again, the diagram shows the number of assertions in the argument, their order of appearance, and which are the premises and which the conclusion. By means of plus signs and a brace, it also shows that the premises are interdependent. Here are some additional examples of casting arguments that contain the series or chain structure.

> **Example:** Capital punishment deters crime. It also ensures that the killer will never strike again. Reasons enough, then, to legalize capital punishment.
>
> **Comment:** Each of the two reasons is an independent point asserted in favor of the legalization of capital punishment.

The argument can be cast as follows:

> **Steps 1 & 2:** [Capital punishment deters crime.][1] [It also ensures that the killer will never strike again.][2] Reasons enough, then, to [legalize capital punishment.][3]
>
> **Step 3:**

For a "balance of considerations" argument, where, say, assertions 1, 2, and 3 support the conclusion, assertion 4, but some assertion 5 does not, a minus sign can be used.

Example: Capital punishment does ensure that a killer can never strike again. But it consists of killing human beings, and killing human beings should never be allowed. Therefore, capital punishment should not be permitted.

Comment: In this argument two interdependent points are offered in support of the conclusion that capital punishment should not be permitted. These points are thought to be convincing despite the fact that capital punishment does ensure that a killer can never strike again (first assertion), which points to an opposite conclusion.

The argument can be cast as follows:

Steps 1 & 2: [Capital punishment does ensure that a killer can never strike again.]¹ But [it consists of killing human beings]² and [killing human beings should never be allowed.]³ Therefore, [capital punishment should not be permitted.]⁴

Step 3:

$$\underbrace{② + ③} - ① \\ ④$$

Example: A college education increases your earning potential. In addition, it makes you aware of interests you didn't know you had. Most important, it teaches one inherent value of knowledge. It is true, of course, that a college education is very expensive. Nevertheless, a college education is of inestimable worth.

Comment: This argument presents a series of reasons, each of which taken independently offers support for the conclusion that a college education is worthwhile. At the same time, the arguer concedes a fact that points away from this conclusion: "A college education is very expensive." Notice that "nevertheless," although appearing in the conclusion, is being used to contrast this concession.

The argument can be cast as follows:

Steps 1 & 2: [A college education increases your earning potential.]¹ In addition, [it makes you aware of interests you didn't know you had.]² Most important, [it teaches you the inherent value of knowledge.]^3 [It is true, of course, that a college education is very expensive.]^4 Nevertheless, [a college education is of inestimable worth.]^5

Step 3:

Example: A college education makes you aware of interests you didn't know you had. This helps you choose a satisfying job. Job satisfaction is itself your best assurance of personal well-being. Certainly personal well-being is a goal worth pursuing. Therefore, a college education is a worthy goal.

Comment: The points of this argument are arranged in a chain. Although the first point may be taken independently as support for the conclusion, only when they are taken together, in their logical sequence, does the arguer's apparent intention to support the claim that a college education is valuable become clear.

The argument can be cast as follows:

Steps 1 & 2: [A college education makes you aware of interests you didn't know you had.]^1 [This helps you choose a satisfying job.]^2 [Job satisfaction is itself your best assurance of personal well-being.]^3 [Certainly personal well-being is a goal worth pursuing.]^4 Therefore, [a college education is a worthy goal.]^5

Step 3:

In each of the preceding arguments the conclusion happened to appear at the end of the passage. Just as often, however, a conclusion can appear at the beginning of a passage:

Capital punishment should not be permitted because it in fact consists of killing human beings, and killing human beings should never be permitted by society.

Bracketing and numbering this version of the argument, we get:

124

[Capital punishment should not be permitted]¹ <u>because</u> [it in fact consists of killing human beings,]² <u>and</u> [killing human beings should never be permitted by society.]³

The tree diagram for this argument would be:

$$\underbrace{②\;+\;③}_{①}$$

Of course, conclusions also can come sandwiched between premises, as in the following version of the same argument:

> <u>Because</u> killing human beings should never be permitted by society, capital punishment should not be permitted; <u>for</u> it in fact consists of killing human beings.

Bracketing and numbering this version we get:

<u>Because</u> [killing human beings should never be permitted by society,]¹ [capital punishment should not be permitted;]² <u>for</u> [it in fact consists of killing human beings.]³

Diagrammed:

$$\underbrace{①\;+\;③}_{②}$$

So far we have cast arguments containing only premises and conclusions. But, as you know, some arguments also contain support for premises as well as unexpressed premises and conclusions. A few refinements will help you to cast these additional structural features.

*Quick Check on Casting (Answers on Page 391)

Cast the following arguments:

1. Since it is only a matter of time before space-based missile defense technology becomes obsolete, and since the funds

earmarked for the development of such technology are sorely needed elsewhere, we should abandon the Star Wars program.

2. "The diet works because it specifically mobilizes fat. [It] also stimulates the release of ketones and fat mobilizers. [It] causes a disproportionately greater loss of fat. It helps eliminate excess water. It stabilizes blood sugar. It lowers insulin levels and cortisol levels. And it delivers a metabolic advantage." (Robert C. Atkins and Shirley Linde, *Dr. Atkins' Super-Energy Diet* [New York: Bantam, 1977], p. 130.)

3. President Reagan promised to balance the federal budget by 1984. But in his first term of office he succeeded in multiplying the budget deficit by more than 250 percent. And he refused to address seriously the issue of the budget deficit throughout the 1984 reelection campaign. Such behavior clearly amounts to a betrayal of the public trust.

4. The Star Wars program is our only realistic option for national defense in the nuclear age. Any defense program that relies on nuclear deterrence raises the risk of nuclear war, and that is not a realistic option for national defense. The Star Wars program is the only option yet proposed that does not rely on nuclear deterrence.

CASTING SUPPORT PREMISES

Let's reconsider two arguments we discussed in Chapter 4:

Argument 1: Censorship is acceptable only if it can be easily enforced. But censorship cannot be easily enforced. Therefore, censorship is not acceptable.

Argument 2: Censorship is acceptable only if it can be easily enforced. But censorship cannot be easily enforced. The main problem with enforcement is determining which works will not be censored. Therefore, censorship is not acceptable.

Following the three-step procedure, we can cast argument 1 as follows:

Steps 1 & 2: [Censorship is acceptable only if it can be easily enforced.]^1 But [censorship cannot be easily enforced.]^2 Therefore, [censorship is not acceptable.]^3

Step 3:

Argument 2 differs from argument 1 in providing support for its second premise. The assertion "The main problem with enforcement is determining which works will not be censored" presumably supports the premise "But censorship cannot be easily enforced." In casting this argument, then, we must show the proper relationship between these two assertions. We must portray the structure of this argument in a way that makes it clear that one assertion is supporting another. This may be done in the following way:

Steps 1 & 2: [Censorship is acceptable only if it can be easily enforced.]¹ But [censorship cannot be easily enforced.]² [The main problem with enforcement is determining which works will not be censored.]³ Therefore, [censorship is not acceptable.]⁴

Step 3:

The solid line between 3 and 2 means that assertion 3 is intended to support assertion 2.

Suppose that the same argument contained additional support material, as in the following passage:

Argument 3: [Censorship is acceptable only if it can be easily enforced.]¹ But [censorship cannot be easily enforced.]² [The main problem with enforcement is determining which works will not be censored.]³ [Another problem concerns who will do the censoring.]⁴ [Still another problem pertains to the standards that will be used.]⁵ Therefore, [censorship is not acceptable.]⁶

In this passage assertions 3, 4, and 5 are offered as support for assertion 2. The arguer believes that assertion 2 can be inferred from assertions 3, 4, and 5. Therefore, the argument can be diagrammed as follows:

The diagram indicates that assertions 3, 4, and 5 are independent reasons offered in support of assertion 2 and that assertions 1 and 2 entail assertion 6, the conclusion.

It should be evident from these examples that in supporting an individual premise, the arguer is actually presenting an argument. Such embedded arguments can be termed "mini-arguments" so as to distinguish them from the main argument of a passage.

The mini-argument in argument 2 has as its premise "The main problem with enforcement is determining which works will not be censored." The conclusion of this mini-argument is "Censorship cannot be easily enforced."

In argument 3 the mini-argument has three premises: "The main problem with enforcement is determining which works will not be censored"; "Another problem concerns who will do the censoring"; and "Still another problem pertains to the standards that will be used." The conclusion of this mini-argument is "Censorship cannot be easily enforced."

In relation to the main argument, then, assertion 2 functions as a premise in both arguments, for it supports the conclusion in each. In relation to the mini-arguments, however, assertion 2 is a conclusion, for it itself is supported by a single premise in argument 2 and by three premises in argument 3. The tree diagrams provide a visual representation of these relationships. For argument 2 the diagram indicates a main argument containing two main premises and one mini-argument containing one mini-premise:

And for argument 3, the diagram indicates a main argument containing two main premises and one mini-argument containing three mini-premises:

A complex argument may have several mini-arguments embedded in the main argument or even in other mini-arguments. A good deal of getting the point of a passage, then, depends on sorting out what roles the assertions are playing in relation to one another in the passage. Following the three-step casting procedure helps you do this.

Here are some further examples with premise support (mini-arguments):

Example: [Most marriages between people under twenty end in divorce.]¹ [This should be enough to discourage teenage marriages.]² But there is also the fact that [marrying young reduces one's life options.]³ [Married teenagers must forget about adventure and play.]⁴ [They can't afford to spend time "finding themselves."]⁵ [They must concentrate almost exclusively on earning a living.]⁶ What's more, [early marriages can make parents out of young people, who can hardly take care of themselves, let alone an infant.]⁷

Comment: This passage offers three assertions—1, 3, and 7—in opposition to teenage marriages (assertion 2). Assertions 1, 3, and 7 thus function as main premises in the main argument. In addition, assertion 3 is further supported by reasons given in assertions 4, 5, and 6. Taken together, assertions 3, 4, 5, and 6 form a mini-argument that can be diagrammed as follows:

The entire argument in turn can be diagrammed as follows:

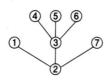

Example: ["Suicide no longer repels us.]¹ [The suicide rate is climbing, especially among blacks and young people.]² What's more, [suicide has been appearing in an increasingly favorable light in the nation's press.]³ [When Paul Cameron surveyed all articles on suicide indexed over the past 50 years in the *Reader's Guide to Periodical Literature,* he found that voluntary deaths . . . generally appear in a neutral light.]⁴ [Some recent articles even present suicide as a good thing to do. . . .]⁵ [They are written in a manner that might encourage the reader to take his own life under certain circumstances."]⁶ [Elizabeth Hall with Paul Cameron, "Our Failing Reverence for Life," *Psychology Today,* April 1976, p. 108.]

Comment: This passage offers assertions 2 and 3 as premises for the conclusion that suicide no longer repels us (assertion 1). In support of assertion 3, the arguer offers assertions 4 and 5, which is supported by 6. Therefore assertions 5 and 6 make up a mini-argument within a larger mini-argument consisting of assertions 3, 4, 5, and 6 and can be diagrammed as follows:

The entire argument can be diagrammed this way:

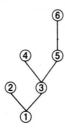

Example: ["... more and more silent evidence is being turned into loudly
damning testimony.] [Over the past ten years, no area has developed faster than
the examination of blood stains.] [Before we used to be satisfied with identifying
a blood sample as type A, B, AB or O.] [Now we have three or more different
antigen and enzyme systems.]. . . [The probability that any two people will share
the same assessment of their blood variables is .1% or less.]. . . [The size,
shape, and distribution of blood spatters tells much about the location and
position of a person involved in a crime.]. . . [The use of bite-mark evidence has
skyrocketed.]. . . [Even anthropology is making a courtroom contribution.] [Some
anthropologists can identify barefoot prints as well as match a shoe to its wearer.]
[Bennett H. Beach, "Mr. Wizard Comes to Court," *Time,* March 1, 1982, p. 90.]

Comment: In this passage assertions 2, 7, and 8 are the premises of the
main argument in support of the claim that "more and more silent evidence is
being turned into loudly damning testimony" (assertion 1). Taken together, the
chain of assertions 3, 4, and 5 provides one piece of evidence for assertion 2.
So one mini-argument in the passage consists of the relationship between assertions 3, 4, 5, and 2. This relationship can be diagrammed as follows:

$$\underbrace{③ + ④ + ⑤}_{②}$$

Assertion 6 provides additional support for assertion 2, thus yielding a second mini-argument.

Assertion 9 supports assertion 8, yielding a third mini-argument.

We can represent the relationships among these various assertions in the argument by means of the following diagram.

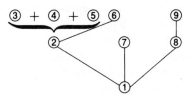

*Quick Check on Casting Premise Support (Answers on Page 392)

Cast the following arguments, all of which contain premise support:

1. "A recent five-year study at a major electronics company indicates that getting fired may have a lot to do with overreaching. Among 2,000 technical, sales and management employees who were followed during their first five years with the company, the 173 people who eventually were fired started out with much higher expectations of advancement than either the 200 people who left voluntarily or the people who remained. On a questionnaire given during their first week on the job, more than half of the people who were fired within the first two years ranked themselves among the top 5% of typical people in their job category. Only 38% of those who stayed with the company ranked themselves that highly." (Berkeley Rice, "Aspiring to a Fall," *Psychology Today*, March 1980, p. 25.)

2. We must stop treating juveniles differently from adult offenders. Justice demands it. Justice implies that people should be treated equally. Besides, the social effects of pampering juvenile offenders have sinister social consequences. The record shows

that juveniles who have been treated leniently for offenses have subsequently committed serious crimes.

3. "The development of a human being from conception through birth into childhood is continuous. [Then] it is said that to draw a line, to choose a point in this development and say 'before this point the thing is not a person, after this point it is a person' is to make an arbitrary choice. [It is further said that this is] a choice for which in the nature of things no good reason can be given. It is concluded that the fetus is . . . a person from the moment of conception." (Judith Jarvis Thomson, "A Defense of Abortion," *Philosophy and Public Affairs* 1:1 [Fall 1971].)

4. It's high time we seriously investigated the impact of television on children. Children spend much of their free time watching television. The average American child by age eighteen has watched thousands of hours of television. The same average viewer has watched thousands of hours of inane situation comedy, fantasy, soap operas, and acts of violence.

5. "The tax cuts will result in higher deficits than would have occurred had the Democrats stayed in office. The result will be blistering inflation. The federal deficits for the last half of the 1970's totalled $310 billion. Without the tax cuts, they would have totalled at least twice that amount for the first half of the 1980's. With the cuts, they will probably total $800 billion for that period." (John Pugsley, "The Deficits Deepen: An Economic Program Disintegrates," *Common Sense*, December 13, 1981, p. 4.)

6. "Such crises [of employees departing with a firm's trade secrets] are not surprising. . . . The highly educated employees of R & D [research and development] organizations place primary emphasis on their own development, interests and satisfaction. Graduates of major scientific and technological institutions readily admit that they accept their first jobs primarily for money. [They also want] the early and brief experience they feel is a prerequisite for seeking more satisfying futures with smaller companies. . . . Employee mobility and high personnel turnover rates are also due to the placement of new large federal contracts and the termination of others. One need only look to the Sunday newspaper employment advertisements for evidence as to the manner in which such programs are used to attract highly educated R & D personnel." (Michael S. Baram, "Trade Secrets: What Price Loyalty?" *Harvard Business Review*, November–December 1968.)

7. "To the extent that it is working at all, the press is always a participant [in, rather than a pure observer of, the events it reports.] Our decisions on where (and where not) to be and what (and what not) to report have enormous impact on the political and governmental life we cover. We are obliged to be selective.

We cannot publish the Daily Everything. And so long as this is true—so long as we are making choices that 1) affect what people see concerning their leaders and 2) inevitably cause those leaders to behave in particular ways—we cannot pretend we are not participants." (Meg Greenfield, "When the Press Becomes a Participant," *The Washington Post Company, Annual Report, 1984*, p. 21.)

CASTING UNEXPRESSED PREMISES AND CONCLUSIONS

As you learned in the preceding chapter, unexpressed premises and conclusions are a structural feature of many arguments. Consider this simple example:

Because [Smith is a ¹police officer,] [he's trained and experienced in the ²use of firearms.]

The stated premise, assertion 1, does not provide conclusive support for the conclusion, assertion 2. It is reasonable to suppose that the arguer is assuming something that, together with the stated premise, entails the conclusion. Suppose the missing premise is "All police officers receive training and experience in the use of firearms."

A convenient way to show an unexpressed premise is by a letter: *a, b, c,* and so forth. The preceding argument, then, with the additional premise could be cast as follows:

Here's another simple argument:

[Phyllis must be a ¹college graduate], for [she's a member of the American ²Association of University Women (AAUW).]

This argument has a single stated premise, assertion 2, and a conclusion, assertion 1. But there is a considerable gap in the inference from assertion 2 to assertion 1. It is reasonable to suppose that the inference depends on an additional premise covering conditions for membership in the AAUW: something like "Membership in the AAUW is restricted to college graduates." Once this premise is flushed out, the gap in the inference is closed. We can now diagram the argument as follows:

Filling in the missing premises correctly is perhaps the most challenging aspect of argument analysis. Because we consider this subject in the next chapter we needn't say anything more about it here.

Unexpressed conclusions can be handled like unexpressed premises. For example, recall this argument from *Julius Caesar:*

["Yond Cassius has a lean and hungry look. . . .][1] [Such men are dangerous."][2]

Although missing, the conclusion of this argument is obvious: "Cassius is a dangerous man." It would appear in the diagram as follows:

$$\underbrace{① + ②}_{ⓐ}$$

Recall this argument:

[Only citizens can vote.][1] But [Jones isn't a citizen.][2]

The expressed premises entail the unexpressed conclusion: "Jones can't vote." The argument therefore yields this diagram:

$$\underbrace{① + ②}_{ⓐ}$$

Of course, the arguments you come across and compose often are far richer in rhetorical devices than the specimens we've been dealing with. As a result, they can raise problems in casting. To handle these kinds of arguments, you'll need a few more guidelines.

*Quick Check on Casting Unexpressed Premises and Conclusions (Answers on Page 395)

Fill in the missing premises or conclusions of the following simple arguments, then cast them:

1. Cows are ruminants because they chew the cud.
2. Liberty means responsibility. That is why most men dread it.
3. Whatever isn't an evil must be a good. Wealth isn't an evil.
4. The American government leaves business on its own. A government that lets business alone is said to be a laissez-faire government.
5. There are no strong philosophical bents on the Supreme Court. Each of the justices is a pragmatist who takes each case as it comes. The philosophical inconsistencies in their rulings is proof of this. Besides, most of the justices themselves have said that they must judge each case on its own merits.

GUIDELINES FOR CASTING RHETORICAL FEATURES

We use a variety of rhetorical devices in argument, including examples, asides, background information, and repetition. The following guidelines tell you how to handle these features, which are common to longer arguments.

1. Cast each assertion separately. Sometimes a sentence makes a single assertion: "All cancer cells have nutritional needs." But a single sentence may contain several assertions: "All cancer cells have certain nutritional needs, all grow in soft agar cultures, all can seed new solid tumors when transplanted into experimental animals, and all contain drastically abnormal chromosomes." This sentence contains four separate assertions. If it were part of the following argument, then, it would be portrayed as follows:

[All cancer cells have certain nutritional needs,]¹ [all grow in soft agar cultures,]² [all can seed new solid tumors when transplanted into experimental animals,]³ and [all contain drastically abnormal chromosomes.]⁴ It follows that [these traits must be common to all cancers.]⁵

2. Don't cast repetitions of the same assertion. When we argue we often repeat or rephrase assertions for emphasis or clarity. In fact it's not uncommon in long arguments for a main premise or a conclusion to be repeated or rephrased several times. Notice for example how the arguer repeats the conclusion in this argument:

Capital punishment is a legitimate punishment. For one thing it deters crime. For another it ensures that a killer can never strike again. Therefore, the death penalty is a permissible form of punishment.

In this passage the conclusion is stated in the first sentence, and repeated in other words in the last. When premises or conclusions are repeated, they needn't be numbered or portrayed in the argument's structure. The preceding argument, then, can be cast as follows:

[Capital punishment is a legitimate punishment.]^1 For one thing [it deters crime.]^2 For another [it ensures that the killer can never strike again.]^3 Therefore, the death penalty is a permissible form of punishment.

3. Don't cast "asides." Often in written and especially in oral discourse, arguers introduce matters that are not relevant to the issue under discussion. Or they may change the subject or interrupt the line of argument. Consider for example this argument:

Women still don't get a fair shake in the workplace. For one thing, they're not paid the same as their male counterparts. This, by the way, is also true of black males in relation to white males. For another thing, women are not as often promoted to upper-level executive positions as men are, which is really unfortunate because women have qualities desperately needed by American business. But beyond this, women continue to be plagued by stereotyping.

The first sentence of this argument is the conclusion. The second, fourth, and fifth are premises. The third sentence and the clause beginning with "which" in the fourth sentence are irrelevant. The argument, then, can be cast as follows:

[Women still don't get a fair shake in the workplace.]^1 For one thing, [they're not paid the same as their male counterparts.]^2 This, by the way, is also true of black males in relation to white males. For another thing, [women are not as often promoted to upper-level executive positions as men are,]^3 which is really unfortunate because women have qualities desperately needed by American business. But beyond this, [women continue to be plagued by stereotyping.]^4

4. Don't cast background information.   In longer arguments arguers sometimes indicate how they became interested in an issue or controversy. They tell the audience what prompted them to address the topic, what the central concerns are, or who the participants are. While such information is useful in placing the argument in context, it is not part of the argument and therefore should not be cast. For example, consider the following argument, which deals with abortions:

> The most fundamental question involved in the long history of thought on abortion is: When is the unborn a human? To phrase the question that way is to put in comprehensive humanistic terms what theologians either dealt with as an explicitly theological question under the heading of "ensoulment" or dealt with implicitly in their treatment of abortion. The answer to the question of when the unborn is a human is simple: at conception. <u>The reason is that</u> at conception the new being receives the genetic code.

The first two sentences of this passage provide background information. While informative, they are not part of the argument, which is to be found in the last two sentences. Accordingly, the argument may be cast as follows:

> [The answer to the question of when the unborn is a human is simple: at conception.]¹ <u>The reason is that</u> [at conception the new being receives the genetic code.]²

Here's another example, followed by a comment:

Example: "In recent years government policies intended to ensure fairer employment and educational opportunities for women and minority groups have engendered alarm. Although I shall in this paper argue in support of enlightened versions of these policies, I nevertheless think there is much to be said for the opposition arguments. In general I would argue that the world of business is now overregulated by federal government, and I therefore hesitate to support an extension of the regulative arm of government into the arena of hiring and firing. Moreover, policies that would eventuate in reverse discrimination in present North American society have a heavy presumption against them, for both justice-regarding and utilitarian reasons. [Tom Beauchamp, "The Justification of Reverse Discrimination," in William T. Blackstone and Robert Heslep (eds.), *Social Justice and Preferential Treatment* (Athens, Ga.: University of Georgia Press, 1977).]

Comment: The first two sentences of this paragraph provide background information. The author's argument is contained in the third and fourth sentences, in which he provides support for his reluctance to extend further the "regulative arm of government into the arena of hiring and firing." Thus the argument can be cast as follows:

In general I would argue that [the world of business is now over[1] regulated by federal government,] and [I therefore hesitate to support an extension of the regulative[2] arm of government into the arena of hiring and firing.] Moreover, [policies that would eventuate in reverse discrimination in present North American[3] society have a heavy presumption against them, for both justice-regarding][4] and [utilitarian reasons.]

5. Do not cast examples that merely illustrate or clarify a point.   We often use examples to illustrate or clarify a point when we argue. Examples used like this should not be considered a formal part of the argument. The following passage contains such strictly illustrative examples. You can use a broken bracket ({ }) to show a break in or interruption of an assertion.

[The average athlete begins to wonder when his career[1] is going to end almost as soon as he starts.] [He knows that it either can be shortened[2] with devastating swiftness by an injury,] or [eventually reach the point at which the great skill[3] begins to erode.] As time goes on . . . [the player has to decide whether to cut it clean and retire at the top— {as Rocky Marciano, the heavyweight champion did}—or wait for some sad moment—{Willie Mays[4] stumbling around in the outfield reaches of Candlestick Park}—when the evidence is clear not only to oneself but one's peers that the time is up.] [George Plimpton, "The Final Season," *Harper's*, January 1972, p. 62.]

In this passage the author uses Rocky Marciano and Willie Mays as outstanding familiar illustrations of the dilemma athletes inevitably face: "retire at the top" or "wait for some sad moment." Because these examples have been used strictly for illustration, they are excluded from bracketing and numbering. The argument can be diagrammed as follows:

That such illustrations or clarifying examples are not a formal part of an argument does not mean that they shouldn't appear in arguments. When well chosen, as in the preceding passage, such examples both elucidate and enliven an argument. They provide a common ground of understanding between arguer and audience. They can thus be most effective rhetorical devices. But for purposes of casting an argument they are irrelevant.

6. Cast examples used to support a point being made, that is, examples that indicate why the point is so. Besides using examples to clarify and illustrate, arguers also use them as support for their claims:

[The ethical code of ancient Greece did not extend to human chattel, as this example shows.][1] [When godlike Odysseus returned from the war in Troy, he hanged on one rope some dozen slave girls whom he suspected of misbehaving during his absence.][2]

The example cited in this passage does more than graphically illustrate the author's point. It also provides support for the claim made about the ethical code of ancient Greece. Thus, the example can be considered a premise in the argument. The argument therefore consists of two assertions. The first assertion is the conclusion, the second the premise. The argument may be diagrammed as follows:

Here is another instance in which examples are used to support a claim:

Example: "We go out for coffee, invite friends over for drinks, celebrate special occasions with cakes or big meals. We can't think of baseball without thinking of hot dogs and beer, and eating is so often an accompaniment to watching TV that we talk of TV snacks and TV dinners. . . . the activities we associate with food can become signals to eat. . . ." [Michael J. Mahoney and Kathryn Mahoney, "Fight Fat with Behavior Control," *Psychology Today*, May 1976, p. 43.]

Comment: This passage uses a series of pithy examples to establish the point that activities we associate with food can become signals to eat. Therefore, these examples can be considered premises in the argument, which can be cast as follows:

[We go out for coffee],[1] [invite friends over for drinks,][2] [celebrate special occasions with cakes or big meals.][3] [We can't even think of baseball without thinking of hot dogs and beer],[4] and [eating is so often an accompaniment to watching TV that we talk of TV snacks and TV dinners].[5] . . . [the activities we associate with food can become signals to eat.][6]

7. Do not cast as a separate assertion information that follows a colon.

In general, information that follows a colon simply extends the point being made in the part of the sentence that precedes the colon. The entire sentence should be treated as a single assertion.

To illustrate, consider this passage:

[There is no scientific proof for the assumption that reading about sexual matters or about violence and brutality leads to antisocial actions, particularly juvenile delinquency.]^1 In the absence of such evidence, [two lines of psycholog-ical approach to the examination of this assumption are possible]^2: (1) a review of what is known about the cause of juvenile delinquency and (2) a review of what is known about the effects of literature on the mind of the reader.

This passage consists of two assertions. The first is the premise, the second the conclusion. The information following the colon simply extends the conclusion; it specifies the "two lines of psychological approach" possible.

8. Cast as separate assertions information separated by a semicolon.

The semicolon typically separates different pieces of information. Each piece of information must be considered an individual assertion and cast as such. The following passage, for example, contains three premises separated by two semi-colons:

Jones is the best-qualified candidate. He is experienced in domestic and foreign affairs, having held positions in both fields; he is extremely dedicated; and he has demonstrated the imagination and creativity that this office requires.

The first sentence of this passage is the conclusion. The second sentence contains three premises, the first of which is supported. The argument can be cast as follows:

[Jones is the best-qualified candidate.]^1 [He is experienced in both domestic and foreign affairs,]^2 [having held positions in both fields;]^3 [he is extremely ded-icated;]^4 and [he has demonstrated the imagination and creativity that this office requires.]^5

***Quick Check on Casting Rhetorical Features
(Answers on Page 396)**

Apply the guidelines you have just learned in casting the following arguments. Ignore unexpressed premises.

1. "Evolution is a scientific fairy-tale just as the 'flat earth theory' was in the 12th century. Evolution directly contradicts the Second Law of Thermodynamics, which states that unless an intelligent planner is directing a system, it will always go in the direction of disorder and deterioration. . . . Evolution requires a faith that is incomprehensible!" (Dr. Edward Blic, *21 Scientists Who Believe in Creation* [Harrisonburg, Va.: Christian Light Publications, 1977].)

2. "Contrary to popular assumption, volcanoes are anything but rare. The Smithsonian Scientific Event Alert Network often reports several dozen [volcanic eruptions] per quarter. America's slice of the volcanic 'ring of fire' includes the Cascades, a mountain range that arcs across the Pacific Northwest. When peaceful, shimmering Mt. St. Helens exploded this past spring, blasting 1.3 billion cubic yards of rock into powder, the people of Washington state received a rude lesson about nature's penchant for change. Bathed in ash every few weeks over the summer, the Washingtonians queasily came to the realization that the mountain might stay belligerent for years, that they had, in a sense, been living on borrowed time between inevitable eruptions. 'There are potential volcanoes all over the Cascade Range where Mt. St. Helens stands,' says geologist Alfred Anderson of the University of Washington. 'There's still a lot of change, a lot of formations, going on in that area of the world.' " (Edward M. Hart, "The Shape of Things to Come," *Next: A Look into the Future,* December 1980, pp. 69–70).

3. "A scientific colleague of mine, who holds a professorial post in the department of sociology and anthropology at one of our leading universities, recently asked me about my stand on the question of human beings having sex relations without love. Although I have taken something of a position on this issue in my book, *The American Sexual Tragedy,* I have never quite considered the problem in sufficient detail. So here goes . . . . In general, I

feel that affectional, as against nonaffectional, sex relations are *desirable*. . . . It is usually desirable that an association between coitus and affection exist—particularly in marriage, because it is often difficult for two individuals to keep finely tuned to each other over a period of years." (Albert Ellis, *Sex Without Guilt* [New York: Lyle Stuart, 1966].)

4. "Scientists are human beings with their full complement of emotions and prejudices, and their emotions and prejudices often influence the way they do their science. This was first clearly brought out in a study by Professor Nicholas Pastore . . . in 1949. In this study Professor Pastore showed that the scientist's political beliefs were highly correlated with what he believed about the roles played by nature and nurture in the development of the person. Those holding conservative political views strongly tended to believe in the power of genes over environment. Those subscribing to more liberal views tended to believe in the power of environment over genes. One distinguished scientist (who happened to be a teacher of mine) when young was a socialist and environmentalist, but toward middle age he became politically conservative and a firm believer in the supremacy of genes!" (Ashley Montagu, *Sociobiology Examined* [Oxford: Oxford University Press, 1980], p. 4.)

Summary

Casting refers to portraying the structure of arguments. Casting is an important skill because (1) it helps you zero in on arguments, which is not always easy to do in longer passages; (2) it trains you to penetrate a passage's rhetorical flourishes; and (3) it minimizes the need to reproduce or keep referring to previous passages when evaluating an argument.

In learning to cast, it's useful to remember how arguments are organized. Arguments typically are organized in series or chains. In a series structure, the argument presents a series of mutually independent reasons, each of which is offered in support of a conclusion. In a chain structure, the argument presents a number of interdependent points that function together in support of a conclusion.

The casting method presented in this chapter consists of three steps:

1. Putting brackets at the beginning and end of each assertion
2. Numbering assertions consecutively in the margin or above the line of type
3. Setting out the relationship between the relevant assertions in a tree diagram to be read down the page.

When diagramming an argument, drawing a single line between assertions means that one assertion implies the other. Here, assertion 1 implies assertion 2:

In this diagram

assertions 1 and 2 imply assertion 3, which in turn implies assertion 4.

A plus sign and brace mean that two or more assertions, taken together, imply a third.

$$\underbrace{① \; + \; ②}_{③}$$

Unexpressed premises or conclusions are represented by letters: *a, b, c,* and so forth. Here, assertion *a* is an unexpressed premise:

$$\underbrace{① \; + \; ⓐ}_{②}$$

Similarly, in this diagram

$$\underbrace{① \; + \; ②}_{ⓐ}$$

assertion *a* is the unexpressed conclusion.

Writers and speakers often use a variety of rhetorical devices in arguing. The following guidelines are useful in casting arguments with such rhetorical flourishes:

1. Cast each separate assertion.
2. Don't cast repetitions of the same assertion.
3. Don't cast "asides."
4. Don't cast background information.
5. Don't cast examples that merely illustrate or clarify a point.
6. Cast examples used to support a point being made; that is, examples that indicate why the point is so.
7. Don't cast as separate assertions information that follows a colon.
8. Cast as separate assertions information separated by a semicolon.

Casting calls for interpretations. This means that two people may differ in how they cast the same argument. The key point to remember is that casting is a means to an end. You cast to familiarize yourself with an argument so that you can raise substantive criticisms of it.

Applications

1. Cast the following arguments.

   a. "Many a reader will raise the question whether findings won by the observation of individuals can be applied to the psychological understanding of groups. Our answer to this question is an emphatic affirmation. Any group consists of individuals and nothing but individuals, and psychological mechanisms which we find operating in a group can therefore only be mechanisms that operate in individuals. In studying individual psychology as a basis for the understanding of social psychology, we do something that might be compared with studying an object under the microscope. This enables us to discover the very details of psychological mechanisms that we find operating on a large scale in the social process. If our analysis of sociopsychological phenomena is not based on the detailed study of human behavior, it lacks empirical character and, therefore, validity." (Eric Fromm, *Escape from Freedom* [New York: Avon Books, 1965], p. 158.)

   b. "Flextime (Flexible Working Hours) often makes workers more productive because being treated as responsible adults gives them greater commitment to their jobs. As a result it decreases absenteeism, sick leave, tardiness and overtime, and generally produces significant increases in productivity for the work group as a whole. For example, in trial periods in three different departments, the U.S. Social Security Administration measured productivity increases averaging about 20 percent. Many companies that have tried flextime have recorded increases of at least five to ten percent and none has reported a decline." (Barry Stein et al., "Flextime," *Psychology Today*, June 1976, p. 43.)

c. "The medical community has long debated the effects of tobacco smoke on non-smokers. Now recent studies have bolstered the contention of many physicians that, apart from the clear health hazard to smokers, tobacco smoke has harmful effects on non-smokers as well. In fact, in 1972 the U.S. Surgeon General devoted fully a quarter of his 226-page report, "The Health Consequences of Smoking," to the other effects of smoke on non-smokers. Other people's smoking, says the report, is retarding fetal growth and increasing the incidence of premature birth; is exacerbating respiratory allergies in children and adults; and is causing acute irritation and taxing hearts and lungs of non-smokers by filling the air in smoky rooms with carbon monoxide, the deadly poison found in automobile exhaust." (*Reader's Digest,* July 1974, pp. 102, 104).

d. "Government control of ideas or personal preferences is alien to a democracy. And the yearning to use governmental censorship of any kind is infectious. It may spread insidiously. Commencing with suppression of books as obscene, it is not unlikely to develop into official lust for the power of thought-control in the areas of religion, politics, and elsewhere. Milton observed that 'licensing of books . . . necessarily pulls along with it so many other kinds of licensing.' Mill notes that the 'bounds of what may be called moral police' may easily extend 'until it encroaches on the most unquestionably legitimate liberty of the individual.' We should beware of a recrudescence of the undemocratic doctrine uttered in the seventeenth century by Berkeley, Governor of Virginia: " 'Thank God there are no free schools or preaching, for learning has brought disobedience into the world, and printing has divulged them. God keep us from both.' " (Jerome

Frank, dissenting opinion in *United States v. Roth,* 354 U.S. 476, 1957.)

e. "While the networks are among the staunchest defenders of free expression . . . they will compromise principles in order to enhance their audience ratings. In an astonishing article the *New York Times* described how ABC subordinated its news division's integrity to an outside influence. Soviet officials were permitted to censor and monitor ABC news stories about life in Russia. Some Soviet officials actually sat in ABC's New York offices reviewing its network reporting. The *Times* article contended that these startling concessions to the Russians were part of the network's effort to secure coverage rights for the 1980 Olympics. . . ." (Marvin Maurer in *Point-Counterpoint: Readings in American Government,* Herbert M. Levine, ed. [Glenview, Ill.: Scott, Foresman, 1977].)

f. "Well, is it true that the black community is edging into the middle class? Let's look at income, the handiest guide and certainly the most generally agreed-upon measurement. What income level amounts to middle-class status? Median family income is often used, since that places a family at the exact midpoint in our society. In 1972 the median family income of whites amounted to $11,549, but black median family income was a mere $6,864.

"That won't work. Let's take another guide. The Bureau of Labor Statistics says it takes an urban family of four $12,600 to maintain an 'intermediate' living standard. Using that measure, the average black family not only is *not* middle class, but it earns far less than the 'lower, non-poverty' level of $8,200. Four out of five black families earn less than the 'intermediate' standard." (Vernon E. Jordan, Jr., "The Truth About the Black Middle Class," *Newsweek,* July 8, 1974.)

g. "American institutions were fashioned in an era of vast unoccupied spaces and preindustrial technology. In those days, collisions between public needs and individual rights may have been minimal. But increased density, scarcity of resources, and interlocking technologies have now heightened the concern for 'public goods,' which belong to no one in particular but to all of us jointly. Polluting a lake or river or the air may not directly damage any one person's private property or living space. But it destroys a good that all of us—including future generations—benefit from and have a title to. Our public goods are entitled to a measure of protection." (Amitai Etzioni, "When Rights Collide," *Psychology Today,* October 1977.)

2. Find two arguments with premise support in a newspaper, magazine, or book. Cast these arguments.

3. Compose five arguments, each of which contains at least three premises and support for at least one premise. Then cast the arguments.

4. Construct arguments for the following castings:

a.

b.
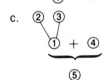

c.
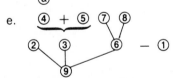

d.
① ③

② ④

ⓐ

e.
④ + ⑤ ⑦ ⑧

②   ③   ⑥ — ①

⑨

5. Construct arguments that illustrate each of the following guidelines. Then cast your arguments.

   a. Cast each separate assertion.
   b. Don't cast repetitions of the same assertion.
   c. Don't cast asides.
   d. Don't cast background information.
   e. Don't cast examples that merely illustrate or clarify a point.
   f. Cast examples used to support a point; that is, examples that indicate why the point is so.
   g. Don't cast as separate assertions information that follows a colon.
   h. Cast as separate assertions information separated by a semicolon.

[1]Michael Scriven, *Reasoning* (New York: McGraw-Hill, 1976).

MISSING PREMISES

So far you've learned about the structure of arguments and how to cast them. Many of the arguments you will read, hear, and compose will be rather lengthy and complex. Such arguments frequently leave premises, and even conclusions, unexpressed. To fully understand, accurately cast, and fairly evaluate the structure of an argument, one must take into account all of its structural elements. Thus, the art of critical thinking hinges in large part on your ability to fill in missing premises correctly, which is the subject of this chapter.

THE IMPORTANCE OF FILLING IN PREMISES

Here's a simple, familiar argument that we'll use to emphasize further the importance of filling in missing premises:

> Because [Smith is a police officer,][1] [he's trained and experienced in the use of firearms.][2]

Taken by itself, assertion 1 does not entail assertion 2. Inferring Smith's training and experience in the use of firearms *solely* from the fact that Smith is a police officer is simply wrong-headed. After all, the expressed premise does not even mention the matter of training and experience in the use of firearms. To make such an inference based only on the expressed premise would be like inferring "*A* is greater than *C*" from "*B* is greater than *C*." If an arguer made such an inference, you'd rightly ask, "How can you infer anything about *A*'s relation to *C* when you don't even mention *A* in your premise?"

The arguer might reply, "Oh, I'm assuming that *A* is greater than *B*." With this additional premise, the connection between the conclusion and the stated premise is clear. You would then see how the arguer proceeded from the premise that *B* is greater than *C* to the conclusion that *A* is greater than *C*, namely with the help of the unexpressed premise "*A* is greater than *B*." You would also understand the structure of the argument: It doesn't consist of a single premise and a conclusion but of the *two* premises and a conclusion. You would realize that the argument should *not* be cast

but

$$\underbrace{① + ⓐ}_{②}$$

It is this latter form that you would eventually evaluate in determining the worth of the argument.

Of course, you rarely can query an arguer about his or her unexpressed premises. The task of filling in missing premises therefore falls to you, the critical thinker: You must reconstruct the assumed premises. When an argument is incomplete, you must determine the premises assumed by the arguer that, together with the expressed premise or premises, entail the arguer's conclusion.

Let's return to the argument about police officer Smith:

Because [Smith is a police officer,]¹ [he's trained and experienced in the use of firearms.]²

This argument appears to have only one premise and a conclusion. More likely, it consists of two premises, one expressed, the other unexpressed. No doubt, the unexpressed premise is "All police officers receive training and experience in the use of firearms." The structure of this argument, then, should be cast as follows:

$$\underbrace{① + ⓐ}_{②}$$

Reconstructed in this way, the premises entail the conclusion: The reasoning process is as legitimate here as it was in "*A* is greater than *B*, and *B* is greater than *C*. Therefore, *A* is greater than *C*."

Whether an argument is a good one depends, of course, on more than this. It depends also on the truth of its premises. For example, is it true that all police officers receive training and experience in the use of firearms? So, the legitimacy of the argument's conclusion—that Smith is trained and experienced in the use of firearms—depends also on the truth of unexpressed premise. But if you never detected this assumed premise, you would not be able to evaluate it to determine whether it is true. Therefore, you would not be able to fully evaluate the argument.

Filling in missing premises is important for another reason. Suppose you take the argument we're discussing at face value. You assume that it has only one premise: "Smith is a police officer." You therefore cast the argument as follows:

You then fault the argument as unsound, because the single premise does not entail the conclusion: That Smith is a police officer doesn't by itself necessarily mean that he's trained and experienced in the use of firearms.

But what have you really done? If the argument *is* based on an additional unexpressed premise, you've misrepresented the argument. When the unexpressed premise is filled in—"All police officers receive training and experience in the use of firearms"—the argument survives your criticism because the expressed premise, when taken together with the unexpressed one, does imply the conclusion. Of course, the argument *may* still be faulty: It may not be true or may at least be doubtful that all police officers receive training and experience in the use of firearms. But in that case the fault would not lie in the reasoning procedure but in the false content on which the reasoning is based.

If we are thinking critically about arguments, we are trying to make fair assessments for the right reasons. Calling an argument faulty for the wrong reason is like a physician's describing a patient as ill for the wrong reason. Without a proper diagnosis of the problem, both the critical thinker and physician are ineffectual.

At this point you may be wondering, "Why should I, the reader or listener, have to fill in missing premises? Isn't that the job of the arguer? I have enough to do sorting out what the argument says without having to worry about what it doesn't say." Certainly it would be less trouble for critical thinkers if all arguments came complete. But they don't, and in some ways it's just as well that they don't. If they did, writing, reading, and listening would be dishwater dull. After all, sometimes premises are too obvious to be stated. For example, when someone says,

> Because you're planning to go to medical school, you'd better get good grades in college,

what is assumed is obvious: "Anyone planning to go to medical school had better get good grades in college." And when you say, "I try to avoid unhealthy habits.

That's why I don't smoke," it is obvious that you are assuming that "smoking is an unhealthy habit." Often, premises are just too obvious to need stating.

Sometimes arguers simply overlook premises. This is especially common in oral arguments. Although failing to express premises may impede communication, there is nothing logically objectionable about an argument with missing premises. It can be as good as one with no missing premises.

Finally, arguers don't always realize what they are assuming and in fact often would prefer to leave their assumptions uninspected. Indeed, concealing questionable assumptions is a common and effective ploy in argument, as we'll see in Chapter 10. If we don't take pains to fill in missing premises, we may invite our own exploitation; we make ourselves easy marks for every huckster who comes down the pike.

These preliminary observations should impress on you the importance of filling in missing premises. Of course, it's one thing to realize that thinking critically requires you to fill in missing premises; it's another to do so correctly. In fact, accurate reconstruction of missing premises is the most challenging aspect of critical thinking and argument analysis. It can also be the most rewarding. To do it well you must be attentive, thoughtful, and clever. In the process you likely will uncover weaknesses in an argument, for falsehoods typically lie more in what is unsaid than in what is said. Discovering these flaws can be an exhilarating problem-solving exercise. Even when filling in missing premises is more exercising than exhilarating, it still is useful, for when done well, it allows you to focus on the essential weaknesses of an argument. An ability to fill in missing premises makes you an incisive and formidable critic; it helps you get on top of the mountain of argumentative material that looms large in your personal and professional life.

THE DIFFICULTIES OF FILLING IN PREMISES

Let's return for a moment to several examples we used earlier. When someone says,

> Since you're planning to go to medical school, you'd better get good grades in college,

we said that what is assumed as an unexpected premise is obvious:

> Anyone planning to go to medical school had better get good grades in college.

How did we know this? How did we know that the unexpressed premise was not something entirely different? And if someone says,

> I try to avoid unhealthy habits. That's why I don't smoke,

we said it is obvious that what is assumed as an unexpressed premise is

> Smoking is an unhealthy habit.

How did we know this? How did we know that the arguer is not assuming

> Smoking is an aesthetically offensive habit?

Suppose you now respond, "The unexpressed premises we filled in are the right ones because they are the ones that make the most sense of what the arguer *did* say." That is a good answer for a couple of reasons.

First of all, it's true. The unexpressed premises we filled in do make sense of what the arguer did say—better sense, no doubt, than anything else we could have come up with. "Anyone planning to go to medical school had better get good grades in college" does make sense of "Because you're planning to go to medical school, you'd better get good grades in college." And "Smoking is an unhealthy habit" does, whereas "smoking is an aesthetically offensive habit" does not make sense of "I try to avoid unhealthy habits. That's why I don't smoke."

Second, it captures the essence of the whole business of filling in premises: When we fill in premises, we are trying to make sense of what people say. The two examples we've been discussing are relatively simple and straightforward. Although they are each incompletely stated, they each embody a sufficient measure of guidance so that it's not at all difficult to identify the unexpressed premises in them. This is part of what we meant when we said that the unexpressed premises were "obvious." But many cases are much more difficult. Frequently there are *several different ways* of "making sense" of what someone says. Then, too, sometimes what people say just doesn't make very much sense. It won't always be possible to know, with certainty, which of several different statements should be cast in the role of missing premise, or whether one should be bothering to look for missing premises at all.

The problems that arise in connection with filling in premises have to do with an inevitable fact about human communication: Making sense of what people say is *non-algorithmic.* This means that it is not governed by any absolute, mechanical, foolproof decision procedures. Rather, it involves the application of multiple criteria that sometimes conflict with one another. Hence, it tends to yield multiple solutions, each with advantages and liabilities. The most one can expect by way of systematic guidance to this sort of process is a set of guidelines—"rules of thumb." That is precisely what we will present in this chapter. But as you work with these guidelines, building experience and cultivating sensitivity and judgment, you should be alert to the exceptions that such guidelines predictably admit of.

You may well sense a second difficulty in learning to fill in missing premises: You may have noticed, for example, when you recognized that inferring Smith's training and experience in the use of firearms *solely* from the fact that Smith is a police officer is simply wrong-headed, you were, in effect, evaluating the argument

> Because [Smith is a police officer,] [he's trained and experienced in the use of firearms.]

You recognize, then, that some of the crucial procedures involved in filling in missing premises are themselves techniques of argument evaluation—something you have yet to study in detail. Don't let this throw you for a loop. In fact, you should congratulate yourself. In recognizing this, you have gained a valuable insight into the nature of thinking critically, one that will help you immeasurably in this chapter and those to come: Ultimately, argument analysis and argument evaluation interpenetrate and depend on each other.

WHEN TO FILL IN PREMISES

In general, you should fill in missing premises whenever an argument is incomplete and you can identify a plausible and relevant assertion that would complete it and that is part of the arguer's position. In an incomplete argument, the stated premise does not entail the argument's conclusion. Before you can fill in its premises, however, you must be able to recognize an argument as incomplete. A strategy you can use to identify incomplete arguments is the "what if" strategy.

The "What If" Strategy

Let's begin with the simple argument "Bill must be a man because he's a father." If you want to determine whether this argument is complete or incomplete, you could ask, *What if* it's true that Bill is a father? Must it follow that he's a man? By definition a father is a male parent. Therefore, if Bill is a father, he must be an adult male. The single premise in this argument thus entails the conclusion. The argument is complete as it appears.

In contrast, reconsider the argument "Because Smith is a police officer, he's probably in favor of gun-control legislation." If you wanted to determine whether this argument was complete, you could ask, *What if* it's true that Smith is a police officer. Must it follow that he's probably in favor of gun-control legislation? Not necessarily, for it may well be that most police officers are opposed to such legislation. Nothing in the stated premise disallows that possibility. If in fact most police officers are not in favor of such laws, then the conclusion would not follow from this premise. Something is missing; the argument is incomplete.

These simple examples should illustrate how the "what if" strategy works. Notice that in applying it you needn't know whether the expressed premise is true to determine whether it implies the conclusion. All you have to do is ask, *What if* it were true? Would the conclusion then have to be true? Thus, the "what if" strategy consists of *assuming* that the expressed premise (or premises) is (are) true and asking whether the conclusion therefore would have to be true. If the answer is yes, the argument is complete; if it is no, the argument is incomplete.

You can look at the "what if" strategy as placing you in the role of a detective who might be testing someone's alibi.

> **Alibiing suspect:** My girlfriend will testify that I was with her in her apartment when the mugging occurred. So I couldn't have committed the crime.

> **Skeptical detective:** *What if* the suspect's girlfriend testifies that he was with her in her apartment at the time of the mugging? Must it be true that he couldn't have committed the crime?

The detective needn't be a Sherlock Holmes to see that even if the girlfriend does so testify, the suspect still could have committed the crime, for she could be lying. On the other hand, let's say that it was established indisputably that the suspect was not at the scene of the crime when it was committed. Then the detective would have to formulate the "what if" question differently: *What if* the suspect was not at the scene of the mugging when it occurred? Must it be true that he couldn't have committed the crime? In this case the alibi given in the expressed premise would warrant the conclusion.

---

*Quick Check on "What If" Strategy
(Answers on Page 398)

Using the "what if" strategy, determine whether the following arguments are incomplete:

1. Because prisons do not rehabilitate inmates, they are an ineffective form of punishment for criminal behavior.
2. The United States should develop solar energy on a widespread basis because it must become energy independent.
3. Abortion involves the taking of a life. Therefore, it should be discouraged.
4. Jane's probably married. She's wearing a wedding ring.
5. Men are not innately superior to women. If they were, they wouldn't establish caste systems to ensure their preferred positions, and they wouldn't work so hard to maintain these systems. But obviously men do both.

GUIDELINES FOR RECONSTRUCTING
PREMISES

The "what if" strategy tells you whether an argument is complete or not as it stands. Suppose a given argument is incomplete as it stands. Do you proceed to fill in a missing premise, and if so, which one? At this stage of the game you will need to determine whether there is some assertion that is both plausible and relevant to the argument, that you may reasonably suppose the arguer would accept or is committed to, and that would, if it were added to the argument as a premise, make the argument complete.

Plausibility

Plausibility literally means deserving of applause. It has to do with the credibility or believability of an idea. This, in turn, is a measure of how well we think an idea is likely to survive critical scrutiny. If we were to devise strenuous tests designed to falsify an idea, how would the idea do? A plausible idea is one that we think would do well. An implausible idea is one that we think would not do so well.

Neither plausibility nor implausibility is "absolute." Rather, they admit of degrees. This means that some ideas are more plausible than others. A good place to look for examples to illustrate this point (implausible though this may sound) is in tabloids like the *National Enquirer.* In these publications you will find a steady diet of very implausible ideas, such as: "Confederate Flag Sighted on the Bottom of UFO" and "Elvis Presley Planning Return to United States from Seclusion in Brazil to Expose His Death as Hoax"; and a good many ideas that are somewhat less implausible, for example, "Hypnosis Cures Urge to Smoke"; alongside a few ideas that are quite a bit more plausible, such as: "Madonna and Husband Sean Penn May Soon Separate" or "Cast of 'Dynasty' Involved in Power Struggle."

Moreover, our estimates of an idea's plausibility or implausibility are not static. Rather, they are subject to adjustment in accordance with new incoming information. What may appear initially to be a plausible idea may, on further investigation, seem more and more or less and less plausible.

And plausibility is only loosely correlated with truth. A plausible idea may well turn out not to be the case. And there are a good many cases throughout history of initially implausible ideas that have nonetheless been confirmed as true. Plausibility, in other words, is a preliminary measure of an idea's worth. This is one reason why it is appropriate as a criterion for filling in missing premises.

Now consider this example:

> Because Smith is a police officer, he's probably in favor of gun-control legislation.

There are a number of distinct alternatives you might consider casting in the role of missing premise. Take, for example, these two:

1. All police officers favor gun-control legislation.
2. Most police officers favor gun-control legislation.

Either of these alternatives will complete the argument. But the first alternative is somewhat less plausible than the second. Remember, this means simply that if we were to devise strenuous tests designed to falsify them, the first would be less likely to survive than the second. This is because the first alternative makes a stronger claim than the second.

In filling in missing premises we generally try to avoid implausible assertions, even if adding them would make the argument complete. This is because we want to give an argument a fair run for its money. It does no service to an argument to reconstruct it on the basis of an implausible premise, when there is a more plausible alternative that would equally well complete it. Similarly, in assessing candidates for the role of missing premise, preference generally goes to the more plausible of two alternatives. This derives from a general principle of fairness, which ought to govern our attempts to make sense of what people say.

*Quick Check on Plausibility (Answers on Page 399)

Rank the following statement pairs in terms of plausibility. Compare your rankings with those of someone else in the class. Wherever your rankings conflict, explain your initial ranking. Compare notes and see whether your ranking is affected.

1. a. There is intelligent life in outer space.
   b. Some nonhuman animals have the capacity for language.
2. a. The use of computer technology in weapons systems increases the risk of a nuclear accident.
   b. The perfection of a space-based missile defense system is feasible.
3. a. Some of the assassins of President Kennedy are still alive.
   b. Some of the assassins of President Kennedy presently hold high office in Washington.
4. a. Human adults generally use less than 10 percent of the capacity of their minds.
   b. The universe is finite.

Relevance

Let's now return to another of our earlier examples.

> I try to avoid unhealthy habits. That's why I don't smoke.

We considered two alternative missing premises for this argument:

> Smoking is an unhealthy habit.
> Smoking is an aesthetically offensive habit.

And we said that "smoking is an unhealthy habit" does, whereas "smoking is an aesthetically offensive habit" does not, make sense of "I try to avoid unhealthy habits. That's why I don't smoke." This was not based on a difference in their relative plausibility. Rather, it was based on the fact that the first alternative is relevant to the argument, whereas the second is not. The first alternative connects the expressed premise to the conclusion, whereas the second alternative, although it may be true, and although it may count as a reason for not smoking, does not link the conclusion to the reason given in the expressed premise.

Here is a strategy you can use to determine the relevance of candidates for the role of missing premise.

Topic Coverage Strategy When we identify an argument as incomplete, we in effect sense a gap or hole in it. But we can be more specific than this. The hole has a more or less definite shape that we can discern, to some extent at least, by paying close attention to what surrounds it—to the argument's conclusion and its expressed premise(s). Think of this as similar to searching for a missing piece in a jigsaw puzzle. You study closely the shapes and colors of the pieces that surround the one you're searching for. This helps you find the missing piece. When the puzzle is an incomplete argument and what we're searching for is a missing premise, we can guide ourselves by close attention to the topics covered in the conclusion and the expressed premise(s) of the argument. This helps us get a better sense of the "shape" of the hole or gap we're trying to fill in and of the missing premise that can fill it.

So, for example, in the argument we've been discussing, the topics covered in the conclusion and the expressed premise are

1. reasons why the arguer doesn't smoke
2. the arguer's policy of trying to avoid unhealthy habits

The gap or hole in the argument, then, is something that relates these to each other. The second alternative we considered, "Smoking is an aesthetically offensive habit," doesn't do this. Although it might fit with topic 1, reasons why the arguer doesn't smoke, it doesn't fit with topic 2, the arguer's policy of trying to avoid unhealthy habits. The first alternative, however, fits with both.

---

*Quick Check on Relevance and Topic Coverage Strategy (Answers on Page 399)

The following arguments are incomplete. Each is followed by a list of possible missing premises. Use the topic coverage strategy to select from each list the missing premise most relevant to the argument.

Argument 1: People who were born at exactly the same time often have vastly different life histories and personalities. Therefore, astrology is not a reliable predictive system.

Reconstruction a: People who believe in astrology are superstitious.

Reconstruction b: If astrology were a reliable predictive system, people born at exactly the same time would not have vastly different life histories and personalities.

Reconstruction c: No two people are born at exactly the same time.

Argument 2: Since no human system of justice is infallible and capital punishment imposes an irreversible penalty, capital punishment is an unacceptable form of punishment.

Reconstruction a: No form of punishment that imposes an irreversible penalty is acceptable.

Reconstruction b: If we could perfect a system of justice so that no mistaken convictions could possibly occur, then capital punishment would be acceptable.

Reconstruction c: No form of punishment that imposes an irreversible penalty is acceptable within a fallible system of justice.

Fidelity to the Arguer's Position

Probably the trickiest part of filling in missing premises is remaining faithful to the arguer's actual position. If, in reconstructing an incomplete argument, we wind up with something that no longer reflects the views of the arguer, our efforts have obviously gone astray. In saying this, we remember that, as we said earlier, sometimes arguers are unaware of all of the premises they may be assuming in their arguments. They may even be unwilling to learn or admit that they are assuming a particular premise in an argument. That's part of what makes this tricky. When we say that in filling in missing premises we should try to remain faithful to the arguer's position, we don't merely mean that we should remain faithful to what the arguer is aware of or willing to admit to. We mean rather that the missing premise should be something that the arguer would accept as part of her view if she were aware of it, or which she must be committed to in order for her reasoning to make sense.

Another thing that makes this tricky is that in filling in premises, we are engaged in interpretive activity that takes us beyond what the arguer actually says. You can see what the difficulty is here by considering the difference between oral and written discourse. In oral contexts, when you are listening to someone present an argument, you at least have the opportunity to question the arguer if you think she is relying on an unexpressed premise. With written arguments you generally cannot do this. You must guide your efforts on the basis of information which is of necessity incomplete.

Consider once again this argument: "Because Smith is a police officer, he's probably in favor of gun-control legislation." The "what if" strategy tells us that the argument is incomplete as it stands. Using the topic coverage strategy, we can see that the missing premise will need to link the category of police officers with favoring gun-control legislation in some way. But this still leaves the field open to several candidates:

> Reconstruction 1: Some police officers favor gun-control legislation.
> Reconstruction 2: Most police officers favor gun-control legislation.
> Reconstruction 3: All police officers favor gun-control legislation.

Let's first consider reconstruction 1: "Some police officers favor gun-control legislation." If "some" is taken to mean at least one, then we can be quite certain that the arguer would accept this premise as part of her position. After all, the argument explicitly commits her to the claim that Smith is a police officer and to the claim that Smith is for that reason probably in favor of gun-control legislation. The arguer must be committed at least to the view that some police officers are in favor of gun-control legislation. But the arguer must be committed to something stronger than reconstruction 1, because the arguer concludes that Smith is *probably* in favor of gun-control legislation and if reconstruction 1 were all that the arguer were committed to, then she would lack an adequate basis for that conclusion. In other words, even with the addition of reconstruction 1 as a missing premise, the argument would remain incomplete.

Reconstruction 3 is the strongest of the three. Certainly if "All police officers favor gun-control legislation," then the conclusion can be inferred: "Smith is probably in favor of gun-control legislation." In fact, reconstruction 3 would allow the even stronger conclusion "Smith *must be* in favor of gun-control legislation." That the arguer qualifies her conclusion with the word "probably" gives us convincing evidence that reconstruction 3 would not be in keeping with the arguer's position. As we earlier said, if we insisted on reconstruction 3, then we'd be saddling the arguer with a needlessly implausible premise, thereby turning her argument into a sitting duck. All you'd have to do to discredit the argument would be to cite a single example of a police officer opposed to gun-control legislation. That single example would disprove the assertion that all police officers favor gun-control legislation, which in turn would prove the argument faulty.

Reconstruction 2 falls between these extremes. In referring to the position of *most* police officers, it avoids the overstatement of reconstruction 3 and the understatement of reconstruction 1. It is strong enough to complete the argument but not so strong as to overstate the arguer's position.

As tricky as it is to faithfully extrapolate an arguer's position from an incomplete expression of it, there is even a risk that we will wind up merely restating the original incomplete argument as our reconstruction of a missing premise. Take this example:

> Most working women don't complain of sexual harassment on the job. Therefore, sexual harassment on the job must not be a widespread problem.

First of all, the "what if" strategy tells us that this argument is incomplete as it stands. Suppose it's true that most working women don't complain of sexual harassment on the job. Must it be true therefore that sexual harassment on the job is not a widespread problem? Not necessarily. What is the missing premise? The topic coverage strategy indicates that the missing premise will need to link the incidence of sexual harassment on the job (the topic of the conclusion) with the incidence of complaints from working women concerning sexual harassment on the job (the topic of the expressed premise). One way to do this would be with the addition of the premise that

> If most working women don't complain about sexual harassment on the job, then it's not a widespread problem.

This premise does complete the argument. Check this with the "what if" strategy. Suppose that this new premise and the original expressed premise are both true. Must it necessarily be true then that sexual harassment on the job is not a widespread problem? Yes. Furthermore, we can be quite sure that the arguer is committed to this assertion. This is because it merely restates the original argument in a single sentence. Indeed, that's what's wrong with this as a candidate for the role of missing premise. To suppose that the arguer had nothing more in mind than a mere restatement of what she did say in the form of a general principle—so as to plug a logical gap in her argument—is neither fair nor reasonable. Such a reconstruction, were the arguer herself to supply it, would be dismissed as *ad hoc*. The term "ad hoc," which derives from Latin, means roughly "without independent reason." We should be wondering if the arguer didn't have some deeper, more independent basis for her conclusion, something like:

> Only that which most people complain about is a widespread problem.

If there is a plausible and relevant alternative that would complete the argument and that goes beyond what is already present in the incomplete original to a broader principle on which the arguer may reasonably be supposed to have based her reasoning, that alternative is preferable.

---

*Quick Check on Filling in Missing Premises (Answers on Page 399)

1. For this exercise, you'll need a study partner, preferably someone who is also taking critical thinking. Formulate and evaluate possible missing premises for the incomplete arguments in the Quick Check on "what if" strategy (p. 155). As you examine possible reconstructions, consider the questions of plausibility and relevance and fidelity to the arguer's position. Compile a list of alternatives for each, along with your assessments of relative advantages and liabilities, for class discussion.

2. Select the best reconstructed premise from the alternatives offered for each of the following arguments:

   a. Some of these people can't be golfers. They're not carrying clubs.

      Reconstruction 1: Some golfers are carrying clubs.

      Reconstruction 2: Everyone carrying clubs is a golfer.

      Reconstruction 3: All golfers carry clubs.

   b. If capital punishment isn't a deterrent to crime, then why has the rate of violent crimes increased since capital punishment was outlawed?

      Reconstruction 1: Because the rate of violent crime has increased since capital punishment was outlawed, it must be a deterrent to crime.

      Reconstruction 2: An increase in the rate of crime following the abolition of a punishment proves that the punishment is a crime deterrent.

      Reconstruction 3: An increase in the rate of crime following the abolition of a punishment usually indicates that the punishment is a crime deterrent.

   c. Constitutionally, only the House of Representatives may initiate a money-raising bill. Thus, when the Senate drafted the recent tax bill, it acted unconstitutionally. Therefore, the proposed tax bill should not be made law.

      Reconstruction 1: Any bill the Senate drafts should not be made law.

      Reconstruction 2: Any bill that originates unconstitutionally should not be made law.

      Reconstruction 3: Any tax bill originating in the Senate should not be made law.

3. Fill in the missing premises of the following incomplete arguments, and cast them. Some may have *more than one* premise missing.

   a. All successful politicians are self-serving, for only ambitious people succeed in politics.

   b. Whatever invades privacy threatens justice. That's why subjecting people to polygraph tests as a condition of employment is so serious.

   c. Resident reacting against a mobile home park's becoming part of the neighborhood: "I have nothing against mobile homes as a way of living, but it's unthinkable to put a mobile home park right in the middle of a residential area. After all, they're usually in outlying areas."

   d. Because they see it as a hedge against malpractice suits, doctors typically welcome a patient's informed consent.

e. "Imperialist is a dirty word, all right, but it hardly fits a nation like the United States which, with all our faults, is ready to give millions of dollars to help starving and dying Cambodians." (William Randolph Hearst, Jr., *Los Angeles Herald Examiner,* November 4, 1979, p. F3.)

f. Former Michigan Governor George Romney in describing the Equal Rights Amendment as a "moral perversion": "Surely this resolution and its supporting statements are designed to legitimize sex and social relationships other than those that form the basis of divinely ordained marriage, parenthood and home." (AP release, January 2, 1980.)

LONGER ARGUMENTS

So far we have restricted our discussion of missing premises to short arguments. But as you know, long arguments can contain many intermediate mini-arguments. Such subarguments require more than filling in a single missing premise. Nevertheless, the strategies for identifying incomplete arguments and the guidelines for reconstruction of missing premises apply with equal force to longer arguments. Here is a slightly longer argument:

[President Reagan promised to balance the federal budget by 1984.] But [in his first term of office he succeeded in multiplying the budget deficit by over 250 percent.] And [he refused to seriously address the issue of the budget deficit throughout the 1984 reelection campaign.] But since [such behavior evidently amounts to a betrayal of the public trust,] [President Reagan was unworthy of reelection.]

This argument contains five explicit claims, the last of which is the argument's main conclusion. The first three claims together support number 4, which in turn supports the main conclusion. On the face of it, the argument could be cast as follows:

Is this argument incomplete? It is if *either* of its conclusions, 4 or 5, is not warranted by the support expressed. To see if there are any unwarranted inferences, we can apply the "what if" strategy.

Both the inference from 1, 2, and 3 to 4 and the inference from 4 to 5 are incomplete. What if premises 1, 2, and 3 are all true? Is assertion 4 necessarily true? Suppose that Ronald Reagan did make a campaign promise to balance the federal budget but instead multiplied the budget deficit by more than 250 percent during his first term in office and that he refused to address this issue seriously during the 1984 reelection campaign. It does not necessarily follow that this adds up to a betrayal of the public trust. It is possible that the rise in the deficit was due to factors beyond the former president's control and that a frank public discussion of the issue during the 1984 campaign would have jeopardized a fragile economic balance. So assertion 4 is still debatable. It is, however, worded somewhat cautiously. It says the president's record *evidently* adds up to a betrayal of the public trust. This gives us some guidance as to possible additional premises that the arguer may be appealing to:

a. In the absence of evidence to the contrary, such a record in office would add up to a betrayal of the public trust.
b. There is no evidence to the contrary.

Now let's consider the inference from 4 to 5. Again, the inference is incomplete as it stands. Even if it's true that Reagan betrayed the public trust, the question remains open whether or not he was worthy of reelection; that is, unless the arguer is also appealing to a general principle to the effect that

c. Any elected officer of the public trust who betrays that trust while in office is unworthy of reelection.

This would complete the argument. It fits in well with the expressed premise 4 and the argument's conclusion. As a principle, it is highly idealistic, although that doesn't make it implausible in the least. It does, however, raise a certain question concerning fidelity to the arguer's actual position. Many people would question the wisdom of c from the point of view of political pragmatism. But people who find c "too idealistic" or "impractical" or "unworkable" would be unlikely to make the sort of argument we're presently considering. It therefore remains reasonable to suppose that the arguer is committed to c, or to something very close to it, in arguing from 4 to 5. Thus, the argument might be cast as follows:

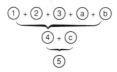

Now let us consider an even longer argument, which connects the increase in premarital sex with a reduction in teenage marriages and a subsequent reduction in the divorce rate:

[Premarital sex¹ is on the rise.] [One study shows that sexual intercourse² is initiated at a younger age] <u>and that</u> [its occurrence among teenagers³ is increasing.] <u>Another shows that</u> [the percentage of married persons between the age of eighteen and twenty-four who had sexual experience⁴ prior to marriage was 95 percent for males and 81 percent for females.] <u>Still another</u> [survey shows that of the sampled adolescents between ages thirteen and nineteen, 52 percent⁵ had had some premarital intercourse.] [This increase in the prevalence of premarital sex is⁶ bound to reduce the number of teenage marriages.] <u>Thus,</u> [there will probably be a substantial decline in the divorce rate.⁷]

This argument consists of seven explicit assertions. (We are taking sentence 2 as two separate assertions.) The main conclusion is assertion 7, which the arguer feels is implied by assertion 6. This assertion is supported by assertion 1, which in turn is supported by assertions 2, 3, 4, and 5. The argument, then, has two mini-arguments, which can be diagrammed as follows:

and

Taken on face, the entire argument may be diagrammed:

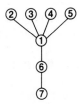

Is this argument incomplete? It is if *any* of its conclusions, 1, 6, or 7, is not warranted by the support expressed. To see if there are any unwarranted inferences, we can apply the "what if" strategy.

Mini-conclusion 1 is inferred from a series of independent statistical references expressed in mini-premises 2, 3, 4, and 5. What if the data are true? Must it then be true that "Premarital sex is on the rise"? If we concede that the data are up-to-date and typify the results of research in the field, then they do entail the inference. There is no point in reconstructing these concessions as assumptions because they merely repeat the argument. After all, the arguer presumably believes that these data are typical and current and that they support the mini-conclusion about the increased incidence of premarital sex. So we can take the data presented in mini-premises 2, 3, 4, and 5 as providing conclusive support for mini-conclusion 1. (Obviously, if we have reason to dispute the data as atypical or dated, then in evaluating the argument, we'd criticize them.)

Let's now turn to the second mini-argument, in which mini-conclusion 6 is inferred from mini-premise 1. *What if* it's true that premarital sex is on the rise? Must it then be true that teenage marriages will be reduced; that is, that the age of the average couple at marriage will be older than it was, say, in the immediately preceding generation? Not necessarily. Why couldn't premarital sex just as likely encourage teenagers to marry *earlier?* It's possible that, having satisfied themselves that they are sexually compatible, a couple might be more inclined to marry than if they hadn't. Or because they are having premarital sex, a couple might be inclined to marry rather than risk having a baby or facing an abortion decision outside marriage. Thus, the mini-premise that premarital sex is on the rise doesn't of itself lead to the mini-conclusion that teenage marriages will decline. What, then, led the arguer from mini-premise 1 to mini-conclusion 6? It must have been an *unexpressed* mini-premise.

Our next job is to decide what mini-premise *a* together with the expressed mini-premise 1 leads to mini-conclusion 6. What must the arguer be assuming that will complete the mini-argument "Premarital sex is on the rise. . . . This . . . is bound to reduce the number of teenage marriages"?

The reconstruction should link premarital sex with a reduction in the number of teenage marriages. It should be strong enough to support the conclusion but not so strong that it overstates the case. And it should not merely repeat the argument in an ad hoc fashion.

Here are three possible reconstructions:

Reconstruction 1: Whenever premarital sex is on the rise, marriages are bound
         to be delayed.
Reconstruction 2: Premarital sex discourages people from marrying.
Reconstruction 3: Premarital sex discourages teenagers from marrying.

Reconstruction 1 merely repeats the argument. We are still left wondering why premarital sex is bound to delay marriage. Reconstruction 2 looks better, but it's too strong. Taken together with mini-premise 1, it would yield the conclusion that there will be fewer marriages, or something to that effect. But the arguer infers only that *teenage* marriages will be reduced. Young people may marry later; they won't stop marrying altogether. Reconstruction 3 expresses what needs to be covered. It connects premarital sex and teenage marriages. It is strong enough to help produce the conclusion without overstating the issue. And, unlike reconstruction 1, it illuminates rather than repeats. With the help of reconstruction 3, we see how the arguer was led to mini-conclusion 6 from the expressed mini-premise 1.

The second mini-argument, therefore, can be diagrammed as follows:

In this case, *a* is taken to mean reconstruction 3 in our list of candidates.

The arguer then moves from premise 6 to conclusion 7, from the assertion that "the prevalence of premarital sex is bound to reduce the number of teenage marriages" to the argument's main conclusion: "There will be a substantial decline in the divorce rate."

You needn't be a professional logician to sense a considerable leap of logic between assertions 6 and 7. The conclusion covers a decline in the divorce rate but the premise mentions nothing of this. Why will a reduction in teenage marriages produce a substantial reduction in the number of divorces? Clearly, the arguer must be making at least one other assumption *b*, which together with premise 6, helps provide support for conclusion 7.

Here are four possible reconstructions for the missing premise *b*:

1. If the number of teenage marriages is reduced, the divorce rate likely will decline substantially.
2. Teenage marriages end in divorce.
3. A substantial number of teenage marriages end in divorce.
4. A substantial number of divorces involve teenage marriages.

Reconstruction 1 merely repeats the argument; it doesn't illuminate it. We're still left wondering, But why will a reduction in teenage marriages likely lead to a substantial decline in divorce? Reconstruction 2 supplies an answer. Teenage marriages result in divorce. The problem, however, is that this reconstruction is a sweeping generalization. It's not very plausible and it overstates the case. Not all teenage marriages end in divorce. And even if they did, a reduction in teenage marriages wouldn't necessarily produce a *substantial* decline in the number of divorces. This last observation applies equally to reconstruction 3, although reconstruction 3 is somewhat more plausible than reconstruction 2.

To illustrate this point, let's say that 75 percent of teenage marriages fail; that is, a substantial number of teenage marriages end in divorce (reconstruction 3). Let's further say that these divorces account for only 2 percent of the total number of divorces; the other 98 percent involve nonteenage marriages. If this were the case, then reducing the number of teenage marriages would not produce a *substantial* decline in the divorce rate. But the conclusion of this argument implies that a substantial percentage of the total divorce rate involves teenage marriages. Reconstruction 3 misses this point; it merely asserts that a lot of teenage marriages end in divorce. Thus, if the number of such marriages can be reduced, then the number of divorces will decline, assuming that everything else remains constant. But will they decline *substantially?* They will do so only if teenage marriages contribute *substantially* to the total number of divorces.

Reconstruction 4 covers this point. It rightly focuses on the contribution teenage marriages make to the total divorce picture and not on the number of teenage marriages ending in divorce, as reconstructions 2 and 3 do. In addition, it is strong enough to help support the conclusion but not so strong that it overstates the case, as does reconstruction 3. If it's true that a substantial number of divorces involve teenage marriages (reconstruction 4) and that the number of teenage marriages will decline (reconstruction 6), it must be true that the divorce rate probably will decline (reconstruction 7). The diagram for this mini-argument, therefore, is

$$\underbrace{ⓆＱ + ⓑ}_{⑦}$$

where *b* is now taken to mean reconstruction 4 in our list of candidates. The diagram for the entire argument is

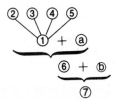

Summary

To fully understand, accurately cast, and fairly evaluate the structure of an argument, one must take into account all of its structural elements. Thus, the art of critical thinking hinges in large part on your ability to fill in missing premises correctly.

When you fill in premises, you are trying to make sense of what people say. Making sense of what people say is not governed by any absolute, mechanical, foolproof decision procedures. Rather, it involves the application of multiple criteria that sometimes conflict with one another. Hence, it tends to yield multiple solutions, each with advantages and liabilities. The most one can expect by way of systematic guidance to this sort of process is a set of guidelines. As you work with these guidelines, building experience and cultivating sensitivity and judgment, be alert to the exceptions that such guidelines admit of.

Some of the crucial procedures involved in filling in missing premises are techniques of argument evaluation—something you have yet to study in detail. Don't let this throw you for a loop. Rather, congratulate yourself on having gained a valuable insight into the nature of thinking critically, one that will help you immeasurably in this chapter and those to come, namely, that argument analysis and argument evaluation interpenetrate and depend on each other.

In general, you should fill in missing premises whenever an argument is incomplete and you can identify a plausible and relevant assertion that would complete it and that is part of the arguer's position.

The "what if" strategy helps you identify incomplete arguments. Ask "what if" the stated premise is true? Would the conclusion have to be true? If the answer is yes, the argument is complete; if it is no, the argument is incomplete.

Plausibility has to do with the credibility or believability of an idea. It is a measure of how well we think an idea is likely to survive critical scrutiny. If we were to devise strenuous tests designed to falsify an idea, how would the idea do? A plausible idea is one that we think would do well. An implausible idea is one that we think would not do so well. In filling in missing premises, we generally try to avoid implausible assertions, even if adding them would make the argument complete. This is because we want to give an argument a fair run for its money. Similarly, in assessing candidates for the role of missing premise, preference generally goes to the more plausible of two alternatives.

The topic coverage strategy is a strategy you can use to determine the relevance of candidates for the role of missing premise. Think of this as similar to searching for a missing piece in a jigsaw puzzle. By paying close attention to the topics covered in the conclusion and expressed premise(s) of the argument, you can get a better sense of the "shape" of the hole or gap you're trying to fill in, and of the missing premise that can fill it.

The trickiest part of filling in missing premises is remaining faithful to the arguer's actual position. When we say that in filling in missing premises we should try to remain faithful to the arguer's position, we don't merely mean that we should remain faithful to what the arguer is aware of or willing to admit to. We mean rather that the missing premise should be something that the arguer would accept as part of her view if she were aware of it, or that she must be committed to in order for her reasoning to make sense.

In trying to remain faithful to the arguer's actual position, try to reconstruct a premise that is just strong enough to help support the conclusion. A reconstruction that overstates the missing premise misrepresents the argument, thereby making it easy to refute. One that understates the missing premise will be too weak to help support the conclusion.

In trying to remain faithful to the arguer's actual position, try to reconstruct a premise that illuminates, and doesn't just repeat in an ad hoc fashion, the original incomplete argument.

Longer arguments generally can be handled like shorter ones. But be sure to pay attention to each of a longer argument's mini-arguments. There may be several gaps in the overall argument.

Applications

The following arguments contain at least one missing premise and possibly more. Fill in the missing premise (or premises) and cast the argument.

1. Prime-time television encourages sexism by stereotyping women.

2. Television news has a penchant for portraying the visual and sensational. As a result, it overlooks many newsworthy stories.

3. It's little wonder that many ads are misleading. They are geared primarily to selling us something.

4. Most news gives us an acquaintance with issues. That's why it's dangerous to assume that we gain knowledge about issues from viewing the evening news.

5. Abortion is legal. It's also a way of preventing unwanted, unloved babies from being born. Abortion is therefore moral.

6. There's no evidence that capital punishment deters crime. So it should be outlawed. Besides, capital punishment is barbaric.

7. Inasmuch as a college education increases one's earning potential, it's wise to get that degree. A degree provides uncommon social opportunities and testifies to one's persistence and self-discipline, two time-honored character qualities.

8. Studies indicate that sexual harassment is increasing, not abating, on the job. So even though we fancy ourselves "enlightened," we have a long way to travel down the road of sexual equality. Employers need to sensitize workers to the many subtle, even unconscious, forms of sexual harassment in order to ensure that we start practicing as individuals what we preach as a nation: fair play in the workplace.

9. "Even though they'll rarely admit it, little boys do like little girls. . . . A little boy, the acknowledged 'tough guy' in the class, found a dead snake on the playground. To the accompaniment of cheers and jeers from the other boys, he picked it up and slung it carelessly around his neck. Then he marched purposefully across the playground to where the girls were huddled, shrieking and squealing. Unerringly he

sought her out, the loudest squealer of them all, and stopped in front of her. In the silence that followed, the young lover cast his trophy at the feet of his beloved. Secure in the knowledge that he had bestowed a gift of inestimable value, he turned and strode away, while behind him the shrieks and squeals of outraged femininity broke out anew. . ." (Joan C. Roloff and Virginia Brosseit, *Paragraphs* [Encino, Calif.: Glenco, 1979], pp. 109–110.)

10. "After thirteen years in universities, trying to teach writing and literature, I am convinced it is impossible to teach anyone to write, compose, paint, sculpt, or innovate creatively. With luck, you might get across minor techniques, or perhaps elementary craftsmanship suitable for low skill level commercial production. And, of course, you can teach about art and creativity and perhaps inspire self-confidence in individuals who already possess innate creative abilities. You can also teach individuals to recognize and appreciate perceptual innovation and significance. And, of course, you can teach about the importance of creativity in our cultural heritage. But no one can be taught to create a significant human experience in any media form." (Wilson Bryan Key, *The Clam-Plate Orgy and Other Subliminal Techniques for Manipulating Your Behavior* [New York: New American Library, 1980], p. 69.)

11. "In spite of the menacing developments (nuclear weapons, overpopulation, biological and psycho-pharmacological engineering, hybernation, changes in the environment), we remain unable to forecast the social consequences of technology. . . . Scientists are aware of the technological possibilities but are not sufficiently sensitive to their social implications. Some of the scientists care only about the success of their favorite projects. Some apply to these problems a personal pseudo-sociology made useless by its arrogance or naivete. And still others dodge responsibility by arguing that technology itself is neither good nor bad, that its virtues are determined by its uses. . . ." (D. N. Michael, "Science, Scientists, and Politics," in Willis H. Truitt and T. W. Graham Solomons, (eds.), *Science Technology and Freedom* [Boston: Houghton Mifflin, 1974], p. 180.)

12. "The medical professional undoubtedly has special skills for determining and applying the specific criteria that measure whether particular body functions have

irreversibly ceased. Whether the Harvard criteria [i.e., criteria that define death largely in terms of the absence of brain activity] taken together accurately divide those who are in irreversible coma from those who are not is clearly an empirical question (although the important consideration of just how sure we want to be takes us once again into matters that cannot be answered scientifically). But the crucial policy question is at the conceptual level: should the individual in irreversible coma be treated as dead?. . . If I am to be pronounced dead by uses of a philosophical or theological concept that I do not share, I at least have a right to careful due process. Physicians in the states that do not authorize brain-oriented criteria for pronouncing death who take it upon themselves to use those criteria . . . should be . . . prosecuted. . . ." (Robert M. Veatch, *Death, Dying and the Biological Revolution* [Englewood Cliffs, N.J.: Prentice-Hall, 1978], p. 75.)

13. "At its heart, the question of whether the sane can be distinguished from the insane (and whether degrees of insanity can be distinguished from each other) is a simple matter: do the salient characteristics that lead to diagnoses reside in the patients themselves or in the environments and contexts in which observers find them. . . . Gains can be made in deciding which of these is more nearly accurate by getting normal people (that is, people who do not have, and have never suffered, symptoms of serious psychiatric disorders) admitted to psychiatric hospitals and then determining whether they were discovered to be sane and, if so, how. If the sanity of such pseudo-patients were always detected, there would be prima facie evidence that a sane individual can be distinguished from the insane context in which he is found. . . . If, on the other hand, the sanity of the pseudo-patients were never discovered, . . . this would support the view that psychiatric diagnosis betrays little about the patient but much about the environment in which an observer finds him." (D. L. Rosenhan, "On Being Sane in Insane Places," *Science* 179 [January 19, 1973], p. 251.)

14. "No matter what my conviction may be as to the advisability of abortion for a given patient, it is overruled by my adherence to the principle of autonomy. By this I mean that we should support the adolescent patient in her autonomous decision making. [We must ask] questions in an unbiased fashion. (If we don't do

this, our obligation is to refer the patient to someone else.) This approach may increase the anxiety and suffering of the patient. . . . The increased anxiety . . . may lead to further exploration, reading of material on abortion, talking to people who agree or disagree with her, etc. She will then make a decision with more understanding. . . . By guiding the adolescent not to avoid stressful questions, . . . a counselor also is preparing her for a better future. The tragedy of the adolescent facing the abortion decision is that she has to choose between the 'sin of aborting' and the 'sin of harming one's life.' In her dilemma the adolescent might have to 'sin boldly.'" (Thomas Silber, "Abortion in Adolescence: The Ethical Dimension," *Adolescence* 15 [Summer 1980], p. 467.)

15. "Let us now examine the Golden Rule ["Do unto others as you would have them do unto you"] in terms of its clarity. . . . We might begin by asking about the unit of action. Are the actions implied by the rule [those of] a person or persons, groups or some larger social [unit]? Are you and the others in the Golden Rule to be seen as representatives of various social units or as independent citizens or persons in their own right, or does it make a difference? Of course the word 'do' in the Golden Rule can mean many things too, and as usually interpreted all behaviors are included. Another thing which is not too clear has to do with the adequacy of resources. In most human situations there is a scarcity of resources. . . . We know from the research in psychology that emotional and situational factors, among others, can alter and distort what is perceived to be done to oneself, this seemingly inviting considerable distortion and error. And of course the Golden Rule is not very clear as to how one measures the consequences which arise by using it. Do we look at both mental and physical consequences, how does the time dimension come in, and so on?. . . I believe that we have demonstrated that the Golden Rule cannot be taken as a categorical imperative. . . ." (Craig C. Lundberg, "The Golden Rule and Business Management: *Quo Vadis?" Economic and Business Bulletin* 20 [January 1968], pp. 39–40.)

PART THREE

EVALUATION

CRITICIZING ARGUMENTS

You have just learned how to identify arguments, cast them, and fill in their missing premises. You are now poised, ready to evaluate arguments.

As we mentioned in the first chapter, many of us don't quite know what to make of the myriad messages that bombard us daily. This is especially true of claims designed to win our assent. On what basis can we intelligently evaluate the arguments we come across daily? What should we accept? What should we reject or reserve judgment about? Furthermore, when can we feel confident that our own arguments are good ones? We take up these questions in this part of our study.

Books have been written about argument evaluation, so what we cover in the next five chapters will hardly exhaust the subject. But it will give you the essentials you need to evaluate your arguments and those of others.

You will notice that this part comprises Chapters 7 through 12. In Chapters 8, 9, and 10 you will learn how to detect fallacious arguments. In Chapter 11 you will learn a simple, brief format for evaluating arguments. And in Chapter 12 you will learn how to handle the argumentative essay.

Before tackling any of these subjects, however, you must learn how to criticize arguments. This requires familiarity with certain key terms and concepts: cogency, validity, truth, and justification. The present chapter provides you with this necessary background.

A final word before starting. Throughout this chapter we use the word "criticize" or some variation of it. Indeed, the title of the chapter is "Criticizing Arguments." In the context of argument evaluation, "to criticize" does not mean "to find fault with" but to make judgments regarding the merits of an argument, and "criticism" refers to the act of judging the quality of an argument. In criticizing an argument, then, we inspect it to determine whether it is good or bad, whether it is what we will term "cogent" or "not cogent."

"I shall now punch a huge hole in your argument."

COGENCY

In assessing an argument's cogency we are interested in two things: (1) the strength or validity of the connection between its conclusion and its premises, and (2) the acceptability of its premises. Put in other words: *A cogent argument is one whose conclusion is properly drawn from true, or justified premises.* Some textbooks in logic and critical thinking use the term "soundness" where we are using "cogency." This is merely a terminological difference. As a first step in developing tools for assessing the connection between conclusion and premises, we must introduce the important notion of argument form.

ARGUMENT FORM

Consider the following argument:

<u>Because</u> [all humans are mortal][1] <u>and</u> [all Americans are human,][2] <u>it follows that</u> [all Americans are mortal.][3]

Casting the argument shows that premises 1 and 2 together support conclusion 3. But now we want to look more closely at the way in which the premises relate to the conclusion. Let us first represent the argument according to a conventional format:

> (1) All humans are mortal.
> (2) All Americans are human.
> ───────────────────────────
> ∴ (3) All Americans are mortal.

In this format the premises are listed in the order of their appearance above the solid line and the conclusion is listed below it. The triangular three-dot symbol can be read as shorthand for "therefore." Notice that in this particular argument there appears to be a very strong connection between the conclusion and the premises: It is impossible to deny the conclusion without denying at least one of the premises (or contradicting oneself). Try it.

Now consider a second example:

> [All sodium salts are water soluble.]¹ [And all soaps are sodium salts.]² So [all soaps are water soluble.]³

Represented in the same conventional format, the argument looks like this:

> (1) All sodium salts are water soluble.
> (2) All soaps are sodium salts.
> ───────────────────────────
> ∴ (3) All soaps are water soluble.

Notice that here too the same very strong connection appears to exist between the conclusion and the premises. You might be less well acquainted with the chemical properties of sodium salts and soaps than with humans and mortality, but if you found out that all sodium salts dissolve in water and all soaps are sodium salts, you would then *know* that all soaps are water soluble. It would be impossible to deny that all soaps are water soluble without also denying at least one of the premises (or contradicting yourself). Try it.

Now consider the following two statements:

> (1) All mammals suckle their young.
> (2) All primates are mammals.

Suppose these two statements are true. What conclusion could you draw from these two statements as premises?

> (1) All mammals suckle their young.
> (2) All primates are mammals.
> ───────────────────────────
> ∴ (3)   ?

If you said, "All primates suckle their young," then notice once again that the same very strong connection appears to exist between your conclusion and the two premises.

Finally, suppose someone argues as follows:

[All propaganda is dangerous.] That's why [all network news is dangerous.]

From what you learned in previous chapters you can see that this argument depends on a missing premise *a*:

(1) All propaganda is dangerous.
(a) ?
_____
∴ (2) All network news is dangerous.

What is missing premise *a*? (Use the topic coverage strategy if you need to.)

No doubt you can see that the missing premise is "All network news is propaganda." Notice once again the very strong connection between the conclusion and the two premises. If you suppose that both premises are true you cannot deny the conclusion without contradicting yourself. Try it. You may have some doubts about the conclusion in this case. But if you doubt the truth of the conclusion, you must also doubt the truth of at least one of the premises.

Now let's reconsider the four examples we have just examined:

(1) All humans are mortal.
(2) All Americans are human.
_____
∴ (3) All Americans are mortal.

(1) All sodium salts are water soluble.
(2) All soaps are sodium salts.
_____
∴ (3) All soaps are water soluble.

(1) All mammals suckle their young.
(2) All primates are mammals.
_____
∴ (3)   ?

(1) All propaganda is dangerous.
(a) ?
_____
∴ (2) All network news is dangerous.

These four examples have something important in common. It is a single and simple common feature that explains how we can arrive at the conclusion in the third example that "All primates suckle their young" and how we can fill in the missing premise in the fourth example that "All network news is propaganda." But most important, it explains the very strong connection that holds between the conclusion of each of the four arguments and its premises. All four arguments follow the same pattern or form. Here is what the form looks like schematically.

(1) All A's are B's
(2) All C's are A's
_____
∴ (3) All C's are B's

or

All .... are _____
All .... are ....
_____
∴ All .... are _____

Deductive Validity

Deductive validity is another name for the kind of connection that holds between the conclusion and premises of arguments that follow this (or any other deductively valid) form. *The essential property of a deductively valid argument form is this: If the premises of an argument that follows the form are taken to be true, then the conclusion of the argument (no matter <u>what</u> it is) must also be true.* Because this is a feature of the *form* (or pattern) that an argument follows rather than of the argument's specific content, deductive validity is sometimes referred to as "formal validity."

Of course, there are very many forms that arguments can follow. Some of them are so commonly used and well known that they have been given names. You just met *Barbara*. Barbara is a deductively valid form. This means that for any argument whatsoever, as long as it follows the form, accepting the premises forces you to accept the conclusion. Try it. Make some up. Even something as absurd as this:

> (1) All fish can fly.
> (2) All snakes are fish.
> ─────────────────
> ∴ (3) All snakes can fly.

---

*Quick Check on the Concept of Deductive Validity (Answers on Page 402)

1. True or false: A deductively valid argument can have a false conclusion. Explain your answer, or give an example.
2. True or false: A deductively valid argument can have false premises. Explain or give an example.
3. True or false: One cannot tell whether a deductive argument is valid without knowing whether its premises are actually true. Explain or give an example.
4. True or false: A deductively valid argument can have false premises and a true conclusion. Explain or give an example.
5. True or false: If a deductive argument is cogent, it may still be invalid. Explain or give an example.

FORMAL FALLACIES

Deductively valid argument forms are important because they provide a guarantee that if the premises of the argument are true the conclusion must be as well. But not every form or pattern is deductively valid. Consider the following example:

> (1) All Americans are human.
> (2) All Californians are human.
> ─────────────────
> ∴ (3) All Californians are Americans.

Many people initially see nothing deficient in this as a piece of reasoning. This is probably because (1) they can see that the claims are in some way related to each other, and (2) they think that all three claims are true. But notice what happens if you ask whether the truth of the premises *guarantees* that the conclusion is true. Try the "what if" strategy here. Suppose the premises are true. Could the conclusion not still be false? For example, suppose that some Californians are not Americans. This possibility conflicts in no way with either premise 1 or premise 2. So, accepting both premises does not *force* you to accept the conclusion.

If this is difficult to take in, consider this next example:

(1) All men are human.
(2) All women are human.
_____
∴ (3) All women are men.

The falsity of this conclusion is obviously compatible with the truth of these two premises. But this argument follows the same form as the argument about Californians. Here is what the form looks like schematically.

(1) All A's are B's
(2) All C's are B's
_____   or
∴ (3) All C's are A's

All _____ are ....
All .... are ....
_____
∴ All .... are _____

Because it is possible for an argument following this form to move from true premises to a false conclusion, it is easy to see that this form is unreliable. The general name for an unreliable inference is *fallacy*. An inference that is unreliable because it follows an unreliable form or pattern is said to be *formally fallacious* or to commit a *formal fallacy*.

A Foolproof Test for Deductive Validity

The two argument forms we've just been studying resemble each other closely, yet one is deductively valid whereas the other is formally fallacious, and this is a crucial difference for the purposes of argument criticism. It is therefore important to be able to distinguish reliably between deductively valid arguments and formally fallacious ones although they may look very much alike. One way to do this is to memorize argument forms. But this proves to be an endless and unmanageable undertaking. Fortunately, there is a simple and absolutely reliable procedure for determining whether a particular argument is deductively valid, which derives from the essential property of deductively valid forms mentioned above. The procedure consists of asking:

Can I assert the premises and deny the conclusion without contradicting myself?

180

If you cannot, *if asserting the permises and denying the conclusion results in a contradiction, then the inference is deductively valid.* If you *can* assert the premises and deny the conclusion without contradiction, the inference is *not* deductively valid.

The best procedure for demonstrating that an inference is unreliable, or *fallacious*, is to compose an inference that is analogous to it and that moves from premises that are obviously true to a conclusion that is obviously false. In the case of the last two examples, the second argument is *formally analogous to,* or follows the same pattern as, the first, but moves from two premises each of which is obviously true to a conclusion that is just as obviously false. By means of this analogy we prove that the original argument—indeed any argument following this pattern—is fallacious.

Let's try these procedures on a couple of examples:

(1) All crooks should be punished.
(2) Some politicians are not crooks.

(3) Some politicians should not be punished.

Is this a deductively valid argument? In other words, if we assert both of the premises and deny the conclusion does a contradiction result? No, it is possible for both of the premises to be true and the conclusion false. We can demonstrate that this inference is fallacious by producing an inference which is formally analogous to it and which moves from premises which are obviously true to a conclusion which is obviously false, for example:

(1) All mothers are female.
(2) Some women are not mothers.

(3) Some women are not female.

Here's another example:

(1) Some books are mysteries.
(2) Some mysteries are entertaining.

(3) Some books are entertaining.

Is this a deductively valid argument? In other words, if we assert both of the premises and deny the conclusion does a contradiction result? No, it is possible for both of the premises to be true and the conclusion false. And again we can demonstrate that this inference is fallacious by producing an inference which is formally analogous to it and that moves from premises which are obviously true to a conclusion which is obviously false, for example:

(1) Some females are parents.
(2) Some parents are male.

(3) Some females are male.

*Quick Check on Testing for Deductive Validity (Answers on Page 402)

Test the following arguments for deductive validity. Demonstrate the unreliability of any that you find formally fallacious by composing a formally analogous inference that moves from obviously true premises to an obviously false conclusion.

1. Some entertainers abuse drugs, and all comedians are entertainers. So it stands to reason that some comedians are drug users.
2. I must necessarily exist, for in order to think, one must exist, and to doubt is to think. And here I am doubting that I exist, so I must really exist after all.
3. In our society the right to life is our most basic human right, and it is considered irrevocable. The revocation of this irrevocable right is illegal. Suicide is the voluntary revocation of one's right to life. It follows, then, that suicide is indeed illegal.
4. Some college professors favor the concept of a faculty union, and the concept of a faculty union is supported by many socialists. So at least some college professors must be socialists.

Some Additional Deductive Argument Forms

Let's try these procedures on some additional argument forms. The two forms we have been studying are called "categorical syllogisms" because they are made up of "categorical statements" (statements about relationships between categories of things). Let us consider two other kinds of statements: *hypothetical* statements and *disjunctive* statements.

Four Forms with Hypothetical Premises　Hypothetical statements assert "a truth-functional relationship" between two component statements. For example, the hypothetical statement

If love is blind, then fools rush in

asserts that if the statement "Love is blind" is true, then so is the statement "Fools rush in." Hypothetical statements most commonly take the form

If *A* then *B* (where *A* represents a statement and *B* represents some other statement).

In a hypothetical statement, the component statement introduced by the word "if" is called the *antecedent* and the component statement introduced by the word "then" is called the *consequent*. In the preceding example, "Love is blind" is the antecedent and "Fools rush in" is the consequent.

Because of their unique structure, hypothetical statements are extremely powerful reasoning tools, and so they play a crucial role in a great many arguments and argument forms. Let's suppose, for example, that an experimental space probe begins with the following hypothetical first premise:

(1) If there is life on Mars, then there is adequate life support on Mars.

Now suppose that the space probe establishes that in fact

(2) There is life on Mars.

From this as an additional premise, together with the first premise, we can conclude that

(3) There is adequate life support on Mars.

Notice first that premise 2 is identical with the antecedent of the hypothetical premise 1, and that the conclusion is identical with its consequent. Notice also that it is impossible to assert premises 1 and 2 and deny conclusion 3 without contradicting yourself. Try it. Thus, this is a deductively valid argument. It follows a form that can be represented schematically as follows:

(1) If A then B
(2) A
_____
∴ (3) B

Logicians most commonly refer to this argument form by the Latin label *modus ponens*, which means "affirmative mood." Because *modus ponens*, like *Barbara*, is deductively valid, for any argument whatsoever, as long as it follows the form of *modus ponens*, accepting the premises forces you to accept the conclusion. Try it. Make some up.

Now let us suppose that our space probe turns up another kind of evidence. Suppose the space probe establishes that

(2*a*) There is adequate life support on Mars.

Suppose we drew the conclusion from this together with premise 1 that

(3*a*) There is life on Mars.

Perhaps conclusion 3*a* is correct. But do our two premises really guarantee it? No, they don't. It is possible to deny 3*a* without contradicting the assertion either of 1 or 2*a*. Try it.

If you're having trouble with this, consider the following analogy:

> If a figure is square, then it has four sides.
> This rhombus has four sides.
> _____
> ∴ This rhombus is square.

Thus, this argument is not deductively valid. And the form it follows, which can be schematically represented as follows, is unreliable, or formally fallacious.

> (1) If A then B
> (2a) B
> _____
> ∴ (3a) A

Logicians refer to this form as the *fallacy of asserting the consequent,* because that's what the second premise does. It asserts the consequent of the hypothetical first premise.

Now let us suppose that our space probe turns up yet another kind of evidence. Suppose the space probe establishes that

> (2b) There is no adequate life support on Mars.

From this, together with our first premise, it is possible to conclude that

> (3b) There is no life on Mars.

Notice here that premise 2b is the denial of the consequent of premise 1, whereas 3b is the denial of its antecedent. And notice that here again it is impossible to assert 1 and 2b and deny 3b without contradicting yourself. Try it. Thus, this inference is deductively valid. It follows a pattern that can be represented schematically as follows:

> (1) If A then B
> (2b) Not B
> _____
> ∴ (3b) Not A

Logicians most commonly refer to this argument form by the Latin label *modus tollens,* which means "denying mood." Because *modus tollens,* like *Barbara* and *modus ponens,* is deductively valid, for any argument whatsoever, as long as it follows the form of *modus tollens,* accepting the premises forces you to accept the conclusion. Try it. Make some up.

Finally, let's suppose our space probe establishes that

> (2c) There is no life on Mars.

Suppose we drew from this and our first premise the conclusion that

(3c) There isn't adequate life support on Mars.

Again, perhaps 3c is correct, but do premises 1c and 2c guarantee it? No they don't. It is possible to assert both 1c and 2c and deny 3c without contradicting yourself. Try it.

Recall the earlier example. You can demonstrate the invalidity of this inference by means of an analogy thus:

> If a figure is square then it has four sides.
> This figure (a rhombus) is not a square.
> ───────────────────────────────
> ∴ This figure (a rhombus) does not have four sides.

Thus this argument is not deductively valid. And the form it follows, which can be schematically represented as follows, is unreliable, or formally fallacious:

> (1) If A then B
> (2c) Not A
> ────────
> ∴ (3c) Not B

Logicians refer to this form as the *fallacy of denying the antecedent,* because that's what the second premise does. It denies the antecedent of the hypothetical first premise.

The following chart summarizes what we've said about these hypothetical forms:

	Valid			*Invalid*	
Modus	(1)	If A then B	**Affirming the**	(1)	If A then B
Ponens	(2)	A	**Consequent**	(2a)	B
	∴ (3)	B		∴ (3a)	A
Modus	(1)	If A then B	**Denying the**	(1)	If A then B
Tollens	(2b)	Not B	**Antecedent**	(2c)	Not A
	∴ (3b)	Not A		∴ (3c)	Not B

A Deductive Form Involving Disjunction   Grammatically, a disjunction is an "either/or" statement, whereas a hypothetical statement is an "if/then" statement. Like hypothetical statements, disjunctions assert a "truth-functional relationship" between the two component statements of which they are made up. These component statements are referred to as *disjuncts.* Normally, the relationship asserted by a disjunction can be expressed as follows: *At least one of the disjuncts is true* (*and possibly both*). For example, the statement

Either the battery is dead or there is a short in the ignition switch

asserts that at least one of the two statements "The battery is dead" and "There is a short in the ignition switch" is true. They can be represented by the formula

Either *A* or *B* (where *A* and *B* represent the two disjuncts).

Like hypothetical statements, disjunctions are extremely powerful reasoning tools, and so they play a crucial role in a great many arguments and argument forms. Let's suppose, for example, that we've been trying to diagnose a mechanical problem with the car, and we have eliminated all possible problems but two: the battery and the ignition switch. So we now have good reason to believe that

(1) Either the battery is dead or there is a short in the ignition switch.

Now suppose we check the battery and find that it's fully charged and functioning properly. We now know that

(2) The battery is not dead.

From this, together with our first premise, it is possible to conclude that

(3) There is a short in the ignition switch.

Notice here that premise 2 is the denial of one of the disjuncts of premise 1, whereas 3 is identical with the other disjunct. And notice that here again it is impossible to assert 1 and 2 and deny 3 without contradicting yourself. Try it. Thus this inference is deductively valid. It follows a pattern that can be represented schematically as follows:

(1) Either *A* or *B*
(2) Not *A*
———————————
∴ (3) *B*

Logicians commonly refer to this argument form as *disjunctive syllogism*.

Quick Check on Valid Deductive Arguments

1. Demonstrate the formal fallaciousness of *affirming the consequent* and *denying the antecedent* by composing arguments

of each form that move from intuitively acceptable or obviously true premises to intuitively unacceptable or obviously false conclusions.

*2. Determine which of the following are valid deductive arguments. Be sure to fill in any missing premises. Then cast the valid ones. For each of the invalid ones compose a formally analogous argument that moves from obviously true premises to an obviously false conclusion. (Answers on page 402.)

a. Since all birds eat worms, and chickens are birds, chickens must eat worms.

b. Marty must be a real male chauvinist. After all, he's an athlete, isn't he?

c. Some reference books are textbooks, for all textbooks are books intended for careful study and some reference books are intended for the same purpose.

d. Most poets drink to excess, and some poets are women. So, some women drink to excess.

INDUCTIVE ARGUMENTS

We just saw how deductively valid arguments guarantee their conclusions. If the truth of the premises of a deductively valid argument can be established, there is no more room for doubt about the argument's conclusion. But many arguments that do not provide deductively valid grounds for the acceptance of their conclusions nevertheless provide some substantial support for their conclusions and are therefore not to be dismissed simply on the grounds that they are not deductively valid. The premises of valid inductive arguments, for example, provide grounds—but not deductively valid grounds—for their conclusions. *The truth of the premises of a valid inductive argument do not guarantee the truth of its conclusion, but they do make this conclusion probable or likely.*

Here's an example of a valid inductive argument:

[Professor Jones has never missed a class.] So [chances are she'll be in class today.][2]

If the premise, assertion 1, is accepted as true, then it would be reasonable to accept the argument's conclusion, assertion 2. Of course, even if the premise is true the conclusion may prove false: Jones may not show up for class. Perhaps she's ill or had an accident or an important conflicting appointment.

Here's another example of a valid inductive argument:

[It's highly unlikely that any female will play football in the National Football[1] League in the near future,] for [none has so far.][2]

Again, if the premise is accepted as true, it provides good grounds—although not deductively valid ones—for accepting the conclusion. The essential difference between deductive and inductive reasoning is this: *Because the conclusion of a valid deduction is "contained within" its premises, the truth of its premises leaves no room for doubt as to the truth of its conclusion. Because the conclusion of any induction "goes beyond" what is contained within its premises, an inductive argument always contains an element of doubt.*

Deductive and Inductive Signal Words

Just as the presence of arguments, premises, and conclusions are frequently indicated by means of signal words, so the modality of the inference, that is, whether it is intended as a deductive or an inductive one, is often indicated by signal words. Deductive signals include

> certainly
> necessarily
> must

Inductive signals include

> probably
> in all likelihood
> chances are
> it is reasonable to suppose that
> it's a good bet that

Quick Check on Valid Inductive Arguments

1. By relating each of the following sets of terms, compose first a valid deductive argument, then a valid inductive argument.

    Sample: jobs, college education, personal fulfillment
    Valid Deductive Argument: College education is necessary to get a good job. Without a good job, a person stands no chance of attaining personal fulfillment. It follows that a college education is necessary to attain personal fulfillment.
    Valid Inductive Argument: Most college-educated people nowadays qualify for good jobs, and a good job is essential to personal fulfillment. So, with a college education, I'll probably attain personal fulfillment.

    a. Students, homework, teachers
    b. Love, sex, marriage
    c. Television, entertainment, relaxation
    d. Reading, thinking, arguing

2*. For each of the following passages, indicate whether it is a deductive argument, an inductive argument, or not an argument. (Answers on page 403.)

    a. Since tests proved that it took at least 2.3 seconds to operate the bolt of the rifle, Oswald obviously could not have fired three times—hitting Kennedy twice and Connally once—in 5.6 seconds or less.

    b. At bottom I did not believe I had touched that man. The law of probabilities decreed me guiltless of his blood. For in all my small experience with guns I had never hit anything I had tried to hit, and I knew I had done my best to hit him. (Mark Twain)

    c. Even God makes mistakes. In the Bible, God says, "It repenteth me that I have made man." Now either the Bible is not the word of God, or we must believe that God did say, "It repenteth me that I have made man." But then, if we are to believe the word of God, we must further conclude that He really did repent making man, in which case, either God made a mistake in making man, or He made a mistake in repenting making man.

    d. The theory of the unreality of evil now seems to me untenable. Suppose it can be proved that all that we think evil was in reality good. The fact would still remain that we think it evil. This may be called a delusion or mistake. But a delusion or mistake is as real as anything else. The delusion that evil exists is therefore real. But then it seems certain that a delusion which hid from us the goodness of the universe would itself be evil. And so there would be real evil after all. (J. M. E. McTaggart)

    e. In a democracy, the poor have more power than the rich, because there are more of them. (Aristotle)

Strength in Inductive Arguments

Since inductive arguments always leave some room for doubt as to the truth of their conclusions, the most important question for evaluating them is, How much room for doubt? In other words, How strong a case do the premises make for the conclusion? A deductive argument is either valid or not valid. But "inductive strength" is relative, by which we mean some valid inductive arguments are stronger than others. Consider the following two arguments:

> The last three cars we have owned have been Chrysler products and they've all been trouble free. So we're probably safe to assume that a new Dodge will be reliable.

> In Consumers' Union nationwide studies of new cars purchased over the last three years, Chrysler had a 30% lower frequency of repair rate than the other manufacturers. So we're probably safe to assume that a new Dodge will be reliable.

Each of these arguments is inductively valid. In other words, in each argument the premise does provide some reason for accepting the conclusion. But the evidence contained in the premise of the second argument makes it much less likely that the conclusion is in error than does the evidence contained in the premise of the first. Thus, the second argument is considerably stronger than the first.

Assessing Inductive Strength

Evaluating the strength of inductive arguments is complicated, because inductive strength depends on a number of variables, including the type of inductive reasoning involved.

The simplest and most common form of inductive reasoning involves generalizing from a number of instances. For example:

> Professor Jones has been on time for each class since the term began, so she is probably punctual

draws a general conclusion about Professor Jones from a number of observations of her past behavior. Here's another example of inductive generalization:

> Every bull market has been followed by a bear market, and vice versa. Therefore, the stock market behaves cyclically.

Here a general conclusion about the behavior of the stock market is drawn inductively from an enumeration of instances of its past performance. In this example, notice that every instance enumerated in the premise is alike.

However, frequently when we enumerate instances for the purpose of drawing inductive conclusions, things are not as simple as in the example about the stock market. Some of the enumerated instances will be one way, and some another. So a variation on simple induction involves projecting trends or percentages observed in the enumeration onto other instances. This is commonly called *statistical induction*. For instance, suppose we're interested in how likely college students with different majors are to gain admission to law school. We might survey law school admissions for a certain period of time. Suppose our survey showed that 20 percent more of the applicants with philosophy majors were admitted than were admitted from the next most successful major. We might then project inductively that philosophy majors are 20 percent more likely to gain admission to law school than other college students.

In both simple inductive generalization and statistical induction the strength of the inference depends in part on the "size of the sample." *The greater the number of instances enumerated (the larger the size of the sample), the stronger the induction.*

In both simple inductive generalization and statistical induction the strength of the inference depends also on how representative the sample is. Suppose our survey of law school admissions was only one year long, or was confined to the state of California. Then we might be overlooking variables that might otherwise show up in a ten-year nationwide survey. Perhaps in a particular year more students with law school aptitude happened to elect philosophy as a major. Perhaps the state of California has particularly strong instructional programs in philosophy. In any case, *the more selective the sample the weaker the induction.*

These two factors help explain why the first of our two examples of induction was weaker than the second. A nationwide comparative study of frequency of repair rates involving not just Chrysler products but those of other manufacturers as well constitutes both a larger and more representative sample than the tiny and highly selective "the last three cars we have owned."

Much more remains to be said about inductive arguments, some of which we will get to in later chapters. It should be apparent by now that criticizing inductive arguments is a more complicated and contingent process than criticizing deductive arguments. Suffice for the present to stress the basic similarity between the two. We have considered one basic ingredient of a cogent argument: the validity, or strength, of its inference. In determining an argument's validity, we have seen that it is *not* necessary to know whether its premises are true. We need only *suppose* that they are true and then determine whether they provide conclusive or probable grounds for the conclusion. If they do, the argument is valid. But although it isn't necessary to know that the premises are true to determine an argument's validity, we do need to know that they are true to determine whether the argument is cogent.

---

*Quick Check on Inductive Strength
(Answers on Page 403)

Rank the following inductive arguments in order of strength. Explain your ranking.

1. Contrary to current media claims, our schools appear to be doing a superb job of teaching our children to read. A leading newsmagazine recently tabulated the results of the thousands of responses it received to the survey it published in its May issue. Readers from every state in the union responded. Ninety percent of the respondents believed that their school-age children's reading skills were good-to-excellent. Eight percent more believed that their children's reading skills were at least adequate. Fewer than 1 percent felt that their children were developing less than adequate reading skills. (One percent of the respondents failed to answer this question.)

2. In all of the studies that have been done over the past thirty years concerning the relationship between standardized test performance and success in school, involving several hundred thousand school-age subjects from a variety of ethnic, regional, and socioeconomic backgrounds, I.Q. tests have been shown to be the single most reliable predictor of success in school. Therefore,

if one scores highly on I.Q. tests, one will probably perform well in school.

3. An hour in a hot tub will probably impair a man's fertility for up to six weeks. According to one study, three men who sat in a hot tub with water heated to 102.4°F (most health clubs heat theirs to 104°F) showed reductions in the number and penetrating capacity of their sperm cells. In samples taken thirty-six hours later, the damage was present, but the most dramatic effects did not show up until four weeks later. This indicated that even immature sperm cells had been harmed by the high heat. (It takes about seven weeks for a newly created sperm cell to mature and pass through a system of storage ducts.) Seven weeks after their dip in the hot tub, the men's sperm returned to normal.

TRUTH

As a concept truth doesn't present much of a problem. It can be defined rather simply as a relationship that may or may not obtain between an idea (or an opinion, or a statement) and what the idea (or opinion, or statement) is about. In the words of the great American philosopher William James, "Truth is a property of certain of our ideas. It means their 'agreement,' as falsity means their disagreement, with 'reality.'" *An assertion is true if (and only if) it reports an actual state of affairs* (that is, some present, past, or future event, condition, or circumstance). Obviously there are many states of affairs in the world. If you're over five feet tall, that's a state of affairs; if the current air temperature is 60°F, that's a state of affairs. And if you *are* over five feet tall, then the idea (or the belief, or the statement) that you are over five feet tall is true—and of course the idea (or the belief, or the statement) that you are not over five feet tall is false. The problem is not defining what truth is, but determining what's true. This too is not *always* difficult. You presumably have no problem determining whether you are over five feet tall. One reason we choose this particular example at this stage is because it is so unproblematic. But determining what's true is where the genuine problems come in. The genuine problems are, however, aggravated by a number of widespread confusions about the nature of truth. So before we deal with the problems of establishing truth, let's dispose of the confusions.

1. Truth is not opinion or belief. Ask somebody what time it is. Chances are she will tell you. If you then said, "That's your opinion," it would be rude (to say the least). But you'd be right. Suppose you ask two people what time it is and they don't agree. Here you can see the distinction between truth and belief or opinion, because obviously the two people cannot *both* be "in agreement with reality." We don't always *observe* this distinction. Indeed sometimes it would be tedious and impolite if we did. But sometimes the distinction is important. And then we should be careful not to confuse opinion or belief with truth. A true statement reports an actual state of affairs; a belief or opinion is a person's attitude toward a particular statement. Unlike truth, an opinion or an assertion could be mistaken. Therefore opinions or beliefs and assertions or statements are subject to "verification," which means simply seeing whether they agree with reality.

2. Truth is not relative.   Sometimes overlooking the distinction between truth and opinion gets compounded with further confusion. Frequently you will hear people say, "that's *only* my opinion" or "that's *just* your opinion," meaning something like "There's no sense trying to verify it." Many people are tempted to think that because opinions can be mistaken, and because they are frequently subject to dispute, and because it is often very hard to know for certain whether such disputes have been resolved, maybe they can't be resolved at all. There's just this person's opinion and that person's opinion and nothing beyond. This is already a confused line of reasoning. But then if we ignore the difference between belief and truth, we may be tempted to make the additional mistake of assuming that truth is "relative," or varies from individual to individual—as when people say (as they often do), "What's true for me may not be true for you." Remember that truth is a characteristic of an assertion that is reporting an actual state of affairs. Thus, "Humans have visited the moon" reports an actual state of affairs. That state of affairs does not depend on what any one of us thinks or believes about it. Humans have either visited the moon or they have not. As it turns out in this instance, they have. If there is someone whose opinion is at odds with this, then that person is mistaken.

Verification

Opinions and assertions are subject to error and dispute and therefore also to verification, which at least in some cases is straightforward and unproblematic. How would you verify the opinion that someone is over five feet tall? Presumably you would measure the person. But verification is not always a matter of simple measurement. For example, consider this common argument:

[The death penalty should be legalized for certain serious crimes]^1 because [it is a deterrent.]^2

Does the death penalty actually deter crime? Is the assertion that it does true? Does it agree with reality? Answering this question probably would require some research. If the research turns up conclusive evidence in favor of the premise, then you can accept the premise as true. But what constitutes *conclusive* evidence? How much evidence do we need to accept a statement as true? There is no simple answer here, for assertions vary in breadth and in other ways, and consequently the amount and quality of the evidence needed to verify them will vary.

But now suppose that your research left no reasonable doubt that capital punishment does in fact deter crime. You would still have to test the truth of the argument's missing premise: Whatever deters crime should be a legal punishment for certain serious crimes. This assertion poses additional problems because it's a value judgment; that is, an assessment of worth. To find out whether the death penalty deters crime, you can introduce all sorts of data discovered in your research. But what can you do to determine the truth of the assertion "Whatever deters crime should be a legal punishment for certain serious crimes"?

The problems involved in verifying assertions depend in part on what type of assertion is involved. It will be useful here to approach different types of assertion in terms of our discussion in Chapter 2 of four common types of dispute: verbal disputes, factual disputes, evaluative disputes, and interpretive disputes.

---

*Quick Check on Verification and Cogency (Answers on Page 403)

1. Which premises of the arguments in the Quick Check on Valid Deductive Arguments would you accept as true?
2. Which arguments would you consider cogent, that is, valid with true premises?

Necessary Truths

Verbal disputes, you'll remember, we set aside as not really genuine disputes, because simple clarification of the meanings or possible meanings of terms involved in assertions dissolves them. Just as we set aside verbal disputes, we can set aside certain types of assertion whose verification is absolutely unproblematic, or raises no problems at all.

For example, the assertion "Either the president knew of the Iran arms deal or he didn't" must of necessity be true, because to deny it would be self-contradictory. Notice that *any* statement of the form "Either *X* or not *X*" must of necessity be true, because to deny it would be self-contradictory (and therefore necessarily false). Statements whose form or structure is such that to deny them would be self-contradictory are called *tautologies* and are *necessarily true*.

The assertions "All humans are vertebrates" and "No circle is square" are also necessarily true, not because of their forms or structures but because of the meanings of their terms. The meaning of "vertebrates" is included in the meaning of "humans," and the statement "All humans are vertebrates" merely asserts this inclusion. Similarly, the meaning of "circle" excludes the meaning of "square," and the statement "No circle is square" merely asserts this exclusion. Such statements are sometimes said to be true *by definition*.

Most interesting assertions are neither self-contradictory nor necessarily true. Assertions that are neither self-contradictory nor necessarily true are called *contingent* statements, meaning that their truth or falsity depends on something beyond them. It is in connection with contingent statements that the problems of verification arise.

Verifying Factual Assertions

Factual disputes concern contingent statements of fact. Consider, for example, the following list of assertions:

1. My best friend is over five feet tall.
2. Your son is suffering from the flu.
3. There's intelligent life in outer space.
4. Lee Harvey Oswald could not have fired three times—hitting President Kennedy twice and Governor Connally once—in 5.6 seconds or less.
5. Capital punishment deters crime.

Because these are contingent assertions, that is, neither self-contradictory nor necessarily true, verifying them is problematic, that is, raises certain problems. Solving the problems in each case involves knowing an appropriate procedure for verification.

Observations   Take the first example. Whether the first assertion is true or not depends on the height of your best friend, something "out there in the world" that can be tested empirically, that is by reference to sense experience, or to what scientists call "observations." Whenever scientists weigh, measure, or take the temperature of something and then record their findings, they are making observations. When can you accept an observation as correct? You can do so when you are satisfied with the conditions under which the observation was made and with the ability of the observer. In this rather basic and simple instance, it would be sufficient to know that your best friend had been measured, when standing erect, by someone using an accurate standard instrument of measurement and who knew how to use it, in circumstances that didn't impair the user's performance—all of which is easily enough established.

It is not hard to imagine more problematic cases of the same kind. Suppose, for example, a doctor makes the observation that someone has a tumor in her thyroid gland. In general, there are five key points to consider in evaluating observations: (1) the physical conditions, (2) the sensory acuity of the observer, (3) the background knowledge of the observer, (4) the objectivity of the observer, and (5) the supporting testimony of other observers.

1. Physical conditions.   *Physical conditions refer to the conditions under which the observations were made.* If a doctor diagnoses someone's condition solely on the basis of a telephone conversation, then her diagnosis would be in serious doubt. But suppose she made her observations during a complete physical examination. In this case the conditions under which she made the observations were conducive to obtaining correct information on the basis of which a diagnosis could be made.

2. Sensory acuity.   *Sensory acuity refers to the sensory abilities of the observer.* Some people can see and hear better than others; some have a more sharply developed sense of smell and taste, and even of touch. Observations always must be evaluated in light of the observer's ability to have made the observations. In science, medicine, and the like, where precise measurements are crucial, instruments heighten the observer's sensory acuity. As a result, in evaluating the reliability of scientific investigations where exact measurements of height, weight, volume, and temperature are crucial, we must evaluate the accuracy of the instruments as well as the sensory abilities of the persons making the observations.

3. Necessary background knowledge. *Necessary background knowledge refers to what an observer must already know to make a reliable observation.* To observe a lump in the thyroid gland is one thing. To infer that the lump is a tumor requires background knowledge of what the normal thyroid gland feels like, looks like in an X ray, and so on.

4. Objectivity. *Objectivity refers to the ability to view ourselves and the world without distortion.* None of us can be totally objective, for as hard as we try, we will always view things according to our own frames of reference. But we can become aware of these biases and minimize their impact on our observations. We can expect the same of others.

Be aware of people's frames of reference, their "taken-for-granteds." This doesn't mean that you should automatically dismiss the views of those who have vested interests. But you should realize that their loyalties—and hence their built-in biases—may be coloring their observations and thus coloring the evidence they present as justification for a claim.

5. Supporting testimony. *Supporting testimony refers to the observations of other observers that tend to support the evidence presented.* Even if an observation meets all the other criteria, it can still prove to be in error, because observers are human and humans make mistakes. Even under ideal observation conditions, with the most sensitive instruments available, expert and detached observers sometimes get it wrong. So it is wise counsel to get a "second opinion," or to seek corroboration in the testimony of other observers. Remember, though, that corroborative evidence itself must meet the above criteria. Although it's impossible to say exactly how many corroborations are required to place an observation beyond reasonable doubt, the more controversial the claim, the more it needs corroboration. In general, the greater the number of corroborations, the greater the evidence.

Hypotheses Now let's take the second example: "Your son is suffering from the flu." The truth of this assertion may depend on certain observations, as we've just discussed. Certain symptoms, for instance, may have been observed. In addition, though, the statement attempts to account for these observations. In other words, it functions as an explanatory *hypothesis*. In other words, it offers an explanatory account of why your son is suffering from the observed symptoms.

How do we determine whether the hypothesis is true or acceptable? Hypotheses are generally tested by seeking confirmation and disconfirmation. This involves supposing that the hypothesis is true and checking its implications. What would we expect to find, and not to find, if the hypothesis was the case? If we find what we would expect to find, that counts toward the confirmation of the hypothesis. Finding what we would expect not to find disconfirms the hypothesis. Thus, on the hypothesis that your son's symptoms are caused by the flu, we would expect the symptoms to disappear in a matter of days. If the symptoms do disappear in a matter of days, that tends to confirm the hypothesis. If the symptoms persist for several weeks, the hypothesis is in trouble.

Frequently confirmation and disconfirmation are sought empirically, that is, by setting up scientific experiments, making observations, and so on. So knowing how to evaluate observations helps in evaluating hypotheses.

Here again it's impossible to say exactly how much confirming evidence is needed to establish a given hypothesis beyond a reasonable doubt. But just as with observations, the more controversial the hypothesis, the more it conflicts with what is already reasonably well established, the more it stands in need of confirmation.

It is easier, theoretically speaking, to disconfirm hypotheses than to confirm them. In general, if we fail to find what we would expect to find, or worse, if we find what we would expect not to find, it's back to the drawing board for the hypothesis. Thus, another way to seek confirmation for hypotheses is to look very hard for disconfirming evidence, hoping and expecting not to find any.

Quick Check on Verifying Factual Assertions

Explain how we might go about verifying the following assertions:

1. There's intelligent life in outer space.
2. Lee Harvey Oswald could not have fired three times—hitting President Kennedy twice and Governor Connally once—in 5.6 seconds or less.
3. Capital punishment deters crime.

Evaluative Disputes and Value Judgments

Evaluative disputes are differences of opinion about matters of value and concern, what we call "value judgments." Ordinarily we think of these as expressing our values in ethics, art, and social and political philosophy. Thus, regarding ethics, someone might claim, "You *shouldn't* lie" or "Murder is *immoral*" or "Abortion is *wrong*." Regarding art: "Beethoven's Fifth Symphony is his *best*"; "Neil Simon's latest plays are *flawed*"; "Steven Spielberg is a *great* film director." Regarding social and political philosophy: "Democracy is the *best* form of government"; "Capital punishment *should* be legalized"; "The United States *should* evenly distribute its wealth among its citizenry."

Sometimes value assertions become premises in arguments. Here's an example:

[Selling illicit drugs to children is reprehensible.]^1 Because [Frank sells children illicit drugs,]^3 [he's doing something reprehensible.]^2

We will call this type of argument a value argument because one of its premises, assertion 1, is a value judgment. Here's another example of a value argument.

[If democracy is the best form of government, then all nations should strive to be democratic.]^1 [Democracy is the best form of government.]^2 Therefore [all nations should strive to be democratic.]^3

Assertion 2 expresses a value.
Here's one final example:

[The film *Stardust Memories* must be worth seeing]^1 because [it's written and directed by Woody Allen.]^2

Here the unexpressed premise is a value judgment: "Any film written and directed by Woody Allen is worth seeing."

As with any argument, the cogency of a value argument depends in part on the truth of its premises. Verifying value judgments raises special problems.

***Quick Check on Value Judgments
(Answers on Page 404)**

1. Which of the following assertions are value judgments?

    a. Stealing is wrong.
    b. Shakespeare is the most effective dramatist in the English language.
    c. Shakespeare wrote comedies, histories, and tragedies.
    d. Oxygen starvation can result in brain damage.
    e. Education is the surest ticket to occupational success.
    f. Sexism is a function of acculturation.
    g. American foreign policy since World War II has been based on a narrow and short-term view of national interest.
    h. Sex without love is a sin.
    i. Honesty is the best policy.
    j. A man who defends himself has a fool for a client.
    k. Polygamy is illegal in California.
    l. If two candidates are equally qualified for a job and one is a woman or a member of a minority group, the job should be given to the woman or minority member.

   m. Photography isn't really art.

   n. Our criminal justice system is a national disgrace.

   o. In part, philosophy studies issues that science cannot fully answer.

   p. Drunk driving is the cause of about half of all traffic fatalities.

   q. The pill shouldn't be taken over a long period of time without medical supervision.

   r. The best government is the one that governs least.

   s. The cooler the light, the less energy it wastes.

2. Write two statements about each subject, one expressing a value judgment, the other not. Then write a third statement that combines a value judgment and a nonvalue assertion in one sentence.

   Sample: sex education
   Value assertion: Sex education *should not* be taught in public schools.
   Nonvalue assertion: Some public schools teach sex education.
   Combination: Sex education, *which is an evil plot devised by our enemies to weaken our nation's moral fiber,* is now being taught in some public schools. [Value judgment italicized]

   a. political parties

   b. legalization of marijuana

   c. advertising

   d. pornography

   e. premarital cohabitation

   f. the military draft

Verifying Value Judgments

Before we approach the problems of verifying value judgments we need to dispose of a confusion at least as widespread as the ones we mentioned earlier about truth and opinion. Let's return for a moment to an example mentioned above:

[Selling illicit drugs to children is reprehensible.][1] <u>Because</u> [Frank sells children illicit drugs,][2] [he's doing something reprehensible.][3]

Clearly there is an important difference between the first and the second premise. The second premise is a factual assertion, whereas the first is a value judgment. But what does this difference really amount to? A great many people seem to think that the difference amounts to this: The second assertion, because it is a factual assertion, can be easily verified; the first, because it is a value judgment, can't be verified at all. Sometimes this idea comes out as a basic distinction between factual and evaluative disputes: Factual disputes are disputes that can be easily settled empirically, whereas evaluative disputes can't be settled at all. But this is a confusion. First of all, as you already know, sometimes it's not so

easy to settle factual disputes, even if the procedures for verifying factual assertions are well enough understood and agreed on. Second, from the fact that
value judgments can't be verified by empirical means, it doesn't follow that they
can't be verified at all. In fact, the truth of some value judgments is much more
firmly established than the truth of some factual assertions. Some evaluative
issues are much more firmly settled than some factual ones. For example, the
assertion

> Gandhi's leadership of his people was morally superior to Hitler's leadership
> of his

is clearly a value judgment. Yet it is also clearly much more easily and firmly
verified than the factual assertion

> There is intelligent life in outer space.

Now, it's undoubtedly true that value judgments can't be weighed or measured
with scientific precision. But it doesn't follow that they cannot be evaluated at
all. The fact is, as we have just seen, people can, do, and must evaluate value
judgments.

For our purposes it probably is most important to acknowledge that values
and value judgments crowd in on us. Like it or not, we must accept some, reject
others, and keep an open mind about most. And this presupposes evaluation.
Just as the verification of factual assertions involves reasoning deductively and
inductively, so the verification of value judgments involves reasoning. We must
weigh the reasons and arguments for accepting a value judgment against those
for rejecting it, just as we must for nonvalue assertions. When there are more
of the right kinds of reasons for accepting it, we can consider it justified. When
there are more of the right kinds of reasons for rejecting it, we can consider it
unjustified.

It is in this sense of justification, then—of having more of the right kinds of
reasons for accepting a value claim than rejecting it—that we can connect truth
with value judgments. In short, when we speak of verifying value judgments, we
have in mind a rational process that aims to determine whether there is reasonable evidence for accepting such a judgment. This process consists of at least
two steps: clarifying language and weighing reasons and arguments.

Clarifying Language   To determine whether a value judgment is justified,
the first order of business is to clarify the language used. Value words such as
"good," "ought," "wrong," "superb," "should not," "best," and "inferior" are vague;
they invite myriad interpretations. Before evaluating a value judgment, then, you
must determine the meaning the arguer is attaching to these terms. Thus, the
italicized value words in these assertions must be clarified before you can tell
whether the assertions are justified: "Abortion is *wrong*"; "Mercy killing *should
be* permitted"; "Capital punishment *should not be* legalized"; "Steven Spielberg
is a *great* film director"; "Capitalism is the *best* economic system"; "Socialism
is *inferior* to capitalism"; "Democracy is the *best* form of government."

Value words can have several different meanings, only some of which will be covered here. Generally, the ordinary value arguments you read and hear have meanings that can be translated into empirical form and then evaluated. Specifically, when appearing in ordinary value arguments, value words typically indicate (1) personal preference, (2) social preference, or (3) conformity to principle, standard, or law.

1. Personal preference. Value words often are intended as expressions of personal approval or disapproval. Take for example the assertion "Abortion is wrong." It's possible that someone asserting this is expressing nothing more than personal disapproval of abortion. Thus "Abortion is *wrong*" means "*I disapprove* of abortion." Likewise, "Steven Spielberg is a *great* film director" translates into "*I like* or *I think highly of* Spielberg's accomplishments as a director." And "Everyone *should* get a college education" would mean "*I'm in favor of* everyone's getting a college education." In each instance the value word is intended as an expression of personal preference, whose verification lies within the person making the assertion (as in "This candy tastes sweet *to me*" or "The leaf looks green *to me*"). Such an interpretation is legitimate, of course, only if the person is not commenting about the nature or quality of the act or thing itself, but merely expressing a belief.

To verify such an assertion, you need only ensure that it does in fact accurately report the person's feelings. But notice also that autobiographical value judgments, assertions that express mere personal preference, make extremely weak and uninteresting premises in arguments relevant to evaluative disputes. Once you realize that the value word is carrying an autobiographical meaning, you can save yourself much time and frustration in fruitless debate. Even more important, you can direct the discussion to a more constructive plane.

Once you have established an autobiographical interpretation of a value word, you're in a position to inquire more deeply into the reasons underlying the preference. This is crucial, because what we are ultimately interested in, in an evaluative dispute, is how much counts for accepting a particular value judgment and how much for rejecting it.

2. Social preference. Frequently people don't mean that only they approve or disapprove of something when they use a value word, but that society does. In other words, value words can be used to indicate social preference. "Whatever will help minimize the number of unwanted children *should be* legalized" may be interpreted as "*Society approves* of the legalization of whatever will help minimize the number of unwanted children."

If a value judgment indicates social preference, then your job of verifying it is again quite simple. All you need do is verify that a majority of society approves or disapproves of whatever it is that is being discussed. Determine the majority view and you determine the truth of the statement. But notice again that value judgments which express mere social preference, that report what is generally approved or disapproved of in society, make relatively weak and uninteresting premises. Remember that what we are ultimately interested in, in an evaluative dispute, is how much counts for or against accepting a particular value judgment.

The mere fact that society generally approves or disapproves of something may count, but it doesn't count for very much. The German theologian Dietrich Bonhoffer, having spoken out against Hitler, was imprisoned and later hanged. Was he wrong and the majority right? Certainly not, for the simple reason that he was out of step with the majority of his society at the time.

3. Conformity to principle, standard, or law. Besides translating value words into expressions of personal or social preference, arguers sometimes identify them with conformity to principle, standard, or law. For example, someone may argue, "Because sexism is *objectionable*, paying women less than their male counterparts simply because they are women is wrong." By "objectionable" the arguer may not intend either personal or social disapproval but nonconformity to the principle of justice as fair play and giving to others what they deserve. Similarly, an arguer who uses "Abortion is *immoral*" as a premise might mean that abortion violates a fundamental moral principle, such as respect for the sanctity of life. Likewise, someone might assert that Spielberg is a *great* film director because Spielberg's skills and talent conform to the artistic standards that define the expert director.

When value words are used this way, verifying the value judgment depends on whether what they are about actually does come under the principle, standard, or law. This frequently involves interpreting both the action, policy, or practice that the judgment is about and the principle, standard, or law. Verifying value judgments of this sort is therefore not as easy and simple as verifying value judgments, which express personal or social preference, because frequently it leads you into interpretive disputes. But notice also that value judgments of this sort make much more interesting and important premises in arguments relevant to evaluative disputes.

In addition, value judgments of this sort focus attention on the principle, standard, or law to which they appeal and raise the question of its acceptability. Thus, verifying the most interesting kind of value judgments involves interpreting both specific actions, policies, or practices and general principles, standards, or laws, and by implication, establishing the acceptability of the principles, standards, or laws appealed to. In short, in the important and interesting cases, verifying value judgments leads you into areas where knowing how to construct and evaluate arguments is more and more important.

***Quick Check on Clarifying Language
(Answers on Page 404)**

Pick out the value words in these statements and indicate what possible interpretations could be put on them. In terms of each meaning, show how the truth of each assertion would be assessed.

1. Needlessly inflicting pain is wrong.
2. Infanticide is evil.

3. A doctor ought never operate on people without their informed consent.
4. Poetry is the highest artistic form.
5. Hypocrisy is immoral.
6. The best form of government is the one that allows the most personal freedom compatible with a like freedom for all.
7. Einstein's theory of relativity is the greatest scientific development of the twentieth century.
8. A government should not underwrite research dealing with in vitro fertilization.
9. No war is ever morally justifiable.
10. You should never disobey those in authority over you.
11. Communism is godless.
12. The women's liberation movement threatens the survival of the family as we've traditionally known it.

Weighing Reasons and Arguments

"Wait just a minute!" some of you may be thinking, "we're going backward, not forward. Before we can fully evaluate an argument with a value judgment as a premise, we have to evaluate the truth of the premise. But before we can do that we have to evaluate other arguments. Does one ever get to the bottom of this?"

That's a good question. At this point some reassurance may be in order. First of all, you already know some very useful and important things about evaluating arguments. So don't be afraid to use the tools at your disposal for the task at hand. Second, don't make the mistake of thinking that value judgments need to be verified *with absolute certainty* in order to be regarded as verified. If what you mean by "getting to the bottom" is establishing the truth of a value judgment with absolute certainty, then very likely one never gets to the bottom. But don't forget, it's just as hard to get to the bottom of some perfectly factual questions. And there's no need to be terrified of deep water as long as you know how to swim. Think again of the example about Gandhi and Hitler. Is it *absolutely certain* that Gandhi's leadership of his people was morally superior to Hitler's leadership of his? No, but the truth of this value judgment can be regarded as well established. Why? Because the arguments one could make in favor of it are so much better than any argument one could make against it. Of course, many value judgments are a lot less firmly established than this one. This is why, as we mentioned earlier, it is so important to keep an open mind to the arguments both for and against them. There are many kinds of arguments that are relevant to verifying value judgments. Let's look at two of the most important and common ones.

Appeal to principle   Value judgments often express evaluations of individual actions, policies, or practices in terms of some general principle, standard, or law. To verify a value judgment of this sort one must express the general principle, standard, or law and show why the specific case is covered by it. This frequently involves interpreting both the action, policy, or practice that the judgment is about and the principle, standard, or law. For example, Adrian is writing a paper in which she argues that it would be *wrong* to disconnect a particular person from a life-support system. In making her case, she should indicate the principle on which she is basing her opinion: "It is always wrong to kill someone intentionally" or "Only voluntary acts of euthanasia are permissible," for instance. She should then show that the case being considered was of a type covered by the principle. To do this she might show, given the first principle, that the person was in fact not dead before being removed from the system, and that removing the person from the system involves knowing that the person would die as a result; or, given the second principle, that neither the consent of the person nor the person's surrogates had been obtained. She would also need to interpret the principles themselves, explaining, for example, what counts as an intentional act of killing or a voluntary consent. Additionally, she might want to spend time supporting the principles, explaining why she thinks they are worth endorsing. As individuals thinking critically about Adrian's position, we have a right to expect these things of her. Should she not meet our expectations, we are entitled to raise them in our criticism.

Adrian can take the same approach to a social policy question. Suppose she is writing a paper in support of the Equal Rights Amendment (ERA). She could appeal to some principle of equality: "Women deserve to be treated equally" or "All people should be treated equally," for instance. Having established the principle and interpreted it, she could then show that women in fact are not treated equally (and how the ERA presumably would right this situation).

Applied to artistic judgment, the approach works the same way. Thus, in arguing that the classical Greek drama *Oedipus the King* is a good play, Adrian might appeal to the classical ideal of unity and catharsis and then show how the play is covered by this ideal.

Appeal to consequences Another common way to lend factual support to value judgments is by appealing to the purported consequences of an action or practice and providing data to justify this forecast. For example, were Adrian arguing that handguns should be prohibited, she might try to show that violent crime would decline if appropriate gun-control legislation was adopted. Of course, she would have to provide information to back up her prediction. If she was arguing that married couples should be required to undergo genetic counseling before having a child, she might show that fewer defective babies would be born if that were the case. Again, she would have to back up her contention.

So providing support is as important in expressing value judgments as it is in expressing nonvalue assertions ("Life exists in outer space"; "Cancer is caused by a virus"; "John F. Kennedy was not killed by a sole assassin"). Two good ways to provide this support are (1) to take a general principle and show that some specific individual, action, or practice is of a type covered by that principle and (2) to predict the consequences of an action or practice and then provide data to support the forecast made. In the best value arguments, these strategies are and should be integrated. For example, arguing against the sale of handguns, Adrian could express a principle (for example, "Society has an obligation to protect the lives of its citizens"). Then, by predicting the consequences of hand-gun control, she could show how the prohibition is covered by the principle. Similarly, in arguing for genetic counseling, she might appeal to the principle that parents have a right to know as much about the health of their unborn as possible. Then, by showing the kind of information prospective parents can glean from genetic counseling and the range of alternatives that counseling thereby opens to them, she could show how genetic counseling is covered by the principle.

Summary

In criticizing arguments you are evaluating them for cogency. A cogent argument is valid and is based on true or justified premises.

Deductive validity is a feature of the form or pattern an argument follows. Deductively valid argument forms are absolutely reliable. If the premises of an argument that follows a deductively valid pattern are true, there is no room for doubt as to the truth of its conclusion. A foolproof test for deductive validity involves seeing whether accepting the premises and denying the conclusion is self-contradictory. If it is, then the argument is deductively valid. If not, the argument is not deductively valid.

Inferences that are unreliable are called "fallacies." An inference that follows an unreliable form or pattern is called a "formal fallacy."

Inductive arguments leave room for doubt as to the truth of their conclusions. A valid inductive argument is one whose premises give probable grounds for its conclusion. Some inductive arguments are stronger than others. The strength of an inductive argument depends in part on the size and representativeness of the sample enumerated in its premises.

A true premise is a statement that describes an actual state of affairs: present, past, or future.

> *Example of a cogent deductive argument:* Because all humans are prone to error, and the president is human, the president is prone to error.

> *Example of a cogent inductive argument:* It's highly unlikely that a woman will be drafted into the National Football League this year, for no woman has ever played in that league in the past.

Do not confuse truth with belief or opinion. Remember that, unlike truth, opinion and belief are subject to error and dispute and therefore also subject to verification, which means simply seeing whether they are true.

For some types of assertions—necessary truths—verification is not a problem. Necessary truths, including tautologies and truths by definition, are statements whose denials are self-contradictory, and therefore necessarily false.

In contrast, verifying contingent statements is problematic. Contingent statements are neither self-contradictory nor necessarily true. Contingent statements can be considered true when there is reasonable evidence to support them. The problems involved in verification depend on the kind of assertion involved.

Factual assertions include observations and hypotheses. Five key points must be considered when evaluating observations: (1) the physical conditions under which the observations were made, (2) the sensory acuity of the observer, (3) the necessary background knowledge, (4) the objectivity of the observer, and (5) supporting testimony. Hypotheses are verified by seeking confirmation and disconfirmation. This frequently involves making observations.

Value judgments are another type of statement whose verification is problematic. Value assertions are judgments of worth: "Murder is *immoral*"; "Capital punishment *should be* legalized for certain serious crimes"; "Steven Spielberg is a *great* film director"; "Democracy is the *best* form of government." In verifying a value judgment, first clarify the value words contained in the assertion, deciding whether (1) personal preference, (2) social preference, or (3) conformity to law, principle, or standard is indicated by their use. Then weigh the reasons and arguments in favor of and against accepting the value judgment.

Applications

Identify the following as value or nonvalue arguments. Then cast them and criticize them for validity of inference and verification of premises, that is, for cogency. Be sure to fill in missing premises if necessary.

1. Fred must be a Republican because he voted for Reagan in the 1980 presidential election.

2. There's no question that Sarah's a Christian. She believes in a personal God, doesn't she?

3. Not all money-making films are made by the Hollywood studios. After all, some pornographic movies are money-makers.

4. Reverse discrimination should be allowed, for it can promote social justice.

5. Premarital sex encourages promiscuity. So it's immoral. It also happens to be a sin.

6. President Bush can't be trusted. He clearly lied about his involvement in the Iran-contra affair, and he reneged on his promise to maintain tuition tax credits for taxpayers sending their children to private or parochial

schools. Besides, he selected as vice president a man totally unfit to be president.

7. How important are professional athletes to society? Not very. They're mere entertainers. They often present bad role models for children—just think of Pete Rose, or Steve Garvey, or José Canseco. And, given the attention they get, they tend to distract us from serious social concerns. At the very least then, the salaries of these prima donnas should be drastically reduced to reflect their social insignificance.

8. Reverse discrimination sometimes occurs in the workplace. If you think not, just read the results of a study recently conducted by the *Harvard Business Review*. Ten percent of the personnel managers polled admitted that their companies did sometimes engage in reverse discrimination. So it's clear that at least in some instances people are judged on criteria not directly related to the job.

9. ". . . according to modern physics, radio is our only hope of picking up an intelligent signal from space. Sending an interstellar probe would take too long— roughly 50 years even for nearby Alpha Centauri—even if we had the technology and funds to accomplish it. But radio is too slow for much dialogue. The most we can hope from it is to establish the existence (or, more accurately, the former existence) of another civilization." (Patrick Moore, "Speaking English in Space: Stars," *Omni*, November 1979, p. 26.)

10. "If a being suffers, there can be no moral justification for refusing to take that suffering into consideration, and indeed, to count it equally with the like suffering (if rough comparisons can be made) of another being. So the only question is, Do animals other than man suffer? Most people agree unhesitatingly that animals like cats and dogs can and do suffer, and this seems also to be assumed by those laws that prohibit wanton cruelty to such animals. ("Animal Liberation," in James Rachels, (ed.), *Moral Problems*, 2d ed. [New York: Harper & Row, 1975], p. 166.)

CRITICIZING ARGUMENTS II: INFORMAL FALLACIES OF LANGUAGE

8

In the last chapter we developed the notion of a *fallacy* as an unreliable inference. This is an extremely important notion for argument criticism. Why? First of all, fallacies are inferences. So they *appear* to be reasonable. Second, their unreliability is not always evident on the surface. In fact, they can be very persuasive. Finally, as a result, they're quite widespread and prevalent in all sorts of everyday discourse, both public and private. So knowing how to spot them and understanding how they work are useful tools for the critical thinker.

INFORMAL FALLACIES

Formal fallacies, you'll remember, are inferences whose unreliability is due to their formal structure. But there are many more things that can go wrong with an argument besides formal structure. Thus, an *informal fallacy* is an inference whose unreliability is due to something other than its formal structure. In this and the next two chapters we will survey a fairly wide range of common informal fallacies. Before we begin, a few general comments and words of caution are in order.

The informal fallacies constitute a large and very mixed bag. The author of one critical thinking textbook estimates that several hundred informal fallacies are covered in one or another logic text. One such text distinguishes more than ninety informal fallacies, far too many for us to cover completely here. In fact, there are so many ways to argue badly that some of them haven't even been given names yet. Moreover, there is no standard classification system for the informal fallacies, nor any generally applicable and mechanically reliable procedure for identifying informal fallacies (as there is for formal fallacies).

As a result, students frequently find the array of informal fallacies bewildering and even intimidating. But don't make the mistake of approaching the informal fallacies as a list of labels to be memorized along with a capsule definition and mechanical application procedure for each. The results of this approach are almost always disastrous.

Here is a much better approach. Think of the informal fallacy categories as tools for doing a certain kind of work. Just as a carpenter has a kit of carpentry tools, you are assembling a set of tools for criticizing arguments. Your goal should be to attain mastery in their employment, and the best way to pursue this goal is by working with the tools. The work of the carpenter is to construct things out of wood. In the course of this work a carpenter will perform a wide variety of tasks, including measuring, cutting, fitting, fastening, finishing, and so on. A good deal of the carpenter's mastery has to do with selecting the right tool for the specific task at hand. The product that argument criticism is aimed at producing is a form of understanding. Just as the carpenter's mastery is evident in the product of the work, so the mastery of argument criticism shows in the understanding it achieves. Your emphasis should be not on labeling fallacies correctly but rather on how well you are able to understand and explain what is wrong with the faulty arguments you encounter, bearing in mind that a given argument can have more than one thing wrong with it. Remember also that it is possible to drive a nail with a screwdriver or a screw with a hammer. In other words, some tools will perform tasks for which they were not designed and which other, more suitable tools will perform much more effectively. Thus, the greater the number of tools you have at your command and the more discriminating you are in their use, the more complete your mastery becomes.

One final word of caution: The informal fallacy categories you will be working with are fault-finding tools. An important liability is inherent in using them. Special care needs to be taken not to find fault where there isn't any. An embarrassing, but revealing, example of this pitfall was reported recently by newspaper columnist Jack Smith. In a column entitled "Critique of an Ironic Writer's Critical Thought," Smith recounts how an earlier column of his, in which he poked fun at transcendental meditation as taught at Maharishi International University, was critiqued in a critical thinking class:

> These [devotees of transcendental meditation] believe, as you may remember, that if enough people meditate together, achieving a state of pure consciousness and connecting with the Unified Field, the basis of all life, they can actually alter events—lowering crime rates, quelling riots, easing international tension and even causing the Dow Jones average to rise.
>
> The theme of my essay was that I did not believe this. However, my tone was irony, which, as we have often seen, is a risky tone to effect.
>
> . . . Pinpointing is my first fallacy, [the student] quotes a paragraph:
>
> "The meditators held a mass meditation . . . thereby raising the temperature and saving the Florida orange crop, lowering drunken driving arrests in Des Moines, influencing Fidel Castro to give up cigars, and causing the stock market to rally."
>
> Obviously, I hope, I am being ironic. I do not for a moment believe that the meditation had any effect whatever on the events cited.
>
> But [the student] comments:
>
> "This is the fallacy of False Cause, or thinking that because someone did

one thing, something else happened as a result. The meditators may have believed that they were the reason for the temperature rise in Florida, but were
probably wrongly justified. . . ."

This is precisely the point Smith was himself trying to make! The moral of this
story for our present purposes is that a prerequisite to good argument criticism
is a fair and accurate understanding of the argument you are criticizing.

It's also important to recognize that an informally fallacious argument may
very closely resemble an argument that is perfectly reasonable, and that the
difference between the two often depends on the context within which each is
offered. So criticisms of arguments themselves need to be critically examined.
Don't overlook the possibility that the argument you find fault with might be
reasonably and persuasively defended against your criticism. Therefore, be especially careful not to condemn an argument too hastily. Be prepared to defend
your criticism, to argue for it, in other words. And in arguing for your criticism
you'll want, of course, to avoid committing any fallacies, formal or informal.

Organization of the Informal Fallacies

For the sake of simplicity we have divided the informal fallacies into three groups.
In this chapter we will survey fallacies of linguistic confusion, fallacies that can
be understood and explained in terms of the peculiarities of language. In Chapter
9 we'll look at fallacies of relevance, and in Chapter 10 we'll look at fallacies of
evidence. The informal fallacies of language can usefully be subdivided into two
subgroups: fallacies of ambiguity and rhetorical fallacies.

"Rose is Rose" by Pat Brady. Reprinted by permission of UFS, Inc.

FALLACIES OF AMBIGUITY

In Chapter 2 we encountered the important notion of ambiguity. An ambiguous expression is one that can be understood in more than one way. There are a number of common informal fallacies that depend on some sort of ambiguity.

Equivocation

If someone were to offer you a choice between eternally increasing ecstatic bliss and a three-day-old Big Mac, which would you choose? Well, consider the following argument:

> Nothing is better than eternally increasing ecstatic bliss, and a three-day-old Big Mac is better than nothing, so a three-day-old Big Mac is better than eternally increasing ecstatic bliss.

Obviously, there's *something* wrong with this argument. But what can it be? It *looks* so logical. The problem here is that the word "nothing," on which the apparently logical comparison hinges, actually changes meaning from the first premise to the second. The first premise can be paraphrased as follows:

> *There isn't anything* better than eternally increasing ecstatic bliss.

And the second premise can be paraphrased as follows:

> *Having* a three-day-old Big Mac is better than *not having anything at all.*

When the premises have been paraphrased in this way, we're no longer tempted to think that eternally increasing ecstatic bliss and a three-day-old Big Mac are both being compared to the same thing, and the apparent logic of the inference falls away. *When an argument depends on switching the meanings of an ambiguous crucial term or expression, as in this example, the argument commits the* **fallacy of equivocation.**

A more serious instance of equivocation is seen in this sometimes-invoked argument for the existence of a Supreme Being:

> The laws of gravitation and motion must have a lawmaker for the simple reason that they are laws, and all laws have a lawmaker.

Here the word "law" is given various meanings. In one sense laws are "artificial" (which means "made by humans") statutes to *proscribe*, or "rule out" certain behavior. This is the sense of "laws" in which the premise "All laws have a lawmaker" is true. But the laws of gravitation and motion are "scientific laws" intended to *describe* regularities in the behavior of the physical universe. Such laws are "discovered" more than "made" and as such do not presuppose law-makers. Therefore the conclusion is unwarranted.

In criticizing an argument as an equivocation, you should be able to identify the term or expression that is being used equivocally and demonstrate its equivocal use by clarifying the distinct senses in which it is employed. A convenient and effective way to do this is to paraphrase the assertions in which it occurs, as we did in the Big Mac example.

A caution: Not every example involving an ambiguous expression is a case of equivocation. Language is rife with ambiguity. And ambiguity is useful. The deliberate use of ambiguity, even in an argument, may be perfectly legitimate as an intentional pun or play on words or double entendre. For example, when baseball pitcher Tug McGraw was asked if he preferred Astroturf to grass he said, "I don't know. I never smoked Astroturf."

Amphiboly

A close cousin of equivocation is amphiboly. Equivocation results from verbal or "lexical" ambiguity, or the capacity of an individual word or expression to support more than one interpretation. By way of contrast, some expressions are "syntactically" ambiguous. They can be understood in more than one way because of their grammatical structure or word order. For example:

> The loot and the car were listed as stolen by the Los Angeles Police Department.

Here there is an ambiguity of reference. The expression is presumably intended to indicate that the police listed the loot and car as stolen, not that the listed property was stolen by the police. *An expression whose ambiguity is due to its grammatical structure or word order is called an amphiboly. An argument that exploits or depends on this sort of ambiguity commits the **fallacy of amphiboly.***

Occasionally this device is used in certain sales gimmicks that verge on fraud. For instance, at the end of a direct-mail sales offer appears the following guarantee:

> We're convinced that you will love your new Acme widget even more than you could begin to imagine. But rest assured. If for any reason you are the least bit dissatisfied, just send it back. We'll give you a prompt and a full refund.

Does this mean that you get a full refund promptly? When a dissatisfied customer applies for the refund and receives a nominal reimbursement along with a statement of "service charges," it becomes evident that this is not what the guarantee meant. Should the customer insist upon a full refund, it may take an indefinitely long time to receive it. (This could be understood as a special case of false implication. See Chapter 2.)

Just as with equivocation, the strategy for exposing amphiboly consists in pointing up the several interpretations of the ambiguous syntax.

Accent

*Ambiguity can also result from the placement of emphasis, or accent, on certain words or phrases in an expression. The **fallacy of accent** consists of drawing an unwarranted conclusion, or suggesting one, by the use of improper emphasis. For example:*

> ***Tom:*** I'm not going to contribute any more to your charity.
> ***Liz:*** Great! I'll just put you down for the same amount as last year.

Here Liz draws the faulty conclusion that Tom is willing to contribute the same as he did the year before because she erroneously accents "more." Without the accent, the colloquial expression "anymore" means "any longer."

The news media and ad writers commonly use accent to get our attention. **PRESIDENT DECLARES WAR,** a headline screams in bold print. Concerned that the country is embroiled in combat somewhere, you buy the paper and anxiously read the article. The "war," you discover, is a "war on inflation." Accent is one of the main devices exploited in the promotion of the tabloids or "scandal sheets." Not to be outdone, television has begun using this tactic ad nauseam. In order to heighten viewer anticipation, talk shows and even the newscasts are routinely promoted by means of ten-, twenty-, and thirty-second "teases," as they are called in the television industry. The tease accents the most sensational, titilating, or alarming aspect of a story or topic and promises "Details at eleven!" or "on the next 'Geraldo'!"

An important variation of the accent fallacy is the out-of-context quote, a device frequently used by candidates for political office to discredit each other. A vivid example of the out-of-context accent fallacy occurred in a statement in which former president Ronald Reagan defended his infamous visit to the Bitburg cemetery in 1985. Reagan said:

> One of the many who wrote me about this visit was a young woman who had recently been bas mitzvahed. She urged me to lay the wreath at Bitburg cemetery in honor of the future of Germany, and that is what we have done.

As the president was later forced to admit, he was here distorting a letter unequivocally opposed to the visit, in which the writer had said that *if* he went to Bitburg, Reagan should do so not to honor the soldiers of the German army and SS buried there, but in honor of the future of Germany.

Composition

A special kind of ambiguity is frequently involved in our references to groups of individuals or things. It is not always clear whether the members of the group are being referred to individually or collectively. This can result in one of two common informal fallacies. *The **fallacy of composition** consists of incorrectly inferring characteristics of the group as a collective whole from characteristics of its individual parts or members.* For example, a man observes that every member of a local club is wealthy and therefore infers that the club itself must be wealthy. Not necessarily. The confusion results from assuming that what is true of the part must also be true of the whole. In fact, the whole represents something different from simply the sum or combination of its parts. Of course, it is sometimes true that a collective whole has the characteristics of its individual members. It may be the case, for example, that a series of good lectures is a good series of lectures. But there is no generally reliable equation here. For example, a program of short pieces of music can be a very long program. A team of highly efficient workers may nonetheless be hopelessly inefficient as a team.

Division

The **fallacy of division** *works in the opposite direction, incorrectly inferring characteristics of the individual parts or members of a group from characteristics of the group as a collective whole.* Observing that a club is wealthy, a man infers that each club member must be wealthy or that a particular member must be wealthy. But just as a property of the part need not imply a property of the whole, so a property of the whole need not imply a property of the part. That a book is a masterpiece doesn't mean that each chapter is also; that an orchestra is outstanding doesn't imply that each member is an outstanding musician. Again, it is sometimes the case that the individual parts or members of a group have some of the characteristics of the group as a whole, but not always. A million-dollar inventory, for example, might be made up of a great many five- and ten-cent items.

*Quick Check on Fallacies of Ambiguity (Answers on Page 404)

1. Identify and explain the ambiguity in the following:

    a. News item: "Some 50,000 undocumented immigrants have gotten a preliminary OK to live legally in America during the first month of the government's unprecedented amnesty offer."
    b. When asked why he robbed banks, notorious bank robber Willy Sutton replied, "Because that's where the money is."
    c. He gave her dog biscuits.

2. Identify and explain the fallacies in the following:

    a. Ronald Reagan, in a speech televised by Worldnet and provided to networks worldwide by the U.S. Information Agency: "[Governments] must move to dismantle trade-distorting subsidies and labor laws that promote unemployment."
    b. National Football League Films, of Mt. Laurel, N.J., chose an all-time NFL team and nominated about a dozen players at each position. Pittsburgh Steeler fans were miffed when former Steelers star Jim Ham was not among the linebacker

nominees. "Everybody has players that they think should be in there," said Steelers president Dan Rooney, "but we did happen to play the best football that was ever played in the NFL for at least six years, if not more."

c. Having missed Veterans Administration deadlines for application for college benefits, two men sued the VA, arguing that under VA guidelines "disabled veterans" had longer to apply, and that their disability—alcoholism—qualified them for the extended deadline.

d. Joseph Dennie was a Federalist. Therefore, the fortunes of Joseph Dennie decayed after 1800." (Paraphrase of historian Vernon Parrington in "Main Currents of American Thought," in David Hackett Fischer (ed.), *Historians' Fallacies* [New York: Harper & Row, 1970], p. 222.)

e. ***Todd:*** Why do you dislike Frank so much, when the Bible says, "Love thy neighbor"?

Ted: But Frank's not my neighbor. He doesn't live anywhere near me.

RHETORICAL FALLACIES

In Chapter 2 we distinguished persuasion as an important function of language. There are a number of common informal fallacies that can best be understood as improper applications of the numerous persuasive capacities of language.

Abuse of Vagueness

In Chapter 2 we developed also the notion of *vagueness*, a lack of clarity in the extensional meaning of an expression. The persuasive power of vague expressions has to do with the fact that they allow one to project onto them meanings determined by one's desires. This helps explain why they have become literally the stock-in-trade of the modern sophists that populate the so-called human potential industry. For example, just as we were composing this chapter, there arrived through the mail an unsolicited flyer that read in part:

> This two-day weekend seminar will open you to the wonders of the contemporary experience of modern High-Tech Serendipity Meditation, as your seminar leader and originator of the High-Tech Serendipity Meditation Experience personally conducts this expansive program, demonstrating the power and potential of this contemporary meditative technology. The weekend includes four power-packed sessions of Holodynamic Serendipity material presented in such a way as to enable each participant to personally experience the contemporary ease and the full potential of High-Tech Meditation.

Sounds exciting, intriguing, beneficial, attractive, but what does all this mean? It is virtually impossible to tell. The terminology, although it sounds very positive and indeed technically precise, is hopelessly vague. That's the important thing to notice here. Because it is so vague, it invites the reader to project onto it whatever meanings are most closely connected with the reader's own search and longings. Of course, if you want to find out in detail what "high-tech holodynamic serendipity meditation" is all about, you can sign up for the two-day weekend seminar for a fee of $250, which, assuming you can afford it, might not be such a bad deal for two full days of whatever you want to believe you're hearing.

(Incidentally, the thought crossed our minds that the timing of the arrival of this flyer, to coincide with the writing of this chapter, might itself have been a case of serendipity. But see the fallacy category Post Hoc in Chapter 9.)

Assumption-Loaded Labels

As we discussed in Chapter 1, labels can be dangerous when they conceal assumptions that may be questionable, leading us to accept uncritically a doubtful or controvertible view of things. When Hitler referred to "the Jewish problem," implied was a freight of questionable assumptions, not the least of which was that a nation's socioeconomic problems could be correctly ascribed to individuals of a particular religion or ethnic background. By systematically using the phrase "the Jewish problem," the Nazis encouraged others to consider the Jews as the source of domestic instability. "The Jewish problem" became a cover for anti-Semitism, and Jews were made scapegoats for Germany's internal strife.

Today we speak of the "welfare problem," even the "welfare mess." "Welfare" means organized efforts to improve the living conditions of needy persons. In what sense, then, is welfare a "problem"? In fact, welfare is the *result* of many problems: unemployment, age, infirmity, racial prejudice, broken homes, limited resources, and so forth. These in turn are likely the results of fundamental problems in our political, social, and economic institutions and philosophies. The label "welfare problem" obscures the complexity of the issue. It is loaded with the assumption that welfare is the disease, not the symptom. As a result it not only encourages us to consider welfare in isolation from its underlying causes but to blame welfare and its recipients for various social ills—for "infecting" the nation, to extend the medical metaphor.

Euphemism

*When certain words are considered too blunt, harsh, painful, or offensive, people sometimes substitute a more acceptable term, a term with fewer negative or with more positive connotations. Such a term is called a **euphemism.*** The tendency to favor euphemisms is a natural and understandable defense mechanism in many cases, but it is also a dangerous tendency in some ways. The dangers inherent in euphemism were almost prophetically envisioned by the writer George Orwell in his famous novel *1984* and in a lesser known but very illuminating essay "Politics of the English Language." Orwell put forward the idea that an effective mechanism of political control is control of the terms of public discussion. Thus for example, rather than "fight a war," we "engage in a conflict" (as in the "Vietnam conflict") or a "police action" (as in the "Korean police action"). Rather than "spy," we "gather intelligence." Rather than "assassinate" people, the CIA "terminates them with prejudice." Rather than "firing" employees, bureaucrats speaking of "selecting out," and instead of "rationing" gasoline, we talk of "end-use allocation." Today in some political circles it is fashionable to speak of a "tax" as a "revenue enhancement."

To be sure, euphemism sometimes is an appropriate adjustment of the language to a situation. We may be better able to deal with the death of a loved one by thinking of the person as having "passed away" rather than having "died." But euphemism can also be used to gloss over unpleasant realities that need attention or to divert us from giving an issue or event the critical inspection it warrants. Worse yet, euphemism is frequently used in place of genuine argument to "settle" controversial issues by controlling the terms of debate. In our times the rhetoric of Vietnam is one of the preeminent examples of this use of euphemism. Here are just a few examples with "translations":

Euphemism	*Word Replaced*
pacification center	concentration camp
protective reaction strike	bombing
incontinent ordnance	off-target bombs (usually when civilians are killed)
friendly fire	shelling friendly villages or troops by mistake
specified strike zone	area where soldiers could fire at anything—replaced "free fire zone" when that became notorious
strategic withdrawal	retreat (when the United States and its allies did it)
advisor	military officer (before the United States admitted involvement)
terminate	kill
infiltrators	enemy troops moving into battle area
reinforcements	friendly troops moving into battle area[1]

More recently, the Reagan administration outdid the notorious Nixon administration in the use of verbal whitewash. It insisted on referring to the rebel forces it sponsored in its attempt to undermine the government of Nicaragua as "freedom fighters"; instead of "deliberate and premeditated cover-up," administration officials prefer to speak of "achieving plausible deniability"; and Oliver North went so far as to describe the secret and illegal diversion of illegally obtained funds to support an illegal war as "the use of collateral assets to support the democratic resistance." Even George Orwell would have been amazed.

Extreme Quantifiers and Intensifiers

Another way writers load language, and thereby communicate bias, is by using extreme quantifiers—terms like "all" or "every"—and extreme intensifiers—terms like "absolutely" or "certainly." When these devices are used in place of reasons in support of controversial claims, the result can be criticized as informally fallacious. Don't misunderstand. We need not qualify everything we say or write. But it is important to frame our assertions with as much accuracy and fairness as possible and to expect the same of others. Such framing is not only conducive to precise and fruitful thinking but also precludes needless disagreement, for frequently controversy is kindled through the use of an immoderate term, an intensifier.

Unfortunately, natural human indolence and intellectual limitations make us eager to view questions in the simplest terms possible, and as we saw in Chapter 1, cultural conditioning encourages this tendency to oversimplify. These factors show up in our approaches to practical problems but even more so in questions of human conduct or social policy. One cannot say with easy assurance, "The environment *certainly* must be cleaned up, even if that means plant shutdowns, unemployment, and a reduced standard of living," "*Surely* the best way to ensure domestic tranquility is to erect the strongest military defense possible," "Abortion should *never* be permitted," or "Drafting young men in peace times *simply* isn't justifiable." Perhaps some of these assertions are warranted, perhaps none is. But before any is adopted as settled conviction, the thinking person must consider its full implications. When the implications are explored, it may be found that these unqualified generalizations don't hold up, that their extreme quantifiers and intensifiers need to be diluted. But the writer who employs these devices ordinarily wants to shut off debate precisely where it needs to be opened up.

Minimizers

A closely related device works in the opposite direction to downplay potential controversy, or to minimize the need for substantial support for a claim. Expressions like "needless to say," "it goes without saying that," "obviously," and the like, lend themselves to this application. They are generally intended and taken to mean that the claims they introduce are so uncontroversial or universally accepted as to require no argument or evidence. To be sure, there are such claims, and it goes without saying that claims which require no argument or evidence need not be argued for or supported with evidence. But when a speaker or writer attempts to slip a controvertible assertion by as though it were "self-evident," it is time to raise an objection.

Rhetorical Questions

A **rhetorical question** *is a question with a built-in answer.* Rhetorical questions *seem* to leave the conclusion up to the reader but are worded in such a way that only one answer is possible. "Would you recommend that the United States not spend every penny necessary to ensure national security?" "Can a law that is opposed to the wishes of millions of honest citizens be fair and just?" "Since students don't know which courses will contribute to their education, should they have a strong voice in curriculum decisions?" It's hard to answer yes to these questions. That's the point: The rhetorical question is intended to elicit a predetermined response. The beauty of the rhetorical question is that it makes you think that you are drawing the inference yourself. The implication of the writer's rhetorical setup is that if we took the time and made the effort to discover the answer, we would arrive at the same conclusion as the writer. Although this device is occasionally used effectively to dramatize an important point for which the supporting evidence has already been laid out, more often it is used to cover up a lack of good arguments.

In a 1983 television address intended to justify the continued presence of the U.S. Marines in Lebanon, Ronald Reagan asked rhetorically:

> "Can the United States, or the free world for that matter, stand by and see the Middle East incorporated into the Soviet bloc? What of Western Europe's and Japan's dependence on Middle East oil for the energy to fuel their industries?"

Here the audience is expected to draw several conclusions—(1) that the incorporation of the Middle East into the Soviet sphere of influence is unacceptable to the free world; (2) that it would curtail the supply of oil to Western Europe and Japan; (3) and that the withdrawal of the Marines would bring all of this about—all without any argument whatsoever. Incidentally, several months after this address the Marines were withdrawn from Lebanon, and to this date none of the dire consequences Reagan predicted has come about. (See the sections "Slippery Slope Fallacy" in Chapter 8 and "False Cause" in Chapter 9.)

Innuendo

Innuendo *consists of drawing or implying a judgment, usually derogatory, on the basis of words that suggest but don't assert a conclusion.* "Has Jones been fired?" someone asks you. You may reply directly, "No." Or you may say, "Not yet." By innuendo, the second response numbers Jones's days. Jones may in fact be on the proverbial block, but you have given no logical grounds for so inferring. Innuendo, then, is dangerous to critical thinking because it encourages us to imply things or draw inferences that we are unable or unwilling to defend.

Innuendo needn't be as obvious as in the preceding example. The person who says, "Most physicians are competent and altruistic health care professionals" probably isn't prepared to substantiate the charge made against the minority of physicians who by implication are incompetent or self-serving. The political candidate who distributes a brochure in which she promises to restore honesty and integrity to an office seldom is prepared to prove that her opponent is by implication a crook.

Indeed, sometimes merely by calling attention to something, we provide enough innuendo to sandbag somebody. Consider this amusing episode—amusing, that is, for everyone except the Captain in question:

> Captain L had a first mate who was at times addicted to the use of strong drink, and occasionally, as the slang has it, "got full." The ship was lying in port in China, and the mate had been on shore and had there indulged rather freely in some of the vile compounds common in Chinese ports. He came on board, "drunk as a lord," and thought he had a mortgage on the whole world. The captain, who rarely ever touched liquor himself, was greatly disturbed by the disgraceful conduct of his officer, particularly as the crew had all observed his condition. One of the duties of the first officer [i.e., the first mate] is to write up the log each day, but as that worthy was not able to do it, the captain made the proper entry, but added: "The mate was drunk all day." The ship left port the next day and the mate got "sobered off." He attended to his writing at the proper time, but was appalled when he saw what the captain had done. He went back on deck, and soon after the following colloquy took place:
> "Cap'n, why did you write in the log yesterday that I was drunk all day?"
> "It was true, wasn't it?"
> "Yes, but what will the shipowners say if they see it? It will hurt me with them."
> But the mate could get nothing more from the Captain than, "It was true, wasn't it?"
> The next day, when the Captain was examining the book, he found at the bottom of the mate's entry of observation, course, winds, and tides: "The captain was sober all day." [Charles E. Trow, *The Old Shipmasters of Salem* (New York: Macmillan, 1905), pp. 14–15.]

Obviously, the mate is hoping that the ship's owners will interpret his entry about the captain as more than the literal truth. Probably they will infer that the mate recorded the captain's sobriety because it was the exception, not the rule. When they do, the mate will gain his revenge.

Complex Question

Sometimes a question is so worded that you can't answer it without granting a particular answer to some other question. Such a construction is called a **complex question,** *sometimes called a "loaded question" or "leading question."* A well-known example is the old vaudeville line "Have you stopped beating your wife (or husband) yet?" Such a question boxes you in because either way you answer, it is presupposed that you are or were beating your spouse. Another example:

> "Why is it that most men prefer beauty to intelligence in women?"

This complex question asks for an explanation of a phenomenon that may or may not be the case but that is presupposed as having already been established.

The Phantom Distinction

Drawing distinctions is often essential to avoiding confusion, and consequently it is often of central importance to arguing about an issue. Moreover, some important distinctions are quite subtle and difficult to make clear. However, *when the linguistic devices useful in drawing and indicating differences are used to suggest differences that do not in fact exist, the **fallacy of phantom distinction** is committed.*

Suppose your next-door neighbor makes some subtle and suggestive threatening gesture toward you in an attempt to get you to move your car from the curb in front of his house. You challenge the unfriendly tone: "Are you threatening me?" And the neighbor responds, "It's not a threat, it's a promise."

Sometimes this rhetorical device is employed with deliberate intent to mislead a discussion, by baffling an essentially accurate description or understanding of some controversial action, or policy, or what have you—often in combination with a more euphemistic description of the same controversial item. For example, suppose that at the annual stockholders' meeting the corporate public relations officer responds to a pointed question about the firm's new tactical approach to labor relations, saying, "We're not talking about union busting here. We're simply reasserting management prerogative in the area of determining compensation."

Summary

Informal fallacies are unreliable inferences whose unreliability has to do with things other than their formal structure. The informal fallacy categories are best understood not as strictly defined and mutually exclusive, but rather as useful terminology for understanding and explaining weaknesses that occur in reasoning. To use them effectively you must bear in mind that a given argument may be fallacious in several ways at once, and that a given argument may look fallacious but not actually be fallacious. Your emphasis, therefore, should be not on labeling arguments as instances of this or that informal fallacy, but rather on explaining and arguing for your account of the weaknesses you think are present in arguments.

Informal fallacies can be divided into three large groups: informal fallacies of language; informal fallacies of relevance; and informal fallacies of evidence.

Informal fallacies of language are those best understood and explained in terms of the peculiarities of language. These can be divided into two subgroups: informal fallacies of ambiguity and rhetorical fallacies.

Informal fallacies of ambiguity are fallacies that arise as a result of the flexibility of language to support multiple interpretations.

Verbal or "lexical" ambiguity is the capacity of individual words or expressions to support more than one interpretation. An argument that depends upon verbal or lexical ambiguity commits the fallacy of equivocation.

An amphiboly is an expression that is grammatically or "syntactically" ambiguous. An argument that depends on an ambiguity of grammar or word order commits the fallacy of amphiboly.

Another form of ambiguity results from placement of emphasis. An argument that depends on this sort of ambiguity commits the fallacy of accent. Quoting out of context is a common form of the fallacy of accent.

A special kind of ambiguity of reference to groups can result in either the fallacy of composition or the fallacy of division. The membership of a group can be referred to collectively or individually. The fallacy of division consists in incorrectly inferring that individual members of a group have some characteristic of the group as a whole. The fallacy of composition consists in incorrectly inferring characteristics of the group as a whole from characteristics of its individual members.

Rhetorical fallacies consist in improper exploitation of the persuasive capacities of language. These include:

The deliberate use of vague language where clarity and substance may legitimately be expected

The use of intensifiers or minimizers in place of arguments

The use of emotionally loaded labels or labels loaded with assumptions, instead of arguments, to communicate a bias or interpretation

The use of euphemism to control the terms of discussion or to misdescribe a set of circumstances whose status is at issue

The use of rhetorical questions in place of arguments to suggest or invite particular conclusions

The use of innuendo in place of arguments to suggest or invite particular conclusions

The use of complex questions, which presuppose particular answers to implicit additional unasked questions

The use of linguistic distinction markers to suggest a difference where no difference exists

Applications

1. For this exercise you'll need a partner, preferably someone who is taking the critical thinking course with you. One of you can play the role of finding and explaining the flaw in the argument or rhetorical appeal, while the other challenges and tests the diagnosis by trying to defend the argument against the proposed criticism. Take turns as you work your way through the following examples. Don't forget, a given argument can

have more than one thing wrong with it. If you arrive at a consensus criticism, move on to the next example.

a. Pushy father-in-law to new bride: "So, when are you kids planning to make us grandparents?"

b. From a political campaign brochure: "Candidate X has resorted to 'name-calling.' She says that our candidate is a 'professional politician.' That's not fair. It is coloring the truth. The truth in black and white is that our candidate was a Deputy Sheriff up until he nearly lost his life in the line of duty. Hardly a 'professional politician.' Our candidate has run for office only once in his life and that was 4 years ago. Hardly a 'professional politician.'"

c. From another political campaign brochure: "What would you call a politician who didn't pay his property taxes on time? We'd call him a little forgetful. What would you call a politician who owned a business but never paid his local business taxes? We'd call him more than a little forgetful. What would you call a politician who owned property but refused to pay his property taxes from 1981 until 1984? We'd call him a lot of the same things you'd call him. But none of us would call him our next Assemblyman."

d. God is love.
   Love is blind.
   _____
   ∴ God is blind.

e. How can you deny that abortion is murder? The fetus is certainly alive, isn't it? And it certainly is human, isn't it? And it hasn't done anything wrong, has it? So you're talking about taking an innocent human life. What else is there to say?

f. People object to sexism and racism on the ground that they involve discrimination. But what is objectionable about discrimination? We discriminate all the time—in the cars we buy, the foods we eat, the books we read, the friends we choose. The fact is there's nothing wrong with discrimination as such.

g. "Most Calvinists were theological determinists. Most New England Puritans were Calvinists. Therefore, most New England Puritans were theological determinists. . . . The fortunes of the Federalists decayed after 1800. (Paraphrase of historian Vernon Parrington in "Main Currents of American Thought," in David Hackett Fischer (ed.), *Historians' Fallacies* [New York: Harper & Row, 1970], p. 222.)

h. What is wrong with the argument in this cartoon?

i. "Should we not assume that just as the eye, the hand, the foot, and in general each part of the body clearly has its own proper function, so man too has some function over and above the function of his parts?" (Aristotle, *Nicomachean Ethics*, trans. Martin Ostwald [Indianapolis: Bobbs-Merrill, 1962], p. 16.)

j. The end of anything is its perfection. Therefore, since death is the end of life, death must be the perfection of life.

k. "Can the universe think about itself? We know that at least one part of it can: we ourselves. Is it not reasonable to conclude the whole can?" (José Silva, *The Silva Mind Control Method* [New York: Pocket Books, 1978], p. 116.)

l. Letter to the editor: "Question for today: How can the federal budget deficits ever be brought under control as long as conservative superpatriots insist that the Defense Department is a sacred cow, despite endless examples of waste and mismanagement? Put another way, how many over-priced ash trays and toilet seats must Congress learn about before it realizes that the Pentagon brass hats are bemedaled equivalents of Imelda Marcos?"

m. During the Iran-contra hearings, Senator Sam Nunn (D. Ga.) queried Rear Adm. John Poindexter, Ronald Reagan's national security advisor, about a recently made White House statement that disputed Poindexter's assertion that the president would have approved the diversion of Iran arms funds to the contras had Poindexter proposed it to him.

Nunn: You said: "I made the decision. I felt I had the authority to do it. I thought it was a good idea. I was convinced that the President would, in the end, think it was a good idea." Is that still your testimony?
Poindexter: It is.
Nunn: That means, Admiral, you must believe the White House is now misleading the American people.
Poindexter: No, I don't think so.
Nunn: How can it not be?
Poindexter: Well, number one, what you have are reports of what (White House spokesman) Marlin Fitzwater said. I don't know exactly . . .
Nunn: You don't believe he's speaking for the President?
Poindexter: Well, I would want to have a personal conversation with the President, which I have not had and which would not be appropriate at this time.

2. With the benefit of the discussions you have had with your study partner, briefly and carefully explain the fallacies you found in each of the preceding examples. You may find it useful in some cases to cast the argument as a first step.

3. Find examples of your own in the public media of the informal fallacies discussed in this chapter. For each example, give a brief but careful explanation of the fallacies you find in it.

[1] See Howard Kahane, *Logic and Contemporary Rhetoric,* 5th ed. (Belmont, Calif.: Wadsworth, 1988), pp. 126–132.

CRITICIZING ARGUMENTS III: INFORMAL FALLACIES OF RELEVANCE

9

Suppose that someone said to you, "Now that I know how to construct a deductively valid argument I can finally settle the abortion issue once and for all! Here's my argument:

> If 'abortion' is an eight-letter word, then abortion should be against the law.
> 'Abortion' is an eight-letter word.
> ___
> ∴ Abortion should be against the law.

Are you convinced? Since the argument is in the form modus ponens it can't be faulted formally. So what's wrong with it? Are the premises false? The second one is true. Count the letters. That verifies that. Which leaves premise 1. Is premise 1 false? Before you answer this question just suppose for a moment that the conclusion of the argument is true. Now, is premise 1 false? Hard to tell, isn't it? You don't know yet whether the conclusion is true, but it might be, and in that case you can't really be sure that premise 1 is false. So what's wrong with the argument? The problem here is that both premises are irrelevant to the issue. Why? Because the number of letters in the word "abortion" is irrelevant to the moral status of abortion and therefore also the question of abortion law.

Here you can see the concept of relevance in bold relief. An important informal consideration in evaluating arguments is whether the premises appealed to are relevant to what is at issue. If they are, so much the better for the argument. If not, some kind of fallacy of relevance, or "irrelevant appeal," has been committed.

A general strategy for exposing irrelevant appeals is to challenge the relevance of the premise(s) to the conclusion of the argument or to the issue under discussion. Bear in mind, however, that to challenge the relevance of a premise

"Let me tell you, folks—I've been around long enough to develop an instinct for these things, and my client is innocent or I'm very much mistaken."

is not the same as establishing that it *is* irrelevant. Relevance is not always obvious on the surface. So it remains open to the arguer to meet the challenge by explaining how the premise bears on the conclusion or issue. But if a premise *is* relevant, it should be possible to explain the connection.

IRRELEVANT APPEALS

A more pointed strategy for exposing irrelevant appeals is to assimilate an argument to one of the common categories of irrelevant appeal that we will survey in this chapter. To keep your criticisms as sharp and clear as possible, remember that there is considerable overlap between many of these categories, and that a given argument can also have more than one thing wrong with it. Most important, take care not to dismiss as irrelevant any considerations whose relevance is just not apparent on the surface.

Ad Hominem

Perhaps the most common, and certainly one of the most objectionable of the informal fallacies of relevance is the ad hominem argument. "Ad hominem" is the Latin phrase for "to the man." *When people argue ad hominem, they attack the person, not the person's position or argument,* a special case of irrelevant reasoning. A most persuasive way of diverting attention from the real issue, ad hominem statements commonly take two forms: *abusive,* which consists of attacking characteristics of the person; and *circumstantial,* which consists of trying to persuade someone to accept a position because of the special facts or circumstances of the person's life.

Abusive Ad Hominem   *The **abusive ad hominem** fallacy is committed when, instead of trying to disprove the truth of what is asserted, one attacks the person making the assertion.* Those using abusive ad hominem pleas attempt to discredit ideas by discrediting the persons who hold them. It's as if they were saying, "Since so-and-so is (*some abusive term*), anything so-and-so says is without merit."

Abusive ad hominem arguments take two principal forms. One is *raising suspicions about a person.* For example, in the 1984 reelection campaign, commenting on the nuclear freeze movement, Ronald Reagan said:

> They were demonstrating in behalf of a movement that has swept across our country, inspired not by the sincere, honest people who want peace, but by some who want the weakening of America and so are manipulating many honest and sincere people.

Besides distorting the actual positions and arguments of those who supported the nuclear freeze and appealing to the public on a level of nationalism and loyalty (see "Straw Person" and "Provincialism" later in this chapter), this comment amounted to an irrelevant attack on the character and motives of the supporters of the nuclear freeze. Even if Reagan's charge had been true, it was beside the point. The relevant question has to do with the merits of the nuclear freeze as an approach to international arms control.

The second ad hominem form is *showing contempt for a person.* For example, "We should reject Rothchild's views on educational reform, because as a banker he can't be expected to know much about anything but making money." Another example: In 1986 a caravan of celebrity activists toured California in support of a clean water ballot initiative. Some voters were quick to dismiss the arguments offered on the grounds that "these people are a bunch of Hollywood actors and rock musicians. What do they know about environmental issues?" Well, as it turned out, many of those involved in the campaign caravan proved to be as knowledgeable as many a state legislator, and this would have been apparent to anyone who had taken the time to pay attention to their arguments. Dismissing the positions and arguments of celebrities, just because they are celebrities, is just as fallacious as accepting as authoritative whatever a celebrity says.

A special kind of ad hominem device has grown increasingly common in the television age: dismissing a person's argument or position because of the person's image or appearance. Consider for example the way in which many viewers and even some television commentators assessed the candidacy of Paul Simon for the 1988 Democratic presidential nomination.

And as you might imagine, ad hominem argument is quite often accomplished by innuendo. That is, by *merely suggesting* something unflattering about an individual, arguers frequently hope in addition to discredit their positions.

You should be aware, though, that not every argument that introduces the character or motives of the parties to the dispute is fallacious. In the political context, for instance, attacking one's opponent is not necessarily ad hominem. If one's attack is on the opponent's record in office, that is not irrelevant to the issue of the campaign. Personal considerations are certainly relevant when deciding whether a person is reliable or conscientious. If people have proven unreliable, we surely have a basis for holding what they say suspect. But suspecting their words is different from rejecting them. Weighing the reliability of a witness differs from assuming that personalities dispose of issues.

Circumstantial Ad Hominem The **circumstantial ad hominem** *fallacy consists of attempting to persuade someone to accept or reject a position because of the special facts or circumstances of the person's life, rather than on the merits of the position itself.* For example, rather than show why a proposed tax bill is a bad piece of legislation and therefore unworthy of support, someone argues, "You're a businesswoman. Don't you realize that the U.S. Chamber of Commerce opposes this measure?" Similarly, Dr. Henry can't understand how a fellow physician can support the new Massachusetts health plan. "Don't you worry about how this will affect your income?" she warns her colleague. In these cases the arguers fail to address the issues, preferring to argue that the measures cannot be consistently supported owing to their supporters' special circumstances. Although such arguments might succeed in placing one's opponent on the defensive, they are quite beside the point.

Guilt by Association The fallacy of **guilt by association,** *a special case of circumstantial ad hominem argument, consists of making negative judgments about people, or their positions and arguments, solely on the basis of their relationships with others.* For example, during the congressional campaigns of 1982 and 1986, many Democratic candidates tried to defeat their Republican opponents by identifying them with President Reagan's economic programs, which in part had contributed to widespread unemployment, farm foreclosures, homelessness, and so on, even though many of the Republican candidates were trying to dissociate themselves from Reagan's policies, and many of these same Democratic candidates had supported Reagan's policies in Congress.

Some Republican candidates used the same tack to discredit Democrats. In the 1982 race for the Senate, for example, California Republican Pete Wilson took every opportunity to identify Democratic candidate Jerry Brown with farm union leader Cesar Chavez, not a popular figure in the powerful California agricultural industry.

The abuse of this fallacy reached epic proportions in the 1986 California races, as numerous candidates sought successfully to tar the images of their opponents by linking their campaigns to State Supreme Court Chief Justice Rose Bird, already the target of a massive negative campaign waged by advocates of stiffer criminal penalties and more liberal procedures for carrying out the death penalty. The campaign to unseat Chief Justice Bird reached such a pitch of hysteria that the question of association with Bird became, in terms of public campaigning and, most of all, in advertising, the top priority issue in many legislative districts and the *only* issue in some. In some thirty-second television spots it was thought sufficient merely to suggest such an association by far-fetched innuendo.

Genetic Appeal   *A similar inference, the fallacy of genetic appeal, consists of evaluating something strictly in terms of its origin.* For example, it is sometimes argued by religious fundamentalists that dancing should be forbidden because it originated as a form of pagan worship, or that day-care centers are insidious because of their socialist origins.

Another kind of example, closer to guilt by association and ad hominem fallacies, involves either endorsing or dismissing an idea simply on the grounds of who its originators or supporters are. For example, in 1988 a struggle was waged through the ballot initiative process over the regulation of the insurance industry in the state of California. One measure that qualified for the election made the insurance industry publicly accountable for rate changes. The insurance industry countered by promoting a measure of its own, called the "No Fault Initiative." Voters were understandably confused. In their confusion, many voters were swayed to "consider the source." It was argued that the No Fault Initiative could not be good for the consumer because the insurance industry had cooked it up and was supporting it. Strictly speaking, this argument commits the fallacy of genetic appeal.

But we should be careful here. Speaking equally strictly, the identity of the source is not entirely irrelevant to the issue, in that one could make a reasonably solid inductive case for conflict of interest between consumer protection (the advertised aim of the No Fault Initiative) and protection of a profitable business climate in which no substantial consumer protection exists. The fallacy consists in closing the issue on the basis solely of the identity of the source, or treating the identity of the source as decisive. At most, the identity of the source constitutes a reason for looking more closely at the measure itself and at the arguments made for and against it. In this case, these are the factors that should be regarded as decisive.

Poisoning the Well   *A similar fallacious argumentative strategy consists of attempting to discredit a position, or its advocate, before the argument for the position has had a chance to get a hearing.* This strategy of attempting to arouse prejudice against an argument that shoud be allowed to stand on its own merits or fall of its own weight is described metaphorically as *poisoning the well* (before anyone can drink from it). In effect, the arguer tries to maneuver an opponent into a position from which he or she cannot reply. For example: "You're not a woman, so it doesn't matter what you have to say about the question of abortion."

Another example: Nineteenth-century philosopher and theologian John Henry Cardinal Newman engaged in frequent disagreements with clergyman and novelist Charles Kingsley. During the course of one of these disputes, Kingsley suggested that Newman could not place the highest value on truth because of his Catholicism. Newman rightly objected that this was poisoning the well, since it made it impossible for him (or any Catholic) to state his case. No matter what reasons or arguments Newman might offer to show that he did value the truth and that this value was basic to his faith, Kingsley would have already ruled out because they had come from a Catholic.

Poisoning the well is a favorite government tactic for managing domestic public opinion about foreign policy. For example, the Reagan administration worked very hard at—and, with the general cooperation of the American press, largely succeeded in—painting a portrait of Nicaraguan leader Daniel Ortega as basically unworthy of trust regardless of what he might have to say. This strategy has been very effective in preventing the American public from arriving independently at an assessment of the Nicaraguan perspective on affairs in Central America.

*Quick Check on Ad Hominem Appeals (Answers on Page 405)

Identify and explain the ad hominem appeal in each of the following passages by using the categories just discussed: abusive ad hominem, circumstantial ad hominem, guilt by association, genetic appeal, and poisoning the well. Remember, a given argument can have more than one thing wrong with it.

1. "Mr. North, a fascist flunkey, wishes by means of his semantics to make meaningless not only the sacred deed of heroism of the fighters against fascism, but the whole past and future struggle for liberty. But he only exposes his reactionary guts, his hatred for liberty and social progress. . . . Stuart Chase, the petty bourgeois American economist, who writes prescriptions for the disease of capitalism, having read the writing of semantics has lost the last remnants of common sense and has come forward with a fanatical sermon of the new faith, a belief in the magical power of words." (Bernard Emmanuilovich Bykhovsky, *The Decay of Bourgeois Philosophy* [Moscow: Mysl, 1947], p. 173.)

2. "Name calling, derogatory articles, and adverse propaganda are other methods used to belittle persons refusing to recommend refined foods. We have long been called crackpots and faddists regardless of training or of accuracy in reporting research. The words 'quack' and 'quackery' are now such favorites that any one using them is receiving benefits from the food processors." (Adele Davis, *Let's Eat Right to Keep Fit* [Los Angeles: Cancer Control Society, 1970], p. 21.)

3. "Every criminal, every gambler, every thug, every libertine, every girl ruiner, every home wrecker, every wife beater, every dope peddler, every moonshiner, every crooked politician, every pagan

Papist priest, every shyster lawyer, every K. of C. [Knights of Columbus, a Roman Catholic lay organization], every white slaver, every brothel madam, every Rome controlled newspaper, every black spider—is fighting the Klan. Think it over. Which side are you on?" (From a Ku Klux Klan circular)

4. "Editor—Let's increase the kid fare on Muni buses by 100% to help pay for the graffiti cleanup program. They are responsible, whether they wield the felt tip pen or spray can or just watch in approval."

5. Letter to the Editor: "I was profoundly dismayed by the badgering of witnesses during the Iran-contra hearings by Senator Rudman. Doesn't he realize that such criticism reflects badly on the President, a fellow Republican? If we can't expect Republicans to support the President in a time of crisis, just who can we turn to?"

Appeal to Authority

As we discussed in Chapter 1, we are understandably reliant on authority in many areas of our lives. Much of what we learn, we are taught by authorities. And since we never arrive at the stage of knowing everything, of being experts in every field, we continue to rely on authority from time to time throughout our lives. But this can lead to error. The risk is that we might rely too heavily on authority or rely on authority when we shouldn't. *If we arrive at conclusions by an improper appeal to authority we commit a fallacy. When is an appeal to authority improper? When the appeal is considered absolutely decisive on its own, when the authority appealed to is not genuinely expert in the relevant field, is not to be trusted, or when the genuine experts in the field are divided on the issue, the fallacy of false or questionable authority is commited.* It's possible to distinguish several specific varieties of this fallacy, including appeal to invincible authority, appeal to authorities with irrelevant expertise, testimonials, appeal to unidentified experts, appeal to experts with axes to grind, and appeal to partisan experts when expert opinion is divided.

Invincible Authority   *When an appeal to authority wipes out all other considerations, it constitutes a fallacious appeal to authority.* Such appeals to **invincible authority** have a notorious kind of currency within cults, or groups whose organization depends on subordinating all personal autonomy. A number of vivid and scary accounts have emerged in recent years of cults such as Scientology, the Moonies, the Rajneeshees and Jonestown (where several hundred followers of Reverend Jim Jones were led to commit mass suicide). These accounts illustrate the danger of allowing reality to be defined by appeal to the unassailable pronouncements of some "spiritual leader."

But such appeals are by no means confined to the dark and sinister world of spiritual fascism. We find fallacious appeals to invincible authority in, of all places, the history of science, where, for example, Galileo's colleagues refused to look into his telescope because they were convinced that no evidence whatsoever could possibly contradict Aristotle's account of astronomy. This is no isolated aberration, by the way. Galileo himself makes a similar argument in *Dialogues Concerning Two New Sciences,* when he says:

> But can you doubt that air has weight when you have the clear testimony of Aristotle affirming that all the elements have weight including air, and excepting only fire?

Irrelevant Expertise   *When the appeal is to an authority whose expertise is in some field other than the one at issue, the appeal is to **irrelevant expertise.*** For example, quoting the political or economic opinions of a distinguished physicist like Oppenheimer or Einstein is fallacious because the massive weight of an Einstein's opinion in the field of physics may not transfer to other fields. Of course, it is entirely possible that a brilliant and distinguished thinker in one specialty might be quite well informed and insightful in other areas as well. But to accept such a person's judgments outside the established area of expertise and on the basis solely of the person's reputation is to commit a fallacious appeal to authority.

Testimonials   *A common variety of appeal to irrelevant expertise is the celebrity **testimonial.*** Examples of testimonials abound in advertising, where celebrities are used to endorse everything from aspirin to presidential candidates. Here are just a few:

> Take it from Bruce Jenner: "You need a good start to get in shape. And I can't think of a better start than a complete breakfast with Wheaties."

> "Elke Sommer knows watching her nutrition counts as much as watching her weight. So she's starting her day with Special K breakfast. That's good for Elke, and good for you, too."

> Don Meredith for Lipton Tea: "What makes me a Lipton Tea lover? Lipton tastes so damn good."

> Robert Young for Sanka: "I think it's important that we take care of ourselves. That's why doctors [remember he used to play Marcus Welby, M.D.] have advised millions of caffeine-concerned Americans, like me, to drink delicious Sanka De-caffeinated Coffee."

That last ad, with its reference to doctors, illustrates not only how the prestige of a profession can take on significance as a testimonial, but also how specialized expertise—in this case medical expertise—can be personified by a famous actor who presumably lacks it. This particular variety of fallacious testimonial hit a new low in the famous ad for an over-the-counter pain reliever, which began:

> I'm not a doctor, but I play one on TV . . .

Celebrity endorsements effectively short-circuit the reasoning process: They are meant to substitute for the scrutiny you should give a product before purchasing, a candidate before voting, or a cause before supporting it.

Unidentified Experts   *Frequently expert opinion is merely alluded to, or is identified in such a vague or incomplete way that its reliability, accuracy, and weight are impossible to verify. This is the* **fallacy of unidentified experts.** This is a favorite device of tabloids such as the *National Enquirer,* which use phrases like "experts agree," "university studies show," "a Russian scientist has discovered," to lend the weight of authority to all sorts of quackery. Here's an interesting one from Anacin:

> Doctors recommend one pain reliever most: the one you get in Anacin.

(Of course you get the same pain reliever, aspirin, in a smorgasbord of other analgesics. But consumers are unlikely to notice this, which is exactly how this sort of testimonial is designed to work. Thus, this example can also be understood as a case of false implication of uniqueness—see Chapter 2.)

Experts with Axes to Grind   *Sometimes claims are advanced by appeal to experts who do have impressive and genuinely relevant credentials, but whose testimony may legitimately be suspected due to a demonstrable conflict of interest. These people are* **experts with axes to grind.** Suppose our attention is directed to an inconclusive study of the effects of secondhand tobacco smoke conducted at a reputable institution under the direction of someone with genuine scientific credentials. Now suppose we learn that the study was underwritten by a research grant supplied by the Tobacco Institute. We should at least look for other studies to compare this one with.

Now you might wonder, What's the difference between this example and poisoning the well or guilt by association? Notice that we are not simply dismissing the evidence on an automatic basis by considering its source, which would amount to well poisoning. We are not refusing to consider the evidence nor are we automatically assuming that it is false. Rather, we are not treating the evidence as decisive; we are suspending judgment and discounting the weight of the authority with which the evidence is introduced pending additional evidence from sources more likely to be objective and impartial.

Division of Expert Opinion   Issues often arise within specialized fields of expertise so that expert opinion is divided. *When the experts disagree, citing the authority of representatives of one side or the other fails to settle the issue and constitutes a fallacy, the* **division of expert opinion.** A good example of controversy among the experts recently occurred within the medical profession. A widely known research team, Masters, Johnson, and Kolodny, challenged the prevailing medical estimates of the rate and risk of the spread of AIDS in the heterosexual population. They went further to claim that there is a significant risk of contracting the virus through mosquito bites and exchange of saliva and other kinds of "casual contact." Their findings were in turn challenged by researchers at the Centers for Disease Control and other recognized experts in epidemiology. In such a climate of controversy it would be inadequate simply to quote Masters, Johnson, and Kolodny, or their critics, in support of an assessment of these risks. What one needs to do, when there is no consensus among the experts, is to look more closely at their competing arguments.

As you can see, there are quite a few pitfalls to watch out for in appealing to authority. However, bear in mind that appealing to authority is not always fallacious. So long as (1) the authority is truly an expert in the field, (2) the authority is trustworthy, (3) there is a consensus of expert opinion to corroborate the claim, and (4) one could in theory verify the claim for oneself, then the appeal to authority is legitimate. For example, suppose someone claimed that smoking was harmful and based that judgment on the opinion of the Surgeon General. The appeal here is presumably legitimate because (1) the Surgeon General is an expert witness, (2) in the absence of any specific evidence to the contrary, the Surgeon General may be presumed trustworthy in this matter, (3) there is agreement among medical experts that smoking is indeed harmful, and (4) in theory one could verify the claim for oneself if one took the time to conduct scientifically valid experiments.

In addition to the six ways of appealing to false or questionable authority just discussed, there are a number of other fallacies closely enough related to authority to deserve mention here: popularity, positioning, tradition, novelty, and provincialism.

Popularity Closely related to the fallacious appeal to authority is the appeal to popular opinion: "Five million people have already seen this movie. Shouldn't you?"; "Why do I think that the president's program is sound? Because the polls indicate that the vast majority supports it"; "By a margin of two to one, shoppers prefer Brand X to any other of the leading competitors. Reason enough to buy Brand X." *In the **appeal to popularity** sheer numbers are substituted for individual testimonial. Popular opinion in effect takes on the weight of authority.* But since it is possible for a large population to be mistaken or misled, as history has amply demonstrated time and again, such an appeal is not a reliable guide to the truth.

Positioning *Just as people sometimes attempt to discredit others through associations, they can just as effectively promote themselves and others by **positioning**, by capitalizing on the reputation of a leader in a field to sell a product, candidate, or idea.* Here's how it works.

Suppose a car rental agency such as Avis advertises, We're the world's second largest car-rental agency. Since we're second, we must try harder. Avis successfully positions itself next to the leader, Hertz, thereby creating through transference a position in the consumer's mind. Goodrich uses this technique masterfully when it reminds us, We're the ones without the blimp.

In advertising, positioning creates a spot for a company in the prospective buyer's mind by invoking not only the company's image but also that of, usually, its leading competitor. The assumption here is that the consumer's mind has become an advertising battleground. So a successful advertising strategy involves relating to what has already been established in the consumer's mind. Thus, although RCA and General Electric tried in vain to buck IBM directly in the computer market, the smaller Honeywell succeeded using the theme "the other computer company."

Positioning is hardly confined to advertising. During presidential election years in which a popular incumbent is running for reelection, many a congressional campaign is based almost entirely on party affiliation with the incumbent president. This is called "riding on the president's coattails." In politics, part of waging a successful campaign often means trading on the reputation of another well-known, popular political figure. Thus, candidates of both parties are forever attempting to appropriate the mantle of a Lincoln or a Kennedy, by invoking lines from their famous speeches and forging all sorts of tenuous connections. In a rather striking case in 1988, Republican presidential hopeful Pat Robertson attempted, unsuccessfully, to overcome public skepticism based on his background as a televangelist by pointing out that JFK had had to overcome anti-Catholic prejudice in his first campaign.

Tradition   *The **appeal to tradition** consists of assuming or arguing that something is good or desirable simply because it is old or traditional.* Jane's friend tells her, "I don't think you should keep your maiden name after marrying. In this culture the woman always takes her husband's name. That's what distinguishes a married woman from a single one." Although there may be good reasons for a woman's not keeping her maiden name after marrying, this isn't one of them. Jane is trying to link her opinion to a long-standing custom, that is, to what has been historically approved by society. But why must custom necessarily dictate present behavior? It needn't, and that's the point.

Recall the frequent appeals to tradition during the attempt to impeach President Richard Nixon in 1974. Many insisted that Nixon should not be impeached because a U.S. president never before had been successfully impeached. In other words, they tried to protect Nixon by invoking a tradition of reluctance to impeach presidents, urging that the future be fashioned in the image of the past. But merely because a president never had been impeached was not reason enough to conclude that Nixon, or any subsequent president for that matter, should not be impeached. Indeed, the fact that a president had never before been impeached was irrelevant to the issue of whether or not to impeach Nixon.

Certain phrases often signal an attempt to summon tradition to the support of a claim. Among them are "tried and true," "the lessons of history," "from time immemorial," "the Founding Fathers," "the earliest settlers," and so on. Of course the appeal to tradition is not always fallacious. The question of whether or not something is in line with tradition is not always irrelevant to the issue. For example, if you are trying to decide whether such and such a costume is suitable for the Founder's Day Parade, appeal to tradition may be legitimate. But most issues are such that tradition in and of itself is irrelevant.

Novelty   In contrast to the appeal to tradition, but just as deadly to correct reasoning, is the **appeal to novelty,** *which consists of assuming or arguing that something is good or desirable simply because it is new.* In the elections of 1980, 1984, and 1988, a number of candidates argued or used slogans like

"Leadership for a change," which, besides suggesting by innuendo that the incumbent was providing no leadership, meant to many people a change in economic and social philosophy. There may be solid reasons for so altering the nation's course, but change for the sake of change is not one of them. Every policy, law, idea, program, or action requires justification independent of its novel character. That a politician represents "new ideas" or a proposal offers a "new approach" is not a logical defense, although it sometimes is an appealing one.

Provincialism *Provincialism occurs when our thinking is dominated by considerations of group loyalty. To appeal to considerations of group loyalty in support of a claim, or to arrive at a conclusion simply on the basis of such considerations, is to commit the fallacy of* ***provincialism.***

During the heated debate in 1980 over the treaty that would transfer responsibility for maintaining the Panama Canal from the United States to Panama, provincialism resounded throughout the land. Most of the arguments against the treaty assumed that (1) the United States had some kind of proprietary claim over the canal, or (2) Americans were uniquely qualified to run the canal. The provincialism came in when it was suggested, as it was frequently, that to question either of these assumptions was unpatriotic and disloyal.

The fallacy of provincialism need not be confined to examples of national loyalty. Sometimes the group identified with is considerably smaller, perhaps a professional, occupational, or religious group, or a school, or a team. Sometimes the group is even larger than a nation: a gender, for example.

***Quick Check on Appeals to Authority
(Answers on Page 405)**

Identify and explain the authority-related appeal, if any, in the following passages in terms of the categories just discussed: invincible authority, irrelevant expertise, testimonials, unidentified experts, experts with axes to grind, division of expert opinion, popularity, positioning, tradition, novelty, and provincialism.

1. Letter to the Editor responding to the question "Do you care about preserving the local July 4th fireworks show?": "My son is a native of this city. After college and the Army his best job opportunity was back East. This summer he plans to spend over two weeks here with his wife and three sons. He deliberately planned his vacation through July 4 just to experience the fireworks display. I will have one disappointed family if the fireworks are cancelled."

2. Letter to the Editor responding to the same question: "Not celebrate the 4th of July with fireworks? What would John Adams say?—having been the very first to advocate the very day after independence was declared, that the birth of our nation ought to be 'celebrated by succeeding generations as the great anniversary

festival'? What would our founding fathers say?—who planted the seeds of liberty and Christianity on a wilderness shore, not for themselves only, but for their children and their children's children?"

3. "According to my dentist, sugar contributes to tooth decay."

4. Owner of a San Francisco restaurant, reacting against a proposed truth-in-advertising ordinance requiring restaurant owners to identify food prepared off the premises and then frozen: "Three-quarters or seven-eighths of the people who come into my place . . . don't give a good goddamn." (*Los Angeles Times*, July 4, 1974, part 1, p. 11.)

5. Speaking in 1983 in front of the Brandenburg Gate, which divides Berlin into East and West sectors, Ronald Reagan struck a chord reminiscent of JFK's famous declaration *"Ich bin ein Berliner"* ("I am a Berliner"). Said Reagan: "I join you as I join our belief: Es gibt nur ein Berlin (There is only one Berlin). . . . Like so many Presidents before me, I come here today because wherever I go, whatever I do: Ich habe noch einen Koffer in Berlin (I still have a suitcase in Berlin [a line from a popular song])."

6. "The picture of reliability. To Magnavox it's the idea that every time you turn on one of our color television sets you know it's going to do what you bought it to do. Our Star® System color television sets combine advanced design concepts, high technology and new manufacturing systems to deliver the highest level of reliability in Magnavox history. Magnavox. For a picture as reliable as it is bright and clear. Time after time. Magnavox. The bright ideas in the world are here today."

7. "We started flying four years ahead of the world's most experienced airline." (ad for Sabena Airline)

8. The Golden Rule is a sound moral principle because it is part of every ethical system ever devised.

Emotional Appeals

A special category of irrelevant appeal involves the invocation of emotion in support of a claim. Emotions can exert a powerful influence over our thinking, but they are not always relevant to the issue at hand. Three of the most common informal fallacies that make irrelevant appeal to emotion are mob appeal, appeal to pity, and appeal to fear or force.

Mob Appeal *The fallacy of **mob appeal** consists in the attempt to win assent to a view by arousing the emotions of a group en masse.* One could say that the fallacy of mob appeal is what happens when the skills of oratory run amok. Oratory is the art of public eloquence, of moving an audience as a body with words. A skillful public speaker will usually understand the common needs and drives likely to be shared by the overwhelming majority of the members of a given audience: the drive for emotional security, for self-esteem, for acceptance, status, and so on, and will naturally couch her argument in terms chosen to appeal to and gratify these needs. But when a public speaker succeeds in stampeding an audience by means of such methods and in the absence of good reasons a fallacious mob appeal has been committed.

Perhaps the best classical example of mob appeal is Mark Antony's famous funeral oration in Shakespeare's *Julius Caesar* (Act 3, Scene 2). Antony is called on by Brutus to address the crowd assembled at Caesar's funeral. He is introduced by Brutus, who with other conspirators had assassinated Caesar and who has already convinced the crowd that the assassination was in the best interests of Rome. Antony's speech, which begins with the famous line "Friends, Romans, Countrymen, . . ." immediately gains the crowd's sympathy and gradually and imperceptibly, but very quickly, subverts Brutus's bid to succeed Caesar and in the end incites the mob against Brutus and his fellow conspirators. The speech is of course a work of art, but it accomplishes its goal by a combination of flattery, innuendo, staging, timing, and repetition, and with a notable lack of real argument. The main engine of its effectiveness, though, is the momentum of the emotional energy generated within the crowd. To the extent that the speech is deliberately designed to fuel, direct, and exploit the crowd's reaction, rather than present an argument in support of rising up against Brutus, it is a case of mob appeal.[1]

Appeal to Pity A device frequently exploited in sales presentations and in attempts to secure special dispensation or exemption from deadlines and penalties, *the* **appeal to pity** *is a fallacious but often effective strategy that attempts to persuade people by making them feel sorrow, sympathy, or anguish, where such feelings, however understandable and genuine, are not relevant to the issue at stake.*

For example, the student who deserves a *C* in History might try to persuade his teacher to raise his grade for a variety of lamentable reasons: It's the first grade below a *B* he's ever received; it spoils a 3.85 GPA; he needs a higher grade to qualify for law school; and his family has taken a third mortgage to finance his pre-law education.

A word of caution. Invoking sympathy is not always irrelevant to the issue. For example, when an attorney asks a judge to take into consideration the squalid upbringing of a client in determining a criminal sentence, this is probably not a fallacious appeal to pity. Although such an appeal would be irrelevant and fallacious in arguing for the person's innocence, it may be perfectly germane to the question of the severity of the sentence. Think of the German youth who in the summer of 1987 flew a small plane into the middle of Red Square in Moscow. That he may have been acting out of simple youthful exuberance rather than some motive more threatening to Soviet national security is irrelevant to whether he acted illegally, but it's not irrelevant to how severely he should be punished.

Appeal to Fear or Force *A similar strategy involves attempting to intimidate people into accepting a position through an* **appeal to fear or force.** The strategy takes the basic form, Believe this (or do this), or else! For example, in the late 1980s, as the public policy issue over secondhand smoke swung more and more in the direction of segregrating smokers and restricting them to designated smoking areas, the Philip Morris corporation launched what became quite a controversial campaign, with full-page ads in major newspapers, such as the one in the *New York Times* that read as follows:

> **$1 trillion is too much financial power to ignore.**
> America's 55.8 million smokers are a powerful economic force. If their household income of $1 trillion were a Gross National Product, it would be the third largest in the world. The plain truth is that smokers are one of the most economically powerful groups in this country. They help fuel the engine of the largest economy on the globe.
> **The American Smoker—an economic force.**

The implication was pretty clear. Municipalities and private businesses (such as restaurants and airline companies) that might be considering the adoption of policies restricting or banning smoking have something to fear: a possible trillion-dollar boycott.

---

*Quick Check on Emotional Appeal (Answers on Page 406)

Identify and explain the fallacious emotional appeal, if any, in the following passages in terms of the categories just discussed: mob appeal, appeal to pity, appeal to fear or force.

1. Ronald Reagan during a radio address: "When you hear talk about a tough trade bill, remember that being tough on trade and commerce, the lifeblood of the economy, will have the worst possible consequences for the consumer and American worker."

2. Shortly after her husband's election to his first Senate term in 1972, the wife of Senator Joseph Biden was killed and his two sons seriously injured in an auto accident. Biden, who remarried and fathered a daughter, has maintained his home in Wilmington, Delaware, and, it is said, commutes there almost every night to be with his family. In introducing Biden on the occasion Biden was to announce what turned out to be his very short campaign for the presidency, fellow Democrat Senator Daniel Inouye of Hawaii referred to that tragedy and to Biden's life-style: "That's fatherhood, that's family. This nation needs a President with a family."

3. In May 1983, George Bush, then vice president, posed dramatically with several hundred pounds of cocaine and stacks of greenbacks confiscated from dope smugglers. Proof positive, said Bush, that Fidel Castro was trying to destabilize the United States by smuggling drugs into Florida and other entry points. Other administration officials staged similar displays, designed to

associate leaders of the Sandinista government in Nicaragua with dope trafficking.

Diversion

A common argumentative strategy consists of attempting to divert attention from an issue, especially where one lacks effective arguments relevant to it. This is a particular favorite of public figures when they find themselves called upon to address delicate or controversial topics and are not well enough prepared. Caught in such a bind, officials (and office seekers) frequently respond to an embarrassing question by answering some other question, usually without explicitly indicating that this is what they are doing. Sometimes a speaker will give explicit indication of a shift in focus: "Before I answer this question, Ted, let me make a few things clear. . . ." This sort of thing, followed by a long and winding excursion through a number of relatively complicated points, may effectively leave the original topic buried in obscurity.

A caution: As we've already discussed, sometimes a question may itself be loaded or slanted or otherwise objectionable, so that an exposé of the assumptions underlying it, in place of a direct answer to it, would be perfectly appropriate. However, if a diversionary tactic is used simply as a means of evading a perfectly reasonable question, this too is worth pointing out as a fallacious move. There are a number of common diversionary strategies worth individual mention.

Humor or Ridicule   A common variety of the diversionary strategy is the **appeal to humor and ridicule.** *When one is stuck for a good argument, and sometimes even when one isn't, getting a laugh out of one's audience can be an effective substitute.* For example, a member of the British Parliament named Thomas Massey-Massey once introduced a bill to change the name of "Christmas" to "Christide." He reasoned as follows: Since "mass" is a Catholic term and since Britons are largely Protestant, they should avoid the suffix "mass" in "Christ*mas*." On hearing the proposal another member suggested that Christmas might not want its name changed. "How would you like it," he asked Thomas Massey-Massey, "if we changed your name to Thotide Tidey-Tidey?" The bill died in the ensuing laughter.

Similarly, a story is told of an incident that occurred at the Yalta meeting of the Allied leaders Franklin D. Roosevelt, Winston Churchill, and Joseph Stalin. Churchill reportedly mentioned that the Pope had suggested a particular course of action as the right one, whereupon Stalin is said to have replied, "And how many divisions did you say the Pope had available for combat duty?" thus diverting attention from the issues through a form of ridicule.

Two Wrongs   *A particularly common fallacy of diversion where moral blameworthiness is at issue involves introducing an irrelevant comparison to other instances of wrongdoing, the fallacy of* **two wrongs.** For example, a police officer stops a speeding motorist. "Why stop me?" the driver asks. "Didn't you see that Jaguar fly by at eighty miles per hour?" The motorist is trying to divert attention from his own infraction, and perhaps to excuse it, by pointing out the wrongdoing

242

of another. But what other motorists are doing is irrelevant to whether this motorist has exceeded the speed limit.

The two-wrongs fallacy takes two general forms:

1. Tu Quoque *Tu quoque* is Latin for "you also," or "you too," or more colloquially, "Look who's talking!" *In its **Tu quoque** form, the two-wrongs fallacy consists of accusing one's critic of what he is criticizing.* For example, Brad advises Beth to get more exercise. Beth reminds Brad that, being the world's greatest couch potato, he's in no position to give such advice. Again, a mother cautions her teenage son against using drugs. "That's a laugh coming from you," he replies. "You smoke, drink, and use caffeine." Even if Brad is sedentary and Mom is addicted to alcohol, nicotine, and caffeine, that doesn't make their advice any less sage. And it is the advice that's at issue, not whether or not those who preach it practice it.

2. Common Practice Sometimes, rather than appealing to a single instance of similar wrongdoing, people appeal to a widely accepted or long-standing practice to divert attention from and excuse their behavior. Caught using company stationery for personal use, a worker may say, Everybody else does it. In other words, since helping themselves to company stationery is a common practice of workers in this office, it's okay for me to do it.

Straw Person *The fallacy of **straw person** consists of so altering a position that the new version is easier to attack than the original, or of setting up a position to attack so that one's alternative position will appear stronger by comparison.* The name of this fallacy says what it accomplishes: It sets up a "straw" that's easy to "blow over." Of course, the straw version is not the original, but that's precisely the point: The altered version makes an easier, although irrelevant target.

A common device for erecting straws is *exaggeration*. For example, suppose a mother objects to her son's going out on a school night before a test. The son responds: "What! You're telling me that I can't ever go out on weeknights? That's unreasonable." The real issue concerns going out on this particular weeknight before a test. The straw issue is not ever going out on a weeknight.

Another way to erect a straw is through *distortion*. For example, wanting to engage students in the electoral process, a school board votes to give students released time during an election to campaign for the candidates and issues of their choice. An angry citizen accuses the board of conspiring to get liberals elected and conservatives thrown out of office. The real issue: political involvement through released time; the straw issue: partisan politics.

Notice how much easier it is in each case to assail the straw issue than the real issue. This is what makes the straw person such an effective and insidious diversion and attack ploy.

A common species of this sort of thing involves the assumption that proponents of the interests of one group are antagonistic to the interests of some other group, as for instance when supporters of the Equal Rights Amendment were characterized as antimale, or when critics of U.S. foreign policy are characterized as pro-Soviet and unpatriotic, or when critics of antipornography leg-islation are labeled as supporters of pornography. One can be in favor of a constitutional amendment guaranteeing against gender discrimination without being antimale. One can be critical of U.S. foreign policy on perfectly patriotic grounds, and equally critical of Soviet foreign policy as well. One can be opposed to antipornography legislation on grounds that it would compromise the principle of freedom of speech, and one might be interested in preserving this principle simply as a crucial hedge against tyranny. When the American Civil Liberties Union took the case of the American Nazi party in its attempt to obtain a parade permit in Skokie, Illinois, they did so not because they were pro-Nazi, but in order to defend the First Amendment from what they argued would be a serious erosion in principle. To attack their position as pro-Nazi, as some did, would have been to attack a straw person.

Since there is a predictable, general human tendency to want to understand one's opponent's position in a way one feels confident to dispute, it is generally wise not to accept, without question, the account or description of a position or an argument given by someone opposed to it. Sometimes opponents do give a fair account of positions they oppose, but certainly not always. The best technique we're aware of for detecting straw person arguments, and for avoiding them in one's own reasoning, is to pretend you're the person whose position is being criticized and ask if the criticism does justice to the position you imagine yourself now to be defending.

Red Herring *A common diversionary tactic consists of presenting facts that do not support the position at issue but some other position that vaguely resembles it. This tactic has come to be known as the* **red herring,** a colorful name that derives from an old ruse used by prison escapees to throw dogs off their trails. The escapees would smear themselves with herring (which turns red when it spoils) to cover their scent.

For example, in charging an executive with embezzlement, a prosecutor quotes harrowing statistics about white-collar crime. Although her statistical evidence may influence the jury, it is irrelevant to establishing the guilt of the defendant. The alarming statistics only support the assertion that white-collar crime is a serious social problem. They give no support to the charge that the defendant is guilty of embezzlement and in fact divert attention from it.

Summary

An important informal consideration in evaluating arguments is whether the premises appealed to are relevant to what is at issue. If they are, so much the better for the argument. If not, some kind of fallacy of relevance, or irrelevant appeal, has been committed.

A general strategy for exposing irrelevant appeals is to challenge the relevance of the premise to the conclusion of the argument or to the issue under discussion. Bear in mind, however, that to challenge the relevance of a premise is not the same as establishing that it *is* irrelevant. Relevance is not always obvious on the surface. So it remains open to the arguer to meet the challenge by explaining how the premise bears on the conclusion or issue. But if a premise *is* relevant, it should be possible to explain the connection.

A more pointed strategy for exposing irrelevant appeals is to assimilate an argument to one of the common categories of irrelevant appeal. Perhaps the most common of the informal fallacies of relevance is the ad hominem argument. When people argue ad hominem, they attack the person, not the person's position or argument.

Ad hominem commonly takes two forms: abusive, which consists of attacking characteristics of the person; and circumstantial, which consists of trying to persuade someone to accept a position because of the special facts or circumstances of the person's life. The fallacy of guilt by association, a special case of circumstantial ad hominem argument, consists of making negative judgments about people, or their positions and arguments, solely on the basis of their relationships with others.

A similar fallacy, called genetic appeal, consists of evaluating something strictly in terms of its origin, sources, or genesis.

A similar fallacious argumentative strategy, called poisoning the well, consists of attempting to discredit a position, or its advocate, before the argument for the position has had a chance to get a hearing.

The fallacy of false or questionable authority is committed when we arrive at conclusions by an improper appeal to authority. An appeal to authority is improper when the appeal is considered absolutely decisive on its own, when the authority appealed to is not genuinely expert in the relevant field, is not to be trusted, or when the genuine experts in the field are divided on the issue. However, bear in mind that appealing to authority is not always fallacious. So long as (1) the authority is truly an expert in the field, (2) the authority is trustworthy, (3) there is a consensus of expert opinion to corroborate the claim, and (4) one could in theory verify the claim for oneself, then the appeal to authority is legitimate.

There are a number of fallacies closely related to authority: popularity, positioning, tradition, novelty, and provincialism.

The appeal to popularity consists of arguing for a position on the basis of popular opinion, which in effect takes on the weight of authority.

Just as people sometimes attempt to discredit others through associations, they can just as effectively promote themselves and others by positioning, by capitalizing on the reputation of a leader in a field to sell a product, candidate, or idea.

The appeal to tradition consists of assuming or arguing that something is good or desirable simply because it is old or traditional.

The appeal to novelty consists of assuming or arguing that something is good or desirable simply because it is new.

Provincialism occurs when our thinking is dominated by consider- ations of group loyalty. To appeal to considerations of group loyalty in support of a claim, or to arrive at a conclusion simply from such con- siderations, is to commit the fallacy of provincialism.

A special category of irrelevant appeal involves the invocation of emotion in support of a claim. Three of the most common informal fallacies that make irrelevant appeal to emotion are mob appeal, appeal to pity, and appeal to fear or force.

The fallacy of mob appeal is the attempt to win assent to a view by arousing the emotions of a group en masse.

Appeal to pity is the attempt to persuade people by making them feel sorrow, sympathy, or anguish, where such feelings, however un- derstandable and genuine, are not relevant to the issue at stake.

Appeal to fear or force involves attempting to intimidate people into accepting a position.

A common argumentative strategy is to attempt to divert attention from an issue, especially where one lacks effective arguments relevant to it.

A common variety of the diversionary strategy is the appeal to humor and ridicule. When one is stuck for a good argument, and sometimes even when one isn't, getting a laugh out of one's audience can be an effective substitute.

A particularly common fallacy of diversion where moral blamewor- thiness is at issue involves introducing an irrelevant comparison to other instances of wrongdoing. The two-wrongs fallacy takes two general forms: In its *tu quoque* form, the two-wrongs fallacy consists of accusing one's critic of what he is criticizing. Sometimes, rather than appealing to a single instance of similar wrongdoing, people appeal to a widely ac- cepted or long-standing practice to divert attention from and excuse their behavior.

The fallacy of straw person consists of so altering a position that the new version is easier to attack than the original, or of setting up a position to attack so that one's alternative position will appear stronger by comparison.

The fallacy of red herring consists of presenting facts that do not support the position at issue but some other position that vaguely re- sembles it.

Applications

1. Once again, with your study partner, take turns critically examining the following examples in terms of the informal fallacy categories you have learned so far, including those covered in the previous chapter, and testing your critical assessments for clarity and fairness.

a. Republican presidential candidate Jack Kemp in a 1988 televised presidential primary debate, attacking the eventual Republican nominee George Bush (who was supporting the ratification of the INF Treaty with the Soviet Union): "I can't believe I'm hearing a Republican say 'Let's give peace a chance'!"

b. Philip Morris vice president for corporate affairs, Guy L. Smith, in defending the Philip Morris ad campaign mentioned in this chapter against the criticism that it was designed to appeal to fear, said the ads were "an attempt to raise the level of awareness, but certainly not to scare anybody."

c. From an editorial: "Because of the unique position of Justice Lewis F. Powell, Jr., at the ideological center of a divided Supreme Court, the person who replaces him will have a major hand in determining the next generation of constitutional law. Judge Robert H. Bork at the D.C. Circuit Court of Appeals, who was nominated by President Reagan, is a rock-solid right-winger in the mold of Chief Justice William H. Rehnquist and Associate Justice Antonin Scalia. . . ."

d. "Precisely what is Nixon accused of doing . . . that his predecessors didn't do many times over? The break-in and wire-tapping at the Watergate? Just how different was that from the bugging of Barry Goldwater's apartment during the 1964 presidential campaign?" (Victor Lasky, "It Didn't Start with Watergate," *Book Digest*, November 1977, p. 47.)

e. "Many of my colleagues in the press are upset about the growing practice of paying newsmakers for news. The auction principle seems to them to strike somehow at the freedom of the press, or at least the freedom of the poor press to compete with the rich press. But I find their objections pious and, in an economy where everything and everybody has its price, absurd." (Shana Alexander, "Loew's Common Denominator," *Newsweek*, April 14, 1975, p. 96.)

f. "Repressive environmentalists and population and economic zero-growthers have requested President Reagan to oust James G. Watt as Secretary of the Interior. Those stop-all-progress destructionists have thick-skinned craniums. They lack the intelligence to realize that the United States of America is no longer a subsidiary of the baby-and-people hating and business-repressive do-gooders. President Reagan and Secretary Watt have done what should have been done long ago. Their critics can go to blazes on a one-way ticket." (Letter to the Editor, *Los Angeles Times,* July 24, 1981, part 2, p. 6.)

g. A Soviet official, commenting on the Reagan administration's unwillingness to negotiate key issues, such as the location of the Soviet Union's SS-20 missiles and a new Strategic Arms Limitation Treaty: "We shall continue to urge real negotiations but our patience is not unlimited. This does not mean, of course, that we would start a war, but ultimately if there is not change we will have to counter measures being taken by your administration with measures of our own. We don't want to do this. It can only result in a dangerous spiral. This would be a very dangerous development." (Fred Warner Neal, "America Frustrates Soviets—and That's Dangerous," *Los Angeles Times,* July 31, 1981, part 2, p. 7.)

h. When the Senate Judiciary Committee, headed by Senator Joseph Biden, began to challenge the nomination of Robert Bork to the Supreme Court, Vice President George Bush said, "I find it ironic that Senator Biden would take issue with Judge Bork's judicial philosophy. That philosophy is one of judicial restraint, and what that means above all else is that Congress should make the laws, not the court."

i. "Everybody complains about the U.S. mail these days—prices going up and service down. But our Postal Service seems like a winner compared with the Canadian one. In fact, our neighbors to the north have elevated post-office bashing into a national sport." ("This World," *San Francisco Chronicle,* July 26, 1981, p. 5. The article goes on to catalog deficiencies in the Canadian postal system.)

j. President Reagan suggesting a way to pacify those who object to the sight of oil rigs off their beaches: "Maybe we ought to take some of those liberty ships out of mothballs and anchor one at each one of the oil platforms between that and onshore, because people never objected to seeing a ship at sea." ("Reagan Backs Watt Stand," *Santa Barbara Evening News Press,* August 5, 1981, p. A4.)

k. "Congress put [members of the Reagan administration] in a no-win situation in its eagerness to hamstring the president. Those who voted Boland [the Boland Amendment, which prohibited U.S. aid to the Nicaraguan contras] into law are men of their party first and their country second. . . ." (Jesse Hill Ford, novelist and free-lance writer)

l. During a speech in which they advocated AIDS testing for immigrants, federal prisoners, and people getting marriage licenses, Ronald Reagan and George Bush were noisily jeered by some of the 7,000 scientists and doctors comprising the audience. "What was that, some gay groups out there?" Bush asked over a microphone he didn't realize was live.

m. "It's amazing that the Constitution of the United States says nothing about the separation of church and state. That phrase does appear, however, in the Soviet constitution. . . . People in the education Establishment, and in our judicial establishment, have attempted to impose Soviet structures on the United States. . . ." (Televangelist Pat Robertson in a 1986 *Conservative Digest* interview)

n. Secretary [of State George P.] Shultz and [Defense] Secretary [Caspar] Weinberger both predicted that the American people would immediately assume this whole plan was an arms for hostages deal and nothing more. Unfortunately, their predictions were right. . . . I let my preoccupation with the hostages intrude into areas where it didn't belong. The image— the reality—of Americans in chains, deprived of their freedom and families so far from home, burdened my thought. . . ." (President Reagan)

o. Lt. Colonel Oliver North on his rationale for exchanging arms for hostages in Iran: "I'll tell you right now, I'd have offered the Iranians a free trip to Disneyland if we could have gotten Americans home for it."

p. ". . . our State department is opposed to punishing diplomats (for crimes committed on U.S. soil). At Senate hearings Selwa Roosevelt, chief of protocol, said the United States should not punish diplomats because 'we are an honorable nation—we are not Iran. . .' Well, I've got news for her: Foreign countries take harmful actions against our diplomats *now*. Our diplomats have been kidnapped and killed all over the world. Iran took our diplomats hostage for 444 days. . . ." (Roger Simon, "For Hundreds, Law Doesn't Matter," *Los Angeles Times*, August 26, 1987, Part V, p. 5.)

2. With the benefit of the discussions you have had with your study partner, briefly and carefully explain the fallacies you found in each of the preceding examples.

You may find it useful in some cases to cast the argument as a first step.

3. With your study partner, take turns critically examining the examples in the Quick Check exercises in this chapter in terms of the informal fallacy categories you have learned so far, including those covered in the previous chapter, and testing your critical assessments for clarity and fairness. See if you can find any fallacies in addition to the ones you found originally when you worked the Quick Checks.

4. Find examples of your own in the public media of the informal fallacies discussed in this chapter. For each example, give a brief but careful explanation of the fallacies you find in it.

5. Remember that a given argument can have more than one thing wrong with it. With that in mind, go back over the examples in the Applications section of the previous chapter. Give a brief and careful explanation of any additional fallacies you can find by using the fallacy categories developed in this chapter.

[1]For a more extensive analysis of this rhetorical classic see S. Morris Engel, *With Good Reason: An Introduction to Informal Fallacies,* 2nd ed. (New York: St. Martin's, 1982), pp. 176–180.

CRITICIZING ARGUMENTS IV: INFORMAL FALLACIES OF EVIDENCE

10

Evidence is information that is relevant to an inference. Thus a great deal of importance attaches to how evidence is evaluated and handled in the process of drawing inferences. The discussion of verifying observation statements and hypotheses in Chapter 6 gives you a basic introduction to reliable procedures for gathering, evaluating, and handling evidence. In addition, though, you should be aware of some of the more common pitfalls in this area. In this chapter, we will survey a number of common informal fallacies that have to do with the gathering, evaluating, and handling of evidence in inferential contexts.

It's probably worth mentioning *jumping to conclusions* at the outset as a useful general fallacy category, simply because it corresponds to such a widespread tendency in human reasoning. The tendency, which results from the longing for closure, the discomfort associated with suspended judgment mentioned in Chapter 1, is to accept a conclusion as settled before all of the relevant evidence is in.

In the most obvious and extreme cases, conclusions are hastily arrived at on the basis of single, if striking, instances. For example, on the basis of one sour romance, a man concludes, No woman can be trusted. Or, having been disappointed in one Raquel Welch movie, the viewer concludes, Obviously the woman can't act.

Several of the the more specific fallacies to be discussed in this chapter fall into this general category. But if you find an inference that doesn't seem to fall neatly into any one of these more specific categories, yet seems questionable, it may be that "jumping to conclusions" is the most accurate way to describe what has gone wrong. In criticizing an inference as a case of jumping to conclusions, it is helpful to be able to identify one or more factors that were left out in making the inference but that ought to have been taken into account.

IRREFUTABLE EVIDENCE

fragments of UFO that crash-landed last week near Lambert's Corner, Saskatchewan

Soil taken from site

Some photos taken just prior to landing of craft

Enlarged photo (B.)

Drawings done by Mrs. Kitty Nederson, witness, while under hypnosis

Tape recording of nearby dog barking uncontrollably at time of visitation

"Irrefutable Evidence." Drawing by R. Chast; © 1988 The New Yorker Magazine, Inc.

FALLACIES OF STATISTICAL INFERENCE

Let's now turn to a group of informal fallacies that plague inductive inferences in general and statistical studies more specifically.

You'll remember that an inductive inference is one in which the premises leave room for doubt as to the truth of the conclusion, although they do lend support to it as probable or likely. The main question, then, in assessing inductive arguments is, Given the evidence presented in the premises, how probable or likely is the conclusion? Accordingly, some of the most common pitfalls to inductive reasoning can conveniently be understood in terms of overestimating the strength of an inductive inference.

In Chapter 6 we explained that the strength of an inductive inference depends most heavily on two factors: the size and representativeness of the sample from which the evidence was taken. We can distinguish several informal fallacies of induction, each of which relates in some way to the size and representativeness of the sample.

Small Sample

Sometimes what appears to be a significant pattern in a small number of cases disappears altogether when we investigate a larger number of cases. For example, suppose we are taking a poll to determine political preferences and, of the first ten responses, seven favor the challenger over the incumbent. But by the time we have interviewed a hundred people we find the incumbent ahead seventy-five to twenty-one with four undecided. *The fallacy of* **small sample** *consists of overestimating the statistical significance of evidence drawn from a small number of cases.*

But one must be careful in applying this as a criticism. The size of the sample relative to the target population is not the only factor involved in determining the reliability of the inductive inference. Even a relatively small sample can be used to reliably project trends on a massive scale, if the study is carefully controlled and based on a representative sample. Thus, it would be insufficient basis for criticism merely to point out, for example, that a national political preference poll had been conducted on the basis of 5000 responses. In fact, a poll of just 1500, adhering to all the criteria of a scientifically respectable sample, can yield accurate information about the nation as a whole with a margin of error of only 3 percent. Doubling the sample would only reduce the margin of error by about 1 percent.

Unrepresentative Sample

But suppose the aforementioned 5000 responses were all taken from one geographical region. This regional bias would greatly increase the inference's liability to error. Fundamentally, the representativeness of a sample is even more important than sample size, since what one is trying to do by means of induction is to project conclusions that are affected by many variables. If one can control all of the relevant variables in a relatively small sample, so much the better for the economy of the study. The important thing is to control all the variables. But this can be very difficult to accomplish in an area such as political preference, which is affected by such a wide range of variables. The problem is made greater by the fact that not all of the relevant variables may be known. *The fallacy of* **unrepresentative sample** *consists of overestimating the statistical significance of evidence drawn from a sample of a particular kind.*

Perhaps the most famous example of a genuine, but failed, attempt to avoid this fallacy is the 1936 *Literary Digest* poll, which incorrectly predicted that Alf Landon would defeat Franklin Delano Roosevelt in the presidential race, on the basis of two million respondents selected at random from telephone directories and auto registration lists. The relevant variable that the poll overlooked was that in 1936 those who could afford a car or even a phone were relatively few and far between and had above-average income as well. In other words, because the sample was far from random it failed to truly represent the target population.

Randomness means that each member of the target population has an equal chance of appearing among the sample. If for example pollsters wish to find out what adult U.S. Catholics think about their church's official teaching on abortion, they must ensure that every U.S. Catholic is equally likely to be among those polled. Notice that this doesn't mean that every Catholic needs to be polled— only that they have an equal chance of being asked. If pollsters ask only California Catholics or New York Catholics, they violate randomness, and thus representativeness. We needn't detail here the techniques pollsters use to ensure randomness. Suffice it to say that professional polling organizations—Harris, Roper, Gallup, and the like—do work hard to ensure randomness in sampling. Informal poll taking often violates this critical criterion of a sound poll.

Slanted Study A statistical study is slanted when the methodology determines its outcome in some particular predetermined direction. An unrepresentative sample can slant a study. But a study can also be misleading if even a perfectly representative sample is asked to respond to leading questions, or questions that restrict the range of available responses. For example, suppose that you live in a community where rapid growth has stretched the existing waste management resources to the breaking point, resulting in environmental pollution serious enough to have raised public concern. Now suppose the local newspaper conducts a readers' poll asking

> Which of the following policy options would you prefer?
>
> 1. A municipal bond issue to construct new sewage treatment facilities.
> 2. A regional bond issue to construct a pipeline to transport excess sewage to the ocean.
> 3. An increase in property tax to pay for improvement and expansion of existing facilities.

Does this exhaust the range of available options? Hardly. Notice that each of the options mentioned presupposes acceptance of the present rate of growth. What about a tax on new development? What about a stiffer zoning policy or a statutory limit on growth? A poll that effectively excludes options from consideration is methodologically slanted against them.

By the same token, a question can be ambiguous or vague. For example, "Do you think it's a good practice for employers to seek out minority members and women for jobs?" Precisely what does "good practice" mean? Or the question can be loaded. For example, *"Given that the future of the free world depends on U.S. military strength,* do you think it's wise to reduce defense spending?"

Respondents can also slant a poll or study, because people often report not what they really think but what they think appropriate. Some years ago interviewers asked respondents, "What magazines does your household read?" A large percentage of households apparently read *Harper's* but not many read *True Story*. This was odd, since publishers' figures clearly showed that *True Story* tremendously outsold *Harper's*. After eliminating other possible explanations, pollsters finally concluded that a good many respondents had not responded truthfully.

Bad Base Line Statistics often invite misinterpretation, particularly in the direction of overestimating the significance of some trend. *The fallacy of **bad base line** consists of deriving an interpretation of statistical results on an inappropriate basis of comparison.* For example, suppose that in some small town the number of car thefts rises from three in one year to four in the next. This represents a 33 percent rise in the incidence of car theft in one year, but indicating it in these terms exaggerates the significance of the increase. Suppose, for example, that over the same period the town's population has doubled. In that case, the incidence of car theft *per capita* (that is, relative to population) has significantly dropped.

Or suppose that studies indicate that the number of teenage drunk driving arrests has risen in three decades from one-out-of-twenty to one-out-of-five of all such arrests. Do such figures indicate that teenagers are drinking and driving more frequently now than they were thirty years ago? Not necessarily. It depends on what is being used as the base line for comparison. Such figures could result equally from an overall reduction in drunk driving arrests, while the incidence of teenage drunk driving remained constant.

Suppressed Evidence

Sometimes relevant evidence is deliberately kept from view because it conflicts with the arguer's intended interpretation of the evidence that is presented, or because it would detract from the arguer's thesis. This constitutes the fallacy of **suppressed evidence.** A common political foible and a particular favorite in the field of advertising, especially when statistical data are used, this is an obviously disreputable argumentative strategy.

For example, advertisers are forever referring to "scientific" studies that "demonstrate" the superiority of their products, but strategically neglecting to mention that they have commissioned the studies themselves, a crucial piece of information relevant to assessing the objectivity of the studies.

Arguably even more sinister are certain common political manipulations of statistics, such as the deliberate understatement of unemployment by obscuring or changing the base line for comparison. For example, suppose some administration was to introduce measures to tighten eligibility requirements for unemployment compensation and reduce the term of eligibility, thereby disallowing claims and eliminating benefits for tens of thousands of unemployed people, and then report the results as a drop in unemployment.

It's worth noting that the fallacy of suppressed evidence is not confined to statistical inference. It occurs any time significant evidence—evidence that makes a difference to the conclusion—is omitted. For example, during the Iran-contra hearings, the Reagan administration argued that on the basis of legal advice provided by White House lawyer Bretton G. Sciaroni (counsel for the presidentially appointed Intelligence Oversight Board, which is supposed to review the legality of intelligence activities) it had every reason to believe it was acting legally in giving U.S. military aid to the Nicaraguan contras. But what neither the administration nor Sciaroni initially mentioned was that in arriving at his finding, Sciaroni had spent no more than five minutes questioning Lt. Colonel Oliver North about possible illicit behavior, and that North misled him; and that he had been denied administration documents directly relevant to the issue and to his finding. This evidence eventually did come to light, undermining the arguments of Sciaroni and the Reagan administration. For the obvious reason that this fallacy involves the *suppression* of evidence, it is a difficult one to spot and to document, which gives more reason to read widely and become as well informed as one can.

Gamblers' Fallacies

Lately it seems that more and more large governmental entities have instituted some form of gambling as a means of raising revenue. There is no doubt that a state lottery can produce an enormous cash flow, and enormous jackpots, particularly in a state the size of California. But when the jackpot goes over the moon, cogent reasoning tends to go out the window. The lottery craze is both producing and feeding on a rising tide of "lottery logic," a family of fallacies about "luck" and "beating the odds."

The most obvious and common fallacy to which gamblers seem prone is superstition about "luck." Lucky days, lucky numbers, lucky socks, lucky hunches, all essentially amount to impotent attempts to predict the unpredictable. (For more on this particular sort of fallacious thinking, see the category Fallacies of Questionable Cause later in this chapter.) Gamblers would do well, however, to bear in mind that the stock market is, like a horse race, in many ways unpredictable and therefore risky. Yet there are a number of responsible ways of gathering evidence relevant to managing and controlling the risks of investment— none of which reduce to occult numerology.

There are also a couple of common gamblers' mistakes that can be assimilated to fallacies of induction, because they have to do with the estimation of probabilities. *One such fallacy consists of thinking that the probability of a certain outcome of a future chance event is affected by past outcomes.* For example, suppose we are gambling on coin flips and the last ten flips have come up heads. Many people are tempted to think that tails are therefore more likely to come up than heads on the next flip. The problem here is failure to recognize that the chances of heads or tails coming up are the same for each flip (50/50), because each flip is an independent chance event. The chances of a run of eleven heads in a row are of course much lower than 50/50, but the odds against such a run have no bearing whatsoever on the outcome of the next flip. And yet people persist in the belief to the contrary. Watch people play the slots in Nevada. Again and again you will see people pumping coins into a machine that hasn't paid off for hours, thinking that this fact alone makes it more likely that the machine will pay off soon.

Just as unreliable is the inference to continue playing because one has been winning. The idea of "riding a streak" involves the same mistake as thinking that the odds against you eventually have to "even out." If chance determines the outcome of the next play, past outcomes have no bearing whatsoever.

Gamblers also tend to be (sometimes pathologically) attracted to "systems" designed to "beat the odds," most of which are completely fallacious products of wishful thinking and don't work at all. (The occasional exception, such as a card counter in blackjack, is very quickly found out and excluded from the premises of gaming establishments.) One such system involves "doubling the bet." Suppose you put $2 on red at even money and lose. Following this system you would put $4 on red on the next play. If you win, you're up $2. If you lose, you're down $6, but you bet $8 on the next play. If you win, you're up $10. The idea is that eventually you win, and when you do, you're ahead of the game. The main trouble with this system is that the odds remain uniformly stacked against you throughout the game as you continue to raise your stake, which has the effect primarily of digging you more deeply and quickly into a hole. In other words, if you follow this "system" the only probability that you raise is the probability that you will run out of scratch before you win.

There is really only one rule of thumb that we can confidently recommend as having any useful validity at all for the person who finds the games of chance appealing: Quit while you're ahead—or cut your losses.

*Quick Check on Fallacies of Statistical Inference (Answers on Page 406)

Identify and explain the fallacies of statistical inference, if any, you find in the following passages:

1. Opinion page editors have a time-honored way of assessing their own performance in reflecting community standards: If they receive a roughly equal number of letters accusing them of liberal and conservative bias, they figure they're hitting the mark.
2. The makers of Zest soap wished to find out what consumers thought of their product. So, they interviewed Zest loyalists and found out that their soap was really popular.
3. A poll is being conducted to find out what students think of their college newspaper. A sample is taken in the cafeteria on a Tuesday between 8 A.M. and noon. Every fifth person who enters the cafeteria is asked his or her opinion. The results are that 72 percent of the students are highly critical of the newspaper. The student government decides to use these results to revamp the editorial board.
4. Professor Smith, wishing to improve his teaching, decides to poll his physics class. He commissions a questionnaire from one of his colleagues in statistics that satisfies all the criteria of a sound polling instrument. He calls each member of his class individually into his office and asks them to complete the questionnaire. What is wrong with his polling methods?
5. Survey question: "Do you favor more educational programs on television?"
6. Survey question: "Whom do you think the U.S. should support in the Middle East: the Israelis or the Arab states?"
7. Manufacturers of a spray deodorant dilute their product, place the results in a thirteen-ounce can and sell it for the same price as the original, undiluted ten-ounce version. Now they launch a media campaign around the slogan: **NOW! 30% MORE FREE!**
8. "My last three blind dates have been bombs. This one's bound to be better!"

FALLACIES OF COMPARISON

Frequently the evidence for an inference depends on the making of some comparison. In such cases, evaluating the inference depends on assessing the merits of the comparison. In general, a good comparison assimilates things that are alike in relevant ways and does not gloss over relevant differences. The general strategy for critiquing an argument based on a faulty comparison consists of pointing out a relevant difference between the items compared.

Note that this is a two-step procedure. First, it has to be established that there is a difference between the items compared. Second, and more important, the relevance of the difference to the point of the comparison needs to be established. Overlooking the second step, in particular, results in a common misapplication of this criticism: One often hears by way of objection, Your argument is like comparing apples and oranges. Notice that to criticize an argument as akin to comparing apples with oranges is to make a comparison of one's own. The point of the comparison *being made in* such a criticism is that the comparison *being criticized* is misleading. Well, let's suppose that the argument being criticized does make a comparison that really is comparable to a comparison between apples and oranges. Let's suppose, in other words, that the argument compares items that can be distinguished in some way. But is such a comparison necessarily misleading? Is a comparison between apples and oranges necessarily misleading? Not if you're trying to sort the fruit out from the vegetables.

The important point here is this: First of all, there are no two items in the universe so different from each other that they cannot be compared in some way and for some purpose. Apples and oranges, for example, have quite a few important things in common and can therefore be usefully and accurately compared for many purposes. But there are also limitations to any comparison between two distinct items. The risks inherent in both arguing on the basis of comparisons and criticizing such arguments are exactly the same. One wants to avoid overestimating the significance of both the common points and the distinctions between the items compared.

Questionable Analogy

An analogy is an elaborate comparison, or a comparison involving several points of similarity. Things which are analogous are alike in several ways. Analogies serve a number of important intellectual purposes. For example, unfamiliar things are frequently explained by analogy to things that are or are presumed to be more familiar. For instance, when we introduced the informal fallacy categories, we did so by means of an analogy to a carpenter's tools. Analogies are also frequently involved as premises in arguments. For example, the eighteenth-century Scottish philosopher Thomas Reid argued:

> We may observe a very great similitude between this earth which we inhabit, and the other planets, Saturn, Jupiter, Mars, Venus and Mercury. They all revolve

round the sun, as the earth does, although at different distances and in different periods. They borrow all their light from the sun, as the earth does. Several of them are known to revolve round their axis like the earth, and by that means must have a like succession of day and night. Some of them have moons, that serve to give them light in the absence of the sun, as our moon does to us. They are all, in their motions, subject to the same law of gravitation, as the earth is. From all this similitude, it is not unreasonable to think that those planets may, like our earth, be the habitation of various orders of living creatures. There is some probability in this conclusion from analogy.

Notice that Reid, good philosopher that he was, recognized that this inference was not deductively valid. He recognized, in other words, that this was a form of inductive inference, and accordingly that there was room in it for doubt and error. Nevertheless, he expressed cautious confidence in it as an inference. We now have enough additional evidence to be pretty certain that the conclusion he was cautiously drawing was in error. But he was not essentialy misguided in placing confidence in the argument. Indeed, he was following a familiar and generally reliable line of reasoning, which a great many of our everyday inferences follow as well.

For example, if you try to enroll in Professor Smith's section of the upper division poetry course because you have taken three of her lower division courses and found her to be a knowledgeable and stimulating instructor, you are following the same analogical line of reasoning as Reid was. In effect, you are reasoning as follows:

I have observed three items: a, b, and c, each of which has the important characteristic 1 in common with as yet unobserved item d. [*I have taken three courses taught by the instructor of the course I'm contemplating.*]

The observed items a, b, and c also have characteristics 2 and 3. [*The three courses I've taken were stimulating and imparted knowledge.*]

Therefore, it is likely that unobserved item d will have characteristics 2 and 3 as well. [*The course I'm contemplating is likely to be stimulating and to impart knowledge.*]

When we argue from analogy we infer on the basis of observed similarities that some further as yet unobserved similarity or similarities will be present as well.

Arguments based on analogies can go astray, however, when they are based on similarities that are irrelevant to the point they are intended to establish and when they gloss over relevant differences. We call these **questionable analogies.**

A particularly blatant example of reasoning by faulty analogy was committed by former president Reagan in his notorious attempt to cover up a glaring inconsistency in his account of the sequence of events in the Irangate scandal. Asked if he had known of the arms sale and the diversion of funds to the contras before the fact or after, he first indicated he had, then that he hadn't. Finally, at a press conference he offered, "I think it's possible to forget. How many of you can remember what you did on April 25, 1985? Raise your hands. . . . I don't see any hands."

Translated, the argument was supposed to work like this: Many people routinely and understandably forget details about what they did on a certain day several weeks or months previously and consequently shouldn't be held responsible for inaccuracies in their recollections. Hence, by analogy, Reagan's "memory lapse" should be excused as perfectly routine and understandable. But there are obvious and crucial differences between what Reagan was unable to consistently account for and the kinds of details he was assimilating it to: The kinds of details that people routinely and understandably forget are mundane trivialities of little or no consequence, whereas Reagan was being asked to account for a series of controversial and illegal events of far-reaching national and international consequence, and for which he bore final responsibility.

Of course it's not always as obvious as in the case of Reagan's "memory lapse" argument that the analogy is faulty. Frequently the question of the merits of an analogy is itself a proper subject for deep and lengthy debate. For example, consider the analogy, which supporters and critics alike of American foreign policy in Central America both appeal to and attack, between the situation in Central America and Vietnam.

Questionable Classification

Similar problems arise when we classify things, which, like our use of analogies, involves making comparisons and drawing distinctions. The difference between classifications and analogies is that classifications have become stable conventions for sorting things into groups. So we hardly notice that we are still operating on the basis of similarities and differences between things and the relevance of these similarities and differences to our purposes. And we might have trouble imagining how a classification could be questionable.

Look around the neighborhood and count the houses and cars. Do you have any trouble deciding which is which? Not likely. But an interesting case in constitutional law called even this seemingly obvious classification into question. It seems that police officers had observed a certain vehicle parked for several days during which time individuals and small groups of people were also observed coming from and going to the vehicle. Suspecting possible drug activity, the police investigated further and indeed found the occupant of the vehicle had drugs in his possession. The occupant was arrested and brought to trial on drug charges. The hitch for the prosecution was that the police had not obtained a search warrant before moving to investigate the vehicle. Why would that be necessary? Police don't need a search warrant to inspect a motor vehicle. But it turned out that the occupant lived in the vehicle, a motor home, and it was argued that because the vehicle was the occupant's place of residence, it should be covered by the Fourth Amendment provision, which protects "the right of the people to be secure in their *houses* . . ." against unreasonable search and seizure. Who was right? Is a motor home to be classified as a house or a motor vehicle? The point is, there is no simple answer that will work here.

*Quick Check on Fallacies of Comparison (Answers on Page 406)

Identify and explain the fallacy of a comparison, if any, in the following passages:

1. Speaker of Iran's parliament, Hashami Rafsanjani, on the occasion of an Iraqi missile attack on the U.S. Navy frigate *Stark*: "It showed that the U.S. Navy was a paper tiger. These paper tigers, which can be destroyed by a missile from twelve miles can pose no threat for regional people [i.e., Iranians] who have missiles in their possession capable of hitting these frigates from a distance of sixty miles."

2. Letter to the Editor: "Our police commissioner says that 'adult' bookstores operate under an 'umbrella of legality.' That's true in cities like this one where the obscenity laws aren't enforced. The same would be true of an illegal drugstore if the drug laws weren't being enforced."

3. An argument for dismissing the fear of nuclear blackmail as a reason for opposing unilateral nuclear disarmament: "Despite the frequency with which blackmail is mentioned in strategic treatises . . . the fact is that since nuclear weapons were introduced in 1945 not a single case of nuclear blackmail has ever even been attempted. Even though the U.S. was the sole possessor of nuclear weapons from 1945 to 1949, the U.S. did not consider blackmailing the Soviet Union to prevent the subversion of democratic governments in Hungary and Czechoslovakia, or the erection of the Berlin blockade in 1948." (P. Lackey, "The Moral Case for Unilateral Nuclear Disarmament")

FALLACIES OF QUESTIONABLE CAUSE

Frequently an issue will turn in some important way upon correctly accounting for the cause of something. But causal relationships, because they are often difficult to observe directly, often need to be inferred. And inferring causal relationships is not as simple as we frequently like to think. The fallacy of questionable cause consists of incorrectly inferring or assuming causal relationships. Superstitions provide the most obvious cases of this kind of fallacious thinking, as for example when a basketball coach refuses to change his "lucky" socks in an attempt to influence the outcome of the game. But there are a number of more subtle pitfalls of causal reasoning to be aware of.

Confusing Correlations with Causes

One of the most common kinds of evidence for a causal connection is a statistical correlation between two phenomena. For example, medical scientists knew for some time of a statistical correlation between cigarette smoking and lung cancer: The incidence of lung cancer in the smoking population was higher than in the nonsmoking population. Such a correlation is genuinely relevant inductive evidence for a causal connection between lung cancer and smoking. The problem is that by itself it is inconclusive. It suggests, but does not establish, the causal link. Notice, for instance, that there is also a strong statistical correlation between the incidence of lung cancer and age. Yet it would be misleading to suggest that age causes lung cancer, or that lung cancer causes aging. So, isolating the causal factor requires further evidence.

Overlooking a Common Cause

Two phenomena may be so closely connected that one of them seems to be the cause of the other, although both are really results of some additional, less obvious factor. Suppose a person suffers from both depression and alcoholism. Does the drinking cause the depression or the depression cause the drinking? Or could it be that the depression and the drinking sustain each other causally? Perhaps so. But one shouldn't overlook the further possibility that there is some additional underlying cause of both the depression and the drinking, for example, a biochemical imbalance or a profound emotional disturbance. *The fallacy of* **overlooking a common cause,** *then, consists of failing to recognize that two seemingly related events may not be causally related at all, but rather are effects of a common cause.*

Post Hoc

A similar fallacy consists of inferring a causal connection from temporal continguity. In other words, *it is fallacious to infer that one thing is caused by another simply because it is preceded by it in time.* For example, someone observes that crime among youth has increased in the United States since the arrival of punk rock from England and concludes, therefore, that punk rock is causing an increase in juvenile crime. Or someone observes that every war in this century has followed the election of a Democratic president, concluding therefore that the Democrats caused those wars. This kind of reasoning came to be known in Latin as *post hoc, ergo propter hoc,* which means literally "after this, therefore because of this."

Causal Oversimplification

The fallacy of **causal oversimplification** *consists of assuming that what merely contributes causally to a phenomenon fully explains it.* For example, intense debates are waged regularly over the wisdom of increased taxation as a means of balancing the federal budget. Opponents of such measures frequently point to the predictable negative effects that taxation will have on the vitality of the consumer economy, whereas proponents of such measures stress the effects on real disposable income of the increasing debt burden on the economy as a whole. It is likely that both sides have a point, but it is at least as likely that both sides are in effect oversimplifying the economic equation in a number of ways. Clearly, tax policy is not the only causal factor that affects the consumer economy. But neither is public indebtedness the only such causal factor. Both factors, and numerous others, are involved and influence one another in a great many ways.

Slippery Slope

A specific kind of causal fallacy consists of objecting to something on the grounds of the unwarranted assumption that it will inevitably lead to some evil consequence that will lead to some even more evil consequence that in turn will lead on down the slippery slope to some ultimately disastrous consequence. For example, it is commonly argued that marijuana is a dangerous drug that inevitably leads to experimentation with harder drugs and eventually to hard drug abuse and addiction. Frequently, the alleged slippery slope is supported by further fallacious causal inferences, such as pointing out that a high percentage of admitted heroin addicts testify to having tried marijuana early in their drug experience. But there is in fact no slippery slope here, as can easily be established by pointing out that numerous people who at one time or another have tried or used marijuana have never experimented with harder drugs, much less become addicted to them, and have moderated or given up their use of marijuana.

A variation on slippery slope reasoning takes the form of posing the rhetorical question, Where do you draw the line? This of course has the effect of suggesting that there is no location for the line to be drawn. For example, some people are moved by arguments like this one:

> If you permit the withdrawal of life support from terminally ill patients, where do you draw the line between this form of "mercy killing" and the convenient disposal of one's sick and burdensome elders, or the "euthanasia" of the mentally or physically or racially "defective"?

Here it is merely assumed that we can't clearly distinguish between cases of "passive euthanasia" (the withholding of extraordinary measures that would forestall or postpone death) and "active euthanasia" (the taking of measures that would hasten death or bring death about), or between euthanasia done to alleviate the pointless suffering of the terminal patient and euthanasia done for selfish reasons or with deliberate disregard for the interests of the patient.

Now it is easy to see that such distinctions *are* possible, for they have just been made. It is not much harder to see that they are relevant distinctions. Indeed, the argument presumes the relevance of such distinctions; otherwise, why assume or suggest that they can't be made? Thus, an effective strategy for exposing this sort of slippery slope reasoning is to draw relevant distinctions.

It is, however, important to recognize that in some contexts the question, Where do you draw the line? rhetorical though it is, makes a good point. These are contexts in which—and there *are* some very important ones—some fundamental principle is at stake that would be irreparably compromised if a certain exception to it were allowed to pass.

A special case of slippery slope reasoning in the political context is the so-called **domino theory,** whose influence can be seen in discussions of U.S. foreign policy pretty much throughout the "cold war" period. During the Vietnam period the argument ran that if South Vietnam "falls" to the communists, then it will, like the "lead domino" in a chain of dominos, bring down Laos, which will topple Cambodia, and so on throughout Southeast Asia and eventually throughout the world until the communists are eventually at our very borders. The argument, refitted for Central American duty, was a Reagan administration favorite.

But the argument's basic analogy is questionable. Political regimes, their stabilities and instabilities, and their interdependencies, are much more complex than can adequately be understood by means of a comparison to a row of standing domino tiles. It is, after all, the political complexities whose causal relationships are at stake here. To be fair to the argument, it should be pointed out that fundamental political changes frequently have impacts reaching far beyond the national borders within which they occur. There is some truth in the idea that political events in one country influence political events in others. For example, the French Revolution was inspired in part by the American Revolution. But this is only one of many factors involved, whose causal significance varies from situation to situation and depends on a host of other variables.

*Quick Check on Fallacies of Questionable Cause (Answers on Page 407)

Identify and explain the causal fallacies, if any, you find in the following passages:

1. Ronald Reagan promised us a balanced budget by 1984. But since taking office he's multiplied the budget deficit by more than 250 percent. And he refused to address seriously the issue of the budget deficit until after the 1984 reelection campaign. But since such behavior clearly amounts to a betrayal of the public trust, Reagan was unworthy of reelection.
2. "If you could get rid of drugs [in the workplace], we'd be far ahead of other countries in productivity." (Ira Lipman, quoted in Stanley Penn, "Losses Flow from Drug Use at the Office," *Wall Street Journal,* July 29, 1981, p. 27.)
3. Presidential counselor Ed Meese explaining why the United States was considering hiding 200 MX missiles among 4600 shelters scattered across the Utah and Nevada desert ". . . a bad idea dictated only because of the Carter administration's slavish

adherence to Salt II. . . . and that was the only reason for 4600 holes in the ground."
4. Argument against a ballot initiative that would impose an additional tax on tobacco products: "Taxing cigarettes encourages interstate traffickers in stolen cigarettes by opening up a whole new and very profitable market for them. A vote for this measure is a vote for increased crime. Vote 'NO.' Vote against the smugglers and traffickers and black marketeers."

UNWARRANTED ASSUMPTIONS

The slippery slope fallacy also illustrates another general problem area in the handling of evidence: Introducing premises that are merely assumed to be the case, but are both important enough to the argument and controversial enough to call for independent verification.

False Dilemma

Another example of this sort occurs when an argument depends on the presentation of what is merely assumed or misleadingly represented as an exhaustive range of alternatives. *Such an argument, called a* **false dilemma,** *erroneously reduces the number of possible alternatives on an issue.* The strategy best suited to exposing instances of this fallacy is to articulate a specific alternative that is left out of the range of alternatives presented in the premise. For example, a bank commits a false dilemma when it suggests "The Logical Alternative to the Stock Market: Madison Savings and Loan." There are of course numerous other investment options.

False dilemma arguments have a great deal of rhetorical force, especially when they presuppose a simple choice between two mutually exclusive states of affairs or courses of action, one of which is painted in extremely favorable terms and the other in equally unfavorable terms. Probably because it appeals so powerfully to the understandable human desire to grasp things in the simplest terms possible, this device is a special favorite of political sloganeers and speech writers. In the 1984 presidential election for instance, Ronald Reagan said things like this:

> The truth is, Americans must choose between two drastically different points of view. One puts its faith in the pipedreamers and margin scribblers of Washington; the other believes in the collective wisdom of the American people. Our opponents believe the solutions to our nation's problems lie in the psychiatrist's notes or in a social worker's file or in a bureaucrat's budget. We believe in the working man's toil, the businessman's enterprise, and the clergyman's counsel.

Not to be outdone, Walter Mondale was saying things like this:

> Our choice is between two futures, between a Reagan future and a better future. It is a choice between expediency and excellence. It is a choice between

social Darwinism and social decency. It is a choice between salesmanship and leadership.

Begging the Question

*The fallacy of **begging the question** occurs when the arguer assumes what is at issue, or when the conclusion or some statement presupposing the conclusion is introduced as a premise.* This is sometimes called "circular reasoning," because its point of origin (the premise) is identical with its terminus (the conclusion). Such arguments are objectionable because the premise is just as questionable as the conclusion it is intended to support (hence the name "begging the question"). What makes this fallacy particularly tricky to deal with is that arguers are rarely so clumsy as to appeal to a premise that is *obviously* the same as the conclusion. More frequently the question-begging premise is a subtle rewording of the conclusion or presupposes the conclusion in a way even the arguer may fail to appreciate.

The strategy one frequently needs to pursue in order to effectively diagnose and expose question begging therefore involves sensitive use of paraphrase. If the premise and the conclusion can be paraphrased into each other without significant loss of meaning, then we have a plausible case of begging the question.

Invincible Ignorance

A related fallacy, which we'll call **invincible ignorance,** *consists of refusing to give due consideration to evidence that conflicts with what one is already committed to believing.* For example, in the Peanuts episode on page 267, Snoopy commits this fallacy twice. In the first instance Snoopy dismisses Lucy's testimony as ignorant; and later he dismisses the evidence of her research on the basis of the farfetched assumption of a massive cover-up. In each case there appears to be no reason for dismissing the information other than that it conflicts with the hypothesis he is initially and, it seems, inflexibly committed to. In what might be called a definitive case of "sleeping dogmatism," Snoopy has closed his mind on this point, which now seems no longer to be open to question or challenge from any quarter.

Arguing from Ignorance

*The fallacy of **arguing from ignorance** consists of treating the absence of evidence for (or against) a claim as proof of its falsity (or truth).* Some of the most common examples of this fallacy have to do with the unknown and "the supernatural." For example, there is the well-known argument for the existence of God that proceeds from the single premise that no conclusive proof has ever been offered that God does not exist, or the similar argument supporting a belief in ESP simply because it has never been disproven.

The fallacy of arguing from ignorance should not be confused, though, with arguments based on legitimate presumption. For example, in our tradition of

"Peanuts," by Charles M. Schulz. From *Charlie Brown's Cyclopedia*, 1975. Reprinted by permission of UFS, Inc.

criminal law the accused is presumed innocent unless and until the prosecution discharges its "burden of proof." This means that if the prosecution fails to present sufficient evidence for a conviction, the accused is to be considered innocent. Suppose the counsel for the defense makes the closing argument "My client must be found not guilty, since the prosecution has not proven him guilty beyond a reasonable doubt." This is not a case of arguing from ignorance. It simply reaffirms the criminal law convention that the prosecution bears the burden of proof. In effect, what the fallacious appeal to ignorance does is to shift (or attempt to shift) the burden of proof where it doesn't belong.

*Quick Check on Unwarranted Assumptions (Answers on Page 407)

Identify and explain the unwarranted assumption, if any, in each of the following passages:

1. **News Anchor:** How do you account for the senator's dramatic come-from-behind victory?
   Commentator: One big factor was that his campaign was on the rise.
   Anchor: You mean it had momentum?
   Commentator: Exactly.

267

2. Since no one can definitively disprove the existence of ghosts, it makes sense to assume that ghosts exist.

3. During the height of the Iran-contra affair, French commentator Patrick Wajsman argued in support of the arms-for-hostages swap and subsequent diversion of funds on the grounds that it is a "menace to be so obsessed with . . . rules and procedures as to ignore the fact that the interests of the state must sometimes override all other considerations." (See William Pfaff, "U.S. System Is Flawed and Likely to Stay So," *Los Angeles Times,* May 14, 1987, part 2, p. 5.)

4. News item: "A San Francisco man, asked to provide unbiased Congressional testimony two years ago by Rep. Robert J. Lagomarsino (R-Ca), received funds from Nicaraguan contra rebels and falsely claimed to be a Roman Catholic priest, Congressional investigators said. . . . Lagomarsino said that he still believes that Thomas Dowling, 38, was a credible witness. . . ."

5. Secretary of Defense Caspar Weinberger commenting on why the United States intended to guarantee the safety of neutral shipping in Persian Gulf waters: "[American warships are] to be tangible representatives of our government's . . . concern over safe navigation in this critically important body of water."

SOME ADDITIONAL INFORMAL STRATEGIES FOR CRITICIZING ARGUMENTS

Remember that in evaluating arguments, in assessing their cogency, you are trying to assess the strength or validity of the connection between the conclusion and the premises offered as support, and the truth or acceptability of the supporting premises. In addition to the tools you have so far, there are two other important informal strategies of argument evaluation worth mentioning.

Checking for Consistency

One of the most powerful notions for both formal and informal argument evaluation is consistency. (Remember the crucial role it plays in determining deductive validity.) Inconsistency is always a sign that there is something wrong. So it is always a good idea to check the arguments you come across for both internal consistency and consistency with what has already been established. For example, if there is a genuine inconsistency among the premises of an argument, then, although you may not know which of the premises is false, you know they can't all be true. Again, if a premise, or the conclusion for that matter, is inconsistent with something you have good independent reason to believe is true, you have also therefore got good reason to doubt the argument's cogency. This is an especially useful device for getting your bearings in areas where the facts remain in dispute and good, hard, incontrovertible evidence is hard to come by.

Consistency is also a powerful tool for assessing the cogency of evaluative arguments. Indeed, in the sphere of ethics and public policy it is frequently invoked as a basic moral principle: that like cases should be treated alike. Thus, sometimes a policy or position can be effectively criticized as a violation of this basic principle, that is, as a case of inconsistency. This is what is meant by the term "double standard." Bear in mind, however, that cases which seem to be alike are sometimes different from each other in subtle, hard-to-recognize, but nonetheless important and relevant ways. Thus, challenging the consistency of a policy is not the same thing as demonstrating that the policy is in fact inconsistent. It can, however, shift the burden of proof onto the advocate of the policy to draw a significant distinction between the apparently similar cases that the policy refuses to recognize as such.

This strategy can also be applied in a global way to assess the overall consistency of a body of beliefs or set of conclusions. If one argues for conclusions that are genuinely inconsistent with each other, again, you may not yet know which of them is false, but they can't all be true. And so the arguments which support them can't all be cogent.

Tracing Implications

Remember also that positions and arguments tend to have further implications. Without knowing for certain that a position is correct or that an argument is cogent, it is often an effective strategy to treat it hypothetically, that is, to assume that it is true, or cogent, and trace out its further implications. If a position or an argument leads by implication to further conclusions that there is good reason to reject, then there is good reason to doubt the position or the cogency of the argument.

This strategy, which has traditionally been known by its Latin name *reductio ad absurdum* (which means to reduce to absurdity), can be effectively used as a powerful general strategy of argument in its own right. In this strategy, one merely assumes that the conclusion one wants to establish is false. One then traces the implications of that assumption, hoping to find that it leads to some conclusion that there is good reason to reject, whereupon one also finds good reason to reject the original assumption. This is sometimes referred to as the "method of indirect proof."

A FINAL WORD OF CAUTION

By now it should be pretty clear that evaluating arguments, particularly in informal terms, can be a pretty messy business. You can expect to encounter a fair number of arguments that can quite clearly be faulted in one way or another, and occasionally you'll find an argument that is pretty clearly impeccable. But a great many arguments are neither clearly fallacious nor clearly not. In such cases, you should consider your criticisms to be essentially contestible, and therefore you should also recognize the need to supply arguments in support of them, to deal with arguments against them, and perhaps to change your mind. In other words, assessing arguments, like verifying value judgments, takes you into areas where knowing how to construct and evaluate arguments becomes more and more important.

Summary

Evidence is information relevant to an inference. A number of informal fallacies can be understood in terms of pitfalls to gathering, evaluating, and handling evidence in drawing inferences.

A useful general fallacy category is *jumping to conclusions,* which consists simply in closing an issue, or regarding it as settled, before all of the evidence is in.

Several important fallacies can be grouped together as fallacies of statistical inference. These include

Small sample, or overestimating the statistical significance of evidence drawn from a small number of cases.

Unrepresentative sample, or overestimating the statistical significance of evidence drawn from a sample that overlooks significant variables in the target population.

Slanted study, or using evidence obtained by means of a methodology that determines the outcome of the study in some particular direction.

Bad base line, or misinterpreting the statistical significance of evidence by reference to an incorrect basis of comparison.

Suppressed evidence, which consists of deliberately obscuring or concealing relevant evidence.

There are also a number of related gamblers' fallacies having to do with "luck," estimating probabilities, and "beating the odds." It is important to remember, first, that "luck" is what can't be predicted, whereas risk can at least be assessed and managed; second, that the outcome of a chance event is not affected by previous outcomes of similar events; and that "systems" for beating the odds should be treated with skepticism.

Frequently the evidence for an inference is drawn from a comparison. In such cases, evaluating the inference involves assessing the merits of the comparison. A good comparison assimilates things that are alike in relevant ways and does not gloss over relevant differences. A general strategy for criticizing a faulty comparison consists of pointing out a relevant difference between the items compared. This is a two-step procedure. First, it must be established that there is a difference between the items compared. Second, and more important, the relevance of the difference to the point of the comparison must be established.

An analogy is an elaborate comparison, or a comparison based on several points of similarity. Analogous items are alike in several ways. When we argue from analogy we infer on the basis of observed similarities that some further as yet unobserved similarity or similarities will be present as well. Arguing from analogies is a generally reliable strategy, but arguments based on analogies can go astray. They are open to legitimate objection when they are based on similarities that are irrelevant to the point they are intended to establish and when they gloss over relevant differences.

Similar problems arise in connection with classifications, which, like analogies, involve making comparisons and drawing distinctions. The difference between classifications and analogies is that classifications have become stable conventions for sorting things into groups.

Frequently an issue will turn in some important way upon correctly accounting for the cause of something. But causal relationships, since they are often difficult to observe directly, often need to be inferred. Fallacies of questionable cause consist of incorrectly inferring or assuming causal relationships. Superstitions provide the most obvious cases of this kind of fallacious thinking. But there are a number of more subtle pitfalls of causal reasoning to be aware of, including confusing statistical correlations with causal relationships; overlooking the possible hidden underlying common cause of events that seem causally linked to each other; inferring that one thing is caused by another simply because it is preceded by it in time (called post hoc); and causal oversimplification.

A specific kind of causal fallacy consists of objecting to something on the grounds of the unwarranted assumption that it will inevitably lead to some evil consequence that will lead to some even more evil consequence that in turn will lead "on down the slippery slope" to some ultimately disastrous consequence. A special case of slippery slope reasoning in the political context is the so-called domino theory. In general, where there is no good reason to believe that the causal chain assumed in such arguments exists, the arguments are objectionable.

Another general problem in the handling of evidence is the introduction of premises that are merely assumed to be the case, but that are both important enough to the argument and controversial enough to call for independent verification. Slippery slope fallacies are examples of this. Other examples include

> False dilemma, which consists of presenting what is merely assumed or misleadingly represented as an exhaustive range of alternatives. The strategy best suited to exposing this fallacy is to specify an alternative that was left out of the range of alternatives presented.

Begging the question occurs when the arguer assumes what is at issue, or when the conclusion or some statement presupposing the conclusion is introduced as a premise. Such arguments are objectionable because the premise is just as questionable as the conclusion it is intended to support. This fallacy is tricky to deal with because arguers rarely appeal to a premise that is *obviously* the same as the conclusion. More frequently the question-begging premise is a subtle rewording of the conclusion or is presupposed by the conclusion in a way even the arguer may fail to appreciate. The strategy to pursue in order to diagnose and expose question begging effectively involves seeing whether the premise and the conclusion can be paraphrased into each other without significant loss of meaning.

A related fallacy, invincible ignorance, consists of refusing to give due consideration to evidence that conflicts with what one is already committed to believing.

The fallacy of arguing from ignorance consists of treating the absence of evidence for (or against) a claim as proof of its falsity (or truth). This should not be confused with arguments based on legitimate presumption, which depend on the placement of the burden of proof.

Remember that in evaluating arguments for cogency you are trying to assess the strength or validity of the connection between the conclusion and the premises offered as support, and the truth or acceptability of the supporting premises. In addition to the tools you have so far, two useful informal strategies of argument evaluation are (1) checking for consistency among the claims and in an argument, between those claims and other things you have good reason to believe, and between the positions involved in a system of beliefs; and (2) tracing the implications of a thesis or argument.

Finally, don't forget that a great many arguments are neither clearly fallacious nor clearly not. So you should consider your argument criticisms to be essentially contestible. This means you may have to argue in support of them, to deal with arguments against them, and perhaps to change your mind. In other words, assessing arguments, like verifying value judgments, takes you into areas where knowing how to construct and evaluate arguments becomes more and more important.

Applications

1. Once again, with your study partner, take turns critically examining the following examples in terms of the informal fallacy categories you have learned so far, including those covered in the previous chapters, and testing your critical assessments for clarity and fairness.

a. Phil Donahue introducing former administration official Hedrick Smith, author of *The Power Game,* as a panelist on a program concerning defense industry influence peddling: "He's not in jail yet. So we can assume he's one of the good guys."

b. From a Letter to the Editor: "Two terms of Republican leadership in the White House have seen a drop in inflation and in unemployment, with modest but steady overall growth in the economy. No sooner has that leadership been replaced by a Democrat, but interest rates and inflation begin to rise, the stock market turns sharply down and signs of depression abound. What further evidence do you need to conclude that Democrats are bad for the economy."

c. The Ayatollah Khomeini speaking in defense of state executions of those convicted of adultery, prostitution, or homosexuality: "If your finger suffers from gangrene, what do you do? Let the whole hand and then the body become filled with gangrene, or cut the finger off? . . . Corruption, corruption. We have to eliminate corruption." [*Time*, October 22, 1979, p. 57.]

d. According to Associated Press reporters covering the 1988 presidential campaign of Vice President George Bush, the candidate endorsed the controversial key recommendation of the president's AIDS commission the day after its final report was submitted to the White House. At the time, President Reagan remained uncommitted regarding the recommendation that AIDS victims should have federal protection from discrimination on the job, in schools, and elsewhere. "I think it is needed . . . to lay to rest some of the fears," Bush said, embracing the recommendation. But he added that Reagan "did the right thing" in withholding judgment. "How can the White House be asked to take an instant position?" he asked. When it was pointed out that Bush himself was doing just that, the vice president replied that Reagan "just saw this thing yesterday. He's not running for president. I've got a different role here. I want to say what I think."

e. "According to folk wisdom in many cultures, redheaded people tend to be a bit temperamental. An Israeli researcher believes that there may be something to the ancient prejudice. At the Honolulu conference, psychiatrist Michael Bar of Israel's Shalvata Psychiatric Center, reported a study showing that redheaded children are three or four times more likely than others to develop 'hyperactive syndrome'—whose symptoms include over-excitabilty, short attention span, and feelings of frustration, and usually, excessive aggressiveness.

"Bar arrives at his conclusion after matching the behavior of 45 redheaded boys and girls between the ages of six and twelve against that of a control group of nonredheaded kids. . . ." (*Time*, September 12, 1977, p. 97.)

f. " 'Before he took B$_{15}$ he [her husband] could barely get up for his meals because of a severe heart condition,' said Jayne Link, a 51-year-old Glen Cove, New York, widow. 'Two weeks after he started taking the vitamin pill he was completely changed.' Then Bill stopped taking the vitamin. Three months later he was dead—victim of a fifth heart attack.' . . . Now Mrs. Link takes B$_{15}$ herself for arthritis. 'I take it constantly, three 50 milligram tablets a day,' she said. 'I have a slipped disc in addition to the arthritis. I tried everything under the sun to relieve the pain. But nothing else has worked.'" (*Globe*, September 11, 1979, p. 22.)

g. Colleges should start paying students for getting high grades. After all, business handsomely rewards its top people with bonuses and commissions, and everybody can see the beneficial effect of that practice on worker productivity.

h. "Are interior decorators necessary? Yes. . . . Since one cannot set one's own broken leg one relies on a doctor. Without a formidable knowledge of legal intricacies one depends on a barrister. Likewise, unless the individual is well versed in the home furnishing field the services of an interior decorator are a distinct advantage." (Helen-Janet Bonelli, *The Status Merchants: The Trade of Interior Decoration* [Cranbury, N.J.: Barnes, 1972], p. 36.)

i. "Subaru and Mercedes, two of the finest engineered cars around. One sells for eight times the price of the other. The choice is yours." (Ad for Subaru)

j. **Ron:** Smoking pot definitely leads to heroin addiction.

Jon: Oh, I don't know.

Ron: Figures don't lie. A report by the U.S. Commission on Narcotics on a study of 2000 narcotics addicts in a prison shows that well over two-thirds smoked marijuana before using heroin.

k. Since more suicides occur during the Christmas season than at any other time of the year, something about Christmas must lead people to take their lives.

l. Egyptian President Anwar Sadat was assassinated immediately after he began to crack down on political dissidents. Proof enough that one of those dissident groups was behind Sadat's murder.

m. "Perhaps intimidated by flak from Capitol Hill, the Social Security Advisory Council has backed away from a proposal to increase the maximum pay subject to Soc-Sec taxation from $14,000 to $24,000 to keep the plan on a pay-as-you-go basis. Instead it has recommended shifting the cost of Medicare to the general fund. The proposal, if adopted, would begin the process of transferring SS into an out-and-out welfare program. Once we start in that direction, where do we stop?" ("A Quick About-Face," *New York Daily News,* January 21, 1975, p. 37.)

n. The federal bailout of big companies such as Chrysler and Pan American is wrong because the government makes no effort to rescue small businesses that are failing.

o. When asked to comment on Iranian threats of retaliation, in the aftermath of the shooting down of an Iranian airliner by a U.S. Navy cruiser, Ronald Reagan said, "You have to think about that, knowing who they are." But he dismissed Iranian allegations that the downing of the civilian plane, which Reagan termed an "understandable accident," had been deliberate, saying, "I don't go much by what the Iranians say, ever."

2. With the benefit of the discussions you have had with your study partner, briefly and carefully explain the fallacies you found in each of the preceding examples. You may find it useful in some cases to cast the argument as a first step.

3. In frame eleven of the Peanuts episode used earlier in this chapter to illustrate the fallacy of invincible ignorance, Lucy makes reference to medical history. Why is her argument *not* an example of the fallacious argument from ignorance?

4. In this cartoon, cartoonist Jules Feiffer takes a satirical look at professional journalists who write op-ed (editorial opinion) columns, in the context of an issue in which the ethics of journalism were involved. *Time* magazine had

been named in a libel suit filed on behalf of Israeli defense minister Ariel Sharon, about whom *Time* had published a controversial story.

How many fallacies can you find in the columnist's argument? We count no less than seven distinct fallacious moves and at least eleven distinctly applicable fallacy categories.

Cartoon copyright 1985 Jules Feiffer. Reprinted with permission of Universal Press Syndicate. All rights reserved.

5. A survey indicated that more than half of all college students with below-average grades smoke pot. In contrast, only 20 percent of nonsmokers have below-average grades. From this, one person concludes that pot smoking causes students to get lower grades. Another person concludes that getting lower grades causes one to smoke pot. Comment.

6. Find examples of your own in the public media of the informal fallacies discussed in this chapter. For each example, give a brief but careful explanation of the fallacies you find in it.

7. Remember that a given argument can have more than one thing wrong with it. With that in mind, go back over the examples in the Applications section of the previous chapters. Give a brief and careful explanation of any additional fallacies you can find using the fallacy categories developed in this chapter.

APPLYING A FORMAT | 11

If you have mastered the material in the preceding chapters, you are well on your way to becoming an effective critical thinker. What you now need is some kind of systematic procedure that integrates argument analysis and evaluation. We now present a seven-step format that achieves this integration.

FORMAT FOR ANALYSIS AND EVALUATION

All evaluation of arguments presupposes some analysis, but the amount of analysis preceding the actual evaluation depends on the complexity of the argument. A short, simple argument may require very little detailed analysis. Also, some of the steps of analysis presuppose preliminary evaluation. The following seven-step procedure, then, is offered with the following qualifications: You may find it useful to reverse the order of certain steps in this procedure or to work back and forth between them on occasion; and it may not always be necessary to work through each step of the analysis for every argument you encounter.

1. Clarify meaning.
2. Identify conclusion and main premises.   }
3. Cast the argument.   **Analysis**
4. Fill in the missing premises.
5. Examine the main premises and support for justification. }
6. Examine the argument for fallacies.   **Evaluation**
7. Give an overall evaluation.

You should view this format as a general guide for thinking critically about what you read and hear. Your instructor may use some variation of it, or you may come across another book that takes a slightly different approach. In short, there's nothing sacred about this procedure; others might serve just as well. But following this format *will* enable you to assess arguments effectively.

Before applying this format, let's take a look at each of the steps. Doing so will serve as a review of much of the material covered in the preceding chapters.

Step 1: Clarify Meaning

Before even attempting to clarify meaning, read a passage all the way through. This will give you a feel for the argument as a whole. Even if you happen to disagree with the position advanced, don't allow your disagreement to color your interpretation. If you don't understand some words, consult a dictionary. Unless otherwise indicated, assume that the words used follow common usage. Beware of blocks to critical thinking in the passage itself and in your own reaction. Recall those clichéd patterns of thinking and of viewing things: cultural conditioning, reliance on authority, hasty moral judgment, labels, and limited frame of reference. (See Chapter 1.) Be sensitive to the functions of language: informative, expressive, directive, performative, and persuasive. (See Chapter 2.) And be alert for (1) vague or ambiguous language, including jargon; (2) shifts in word meaning; (3) bias communicated by highly emotive words, assumption loaded labels, rhetorical questions, innuendo, extreme quantifiers (such as "all" or "no") or intensifiers (such as "absolute" or "certainly"); and (5) euphemism. (See Chapters 2 and 7.) If the passage includes a definition, note what kind it is (denotative, logical, stipulative, or persuasive). Be particularly alert to the use of persuasive definition—redefining a term while at the same time preserving its old emotive impact. Lastly, make sure you can state precisely what the argument is attempting to demonstrate.

Step 2: Identify Conclusion and Premises

Recall that signal words such as the following are helpful in identifying premises and conclusions:

> **Conclusion signals:** then, therefore, consequently, it follows that (and so forth)
> **Area premise signals:** since, because, for, insofar as (and so forth)
> **Specific premise signals:** first, . . . second, . . . third; for one thing . . . for another (and so forth)

When an argument contains no such words, ask yourself, What is being advanced? What is the arguer trying to demonstrate as true? The answer to these questions most probably is the argument's conclusion. Similarly, to locate premises in the absence of signals, ask yourself, Why should I accept the conclusion as true? What basis does the arguer give for drawing the conclusion? (See Chapter 4.)

Step 3: Cast the Argument

Short, simple arguments don't need to be cast, but with longer, more involved ones casting can be very useful both in grasping the argument's overall structure and in keeping track of its many details. The casting method developed in this book consists of three steps: (1) putting brackets at the beginning and end of each assertion, (2) numbering assertions consecutively, and (3) setting out the relationships among the assertions in a tree diagram to be read down the page. When casting a passage with rhetorical devices,

1. Cast each separate assertion.
2. Don't cast repetitions of the same assertion.
3. Don't cast asides.
4. Don't cast background information.
5. Don't cast examples that merely illustrate or clarify a point.
6. Cast examples used to support a point being made, that is, examples that indicate why the point is so.
7. Don't cast as separate assertions information that follows a colon.
8. Cast as separate assertions information separated by a semicolon. (See Chapter 5.)

Step 4: Fill in Missing Premises

In general, you should fill in missing premises whenever an argument is incomplete and you can identify a plausible and relevant assertion that would complete it and that is part of the arguer's position.

The "what if" strategy helps you identify incomplete arguments. Ask "what if" the stated premise(s) is true? Would the conclusion have to be true? If the answer is yes, the argument is complete; if it is no, the argument is incomplete.

Plausibility has to do with the credibility or believability of an idea. It is a measure of how well we think an idea is likely to survive critical scrutiny. If we were to devise strenuous tests designed to falsify an idea, how would the idea do? A plausible idea is one that we think would do well. An implausible idea is one that we think would not do so well. In filling in missing premises we generally try to avoid implausible assertions, even if adding them would make the argument complete. This is because we want to give an argument a fair run for its money. Similarly, in assessing candidates for the role of missing premise, preference generally goes to the more plausible alternative.

The topic coverage strategy is a strategy you can use to determine the relevance of candidates for the role of missing premise. Think of this as similar to searching for a missing piece in a jigsaw puzzle. By paying close attention to the topics covered in the conclusion and expressed premise(s) of the argument, you can get a better sense of the "shape" of the hole or gap you're trying to fill in, and of the missing premise that can fill it.

The trickiest part of filling in missing premises is remaining faithful to the arguer's actual position. When we say that in filling in missing premises we should try to remain faithful to the arguer's position, we don't merely mean that we should remain faithful to what the arguer is aware of or willing to admit to. We mean rather that the missing premise should be something that the arguer would accept as part of her view if she were aware of it, or that she must be committed to in order for her reasoning to make sense.

In trying to remain faithful to the arguer's actual position, try to reconstruct a premise that is just strong enough to help support the conclusion. A reconstruction that overstates the missing premise misrepresents the argument, thereby making it easy to refute illegitimately. One that understates the missing premise will be too weak to help support the conclusion.

In trying to remain faithful to the arguer's actual position try to reconstruct a premise that illuminates, and doesn't just repeat in an ad hoc fashion, the original incomplete argument.

Longer arguments may contain many missing premises that when reconstructed help generate mini-arguments. (See Chapter 6.)

Step 5: Examine the Main Premises and Support for Justification

Remember, in criticizing arguments you are evaluating them for cogency. And a cogent argument is one that is both valid and based on true or justified premises. A true premise is a statement that describes an actual state of affairs: present, past, or future. Generally, premises are subject to dispute and therefore also to verification.

For some types of assertions—necessary truths—verification is not a problem. Necessary truths, including tautologies and truths by definition, are statements whose denials are self-contradictory, and therefore necessarily false.

In contrast, verifying contingent statements is problematic. Contingent statements are neither self-contradictory nor necessarily true. Contingent statements can be considered true when there is reasonable evidence to support them. The problems involved in verification depend on the kind of assertion involved.

Factual assertions include observations and hypotheses. Five key points must be considered when evaluating observations: (1) the physical conditions under which the observations were made, (2) the sensory acuity of the observer, (3) the necessary background knowledge, (4) the objectivity of the observer, and (5) supporting testimony. Hypotheses are verified by seeking confirmation and disconfirmation. This frequently involves making observations.

Value judgments are another type of statement whose verification is problematic. Value assertions are judgments of worth: "Murder is immoral"; "Capital punishment should be legalized for certain serious crimes"; "Steven Spielberg is a great film director"; "Democracy is the best form of government." In verifying a value judgment, first clarify the value words contained in the assertion, deciding whether (1) personal preference, (2) social preference, or (3) conformity to law, principle, or standard is indicated by their use. Then weigh the reasons and arguments in favor of and against accepting the value judgment.

Step 6: Examine the Argument for Fallacies

Again, remember that in evaluating arguments for cogency you are trying to assess the strength or validity of the connection between the conclusion and the premises offered as support, as well as the truth or acceptability of the supporting premises. Determine whether the argument should be understood as a deductive or an inductive one.

Deductive validity is a feature of the form or pattern an argument follows. Deductively valid argument forms are absolutely reliable. If the premises of an argument that follows a deductively valid pattern are true, there is no room for doubt as to the truth of its conclusion. A foolproof test for deductive validity involves seeing whether accepting the premises and denying the conclusion is self-contradictory. If it is, then the argument is deductively valid. If not, the argument is not deductively valid.

Inductive arguments leave room for doubt as to the truth of their conclusions. A valid inductive argument is one whose premises give probable grounds for its conclusion. Some inductive arguments are stronger than others. The strength of an inductive argument depends in part on the size and representativeness of the sample enumerated in its premises.

Inferences that are unreliable are called "fallacies." An inference that follows an unreliable form or pattern is called a "formal fallacy."

Informal fallacies are unreliable inferences whose unreliability has to do with things other than their formal structure. The informal fallacy categories are best understood not as strictly defined and mutually exclusive, but rather as useful terminology for understanding and explaining weaknesses that occur in reasoning. Bear in mind that a given argument may be fallacious in several ways at once, and that a given argument may look fallacious but not actually be fallacious. Be alert to the strategy that the argument employs. Does it try to make its point on the basis of a comparison or analogy? Does it depend heavily on criticizing an opposing position? Does it involve a causal hypothesis? Use your insights into the argument's strategy to guide your search for possible weaknesses. Is the comparison a good one? Is the argument's representation of the opposing position fair? And so on. Be alert for possible ambiguity and abuse of rhetorical features of language, and check the relevance of the support to what is supported.

Don't forget to check for consistency among the claims made in an argument, between those claims and other things you have good reason to believe, and between the positions involved in a system of beliefs; and don't forget to trace the implications of a thesis or argument.

Finally, don't forget that evaluating arguments, particularly in informal terms, can be a pretty messy business. You can expect to encounter a fair number of arguments that can quite clearly be faulted in one way or another, and occasionally you'll find an argument that is pretty clearly impeccable. But a great many arguments are neither clearly fallacious nor clearly not. In such cases, you should consider your criticisms to be essentially contestible, and therefore you should also recognize the need to supply arguments in support of them, to deal with arguments against them, and perhaps to change your mind.

Step 7: Give an Overall Evaluation

Having completed the preceding steps, you are now in a position to give the argument an overall assessment. Does it have force? If so, how much? Are you ready to go with the argument on balance, or against it? Has the arguer won you over? To answer questions like these, return to your criticisms, especially to steps 5 and 6. Are the argument's essential premises so flawed that they provide little or no support for the conclusion? Or are there flaws contained in premises that are not essential to the claim? In a very short argument, it's rarely necessary to ask questions like these, for the judgments made in step 6 will dictate the overall evaluation. But a complicated argument poses the same problem of overall judgment that the intelligent voter faces when voting. Inevitably there are reasons that argue for a vote and reasons that argue against it. Your job and ours is to decide whether, when all things are considered, we should endorse one candidate rather than another. Similarly, a long sophisticated argument may offer many reasons for advancing its claim, some fair and legitimate and others unfair and illegitimate. We must decide which reasons are legitimate and whether they are sufficient to endorse the claim.

Rendering an overall evaluation is an important part of the evaluative process, for—if nothing else—it keeps critical thinking from becoming a bloodless, abstract exercise. It allows you to decide whether or not to believe, to endorse, and possibly to act on a claim. It also gives you an opportunity, which you should take, to show how the argument could be improved. Finally, it allows you to clarify your own beliefs as you respond to the argument in a creative and constructive way, and perhaps most important of all, to study and reflect critically on your own beliefs and procedures.

APPLYING THE SEVEN STEPS

It's now time to apply the seven-step format in argument analysis and evaluation. The following examples, which present arguments exhibiting a variety of defects, show how you can use the format to detect these defects and assess the arguments. Although we will proceed through each of the steps, keep in mind that it is not always necessary to do so.

Argument 1

The Argument: Surely life exists elsewhere in the universe. After all, most space scientists today admit the possibility that life evolved on other planets. Besides, other planets in our solar system are strikingly like Earth. They revolve around the sun, they borrow light from the sun, and several are known to revolve on their axes, and to be subject to the same laws of gravitation as Earth. What's more, aren't those who make light of extraterrestrial life soft-headed fundamentalists clinging to the foolish notion that life is unique to their planet?

Step 1: Clarify Meaning
"Life" is ambiguous: What kind of life is meant—vegetable, animal, human, amino acids? "Surely" is an extreme intensifier. The last sentence is directive and expressive but also informative. It's also a rhetorical question. The arguer is claiming that life exists somewhere other than Earth.

Step 2: Identify Conclusion and Premises
Conclusion: Life exists elsewhere in the universe.

Premise: Space scientists admit the possibility that life has evolved on other planets.

Premise: Other planets in our solar system are strikingly like Earth.

Premise: Those who make light of extraterrestrial life are soft-headed fundamentalists clinging to the foolish notion that life is unique to this planet.

Step 3: Cast the Argument
Surely [life exists elsewhere in the universe.]¹ After all, [most space scientists today admit the possibility that life has evolved on other planets.]² Besides, [other planets in our solar system are strikingly like Earth.]³ [They revolve around the sun,]⁴ [they borrow light from the sun,]⁵ and [several are known to revolve on their axes]⁶ and [to be subject to the same laws of gravitation as Earth.]⁷ What's more, [aren't those who make light of extraterrestrial life soft-headed fundamentalists clinging to the foolish notion that life is unique to this planet?]⁸

Step 4: Fill in Missing Premises
There are none that aren't obvious, although the arguer might disagree, as we'll see in step 7.

Step 5: Examine the Main Premises and Support for Justification
Assertion 2 is a true contingent statement. Mini-premises 4, 5, 6, and 7 are true contingent statements. The justification of assertion 3 depends on whether the arguer has overlooked significant differences between Earth and other planets that are relevant to the claim that life exists elsewhere in the universe. Assertion 8 is a false contingent statement because not everyone who makes light of extraterrestrial life is a "soft-headed fundamentalist clinging to the foolish notion that life is unique to this planet."

Step 6: Examine the Argument for Fallacies
Assertion 2, which supports assertion 1, contains a legitimate appeal to authority or expert opinion. There is general agreement among the experts about the *possibility* of extraterrestrial life. However, assertion 2 is a red herring because it only supports the claim that there *may be* life elsewhere in the universe and *not* the argument's claim, made in assertion 1, that such life "surely exists." So assertion 2 does not entail assertion 1. Assertion 3 draws an analogy between Earth and other planets such that other planets likely share with Earth an additional characteristic: the existence of life. But the arguer omits at least one significant difference between Earth and other planets: Not all planets revolve around the sun at the same distance from it that Earth does, and a difference in distance could produce such a difference in temperature that life as we understand it would be impossible. Given this consideration alone, the analogy is questionable. Besides this, the arguer omits the fact (thereby offering a half-

truth) that space probes to some other planets, for example Mars, have provided no substantial evidence to support a claim for extraterrestrial life. It's possible that the arguer will object to the criticism that assertion 2 is a red herring by saying, "You've overlooked my assumption, which is 'What most space scientists believe to be the case is actually the case.' Given the unexpressed premise *a*, my claim that most space scientists believe in the possibility of life elsewhere in the universe is altogether relevant to the conclusion." Suppose we concede that assertion 2, together with unexpressed premise *a*, does entail assertion 1. However, unexpressed premise *a* is also very implausible. Similarly, with respect to the inference from 8, the arguer might say, "I'm assuming that 'Whatever only fundamentalists believe is actually false.' This unexpressed premise *b*, when added to premise 8, does logically entail assertion 1." Fine, but this assumption also is preposterous, and question begging. The main point is that even if the reasoning process from premises 2 + *a* to conclusion 1, and from premises 8 + *b* to conclusion 1 are valid, the assumptions themselves are false or highly questionable. And of course premise 8 itself is false (as well as an example of abusive *ad hominem* and question begging). The reason we did not include these assumptions under step 4 (filling in missing premises) is that they, or something like them, would not redeem the argument. More important, they divert attention from the gross fallacies the arguer commits. Furthermore, the inference to 1 from 3 is invalid because even the best analogy doesn't prove anything conclusively. Good analogies offer at best a high probability. Thus, if this analogy were a good one, the strongest conclusion it would warrant would be something like "Life *probably* exists somewhere else in the universe."

Step 7: Give an Overall Evaluation

There is nothing to weigh in balance concerning this argument. It is clearly a bad one. Although there may be good reasons for believing that life exists elsewhere in the universe, this argument doesn't provide any of them. As a matter of fact, given current evidence, there is no basis for arguing that such life *certainly* exists. A good argument for the *probability* of extraterrestrial life would begin by indicating what kind of life is intended and then show through statistics culled from the study of astronomy that the chances of that life-form existing elsewhere in the universe are extraordinarily high.

Argument 2

The Argument: In the fury that surrounds the debate about school prayer, it is sometimes forgotten that prayer is an essential part of religion. To permit school prayer is virtually the same as endorsing religion. What can be said, then, for religion? Not much, I'm afraid. Indeed, religion is dangerous. It has spawned numerous wars throughout history. Today it continues to sow the seeds of discontent and destruction in Northern Ireland and the Middle East. It divides people by emphasizing their differences rather than their similarities. It breeds intolerance of people of opposed views. Is there any doubt, therefore, that the responsible citizen should oppose school prayer?

Step 1: Clarify Meaning

"Prayer" and "religion" are ambiguous. Let us take "prayer" to mean a spiritual communion with God or an object of worship and "religion" to mean an organized system of belief in and worship of that God or object of worship. "Virtually" is a weasel. Every assertion made about religion in this argument is an unqualified generalization. "Spawns," "breeds," and "sows the seeds" are emotive. The last sentence is directive but also informative, a rhetorical question and a persuasive definition.

Step 2: Identify the Conclusion and Main Premises
Conclusion: The responsible citizen should oppose school prayer.
Premise: To permit school prayer is virtually the same as endorsing religion.
Premise: Religion is dangerous.

Step 3: Cast the Argument
In the fury that surrounds the debate about school prayer, it is sometimes forgotten that [prayer is an essential part of religion.][1] [To permit school prayer is virtually the same as endorsing religion.][2] What can be said, then, for religion? Not much, I'm afraid. Indeed, [religion is dangerous.][3] [It has spawned numerous wars throughout history.][4] [Today it continues to sow the seeds of discontent and destruction in Northern Ireland and the Middle East.][5] [It divides people by emphasizing their differences rather than their similarities.][6] [It breeds intolerance of people of opposed views.][7] Is there any doubt, therefore, that [the responsible citizen should oppose school prayer?][8]

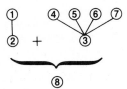

Step 4: Fill in Missing Premises
Mini-conclusion 2 follows from mini-premise 1 plus the unexpressed premise *a*: "Permitting an essential part of religion to be practiced in school is virtually the same as endorsing religion." Thus:

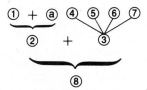

Step 5: Examine Main Premises and Support for Justification
It's difficult to evaluate mini-premise 1 because "prayer" and "religion" are ambiguous. But if these terms are stipulated as in step 1, then we might accept the assertion as true. Unexpressed premise *a* is vague and misleading. "Endorsing" literally means "supporting." If the state allows school prayer and if prayer is an essential part of religion, then presumably it could be argued that the state "supports" religion in the sense that it provides a constitutional basis for the practice of religion in the classroom. More about this unexpressed premise in the next step. Mini-conclusion 3 is a value judgment ("dangerous") that needs

considerable support, which presumably is provided by mini-premises 4, 5, 6, and 7. An evaluation of these support assertions is best left to the next step. In sum, assertion 1 is acceptable; assertions 2 and 3 (together with assertions 4, 5, 6, and 7) warrant closer inspection.

Step 6: Examine the Argument for Fallacies

Returning to unexpressed premise *a*, and by implication mini-conclusion 2, we find "endorsing" loaded with subjective connotations. An example will illustrate. The state permits the publication and sale of pornographic materials. Can it be said, then, that the state "endorses" pornographic enterprises? Yes, but only if "endorses" is taken to mean "support," and "support" in turn is taken to mean providing a judicial basis for the manufacture and sale of pornographic materials. But "endorsing" carries the subjective connotation of "approval" or "actively advancing the interests of." But the state does not endorse pornographic enterprises in either of these senses. In fact, if you read the Supreme Court rulings on pornography, you'll find that the justices who comment without exception express revulsion toward pornography. The court's "permission," then, is based not on approval, and certainly not on active support of the interests of pornographers, but on an interpretation of the constitutional right to freedom of expression. Therefore, to say that the state "endorses" pornography is, at the very least, misleading. Similarly, it seems just as misleading to argue that permitting school prayer is tantamount to endorsing religion in the sense of approving of or actively supporting the interests of religion. For this reason, we're calling "endorsing" in unexpressed premise *a* and mini-conclusion 2 a loaded word.

But even if the arguer insists that "permit" implies "endorse" and "endorse" in turn implies "approval of" or "actively advancing the interests of," then we must be clear about what it is that's being approved or advanced. It isn't religion but individual freedom, specifically the opportunity for the individual to say (or refrain from saying) a prayer in a public classroom, so long as that practice does not conflict with the constitutional doctrine of church-state separation. Stated another way, if school prayer does not violate church-state separation, then there is no constitutional basis for restricting individual freedom to worship. Consider the pornography example again. If the manufacture and sale of pornographic material is permitted, what is being approved of and actively advanced is the individual right to freedom of expression. To say that what is being underwritten is the pornography industry is a distortion, a straw person. It is as much a straw, arguably, to say that permitting school prayer is tantamount to endorsing (that is, approving or actively advancing) religion. And the straw lies in the connotations of "endorsing."

The judgment that unexpressed premise *a* and mini-conclusion 2 introduce a straw is supported by what follows in the argument, namely, an attack on religion. Having identified prayer with religion, the arguer then attempts to show why religion is dangerous. The diversionary tack here is to discredit school prayer by discrediting religion. Whether or not this strategy proves effective very much depends on the audience's perceptions of religion. But is it really easier to "blow over" religion, and with it school prayer, than to repudiate school prayer on legitimate grounds, namely, by attempting to show how school prayer violates the doctrine of church-state separation? In other words, even if mini-premises 4, 5, 6, and 7 are true, so what? All they would do is support the claim that religion is dangerous, mini-conclusion 3. But how does this address the school prayer issue? The arguer undoubtedly will point to mini-argument which is intended to identify prayer with religion and school prayer with endorsing religion. We have already seen that this argument is open to criticism on grounds of ambiguity, loaded language, and straw person.

If we wanted to be extremely charitable, we could concede the legitimacy of

and then closely inspect the mini-argument

Mini-premises 4, 5, 6, and 7 are generalizations that need qualification. They are also half-truths, for they omit to mention that religion has contributed to understanding and human betterment, to the establishment and maintenance of social services (such as schools, orphanages, hospitals, and disaster relief agencies), and the formation of humanity's highest ideals. Moreover, 4 and 5 are causal oversimplifications. Beyond this, in the context of the main argument, all these mini-premises are diversionary appeals to fear and slippery slope, such that if school prayer is permitted, presumably those dreadful things associated with religion will inevitable follow.

Step 7: Give an Overall Evaluation

The argument is not cogent. The premises and their support exhibit a variety of fallacies, including half-truth, straw person, appeal to fear, causal oversimplification, as well as loaded and ambiguous language. When the premises and support are stripped of these ploys, they collapse, thus rendering the conclusion unwarranted. A much more powerful argument against school prayer would attempt to establish that permitting school prayer violates the doctrine of church-state separation and that this doctrine is worthwhile. The preceding argument doesn't do this, nor does it develop an alternatively compelling argument against school prayer.

Argument 3

The Argument: When you call 911 in an emergency, some police departments have a way of telling your telephone number and address without your saying a word. The chief value of this, say the police, is that if the caller is unable to communicate for any reason, the dispatcher knows where to send help. But don't be duped by such paternalistic explanations. This technology is a despicable invasion of privacy, for callers may be unaware of the insidious device. Even if they are, some persons who wish anonymity may be reluctant to call for emergency help. Remember that the names of complainants and witnesses are recorded in many communities' criminal justice systems. A fairer and more effective system seemingly would include an auxiliary number for callers who wish anonymity.

Step 1: Clarify Meaning

Some highly emotive language is used: "duped," "despicable," "insidious." "Paternalistic" is used accurately, but it does have negative connotations. The sentence beginning "This technology . . ." is both informative and expressive; the one beginning "Remember . . ." is both informative and directive. The arguer carefully qualifies generalizations by using words such as "some," "may be," "many," and "seemingly." The term "emergency help" seems vague. What kind of emergency is intended: a heart attack, an accident, a fire, a crime? What is clear is that the arguer doesn't want to scrap the emergency phone system by which telephone numbers and addresses of callers are recorded but to supplement it with a system that protects caller anonymity.

Step 2: Identify Conclusion and Main Premises

Conclusion: A fairer and more effective system seemingly would include an auxiliary number for callers who wish anonymity.

Premise: This technology (i.e., the system that records personal information about callers) is a despicable invasion of privacy.

Premise: If they are aware, some persons who wish anonymity may be reluctant to call for emergency help.

Step 3: Cast the Argument

When you call 911 in an emergency, some police departments have a way of telling your telephone number and address without your saying a word. The chief value of this, say the police, is that if the caller is unable to communicate for any reason, the dispatcher knows where to send help. But don't be duped by such paternalistic explanations. [This technology is a despicable invasion of privacy,][1] for [callers may be unaware of the insidious device.][2] [Even if they are, some persons who wish anonymity may be reluctant to call for emergency help.][3] [Remember that the names of complainants and witnesses are recorded in many communities' criminal justice systems.][4] [A fairer and more effective system seemingly would include an auxiliary number for callers who wish anonymity.][5]

Assuming the first three sentences are background and not part of the argument proper, the argument can be cast as follows:

Step 4: Fill in Missing Premises

Underlying mini-conclusion 1 seems to be the unexpressed premise *a* that collecting information about people without their informed consent is an invasion of privacy. The argument, then, could be recast as follows:

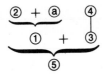

Step 5: Examine the Main Premises and Support for Justification

Unexpressed premise *a* poses no problems: When data about people are collected without their knowledge and agreement, their privacy is indeed invaded. One might say that this is part of what "privacy" means, and thus that premise *a* is acceptable on semantic grounds. Assertion 2 is a true contingent statement. Mini-conclusion 1, then, devoid of the inflammatory terms "despicable" and "insidious," is true, since it is validly deduced from 2 + *a*. If 2 and *a* are justified, it would be contradictory to deny this conclusion. (Of course, we assume that the arguer doesn't mean that the technology itself is an invasion of privacy, but that certain acts involving the use of it are.) Mini-conclusion 3 is a contingent statement. Studies do show that people are most reluctant to get personally involved in reporting crimes. But are people equally reluctant to report things like accidents and fires? That's doubtful. It's even more doubtful that they are reluctant to identify themselves in seeking emergency help for something like a heart attack. Despite these reservations we may accept 3, giving the arguer the benefit of the doubt since she has carefully qualified the generalization with the words "some" and "may be." Mini-premise 4, which supports mini-conclusion 3, is a fact.

Step 6: Examine the Argument for Fallacies

The sentence "But don't be duped by such paternalistic explanations" is a case of well poisoning, but is not essential to the argument. Assertions 1 and 2 contain the highly emotive "despicable" and "insidious." "Emergency help" in assertion 3 is ambiguous.

Step 7: Give an Overall Evaluation

It is true that assertions 1 and 2 use emotive language and assertion 3 is ambiguous ("emergency help"). But the argument doesn't rely exclusively or even primarily on either of these devices. In other words, stripped of these devices, the premises are justified and do provide legitimate support for the qualified conclusion that a fairer and more effective system *seemingly* would include an auxiliary number. (Remember, even though an argument may stoop to a fallacious device or two, it may nevertheless rest on strong enough additional bases to qualify as cogent. The key point is whether the argument relies solely or chiefly on the objectionable features. If it does, it's fallacious. If not, then it may yet be cogent. This argument appears to be cogent.) This argument appears to carve out some middle ground regarding an emergency telephone system. It reminds us that the system needn't be construed in black-and-white terms as one that either (1) records information about callers and thus violates privacy and discourages calls or (2) does not record information, which would respect privacy and encourage the otherwise reluctant to call but would leave in the lurch those unable to communicate. The argument's few intensifying devices do not undercut the support for its conclusion. In brief, subject to the possibility of overriding counterarguments, the argument makes a convincing case that the auxiliary number approach probably would make a fairer and more effective call system.

Summary

The format for argument analysis and evaluation that was developed in this chapter consists of the following seven steps:

1. Clarify meaning.
2. Identify conclusion and main premises.
3. Cast the argument.
4. Fill in the missing premises.
5. Examine the main premises and support for justification.
6. Examine the argument for fallacies.
7. Give an overall evaluation.

All evaluation of arguments presupposes some analysis, but the amount of analysis preceding the actual evaluation depends on the complexity of the argument. A short, simple argument may require very little detailed analysis. Also some of the steps of analysis presuppose preliminary evaluation. The seven-step procedure, then, is offered with the following qualifications:

1. You may find it useful to reverse the order of certain steps in this procedure or to work back and forth between them on occasion; and it may not always be necessary to work through each step of the analysis for every argument you encounter.
2. Although an argument may contain fallacies, it doesn't therefore necessarily fail to be cogent. Fallacies are fatal only when they are relied on exclusively or primarily to make a point. If when stripped of an objectionable device an assertion can still be evaluated for truth and is relevant to the argument, then the device does not invalidate it. But if the assertion collapses when the device is knocked out from under it, then the assertion is illegitimate.
3. When in doubt about the arguer's meaning or intent, always give the arguer the benefit of the doubt. This especially applies to reconstructing missing premises. Remember, critical thinking doesn't aim to embarrass or humiliate. It does not entail nitpicking. Rather, it aims to make sense of written and oral communication and raise *substantive* points of criticism about it.
4. In giving an overall evaluation, state whether the argument has force for you and explain why it does or does not. Since critical thinking aims to raise the level of discussion on issues, you should also indicate how the argument could be improved, that is, what points it would need to make to win you over.

Applications

Application 1. Apply the seven-step format to the following arguments.

1. There's no question that everyone should take vitamin E daily. For one thing, vitamin E increases the sex drive. Not only have I noticed this myself, but friends who have taken the vitamin regularly for a year report the same thing. Studies confirm that this wondrous elixir also strengthens the heart muscles. Besides, if you don't take vitamin E regularly, then your cells will lose vital oxygen, thereby depriving your body of critical restorative powers. The upshot will be a general deterioration in your health.

2. *"The prayer for others.* Such prayers are potent because, first of all, they are a wonderful way of getting ourselves off our hands. And they are powerful because they *can* change the lives of others.

   "An elderly woman once told me how she had been dangerously ill in the hospital and in pain. She had lost her courage and was fighting against tests she needed because it seemed to her that she could bear no more pain. But one day a note came from her church—a place where prayer meetings had long since gone out of fashion—to tell her that her friends had formed a prayer circle and would pray all night for her. 'About one o'clock,' she said, 'I fell asleep and slept as soundly as a child.' The next day she went cheerfully to take her tests and began a slow but steady convalescence." (Ardis Whitman, "Six Special Powers of Prayer," *Reader's Digest,* May 1980, p. 71.)

3. "Although men as well as women struggle with extra pounds, in our culture fat seems to be particularly a woman's problem. I do not know whether there are more fat women than fat men, although women's bodies do contain a higher proportion of fat. But women far outnumber men in organizations like Weight Watchers or Overeaters Anonymous. Almost every issue of most women's magazines announces the 'newest diet,' not so magazines for men. Whether or not women are fatter than men, they worry about it more." (Elsa Dixler, "Fat Liberation," *Psychology Today,* May 1980, p. 110.)

4. "Most Americans . . . will argue that technology is neutral, that any technology is merely a benign instrument, a tool, and depending upon the hands into which it falls, it may be used one way or another. [So] the

argument goes that television is merely a window or a conduit through which any perception, any argument or reality may pass. It therefore has the potential to be enlightening to people who watch it and is potentially useful to democratic processes." (Jerry Mander, *Four Arguments for the Elimination of Television,* p. 43)

5. "[T]hese assumptions about television, as about other technologies, are totally wrong. If you once accept the principle of an army—a collection of military technologies and people to run them—all gathered together for the purpose of fighting, overpowering, killing and winning, then it is obvious that the supervisors of armies will be the sort of people who desire to fight, overpower, kill and win, and who are good at these assignments: generals. . . .

"If you accept the existence of automobiles, you also accept the existence of roads laid upon the landscape, oil to run the cars, and huge institutions to find the oil, pump it and distribute it. In addition you accept a sped-up style of life and the movement of humans through the terrain at speeds that make it impossible to pay attention to whatever is growing there. Humans who use cars sit in fixed positions for long hours following a narrow strip of gray pavement, with eyes fixed forward, engaged in the task of driving. . . . Slowly they evolve into car-people. "If you accept nuclear power plants, you also accept a techno-scientific-industrial-military elite. Without these people in charge, you could not have nuclear power. You and I getting together with a few friends could not make use of nuclear power. We could not build such a plant, nor could we . . . handle or store the radioactive waste products which remain dangerous to life for thousands of years. The wastes, in turn, determine that *future* societies will have to maintain a technological capacity to deal with the problem and the military capability to protect the wastes. . . .

"If you accept mass production, you accept that a small number of people will supervise the daily existence of a much larger number of people. You accept that human beings will spend long hours, every day, engaged in repetitive work, while suppressing any desires for experience or activity beyond this work. . . . With mass production, you also accept that huge numbers of identical items will need to be efficiently distributed to huge numbers of people and that institutions such as advertising will arise to do this. . . .

"If you accept the existence of advertising, you accept a system designed to persuade and to dominate minds by interfering in people's thinking patterns. You also accept that the system will be used by the sorts of people who like to influence people and are good at it. . . .

"In all of these instances, the basic form of the institution and the technology determines its interaction with the world, the way it will be used, the kind of people who will use it, and to what ends.

"And so it is with television.

"Far from being "neutral," television itself predetermines who shall use it, how they will use it, what effects it will have on individual lives, and, if it continues to be widely used, what sorts of political forms will inevitably emerge." (Jerry Mander, *Four Arguments for the Elimination of Television,* pp. 43–45).

Application 2. Apply the seven-step procedure to the following arguments from this text:

a. Part of believing something is believing that it's true. So if I were to do an inventory of my beliefs, they'd all seem true to me. Or, to put it another way, if I knew something was false, I wouldn't believe it. So what sense does it make for me to say that some of my own beliefs are false?

b. I've been mistaken in the past. I've learned on numerous occasions, and pretty much throughout my life, that things that I believed to be true were really false. Why should it be any different now? So if I were to do an inventory of my beliefs I probably wouldn't notice the false ones, but I'd still bet there are some in there somewhere.

c. When you argue for a position, you imply that another position exists. After all, if an issue were one-sided, arguing about it would be as pointless as trying to prove a widely known fact. Whether or not you argue effectively for your position depends largely on how well you understand and how deeply and sympathetically you consider the other side or sides to the issue.

"But," you might wonder, "how do I know for sure that my audience holds an opposing position?" True enough. In many cases you don't. But like yourself, your readers are critical thinkers. As such, they can be expected to raise challenging questions, just as you would. And chances are that most of the time your readers won't be in complete agreement with the position you're advancing. Inevitably, if you're arguing for an interesting position on an issue of any depth and complexity at all, and you're trying to be rationally persuasive, you'll need to confront the opposition. You'll need to address yourself to readers who presumably disagree with you, and who disagree with you on some basis or other for which they would themselves presumably be prepared to argue. In what spirit should you confront such opposition?

Thomas Aquinas once remarked that when you want to convert someone to your view, you go over to where he is standing, take him by the hand (mentally speaking), and guide him to where you want him to go. You don't stand across the room and shout at him. You don't call him nasty names. You don't order him to come over to where you are. You start where he is, and work from that position. To put it another way: When you think that someone is wrong, and you disagree with her, your first task is to determine in what way she is right. This is not as paradoxical as it sounds. Suppose you're firmly convinced of some particular position on a complex and controversial subject like the death penalty. Are you absolutely certain that you're 100 percent correct? Can you be absolutely certain that someone who disagrees with you is entirely wrong in everything they might have to say? Wouldn't it be wiser to consider thoughtfully what your opponent might have to say, and to concede as much as you honestly can? Then when you go on to offer criticisms of your opponent's position, you can reasonably expect them to be given thoughtful consideration as well. After all, think how you would react as a reader to a criticism of your position. If the criticism starts out by identifying your position as out-to-lunch, you're not likely to be very receptive, are you? You'd be much more open to a criticism which began by stating your position in a way that you would yourself state it, recognizing its intuitive plausibility, or its explanatory power, or the weight of evidence in its favor, or whatever strengths it may have. Thus, when you oppose a position and undertake to criticize it you enhance your chances of being persuasive if you can state that position in a way that would fully satisfy someone who holds it—even more so if you can make out a better case for it than the proponent herself can.

Just as you should be aware of the possibility that your opponent's position may embody certain strengths, you should be aware of the possibility that your own position may have certain weaknesses— weaknesses which very likely will be more apparent to your opponent than to you. Thus an additional strategic advantage for the writer of an argumentative essay flows from making a genuine attempt to appreciate the opponent's position. Your opponent's position affords you a much better vantage point from which to troubleshoot your own position and argument—to make yourself aware of points at which your argument stands in need of additional support, or of needed qualifications and refinements of the thesis itself.

d. Perhaps the most disturbing of the detectable effects of television is the impact it has apparently had on journalism, upon the news as it is gathered, reported, and interpreted in our society. Neil Postman, Professor of Communications at New York University, and a media analyst who has taken considerable interest in critical thinking, notes in his most recent book *Amusing Ourselves to Death: Public Discourse in the Age of Show Business* that news and public affairs programming on television has degenerated almost entirely into entertainment, and that more traditional print journalism is being dragged along in the same direction. We have already discussed the centrality of entertainment as a dominant value in television programming generally. One look at a typical national or local newscast will quickly confirm Postman's observations that television news consists almost entirely of discontinuous fragments presented in an essentially entertaining format and that it effectively trivializes everything it touches. In case this assessment sounds uninformed or too harsh, Postman goes on to quote from Robert MacNeil, executive editor and co-anchor of the "MacNeil-Lehrer News Hour" who writes that the essential idea in television news production is "to keep everything brief, not to strain the attention of anyone but instead to provide constant stimulation through variety, novelty, action, and movement. . . . [The assumptions controlling the production are] that bite-sized is best, that complexity must be avoided, that nuances are dispensible, that qualifications impede the simple message, that visual stimulation is a substitute for thought, and that verbal precision is an anachronism."

There are, to be sure, some notable exceptions to this general rule: Ted Koppel's "Nightline" program, particularly the week-long series of programs he produced in 1988 in the Holy Land; and the occasional "MacNeil-Lehrer Report." But such exceptions tend to prove the rule.

If we assume Postman's account to be a fair assessment of the general trend in television journalism, what evidence is there of a similar tendency in journalism as a whole? Postman notes the emergence of *USA Today* and its rapid rise in its first two years of publication to the position of the nation's third largest daily newspaper. Its stories are uncommonly short, frequently no longer than a single paragraph, approximating the level of demand on reader attention typical of television. Its design is colorful and emphasizes graphics over verbal text. It is even sold on the streets through dispensers which resemble television sets. The successful *USA Today* format has begun to penetrate the approach of more traditional dailies, chiefly local and regional dailies, particularly as they have become absorbed into larger organizations like the New York Times chain and undergo editorial and management changes.

Application 3. Revise one of the preceding arguments that you found inadequate. Construct a version of it that you think is cogent and has force. (Your instructor may then have class members swap arguments for analysis and evaluation, using the seven-step procedure.)

Application 4. Apply the seven-step format to five arguments that you find in the newspapers or news magazines.

THE EXTENDED ARGUMENT | 12

So far we have considered relatively short arguments, ones consisting of no more than a paragraph or two. But many arguments come in multiparagraph form and are commonly termed "argumentative essays" or (when oral) "speeches of conviction." Open a newspaper to the opinion-commentary page, look at an article in some magazine, or listen to a policy address made by an important public figure, and chances are you'll find an extended argument. Indeed, it is the extended argument that you will most have occasion to ponder. Any introduction to critical thinking that aims to make you a more searching reader and thinker therefore would be incomplete without consideration of this widespread argumentative form.

The extended argument contains all the elements of a short argument: signal words, unexpressed premises, premise support, and occasional objectionable devices, or fallacies. In fact, the extended argument can be viewed as a string of shorter arguments, all of which support a main idea. As a result, if you have mastered the seven-step procedure developed in the preceding chapter, you should be able to respond intelligently to longer discourses.

This chapter shows how the seven-step format applies to extended arguments. It also covers an alternative approach to assessing arguments that makes use of the outline. As a convenience, we will use the terms "argumentative essay" or simply "essay" to mean "extended argument." This convention seems warranted since you typically will encounter the extended argument in essay form.

ORGANIZATION

The **organization** of an argumentative essay refers to how it is structured. In the next chapter we will discuss organizational strategies from the point of view of the developing writer. Here, however, we are concerned with organization from the point of view of the reader.

Understanding the organization or logical structure of an argumentative essay is analogous to understanding the structure of an argument. Essentially, each involves grasping and appreciating the relationships of support that obtain between individual structural elements, the most important of which is the conclusion or thesis. Just as the conclusion of a short argument can appear at any point from the beginning to the middle to the end, so can the thesis of an argumentative essay. Typically though, one can expect to find the thesis at or near the beginning of the essay, in its opening paragraphs, which hereafter we'll take to mean the first two or three paragraphs. These paragraphs are then followed by paragraphs that provide supporting materials. Occasionally however, writers present their supporting materials first, especially when dealing with highly controversial topics. It is not until the closing paragraphs—hereafter taken to mean the final two or three paragraphs—that they state or imply their thesis.

In an argumentative essay a great many points typically will be made, some will be offered as direct support for the thesis, others will be offered in support of these main points, and still others offered in support of these. A considerable number of mini-arguments may typically be found embedded in a given argumentative essay. Thus, understanding the organization or logical structure of an argumentative essay typically involves analysis at several levels or layers of detail. It's best to start with the most basic—what might be called the "macrostructure" of the essay—the essay's main argument. The main argument consists of the essay's thesis and main points, or those points that are offered to support the thesis *directly*. When you have sketched out the main argument, you'll find it easier to proceed with "microanalysis," focusing more closely on the details of the embedded mini-arguments.

Thesis

*The **thesis** is a statement of the main idea of the essay.* It resembles the theme in fiction, in which an underlying idea or moral is expressed through dialogue and action. Because the whole purpose of the essay is to compel the audience to accept a position, the thesis is really what the essay is all about. Without a thesis, or main idea, an essay would be a snarl: a collection of incoherent paragraphs and sentences. The thesis, then, is the essay's counterpart to the conclusion in short arguments.

As you can imagine, if you're seriously interested in evaluating an essay, you must first determine its thesis. This is crucial because everything offered in support of the thesis can be assessed only in terms of whether or not it in fact supports it. If you don't know what the thesis is, or if you misrepresent it, you can't intelligently evaluate the essay.

There is no single foolproof way of determining the thesis, or main idea, of an extended argument. Sometimes an author states it directly by providing a thesis statement in the essay. But even when the author doesn't expressly state the thesis, but only implies it, you can infer what the thesis must be from a close and intelligent consideration of the argument. *The reason is that an argumen-*

tative essay deals with some topic, and its author always has an attitude toward that topic. When you combine topic and attitude, you come up with the main idea. And when you state the main idea, you have a statement of the thesis.

If the essay is written in response to a particular issue, a very good way to identify the thesis is to orient yourself to the issue. Remember, an issue is simply a genuinely disputable topic. Issues can usually be conveniently captured in the form of a question.

> Should the human fetus be considered a person from the moment of
>   conception?
> Is the publication of racist material subject to First Amendment protection?
> Under what circumstances, if any, should the government in a democracy be
>   permitted to conduct covert operations?

The thesis of an essay addressed to an issue should be understandable as a direct response to the question.

> The human fetus should (should not) be considered a person from the moment
>   of conception.
> The publication of racist material is (is not) subject to First Amendment
>   protection.

Notice, by the way, that some questions admit of more answers than yes or no; accordingly, sometimes there are more than two positions available on a given issue.

> A democratic government should not under any circumstances be permitted to
>   conduct covert operations;
> A democratic government should be permitted to conduct covert operations at
>   the discretion of duly elected constitutional officers;
> A democratic government should be permitted to conduct covert operations
>   only to protect national security and only in such a way as is ultimately
>   subject to strict procedures of public accountability; and so on.

The topic is the subject that the essay deals with. But how do you determine the topic of an essay? If the essay has a title, that's the place to look first. The main function of an essay's title is to identify the topic. But not all essays have titles. And essay titles also have other functions—such as to intrigue, or entertain—which can sometimes obstruct access to the topic. If the topic is not otherwise revealed, scrutinize the paragraphs. Paragraph scrutiny is the key to extended argument analysis. Paragraphs always are about somebody or something. And somebody or something is the topic of the paragraph. To find out what the topic of the argument is, discover the common concerns of the paragraphs. Once this is apparent find out what the author is interested in telling you about it. That will reveal author attitude or viewpoint. Thus, having isolated topic and attitude, you'll have the main idea, the thesis.

What we've said so far can be graphically illustrated by a simple tree diagram, to be read from top to bottom:

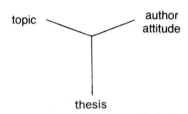

If we were dealing with actual essays, we might get relationships such as these:

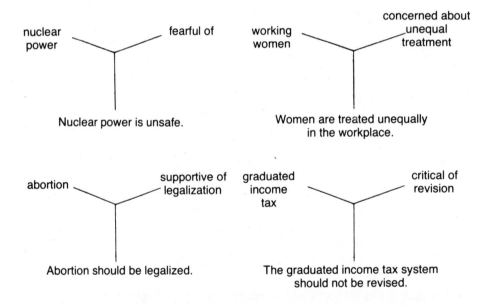

***Quick Check on Thesis Identification
(Answers on Page 407)**

These passages are excerpts from essays. For each, identify the topic and the author's attitude, then write an appropriate thesis statement.

1. Capital punishment is meted out to some groups in society more than to others. Minority groups are hit hardest by this imbalance

of justice. In addition, wealthy people seldom receive the death penalty because they can afford better counsel. All the people executed in the United States in 1964 were represented by court-appointed attorneys. Finally, the death penalty can wrongfully execute an innocent person. There are documented cases of this happening.

2. We have seen "hunting" rifles used to kill a president, Martin Luther King, and numerous others. It is said that these and other guns would not kill if there were not people to shoot them. By the same token, people would rarely kill if they lacked the weapons to do so. But there is an even more pressing threat to our lives than the sniper or assassin. Blacks, after centuries of exploitation, are openly rebellious. Given the weapons, young blacks could ignite the bloodiest revolution in this country since the Civil War. On the other side are white racists arming in fear. And don't forget the militant right-wingers storing up arsenals against the Reds, whom they see under every bed.

3. "This weekend, the city of Indianapolis is hosting approximately 500,000 people to create a two-day saturnalia out of the annual celebration of grease, gasoline, and death.

   ". . . the stands inside the Indy Speedway will be filled on Monday with hundreds or thousands of real racing fans. I can't help but think of them as vultures who come to watch the 500-mile race on the highway of death to nowhere, hoping that the monotony of watching cars flick by at speeds in excess of 190 mph will be relieved by mechanical—and human—catastrophe.

   "The beltway around Indianapolis is staked with grim white crosses, mute reminders to travelers of the fatal consequences of a too-heavy foot on the accelerator.

   "Watching the race from the Indy grandstand is a little like watching hyperactive hamsters tread a cage wheel. The cars fly by like brightly painted berserk vacuum cleaners sucking the ground. . . ." (Joan Ryan, "Grease, Gasoline and Death," *Washington Post*, May 1979)

4. "Feminists have long complained that playing with dolls is one way of convincing impressionable little girls that they may only be mothers or housewives. . . . But dollplaying may have even more serious consequences for little girls than that. Do girls find out about gravity and distance and shapes and sizes playing with dolls? Probably not.

   "A curious boy, if his parents are tolerant, will have taken apart a number of household and play objects by the time he is ten, and, if his parents are lucky, he may even have put them back together again. In all this he is learning things that will be useful in physics and math. Sports is another source of math-related concepts for children which tends to favor boys. Getting to first base on a not very well hit grounder is a lesson in line, speed and distance. Intercepting a football thrown through the air requires some rapid intuitive eye calculations based on the ball's direction, speed and trajectory. . . ." (Sheila Tobias, "Who's Afraid of Math, and Why?" *The Atlantic Monthly,* November 1979)

Macroanalysis and Microanalysis

Main points are the principal assertions offered to advance the thesis. Elsewhere we've called them main premises. They are crucial to any extended argument, for the argument's thesis stands or falls on the strength of these underpinnings. Furthermore, these main points are the object of the bulk of your analytical work. Usually it's not difficult to isolate the main points of an argument, especially when the essay is tightly organized. The *main points* are those points that are offered as direct support for the thesis. They are themselves usually argued for, sometimes at considerable length. Thus, they can usually be identified as the mini-conclusions that serve as direct support for the thesis.

In evaluating the essay you will have to determine how well each of the main points is justified. That in turn requires a close and critical inspection of the paragraphs in which the main points are made. Having sketched out the main argument, you can now proceed with microanalysis, focusing more closely on the details of the embedded mini-arguments.

Since a well-constructed argumentative paragraph is really a microcosm of a well-constructed extended argument, macroanalysis and microanalysis are essentially the same, only applied at different levels of depth and detail. Your main difficulty in moving from one to the other is likely to be one of keeping your bearings. Use the thesis as your landmark. Periodically it's a good idea to see if you can trace your way from where you are in your microanalysis back to the thesis, by asking questions like, How is this point relevant to the thesis? A casting of the argument as a whole will also help you to stay oriented within the overall macrostructure as you focus more and more closely in your microanalysis.

AN ESSAY CRITIQUED

With these preliminary remarks behind us, let's now see how the seven-step format can be applied to argumentative essays. We want to start with an example in which the author assigns high priority to strength of argument and clarity of presentation. So we have selected as our first example a piece of legal reasoning, an excerpt from an important judicial opinion that is both clearly articulated and forcefully argued. Here is an excerpt from the decision of the U.S. Supreme Court in the case of *Wyman v. James.* It concerns an issue of constitutional interpretation. The question that came before the Court in this case was whether the right to be secure against unreasonable search and seizure, guaranteed under the Fourth Amendment, is violated by a practice of a state welfare agency requiring periodic official visits in the homes of welfare recipients as a condition of eligibility for welfare benefits. The opinion of the majority was written by Justice Blackmun:

> This appeal presents the issue whether a beneficiary of the program for Aid to Families with Dependent Children (AFDC) may refuse a home visit by the caseworker without risking the termination of benefits.
>
> The New York State and city social services commissioners appeal from a judgment and decree of a divided three-judge District Court. . . .
>
> The district court majority held that a mother receiving AFDC relief may refuse, without forfeiting her right to that relief, the periodic home visit which the cited New York statutes and regulations prescribe as a condition for the continuance of assistance under the program. The beneficiary's thesis, and that of the District Court majority, is that home visitation is a search and, when not consented to or when not supported by a warrant based on probable cause, violates the beneficiary's 4th and 14th Amendment rights. . . .
>
> When a case involves a home and some type of official intrusion into that home, as this case appears to do, an immediate and natural reaction is one of concern about 4th Amendment rights and the protection which that Amendment is intended to afford. Its emphasis indeed is upon one of the most precious aspects of personal security in the home: "The right of the people to be secure in their persons, houses, papers, and effects. . . ." This Court has characterized that right as "basic to a free society. . . ." And over the years the Court consistently has been most protective of the privacy of the dwelling. . . .
>
> This natural and quite proper protective attitude, however, is not a factor in this case, for the seemingly obvious and simple reason that we are not concerned here with any search by the New York social service agency in the 4th Amendment meaning of that term. It is true that the governing statute and regulations appear to make mandatory the initial home visit and the subsequent periodic "contacts" (which may include home visits) for the inception and continuance of aid. It is also true that the caseworker's posture in the home visit is, perhaps, in a sense, both rehabilitative and investigative. But this latter aspect, we think, is given too broad a character and far more emphasis than it deserves if it is equated with a search in the criminal law context. We note, too, that the visitation in itself is not forced or compelled, and that the beneficiary's denial of permission is not a criminal act. If consent to the visitation is withheld, no visitation takes place. The aid then never begins or merely ceases, as the case may be. There is no entry of the home and there is no search.
>
> If however, we were to assume that a caseworker's home visit, before or subsequent to the beneficiary's initial qualification for benefits, somehow (perhaps because the average beneficiary might feel she is in no position to refuse consent to the visit), and despite its interview nature, does possess some of the characteristics of a search in the traditional sense, we nevertheless conclude that does not fall within the 4th Amendment's proscription. This is because it does not descend to the level of unreasonableness. It is unreasonableness which is the 4th Amendment's standard.
>
> There are a number of factors that compel us to conclude that the home visit proposed for Mrs. James is not unreasonable.
>
> The public's interest in this particular segment of the area of assistance to the unfortunate is protection and aid for the dependent child whose family requires such aid for the child. . . . The dependent child's needs are paramount, and only with hesitancy would we relegate those needs, in the scale of comparative values, to a position secondary to what the mother claims are her rights.

The agency, with tax funds provided from federal as well as from state sources, is fulfilling a public trust. The State, working through its qualified welfare agency, has appropriate and paramount interest and concern in seeing and assuring that the intended and proper objects of that tax-produced assistance are the ones who benefit from the aid it dispenses. . . .

One who dispenses purely private charity naturally has an interest in and expects to know how his charitable funds are utilized and put to work. The public, when it is the provider, rightly expects the same. . . .

Step 1: Clarify Meaning

Many of the crucial terms in this passage are subject to rather precise definition. An important preliminary to clarifying the meanings involved in this passage would be the Fourth Amendment itself. The Fourth Amendment to the Constitution reads:

The right of the people to be secure in their persons, houses, papers, and effects, against unreasonable searches and seizures, shall not be violated, and no warrants shall issue, but upon probable cause, supported by oath or affirmation, and particularly describing the place to be searched, and the persons or things to be seized.

In common vernacular this means that the government cannot search or seize a person or a person's house or private property without a warrant, and that a warrant must be obtained from a judge on the basis of sworn testimony that there is reason to suspect that something criminal is going on. "Probable cause" means "reason to suspect that something criminal is going on."

There is one crucial term whose vagueness we should notice right away as a matter of central importance not only to the argument but to the issue. The term "unreasonable" is vague.

Step 2: Identify Thesis and Main Points (Macroanalysis)

Remember that one good way to find the thesis of an extended argument is to orient yourself to the issue to which the argument is addressed. In this case the issue can be formulated with a good deal of precision: Does the practice of the New York State welfare agency requiring periodic official visits in the homes of welfare recipients as a condition of eligibility for welfare benefits violate the welfare recipient's right to be secure against unreasonable search and seizure, as guaranteed under the Fourth Amendment? Once the issue has been formulated in this way, it is quite clear what the thesis of the passage is:

Thesis: The New York State welfare agency practice does not violate the Fourth Amendment.

There are two main lines of argument offered in support of the thesis. One is based on the point that the practice of the welfare agency does not constitute a search. The other is based on two main points: (1) that (even if it *does* constitute a search) the practice of the welfare agency is not unreasonable, and (2) the Fourth Amendment is concerned only with *unreasonable* searches.

Step 3: Cast the Argument

This appeal presents the issue whether a beneficiary of the program for Aid to Families with Dependent Children (AFDC) may refuse a home visit by the caseworker without risking the termination of benefits.

The New York State and city social services commissioners appeal from a judgment and decree of a divided three-judge District Court. . . .

The district court majority held that a mother receiving AFDC relief may refuse, without forfeiting her right to that relief, the periodic home visit which the cited New York statutes and regulations prescribe as a condition for the continuance of assistance under the program. The beneficiary's thesis, and that of the District Court majority, is that home visitation is a search and, when not consented to or when not supported by a warrant based on probable cause, violates the beneficiary's 4th and 14th Amendment rights. . . .

[When a case involves a home and some type of official intrusion into that home, as this case appears to do, an immediate and natural reaction is one of [1] concern about 4th Amendment rights and the protection which that Amendment is intended to afford.] [Its emphasis indeed is upon one of the most precious [2] aspects of personal security in the home:] "The right of the people to be secure in their persons, houses, papers, and effects. . . ." [This Court has characterized that right as "basic to a free society. . . ."] [And over the years the Court con-[3] sistently has been most protective of the privacy of the dwelling. . . .] [4]

[This natural and quite proper protective attitude, however, is not a factor [5] in this case,] for the seemingly obvious and simple reason that [we are not [6] concerned here with any search by the New York social service agency in the 4th Amendment meaning of that term.] It is true that [the governing statute and [7] regulations appear to make mandatory the initial home visit and the subsequent periodic "contacts" (which may include home visits) for the inception and continuance of aid.] It is also true that [the caseworker's posture in the home visit [8] is, perhaps, in a sense, both rehabilitative and investigative.] But [this latter [9] aspect, we think, is given too broad a character and far more emphasis than it deserves if it is equated with a search in the criminal law context.] We note, too, that [the visitation in itself is not forced or compelled,] and that [the beneficiary's [10] [11] [12] denial of permission is not a criminal act]. [If consent to the visitation is withheld, no visitation takes place.] [The aid then never begins or merely ceases,] as the [13] case may be. There is no entry of the home and there is no search.

If however, we were to assume that a caseworker's home visit, before or subsequent to the beneficiary's initial qualification for benefits, somehow (perhaps because the average beneficiary might feel she is in no position to refuse consent to the visit), and despite its interview nature, does possess some of the characteristics of a search in the traditional sense, <u>we nevertheless conclude</u> [that does not fall within the 4th Amendment's proscription.]^5 <u>This is because</u> [it does not descend to the level of unreasonableness.]^14 [It is unreasonableness which is the 4th Amendment's standard.]^15

There are <u>a number of factors that compel us to conclude</u> that the home visit proposed for Mrs. James is not unreasonable.

[The public's interest in this particular segment of the area of assistance to the unfortunate is^16 protection and aid for the dependent child whose family requires such aid for the child. . . .] [The dependent child's^17 needs are paramount,] <u>and</u> [only with hesitancy would we relegate those needs, in the scale of compar-^18 ative values, to a position secondary to what the mother claims as her rights.]

[The agency, with tax funds provided from federal as^19 well as from state sources, is fulfilling a public trust.] [The State, working through its qualified welfare agency, has appropriate and paramount interest and concern in seeing and^20 assuring that the intended and proper objects of that tax-produced assistance are the ones who benefit from the aid it dispenses. . . .]

[One who dispenses purely private charity naturally has an interest in and^21 expects to know how his charitable funds are utilized and put to work.] [The public, when it is the provider,^22 rightly expects the same. . . .]

The first three paragraphs give important background information on the history of the case that, although it helps orient us to the issue, is not part of the argument. Paragraph 4, however, contains claims that, although they too are part of the background, are also relevant to the argument's thesis. The author acknowledges them as weighing against the thesis. Thus, we would cast them as balance of considerations claims. We find the thesis stated at the beginning of paragraph 5 followed by the first main point, and restated again in paragraph 6, followed by the two other main points. Thus, the main argument can be sketched as follows:

The beginning of paragraph 6, "If we were to assume . . . we nevertheless conclude," indicates that assertion 6 functions independently as support for the thesis, whereas assertions 14 and 15 function together interdependently in support of the thesis. The remaining claims relate to assertions 6 and 14:

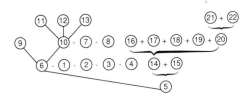

Step 4: Fill in Missing Premises

The inference from 9 to 6 is incomplete, and so is the inference from 16, 17, 18, 19, and 20 to 14. Two premises need to be added to the inference from 9 to 6:

    a: The investigative aspect of the home visit should neither be given too broad a character nor be overemphasized.
    b: The Fourth Amendment sense of the term "search" is confined to the criminal law context.

The inference from 16, 17, 18, 19, and 20 to 14 seems to depend on the additional premise:

    c: A policy or practice for which there are good reasons is not unreasonable.

Thus the argument may finally be cast:

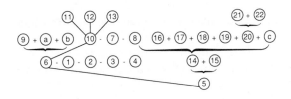

Step 5: Examine Main Points (Premises)
and Support for Justification

One of the strengths of this passage is the degree to which the author has made clear where the main points stand in need of support, and the lengths to which the passage goes in attempting to supply the needed support.

    Of the three main points—6, 14, and 15—the most vulnerable seems to be 6: that the welfare agency practice does not constitute a search. The author acknowledges some six separate considerations that might be thought to weigh against it. Its acceptability depends on premises 9, 10, 11, and 12, as well as unexpressed premises *a* and *b*. Premise 9 makes an interpretive claim that, especially in view of the points that the author concedes as weighing against main point 6, must be regarded as open to serious challenge. Premise 9 is left unsupported, and in the context of an issue concerning the interpretation of the Fourth Amendment, this might well be regarded as question begging (see Step 6). Without 9, unexpressed premise *a*, that the investigative aspect of the welfare agency visit should be neither too broadly construed nor overemphasized, would be reduced to a vague truism of little use to the argument. And unexpressed premise *b*, like premise 9, makes an interpretive claim that in the context of this issue needs independent support. Support for 6 also comes from 10, 11, 12, and 13. Although 11, 12, and 13 are probably acceptable as accurate accounts of the official consequences for the welfare recipient of refusal of consent to the visit, they do not make a very convincing case for 10, that the visit is not compelled. Indeed, the author acknowledges the weakness here when he says in making the transition to the second line of argument, "the average beneficiary might feel she is in no position to refuse consent to the visit."

Main point 15 is little more than a verbatim quotation from the text of the Fourth Amendment itself. Thus, it is hard to imagine how it might be objected to in any substantive way. Nevertheless, it does bring one crucial vague element to the center of attention: the term "unreasonable." The acceptability of main point 14, that the visit prescribed for Mrs. James is not unreasonable, and consequently the cogency of the entire second line of argument turns on the question of what is meant by "unreasonable." This is never made explicit in the passage. However, the support that is offered for 14 seems to imply the understanding of "unreasonable," which is formulated in unexpressed premise *c*. If we assume for the moment that claims 16 through 20 do constitute good reason for the state agency's practice of conducting mandatory home visits, we can see once again how important it is to fill in missing premises, for now it becomes apparent that, with main point 6 in trouble, the entire argument hinges on the acceptability of unexpressed premise *c*. So what about the unexpressed premise? Initially it seems a perfectly plausible idea. However, on closer inspection a serious question might be raised to challenge it: Is it not possible that a policy or practice for which there are good reasons is nevertheless still an unreasonable policy or practice because there are overriding and even more compelling reasons for objecting to it? For example, today in the United States there might be several very good reasons to raise taxes 200 percent across the board for the next five years. Does this mean that it would not be unreasonable to so so? Not if there are even better reasons for not doing it.

Now let us return to premises 16 through 20. Here we find the reasons for the welfare agency practice spelled out. The agency is charged with a responsibility to look after the welfare of a dependent child and to monitor the disbursement of public funds. We may accept these both as legitimate public concerns for which the agency has properly been made responsible—even without the additional support offered in the form of the analogy between public assistance and private charity (premises 21 and 22). But this may still be a bit of a red herring, because what they constitute good reason for is *some* policy or practice designed to discover cases of child abuse and neglect and cases of welfare fraud, but not necessarily *this* one: a practice that, in addition to raising the privacy issue, also seems to go against the constitutionally guaranteed presumption of innocence. Is there no way for the welfare agency to fulfill its legitimate public responsibilities other than by means of a practice that raises such serious issues of constitutional principle? These, it might be argued, constitute overriding reasons for reforming the agency policy, in spite of the legitimacy of the reasons that underlie it. Notice how this brings us around once again to the acceptability of unexpressed premise *c*.

Step 6: Examine the Argumentative Essay (the Argument) for Fallacies

This passage is relatively free of fallacies, as one would naturally expect. It was composed, after all, by a ranking member of the judiciary, which maintains very high standards in the area of argumentation. Nevertheless, it is possible to detect a few inferences whose reliability might be called "substandard."

In premise 9 we are asked to accept that the admittedly investigative posture of the welfare caseworker in the home of the recipient is "too broadly construed" and "overemphasized" if we think of it as like a criminal search. Notice that this premise therefore makes an interpretive claim. It interprets the welfare caseworker's visit. Now, that's not by itself an objectionable thing. But remember what's at issue in this case. What's at issue is whether or not the visit constitutes a Fourth Amendment violation. So the question of how the caseworker's visit is to be interpreted or understood is absolutely central to the issue. Thus, to simply assume, without independent support, that the visit can't be construed as a search amounts to assuming, again without independent support, that it isn't covered by the Fourth Amendment. But that's what's at issue. Consequently, premise 9 can be faulted as a case of question begging.

Similarly, unexpressed premise *b* makes an interpretive claim that in the context of this issue requires independent support. Unexpressed premise *b* tells us that the Fourth Amendment sense of the term "search" is confined to the criminal law context. Here what is interpreted is not the caseworker's visit, but the Fourth Amendment. Again, this isn't by itself an objectionable thing. After all, the case calls on the Supreme Court to do precisely that: interpret the Fourth Amendment. Specifically, the Court is asked to determine whether the Fourth Amendment's protection extends to cover cases like that of Mrs. James. If we now assume for a moment that the visit prescribed for Mrs. James is not a criminal search, we can see again that the question of whether the Fourth Amendment extends beyond the criminal law context is precisely what's at issue. Consequently, to assume without independent support that it doesn't extend beyond the criminal law context simply begs the question.

We should be cautious in making these criticisms, however. We should bear in mind that there is a considerable body of literature from which powerful arguments could be constructed to support something like premise *b*. In other words, we should not presume that we have blown the Supreme Court's argument out of the water just yet. And we should not overlook the fact that the Court recognizes a certain vulnerability in this first line of argument, and that, as a consequence, the Court attaches greater weight to the second line of argument.

There remains the matter of the possible red herring in support of main point 14. But we feel that this should not be separated from the question of the acceptability of unexpressed premise *c*. And that's too deep an issue to be dismissed as a mere fallacious inference. So we'll come back to it in step 7.

Step 7: Give an Overall Evaluation

Although there are a number of flaws in this argument and some may feel that ultimately it fails to secure its thesis, we must recognize its overall respectability as an argument. It is generally very clear and forcefully argued, again, as one would naturally expect it to be.

Moreover, the points at which it is most vulnerable to challenge or objection are fairly and accurately represented as such to the reader. And some of these are subject to additional support. For example, the assumption that the Fourth Amendment sense of the term "search" is confined to the context of criminal law, which we objected to as a case of question begging, could no doubt be supported. Such support might take the form of a survey of relevant legal precedent: For example, if the Fourth Amendment has always, or traditionally, been interpreted as confined to or rooted in the criminal law context, this would be relevant (although not by itself decisive) support.

We should also recognize certain specific strengths in the second and most important line of argument. First of all, the main inference from 14 and 15 to the thesis is deductively valid. If both of its premises are acceptable, that puts the thesis beyond question. Similarly, with the addition of unexpressed premise *c* the mini-argument in support of 14 is deductively valid. If its several premises are acceptable, then main point 14 is also established beyond question.

The problems that arise for the argument turn out, in the final analysis, to be rather subtle and deep ones. This highlights an important point about argument analysis and evaluation. When we're dealing with issues of depth and substance, as we are in this case, we cannot expect to arrive at complete and final closure of the issue, at least not very often. Notice how this important insight is recognized in the structure and procedures of the Supreme Court. The Court is made up of nine justices in part because it is recognized that the issues which come before the Court will predictably admit of persistent disagreement among rational and reasonable people. This means that one cannot expect to arrive at complete and final closure of the issues, at least not very often. This is one reason why the majority presents its decision as an "opinion," and why there is also in the typical case at least one dissenting "opinion" presented as well. Yet this hardly means that there is no point to constructing, analyzing, and evaluating arguments about such issues. This is also recognized in the structure and procedures of the Court, for that is precisely what the Court does: argument analysis, argument evaluation, and argument construction. Perhaps it would be nice if we could use these methods to arrive at complete and final closure of all of the deep issues that divide people, but the point of these activities and methods is not lost when we fail to reach that goal (which is most of the time). The point of these activities and methods is that they are essential to the pursuit of truth and the accumulation of wisdom in these areas. Even when the issue remains open, as we think it does in this case, what the exercise of analyzing and evaluating the arguments does is deepen the discussion and deepen our understanding and appreciation of the depths and complexities of the issue.

A SECOND ESSAY CRITIQUED

Let us look now at a second extended argument, one with its own difficulties. The following piece deals with voluntary euthanasia, the practice of allowing the terminally ill to elect to die.

AGAINST LEGALIZING EUTHANASIA

The Karen Ann Quinlan case once again has raised the issue of euthanasia. A number of voices have been heard advocating the legalization of voluntary euthanasia. While the agonizing plight of many of our terminally ill makes this proposal understandable, there are good reasons to resist liberalizing our euthanasia laws.

First of all, no matter how you look at it, euthanasia is killing and thus is wrong. The Bible is clear on that point, and our society has always forbidden it.

Second, it is questionable whether a terminally ill patient can make a voluntary decision to begin with. Those who advocate voluntary euthanasia believe that patients should be allowed to die on request when they've developed a tolerance to narcotics. But exactly when are those patients to decide? When they're drugged? If so, then surely their choices can't be considered voluntary. And if they're to decide after the drugs have been withdrawn, this decision can't be voluntary either. Anyone who's had a simple toothache knows how much pain can distort judgment and leave us almost crazy. Imagine how much more irrational we'd likely be if we were suffering from some dreadful terminal disease and suddenly had our ration of morphine discontinued.

But even if such a decision could be completely voluntary, isn't it really unwise to offer such a choice to the gravely ill? I remember how, before she died of stomach cancer, my mother became obsessed with the idea that she was an emotional and financial burden on her family. She actually kept apologizing to us that she went on living! Had she had the option of euthanasia, she might have taken it—not because she was tired of living but because she felt guilty about living!

I shudder to think of the stress that such a choice would have put on us, her family. Surely we would have been divided. Some of us would have said, "Yes, let Mother die," while others would have resisted out of a sense of love or devotion or gratitude, or even guilt.

Then there's the whole question of mistaken diagnoses. Doctors aren't infallible. Even the best of them errs. The story is told of the brilliant diagnostician Richard Cabot, who, when he was retiring, was given the complete medical histories and results of careful examinations of two patients. The patients had died and only the pathologist who'd seen the descriptions of their postmortems knew their exact diagnoses. The pathologist asked Cabot for his diagnosis. The eminent Dr. Cabot muffed both of them! If a brilliant diagnostician can make a mistake, what about a less accomplished doctor? Let's face it: There's always the possibility of a wrong diagnosis.

But suppose we could be sure of diagnoses. Even so, there's always the chance that some new pain-relieving drug, or even a cure, is just around the corner. Many years ago the president of the American Public Health Association made this point forcefully when he said, "No one can say today what will be incurable tomorrow. No one can predict what disease will be fatal or permanently incurable until medicine becomes stationary and sterile."

But what frightens me the most about legalizing voluntary euthanasia is that it will open the door for the legalization of *involuntary* euthanasia. If we allow people to play God and decide when and how they'll die, then it won't be long before society will be deciding when and how defective infants, the old and senile, and the hopelessly insane will die as well.

Step 1: Clarify Meaning

The arguer clearly opposes easing euthanasia laws to allow even voluntary euthanasia. Although the position is clear, the language used is often fuzzy. "That point" (paragraph 2), "killing" (paragraph 2), "voluntary decision" (paragraph 3), "just around the corner" (paragraph 7) all are ambiguous. The sentence beginning "Imagine how much . . . " (paragraph 3) is both directive and informative. The opening sentence of paragraph 4 is a rhetorical question. "No matter how you look at it" (paragraph 2) and "Let's face it" (paragraph 6) are extreme intensifiers.

Step 2: Identify Thesis (Conclusion) and Main Points (Premises)

One of the most efficient ways to identify the thesis and main points of argumentative essays is to paraphrase them. Of course, make sure that your paraphrase does not distort or omit important details.

Thesis: Voluntary euthanasia should not be legalized.
Point: Euthanasia is wrong.
Point: It's impossible to ascertain that consent is voluntary.
Point: Allowing a death decision is unwise.
Point: Diagnoses can be mistaken.
Point: Relief or cures can be imminent.
Point: Abuses will follow the legalization.

(You might conceivably consider the third point as support for the second, in which case the essay could be viewed as having five, rather than six, main points.)

Step 3: Cast the Argument

AGAINST LEGALIZING EUTHANASIA

The Karen Ann Quinlan case once again has raised the issue of euthanasia. A number of voices have been heard advocating the legalization of voluntary euthanasia. While the agonizing plight of many of our terminally ill makes this proposal understandable, [there are good reasons to resist liberalizing our euthanasia laws.][1]

First of all, no matter how you look at it, [euthanasia is killing][2] and thus [is wrong.][3] [The Bible is clear on that point,][4] and [our society has always forbidden it.][5]

Second, [it is questionable whether a terminally ill patient can make a voluntary decision to begin with.][6] Those who advocate voluntary euthanasia believe that patients should be allowed to die on request when they've developed a tolerance to narcotics. But exactly when are those patients to decide? When they're drugged? [If so, then surely their choices can't be considered voluntary.][7] And [if they're to decide after the drugs have been withdrawn, this decision can't be voluntary either.][8] [Anyone who's had a simple toothache knows how much pain can distort judgment and leave us almost crazy.][9] [Imagine how much more irrational we'd likely be if we were suffering from some dreadful terminal disease and suddenly had our ration of morphine discontinued.][10]

[But even if such a decision could be completely voluntary,][11] [isn't it really unwise to offer such a choice to the gravely ill?][12] I remember how, before she died of stomach cancer, my mother became obsessed with the idea that she was an emotional and financial burden on her family. She actually kept apologizing to us that she went on living! [Had she had the option of euthanasia, she might have taken it—not because she was tired of living but because she felt guilty about living!][13]

[I shudder to think of the stress that such a choice would have put on us, her family.][14] Surely [we would have been divided.][15] [Some of us would have said, "Yes, let Mother die,"][16] while [others would have resisted out of a sense of love or devotion or gratitude, or even guilt.][17]

Then [there's the whole question of mistaken diagnoses.][18] Doctors aren't infallible. Even the best of them errs. The story is told of the brilliant diagnostician Richard Cabot, who, when he was retiring, was given the complete medical histories and results of careful examinations of two patients. The patients had died and only the pathologist who'd seen the descriptions of their postmortems knew their exact diagnoses. The pathologist asked Cabot for his diagnoses. The eminent Dr. Cabot muffed both of them! If a brilliant diagnostician can make a mistake, what about a less accomplished doctor? Let's face it: There's always the possibility of a wrong diagnosis.

But suppose we could be sure of diagnoses. Even so, [there's always the chance that some new pain-relieving drug, or even a cure, is just around the corner.][19] Many years ago the president of the American Public Health Association made this point forcefully when he said, "No one can say today what will be incurable tomorrow. No one can predict what disease will be fatal or permanently incurable until medicine becomes stationary and sterile."

But what frightens me the most about legalizing voluntary euthanasia is that [it will open the door for the legalization of *involuntary* euthanasia.][20] [If we allow people to play God and decide when and how they'll die, then it won't be long before society will be deciding when and how defective infants, the old and senile, and the hopelessly insane will die as well.][21]

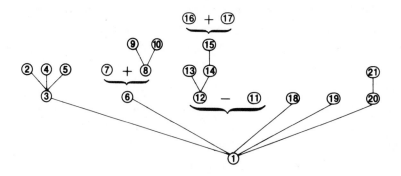

Step 4: Fill in Missing Premises

In the mini-argument

The arguer must be assuming that killing is wrong (unexpressed premise *a*). Thus

$$\underbrace{②~+~ⓐ}$$
$$③$$

In the mini-argument

$$\underbrace{⑦~+~⑧}$$
$$⑥$$

the arguer must be assuming that only one of the two alternatives is possible: that the choice be made either under the influence of powerful drugs, in which case it wouldn't be free because the person's judgment would be clouded; or after the drugs were withdrawn, in which case the choice wouldn't be free because the person would be racked with pain (unexpressed premise *b*). Thus

In the mini-argument

the arguer must be assuming that to choose out of guilt for depleting a family's emotional or financial resources is wrong (unexpressed premise *c*). Thus

Step 5: Examine Main Points (Premises) and Support for Justification

Main point 3 is a value assertion whose justification depends on the meaning of "wrong" and the support provided for that meaning. Mini-premise 2 is a fact, for euthanasia can be considered a form of killing. But unexpressed premise *a* is in doubt. What about self-defense or capital punishment or soldiers in combat? If the arguer allows that these or any other form of killing is justifiable, then she can't hold that killing is *always* wrong. If killing is not always wrong, then euthanasia may not be wrong. Should the arguer admit that killing is not always wrong but that euthanasia is an unacceptable form of killing, then she must demonstrate why. In any event, the arguer leaves this crucial value judgment unsupported. Well, not entirely. The arguer does mention the Bible in mini-premise 4. But is the Bible "clear on that point"? If "that point" refers to killing, then it's not at all certain that the Bible prohibits all forms of killing. In fact, most interpretations of the Bible find exceptions to the commandment "Thou shalt not kill." If on the other hand "that point" refers to euthanasia, it is not true that the Bible clearly takes a stand against euthanasia. As for mini-premise 5 offered in support of main point 3, the reference to "it" in "our society has always forbidden it," must refer to euthanasia, for our society has not always forbidden every form of killing. Although some might question the literal truth of this assertion, let's grant it and reserve further comment until the next step. In short, mini-premises 2 and 5 are acceptable with qualifications, but unexpressed premise *a* and mini-premise 4 are not acceptable.

Whether or not main point 6 is true depends largely on mini-premises 7 and 8 and unexpressed premise *b*. The mini-premises probably are true hypothetical statements, and the arguer has made fair use of an analogy in assertion 9 to make point 8. But is the unexpressed premise true? Must consent be obtained only when patients are drugged or when they're crazed with pain after the drugs have been withdrawn? If these are the only two alternatives, the arguer has good grounds to assert that the death decision may not be voluntary (main point 6). But are there not also other possibilities: Suppose patients make a decision when they are faced with imminent death but have not yet lapsed into excruciating pain or been heavily sedated; or suppose they make a decision during a period of remission. The arguer could reply that consent in such situations is an uninformed and anticipatory consent and that patients can't or shouldn't commit themselves to be killed in the future. Still, there may be cases where patients not in pain indicate a desire for euthanasia and reaffirm that request when in pain. In any event, the question of what constitutes consent is a tricky one that cannot be dismissed by what amounts to a false dilemma. This doesn't mean that the arguer is necessarily incorrect in making point 6, but simply that she hasn't examined those cases in which consent seems at least possible. Nor has the arguer attempted to define precisely what is meant by "consent" and "voluntary decisions." Therefore main point 6 stands in need of stronger support.

Main point 12 is a value assertion ("unwise") whose justification depends on the support offered by mini-premises 13 + *c* and 14, which follows from assertion 15, together with assertions 16 + 17. Given the qualifying "might have," mini-premise 13 asserts at best a possibility. There's no way of knowing for sure that the arguer's mother would have chosen euthanasia, or if she had, that she would have done so for the reasons given. Unexpressed premise *c*, which is a value assertion, needs considerable support before it can be taken as justified. Mini-premise 14 can be considered justified on the basis of a confirmation found within the arguer and supported by the similarly justified assertions 15, 16, and 17. Whether these assertions and mini-premise 13 give enough support to main point 12 are questions best taken up in the next step.

Main point 18 is not in doubt: Diagnoses can be mistaken. (Incidentally, we didn't cast the example because it seems intended to reinforce the point, not to demonstrate it.)

The truth of main point 19 cannot be determined because "around the corner" is so vague. The example cited merely repeats the point.

There is no evidence to support main point 20. Mini-premise 21, which is offered in support of it, is purely speculative, an observation that we'll return to presently.

Step 6: Examine the Argumentative Essay (the Argument) for Fallacies

Regarding mini-arguments

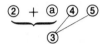

mini-premise 4, besides being ambiguous and doubtful, is a questionable testimonial. Mini-premise 5 is an appeal to tradition: Even if society has always forbidden euthanasia (itself a questionable assertion), that fact doesn't demonstrate that society has been justified in doing so or that the tradition is worth following. Stripped of these devices, mini-premises 4 and 5 provide no support for main point 3. This, together with unexpressed premise *a*'s problems, noted earlier, leaves main point 3 a controversial value assertion that the arguer has not established. Until the arguer does, main point 3 can't be regarded as entailing the argument's thesis, 1.

We have already indicated the false dilemma evident in unexpressed premise *b* of mini-argument

This mini-argument also seems to involve a half-truth. The arguer overlooks cases falling between the two extremes that have been set up. Admittedly, the question whether anyone suffering from a terminal disease can make a "voluntary decision" may remain. So the argument may be rescuable from these criticisms. Nevertheless main point 6 is at best only tenuously related to the thesis. Even if we can question whether a terminally ill patient is capable of making a voluntary decision, that only suggests that we should determine the conditions under which we reasonably can assume that a person is making a voluntary decision. It doesn't support the claim that euthanasia should not be permitted. Maybe society should not allow death decisions made under the influence of powerful drugs or when people are mad with pain. But it doesn't follow that society shouldn't allow death decisions at all. So even if main point 6 is true, we'd consider it a red herring and thus irrelevant to thesis 1.

The support offered for main point 12 consists of intensifying through provincialism. The personal illustration is insufficient to support the implied unqualified generalization in main point 12. Furthermore, in writing about the stress death decisions place on families (mini-premise 14) the arguer omits to mention the fact that under existing circumstances families already experience stress that sometimes strains the limits of human financial, emotional, and spiritual endurance. (Curiously, the arguer betrays awareness of this in arguing earlier that patients will choose euthanasia out of concern for their suffering families.)

Another thing. Mini-argument

is a straw person. The real issue is whether the dying should be allowed to choose death; the straw is whether family should be allowed to choose death for a dying loved one. Although legislation concerning voluntary euthanasia could be so written as to allow a proxy death decision, it needn't be. Up to this point in the essay, the arguer clearly is discussing voluntary euthanasia in the context of terminal patients making their own decisions. This mini-argument raises the possibility of others making the decision for them. It would have been perfectly legitimate to raise this matter if earlier the arguer had defined voluntary euthanasia to include cases of proxy decisions. But in the absence of such stipulation and in the context of the rest of the essay a narrower interpretation of "voluntary euthanasia," to include only decisions made by the patient in his or her own behalf, seems justified. We think this interpretation is correct because, even in cases of proxy decisions, individual patients have expressly indicated (for example, through a so-called living will) that under carefully circumscribed conditions, they prefer death to artificially sustained life and have designated someone to implement their wishes if they themselves can't. So to raise the specter of a family battle over whether to allow Mother a quick and painless death is unfair. It's a straw person and an appeal to fear. By this account mini-premise 14 provides no support for the value assertion made in main point 12. Since the premises 13 + c don't either, the value assertion is left unsupported and consequently fails to support the thesis.

Although main point 18 is true, it smacks of fear. It also can be considered a half-truth because the vast majority of diagnoses are correct ones. But the arguer's reason for using this point to support the thesis obviously is that even the slightest possibility of miscalculation should discourage the relaxation of prohibitions against euthanasia. Fair enough. But what are we to say about the many medical procedures and operations that are performed daily? These always carry a risk of wrong diagnosis, in which case patients can be harmed, sometimes irreparably. Indeed, any operation carries risk to life, and often the risk is grave. The medical profession itself admits that too many operations and other medical procedures are unnecessary. What are we to say to all this? That medical procedures shouldn't be allowed? It is true that euthanasia is unique in that its object is not to save or prolong life but to end it. But euthanasia also aims to alleviate pain, and alleviating pain is widely considered to be a legitimate aim of medical practice. The arguer could object that we don't know for sure that euthanasia in fact effects a net reduction of pain. True enough, but how are we to find out? Apparently by trying voluntary euthanasia. To dismiss summarily the possibility that voluntary euthanasia may result in a net reduction of pain would be arguably a case of invincible ignorance. Finally, it's possible to question the relevance of the arguer's whole point about mistaken diagnoses, that is, to see it as a red herring. After all, the issue of mistaken diagnoses is a medical, not legal, one. Even if mistaken diagnoses of terminal diseases were highly likely, is that relevant to the question of whether or not individuals should have the legal right to euthanasia? So although main point 18 obviously is true, the arguer has failed to demonstrate why the possibility of mistaken diagnoses argues against permitting voluntary euthanasia. Thus the thesis cannot be inferred from this point.

In main point 19 the phrase "just around the corner" is vague and confusing. Will a day, week, month, year, or several years pass before relief or a cure is found? Not only is "just around the corner" obscure, it's a half-truth concealing the fact that when medical discoveries are made usually several years pass before the new drug or therapy is available for widespread use. It's not as if one day we can't perform liver transplants, for example, but the next day we can. In the interim between discovery and general availability of a drug or therapy, the euthanasia option could be halted for those affected, or at least those affected could be informed of the possible new treatment. Moreover, the arguer conceals the fact that relief or cure would apply only to those in the group to whom the discovery applies. Are we to leave the remainder to suffer to preclude risk to these patients? The arguer leaves this point underdeveloped, citing instead a testimonial that, while legitimate, repeats main point 19 instead of illuminating it. In short, the arguer relies totally on ambiguity and half-truth in asserting this point. Therefore 19 doesn't entail 1.

The last mini-argument

is a "wedge" defense. The arguer claims that should voluntary euthanasia be permitted, various forms of involuntary euthanasia are bound to follow. But there's nothing inevitable about this anticipated chain of events. This mini-argument, then, amounts to a slippery slope fallacy. The thesis cannot be inferred from it.

Step 7: Give an Overall Evaluation

Although there may be good reasons for not permitting voluntary euthanasia, this essay has not marshaled them. It has relied heavily on ambiguity, straw person, half-truth, and red herring in an attempt to demonstrate its thesis. Perhaps a more fruitful approach would be to present an alternative care system for the dying that would greatly reduce, if not dissolve, the desire and need for death decisions. The hospice approach is an alternative that has gained widespread attention in England and the United States. Hospices are special settings devoted exclusively to the care of the terminally ill. The hospice approach to the care of the dying differs from conventional care in a number of ways. Most important, hospices stress comfort and care, which includes pain and symptom control and assistance at all levels to patients and their families during and after death. Specifically, hospice practitioners contend that pain, especially chronic pain, is a complex phenomenon that involves emotional, social, and spiritual dimensions of the patient as well as the physical. Drawing on this view, they take a preventive rather than reactive approach to pain and symptom control. Thus every attempt is made to keep patients pain-free. Is this possible? Medical experts claim that most of the painful symptoms connected with terminal disease can be treated effectively but are not because health care professionals have not received proper training in symptom control. (See J. M. Hinton, "The Physical and Mental Distress of Dying," *Quarterly Journal of Medicine* 5 (1963): 1–21; W. D. Rees, "The Distress of Dying," *Nursing Times* 68 (1972): 1479–1490; and M. A. Simpson, "Planning for Terminal Care," *Lancet* 1 (1976): 192–193.) If in fact the pain connected with terminal disease can be reduced to a tolerable level, then the major reason for allowing death decisions loses much of its force. Of course, the hospice approach is not applicable in cases of extremely debilitating chronic disease. For such patients mercy death may still be a viable alternative.

Notice that what we've done in this overall evaluation is present points that the arguer could have presented in discussing voluntary euthanasia and also taken the opportunity to clarify a viable alternative approach to the difficult issue that the argument addresses. By so doing, we have attempted to move the discussion of this important social issue to what appears a more constructive level of discourse.

AN ALTERNATIVE CASTING METHOD: THE OUTLINE

The casting method we've been using throughout our study is just one way an essay's structure can be portrayed. Another is the outline, with which you're probably familiar from your writing and speech courses. An outline presents the thesis of an essay and then lists in their order of appearance the main points (represented by roman numerals) and support materials (represented by capital letters).

If you prefer the outline to the tree-diagram method, use it in step 3 of the seven-step format. Indeed, if you have properly identified the thesis and main points in step 2, you have the basis for an outline, which you must complete with any support material given in the argument. In implementing step 4 you will then insert in the outline any missing premises that are not obvious.

Here is an outline of the essay under discussion. Notice that the missing premises, when inserted, have been indicated with a wedge (< >).

Thesis: Voluntary euthanasia should not be legalized.

I. Euthanasia is wrong.
 A. Euthanasia is killing.
 + <Killing is always wrong.>
 B. The Bible says so.
 C. Society forbids it.

II. It's impossible to ascertain that consent is voluntary.
 A. If patients are drugged the consent cannot be voluntary.
 B. If the drugs are withdrawn the consent cannot be voluntary because the patients will be mad with pain.
 + <These are the only two options.>
  1. A common toothache illustrates how much pain interferes with judgment.
  2. The excruciating pain associated with terminal illness would blur judgment even more.

III. Allowing a death decision is unwise.
 A. Had she the choice, my mother might have chosen euthanasia out of guilt.
 + <Choosing out of guilt is wrong.>
 B. Families will be strained.
  1. My family's experience is a case in point.

IV. Diagnoses can be mistaken.

V. Relief or cures may be imminent.

VI. Abuses will follow the legalization.
 A. Permitting voluntary euthanasia wil lead to death decisions imposed on defective infants, the old and senile, and the hopelessly insane.

Once you have outlined the essay and inserted the missing premises, you can then proceed with steps 5, 6, and 7—the evaluation. In fact, if your outline is complete, you may not have to refer to the essay at all. You may be able to rely exclusively on the outline to determine whether the premises and support are justified and what informal fallacies there may be present. Used properly, then, the outline is an economical way of portraying the structure of argumentative essays and evaluating them.

Summary

Many arguments come in multiparagraph form and are commonly termed "argumentative essays" or (when oral) "speeches of conviction." Understanding the organization or logical structure of an argumentative essay is analogous to understanding the structure of an argument. Each involves grasping and appreciating the relationships of support that obtain between individual structural elements.

Understanding the organization or logical structure of an argumentative essay typically involves analysis at several levels or layers of detail. It's best to start with the most basic macrostructure of the essay, the essay's main argument. The main argument consists of the essay's thesis and main points, or those points that are offered to support the thesis *directly*.

In identifying the thesis, determine the essay's topic and the author's attitude toward it. If the essay is written in response to a particular issue, a very good way to identify the thesis is to orient yourself to the issue. Remember, an issue is simply a genuinely disputable topic. Issues can usually be conveniently captured in the form of a question. The thesis of an essay addressed to an issue should be understandable as a direct response to the question.

In the typical argumentative essay the thesis is likely to be stated in the opening paragraphs, followed by support material; occasionally, the support material may come first, followed in the closing paragraphs by the thesis.

The main points are those points that are offered as direct support for the thesis. They are themselves usually argued for, sometimes at considerable length. Thus, they can usually be identified as the mini-conclusions that serve as direct support for the thesis.

When you have sketched out the main argument, you'll find it easier to proceed with microanalysis, focusing more closely on the details of the embedded mini-arguments. Macroanalysis and microanalysis are essentially the same, only applied at different levels of depth and detail. Your main difficulty in moving from one to the other is likely to be one of keeping your bearings. Use the thesis as your landmark. From time to time, trace your way from where you are in your microanalysis back to the thesis, by asking questions like, How is this point relevant to the thesis? A casting of the argument as a whole will also help you to stay oriented within the overall macrostructure as you focus more and more closely in your microanalysis.

Being aware of the anatomy of an essay provides a departure point for analysis and evaluation. The seven-step format can be applied as profitably to the extended argument as it can to the shorter one. If you prefer, you may cast the essay (step 3) in the form of an outline rather than a tree diagram, making sure to add to the outline the missing premises (step 4).

Applications

Apply the seven-step format to the following argumentative essays:

LET'S STOP GIVING RICH KIDS A FREE RIDE THROUGH COLLEGE[1]

When Gov. George Deukmejian took office last month, he inherited a budget crisis of the first magnitude. The imminent deficit of the state of California was measured in billions rather than hundreds of millions. Clearly, this looming disaster was not the new governor's fault. After all, he had just been inaugurated.

It would have been easy for Deukmejian to get in front of the television cameras and say, "Now look at this mess. I inherited it, but it's not my fault. It's Jerry Brown's fault. So, I'm going to ask for a large income-tax increase and I will send to the Legislature a bill which I call the 'Jerry Brown Tax Rescue Act of 1983.' "

That would have been easy, but it would have been wrong, and that's for sure.

I think that before long, the governor will have to ask for a tax increase. But in the meantime, he is making a heroic effort to cut the budget without worrying about whether what he does is politically appealing. One aspect of that struggle shows what a fine mind and independent spirit George Deukmejian has in a day of conformers and me-tooers.

Deukmejian has suggested to the Legislature that a modest fee be attached to attending state universities and colleges. This idea is the beginning of an avalanche of good sense that has been due for some time. Students attending state institutions of higher education should absolutely pay tuition and fees unless they come from poor families. This is a matter of the most elementary justice and fairness to the working people of California.

Ten years ago, I was a teacher at the University of California at Santa Cruz. There was no tuition to speak of. There was only a trivial charge for room and board. The students lived in the most fabulous, incredibly beautiful dormitories on Earth, overlooking magnificent Monterey Bay, framed by towering redwoods, gardens and pathways tended ceaselessly by armies of landscapers.

All of this was paid for by the taxpayers of the state of California. In my classroom were mostly children of doctors and lawyers, IBM computer executives, proprietors of large and small businesses. For their Christmas vacations, the students took planes to Hawaii, Puerto Vallarta, Mazatlan, New York City. In the summer, the kids went to Europe, to South America, to artists' retreats.

In other words, these were well-to-do kids. It nearly drove me mad to think that the ordinary dime-store clerk, agricultural laborer, retired policeman, school janitor, assembly-line worker at Lockheed, typist at the Bank of America or oilfield roustabout in Bakersfield were paying for these upper-class school-children to loll about in the redwoods, blowing pot and talking about revolution.

Now I admit that my case was extreme. But, as a fact of life, the mean income of families of students at all UC campuses exceeds the mean income of all California taxpayers. That means the poor of California are subsidizing the rich kids' education. This is a fundamental attack on fairness and equity in a free society. To soak the poor for the benefit of rich children insults the whole idea of a society in which persons are helped or assessed according to their means.

(For the students to say that they do not want to be dependent on their parents is just a rich kid's whine echoing a rich parent's whine. The kids are legally dependent in any event, and the "I want to be independent" nonsense would legitimize giving food stamps to the wife of a Rockefeller.)

I heard reports of a rally at UCLA at which state Sen. Alan Robbins said we should give a "free" education because we get a more highly skilled and productive labor force from a free state university system. Alas, that, too, is nonsense. If students are made more productive by their educations at UC or Cal State, the primary beneficiaries are the students themselves. Their incomes are raised, not the income of the state taxi driver or the factory worker, except by the most remote form of trickle-down theory.

Since the college education of young Californians benefits them and is an investment in their future, they should pay for it themselves. I have to pay for a new typewriter that raises my productivity. The *Herald* has to pay for new delivery trucks that raise its productivity. Why shouldn't well-to-do California kids pay for investments that will increase their productivity? The child of the doctor or small-business owner or lawyer is madly ripping off the ordinary taxpayer of California if he or she does not pay for his or her own education, and if the parents do not chip in a lot of that money.

Of course, there will be some students too poor to pay for their education. For those with genuine need, both social compassion and the welfare of the state dictate public assistance. But for the poor to pay the bills of the rich at the university level is simply not fair. Gov. Deukmejian has made a start toward correcting this basic inequity. More power to him.

WOMBS FOR RENT: NEW ERA ON THE REPRODUCTION LINE[2]

Admittedly, the economy is in bad shape, but somehow I never expected to see a new breed of entrepreneurs arrive on the scene hanging out shingles that offer Wombs for Rent.

Remember when the real-estate moguls of the 1970s dealt in houses? It appears that their 1980s counterparts are dealing with uteri. While they aren't doing a land-office business quite yet, surrogate motherhood is an expanding market.

At the moment, the star of the surrogates is Judy Stiver of Lansing, MI, who was set up by a lawyer in her own cottage industry. According to Judy's testimony, surrogate motherhood, pregnancy and delivery were a little bit like taking in a boarder. She was promised $10,000 to give womb and board to a fetus for nine months and then deliver the baby to its reputed biological father, Alexander Malahoff of Queens, N.Y.

When asked why she decided to take this moonlighting job, Judy explained that she and her husband wanted some money to take a vacation and maybe fix up the house a bit—that sort of thing.

Would I buy an egg from a lady like that? Frankly, I wouldn't even buy a pair of genes from her.

But that was just the beginning, or the conception, of this tale. The baby was born last month with microencephaly, a head smaller than normal, which usually means that he will be retarded. Suddenly, this most wanted child was a pariah. Baby Doe was put in a foster home. The Stivers claimed that he wasn't theirs. Malahoff claimed that he wasn't his.

Pretty soon there were blood tests and lawsuits all around and a climactic scene on a Phil Donahue Show that looked like a parody of a Phil Donahue Show. Live and in color from Chicago—Whose baby is Baby Doe? Will the real father stand up, please?—we learned the results of the blood test. Hang onto your seats: Malahoff was not the father; Judy's husband, Ray Stiver, was.

By any standards, this was a thriller with more identity crisis than *H.M.S. Pinafore.* The fate of the baby was resolved right there on camera as the Stivers promised to bring him up just as if he were their own. So much for their vacation.

But, for all its freakishness, I don't want to dismiss the story as just another human sideshow. This one was a long time in the making.

I don't know a soul who can't symphathize with the feelings and desires of an infertile couple. Over the past several years, we have grown used to reading about dramatic help for infertile couples. By now, artificial insemination seems routine, and in vitro fertilizations have been eased off the front page. We applaud their births as happy endings.

We have been, I think, numbed into regarding motherhood-for-hire as just another option. There are now at least eight and perhaps as many as 20 surrogate-parenting services in the country. Anywhere from 40 to 100 children have been born by surrogate mothers paid $5,000 to $15,000 in states where such payment is legal. At least one entrepreneur aims to become "the Coca-Cola of the surrogate-parenting industry."

The tale out of Michigan was a jarring reminder that surrogate mothering is something qualitatively different, with hazards that we are just beginning to imagine.

Being a surrogate mother is not, as has been suggested, the "flip side" of artificial insemination. The infertile couple have contracted for more from a woman than infusion of sperm. The pregnant woman has a stronger relationship with a fetus than a man has with a vial. The law governing this business, governing this web of parenting, is far murkier.

If the Stiver story has a bizarre twist, there are other and equally mind-boggling risks. What if the biological mother decides, as at least two have done, to keep the baby? Would a court hold that the contract was more sacred than the mother's rights?

What effect is there on a couple when the man seeks another woman to bear his child? The Malahoffs, it should be noted, separated when the child he believed was his was conceived.

What do you tell a child when he asks, "Where did I come from?" And what if the baby isn't perfect? Who holds the final responsibility for a child conceived through a contract?

In the Stivers' home, the boarder is now a son. They've learned something about chance.

We've learned something about a business and an idea that encourages people to regard parents as customers rather than as caretakers. We've learned something about people who look on motherhood as biological work on a reproduction line. We've learned to be wary of people who regard babies as just another product for an eager and vulnerable market.

WHY NOT SEND KIDS TO SCHOOL AT AGE 4, CUT GRADES TO 11?[3]

New York state's commissioner of education proposed recently that kindergarten begin at age 4 and first grade at age 5, and that the public-school curriculum be completed at the end of the 11th grade. These are the first really new ideas in public education since former California Supt. of Public Instruction Wilson Riles made it economically feasible a decade ago for schools to provide pre-kindergarten programs.

Both ideas are sound, and should be implemented. Experience and research tell us that an earlier start makes sense, saves dollars and is long overdue. There is no magic, or special developmental, reason for formal schooling to begin at age 6. That age was selected for political, not educational reasons.

Nineteenth-century factory owners found that most 5-year-olds could not reliably work a 12-hour day, and so the people trying to end child labor selected 6 as the age for beginning compulsory education. It is true that a 5-year-old is unlikely to stand up to 12 hours a day of repetitive labor, but, unless we want to run classrooms like factories for 12-hour days, that fact is irrelevant. Limiting schooling to age 6 and above makes no more sense, educationally, than does the nine-month school year— few of our children are needed for chores on the family farm anymore.

Experimental studies of pre-school education have demonstrated clearly—and with disadvantaged children—that an early start can reduce the need for later special education or for repeating grades, and that children who have been in good pre-schools are more likely to graduate from high school and, subsequently, to find and hold jobs and go on to post-secondary education.

The differences in later performance of pre-school graduates and those who did not attend pre-school are so great that the savings resulting from pre-school exceed its costs.

An earlier start in school offers additional advantages: It capitalizes on the eagerness to learn that 4-year-olds usually display; it establishes a greater commitment to learning and valuing of education, which is essential to school success; and it provides an opportunity for earlier identification of both the talented and the handicapped, permitting more effective schooling for each. Then, too, parents of younger pupils are far more likely to get involved in their education. The cost of re-tooling lower grades will be more than made up by the savings in remedial education and by the elimination of the 12th grade.

The proposal to contract the length of schooling by 8%—from 12 grades to 11—is another sensible idea. About half our youngsters drop out of school by the 12th grade, making it the most costly and least productive year in school. Of those who remain, about half go to college. The normal age for college entrance in the United States used to be 16, and it still is in most of the world. On the other hand, 12th grade has become a bore for able students and simply a "holding tank" for the rest.

Compressing the curriculum by 8% would make high school more challenging, and would result in a higher percentage of students graduating. Reducing the number of years in school wouldn't mean that we would have to teach less. A more efficient curriculum could more than compensate for the difference, and the addition of one class period a day would make up the time. Japanese children are in school eight hours a day and 11 months a year, with results that we feel in our pocketbooks.

Both of these ideas offer real benefits to our society—and our economy:

—Our school resources would better match the age distribution in our country.

—The need for, and costs of, special and remedial education would probably be reduced.

—We would have a better-educated labor pool 12 years from now.

—An earlier start would free more mothers for work. The shortage of decent day care is so acute that the day-care industry would not suffer at all if the number of 4- and 5-year-old users were gradually reduced. The resulting increase in family income would have a beneficial effect on tax receipts and commerce.

Taking into account current dropout rates and college enrollments, the New York commissioner's plan would increase the number of teenagers in the labor market by about 20% a dozen years from now. In today's economy, that would be awful. But if our economy is still in the doldrums a dozen years from now, it wouldn't make any difference anyway.

This plan would not solve all our educational problems. We would still need real curriculum reform, more sensible parental involvement and other changes, such as a more constructive use of summer months.

But an earlier start and earlier graduation are ideas that merit serious consideration.

THESE TESTS ARE MEANT TO SCARE PEOPLE[4]

Sen. Sam Ervin Jr. was right when he called polygraph interrogations "20th Century witchcraft." But despite the frequency with which these examinations fail to detect deception and wrongly accuse people of lying, they do "work."

They work for the same reason that torture works—because the subject decides that resistance is futile.

Polygraphy is little more than a form of psychological one-upmanship enabling an interrogator to intimidate a person into revealing highly private information most of us would regard as nobody else's business. Afraid that his emotions will cause the needles to jump and thus "incriminate" him, the subject will pour out embarrassing admissions to questions that have nothing to do with his job, in hope of producing a smooth graph.

President Nixon, during an effort to stem leaks, said to his staff, "I don't know anything about polygraphs and I don't know how accurate they are, but I know that they'll scare hell out of people."

Like Nixon, the people who inflict polygraph interrogations on employees and applicants know the procedure is unreliable and produces false accusations. They don't care, so long as the test scares people.

Polygraph interrogations are unfair. They deny due process not only by being unreliable but by violating the privacy of beliefs and associations, the freedom from unreasonable searches, the privilege against self-accusation, and the presumption of innocence.

Polygraphers claim that their subjects voluntarily waive their rights, but there's nothing voluntary about waiving basic human rights to keep or get a job. Moreover, no waiver can be voluntary if it's made without full knowledge of the risks, and few polygraph subjects know what they're getting into.

Polygraphers should be required to give subjects this warning: "Before you waive your rights, you should know that many decent people have come out of these interviews feeling demeaned.

"You should also know that your superior or personnel manager will receive my report, and, if he is typical, will rarely risk his career by employing a person who has damaging information of any kind in his record. If you reveal embarrassing information, it may remain in somebody's file for years and you can never be sure who will see it or use it against you. And you should know that polygraphers have been known to wrongly accuse more than 10% of those they question.

"That said, are you sure you want to go through with this?"

LIE DETECTORS ARE ACCURATE AND USEFUL[5]

When used responsibly, the lie detector can be an effective, reliable tool for business and law enforcement agencies to screen prospective employees.

Since the 1960s, the nation's population has become tremendously mobile. An applicant is less likely to come from the community where he or she seeks a job, or to have lived there long enough to establish an easily verifiable record.

The polygraph is particularly useful for small businesses that cannot afford to employ large security, personnel or audit departments. It may cost a business or law enforcement agency up to $1,500 to check an applicant's background; by using a polygraph, the employer can get the answers he needs for $50 to $100.

It's a simple, cost-efective way to verify the information a prospective employee has put on an application form. It's also useful in our litigious society, when many counsels advise their corporations not to respond at all to reference requests, for fear the subject of an inquiry will later sue.

Businesses which require their employees to handle cash or valuables find polygraphs useful. Convenience stores, jewelry retailers, drug chains and trucking firms have all begun using polygraph tests.

When administered correctly by qualified operators, the tests are accurate more than 90% of the time. Responsible operators bend over backwards to avoid asking questions which embarrass, demean or upset the subject. And 40 states have passed laws regulating polygraph use, to ensure responsible operation.

And the great majority of employers are responsible—they use the tests as one indicator among many indicators in the employee selection process. Few job applicants are denied jobs on the single criterion of failing a polygraph test.

Legislation we support will be reintroduced in this Congress to set minimum standards for polygraph operators and prevent abuses. It sets guidelines: No inquiries can be made concerning sexual or religious preference or union relationships, or about activities that occurred more than seven years before the interview. And I would support rules that, as a part of informed consent, would let subjects approve question areas in advance.

There are an estimated 200,000 to 400,000 polygraph tests a year in this country. They save employers money and help them make informed decisions about whom to hire; for the applicants, the test speeds up the process—within a couple of hours, they know whether they'll get the job.

[1]Ben Stein, "Let's Stop Giving Rich Kids a Free Ride Through College," *Los Angeles Herald Examiner,* February 7, 1983, p. A9.

[2]Ellen Goodman, "Wombs for Rent: New Era on the Reproductive Line." © 1983, the Boston Globe Newspaper Company/Washington Post Writers Group; reprinted with permission.

[3]Irving Lazar, "Why Not Send Kids to School at Age 4, Cut Grades to 11?" *Los Angeles Times,* February 7, 1983, part 2, p. 5. Reprinted with permission.

[4]Christopher H. Pyle, "These Tests Are Meant to Scare People," *USA Today,* February 17, 1983, p. A10. Reprinted with permission of *USA Today.*

[5]Lynn Marcy, "Lie Detectors Are Accurate and Useful," *USA Today,* February 17, 1983, p. A10. Reprinted with permission of *USA Today.*

PART FOUR

GENERATION

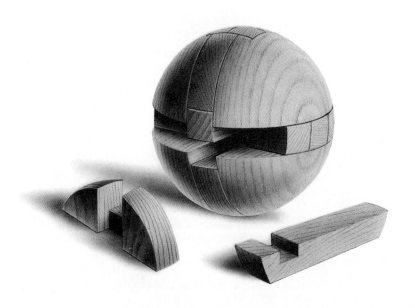

WRITING THE ARGUMENTATIVE ESSAY

13

So far this book has taught you how to analyze and evaluate ordinary arguments, long or short. You should now be able to respond critically to what you read and hear. You should not, however, confine your critical thinking skills to the information you receive. You should also apply them to the arguments that you yourself generate.

As you make your way through college, you will have many occasions to express yourself. Probably there is no single expressive activity you will be called on to do more often than write. And the kind of thing you will be called on to write more often than not will be an argumentative essay.

This chapter is intended to help you write good argumentative essays. It not only shows you what argumentative essays consist of but also gives you strategies for writing them that are based on the critical thinking skills you have acquired.

You might wonder why the essay is so central to schooling. There are so many kinds of writing: fiction, biography, poetry, jokes, news reports, letters, screenplays, ad copy, and so forth. Why always an essay?

Probably the best immediate explanation is that the essay's elements and format are basic to so many practical applications. Indeed, a good many instances of the kinds of writing just mentioned—fiction, biography, humor, news reports, letters, ad copy—are influenced by the essay. In editorial pieces, in art criticism, in business reports, in scholarly papers, in political speeches, in corporate memos, just about anywhere you care to look, you'll see the elements and organizational format of the essay cropping up. This means that learning how to write essays gives you one of education's most useful tools.

Perhaps this explanation doesn't go deep enough. What makes the essay so important in so many areas? The answer is that the essay is so flexible a framework and so well suited to the related and essential human tasks of exploring and communicating ideas. We stress the fact that the essay is suited to *both* these tasks, not just to the task of communicating. Writing is at least as much a process of discovering what one thinks as it is a matter of composing the results of prior thinking. Thus, the importance and value of the essay is not merely as a format for the presentation of the results of your explorations, a sort of literary mold into which you pour your thoughts when they're ready to go to market. The essay has an even more basic value as an organizational framework for finding out or figuring out what one thinks—what one has to say—about a subject.[1]

ARGUMENT AND PERSUASION

Rhetoric is the classical discipline devoted to the general study of expressive discourse. Indeed, the term "rhetoric" derives ultimately from the Greek expression for "I say." Classical rhetoric distinguished four forms of discourse under which all kinds of writing could be classified: narrative or "storytelling"; description, or telling how something looks, sounds, feels, tastes, or smells; exposition, the setting forth or clarification of facts and ideas; and finally, persuasion, intended to induce readers to accept the opinion of the writer or speaker.

Of the four categories, rhetoric's main traditional concern has been the development and systematic refinement of skills, techniques, and strategies of persuasion. Historically, rhetoric's traditional emphasis on persuasion arose in ancient Greece. In the developing political context of the city-states, citizens found it increasingly important to learn how to make effective and persuasive presentations in the assemblies and law courts, the principal institutions of self-government, where the laws were made and interpreted.

There is, then, a deep historical connection in rhetoric between persuasion and argument. Argumentative essays, although they may employ narrative, descriptive, and expository discourse, fall into the persuasive category. This is because argument is essentially a persuasive device. It is aimed at *rational* persuasion—persuasion by appeal to reason.

But as you are already well aware, argument and persuasion are not identical. Nor do they always go hand in hand. A rational approach may fail to persuade; and it is possible to be persuasive without being very rational. A perfectly cogent argument may well turn out to be less persuasive than some blatant fallacy. The central aim of the argumentative essay is to be rationally persuasive. The best argumentative essays combine a good argument with a persuasive presentation.

But before we can usefully address this as a goal, we have to have a writing project. The first questions you will need to ask as a writer are, What do I want to write about? and What do I want to say about it? These questions correspond to two essential preliminary steps in the writing process: (1) selecting—and focusing—a subject, and (2) formulating a thesis about it.

THE THESIS

As you learned in Chapter 12, every argument has a contention, which in an argumentative essay usually is termed the "thesis." The thesis is the argument's main idea, that is, the main point being advanced. Thus, formulating a thesis is an essential early step in the writing process. The thesis gives an essay purpose and direction, without which the essay would be little more than a random collection of sentences and paragraphs.

But, as anyone who has confronted a blank sheet of paper—especially under the added pressure of a deadline—can tell you, formulating a thesis presents a number of stumbling blocks. Without some effective strategies for overcoming them, these can easily add up to the dreaded form of mental paralysis known as "writer's block." Here, then, are some strategies to help you keep the wheels turning in a productive direction. We have organized them sequentially, although it is not essential that they be followed in precise sequential order.

Step 1: Selecting Subjects

Every thesis relates to some subject. The subject is the area of concern or interest. "Education in the United States," "the electoral process," "drugs," "feminism," "the penal system," "religion," and "conflict between the generations" all represent subjects or areas that are ripe for argumentative exploration. The first job of the argumentative writer, then, is to decide on a subject. Often, instructors do this for students. When instructors assign you a subject, or even a more narrow topic within a subject, your job of formulating a thesis is simplified. But often they leave the choice up to you; they assign what is termed a "free-choice subject," which means that you can write on whatever you choose. Faced with no subject limitations, students sometimes falter; they can't formulate a thesis because they can't even select a subject, let alone some aspect of it they may wish to write about.

Have you ever noticed how much longer it takes to make a decision and place an order in a restaurant with a huge menu than it does in a restaurant with only three choices? Whatever one winds up choosing, there are *so many things one will not get to eat.* Baffled by an overabundance of options, we frequently don't know what we want—and sometimes even start to wonder if we were hungry at all! When the array of options is unlimited, as it is in a free-choice assignment, we might wonder what it is that we really want to address. But don't forget: It's not as if you have a shortage of interests, or of opinions about interesting and controversial topics. And it's not as if you have to write about all of them at once. All you have to do is choose one. Here are four things you can do when stymied by a free-choice assignment.

First, you can select something that you are familiar with and about which you would like to learn more. Perhaps you've had a health course and learned something about vitamin therapy in the treatment of disease. If you want to learn more, why not make vitamin therapy your subject? Or maybe you recently read a newspaper article entitled "The American Indian: The Forgotten Minority." You remember being moved by the piece and wishing that you had the time to explore the plight of American Indians further. Here again is a possible subject. Or perhaps one of your outstanding gripes with colleges is the weight that admissions officers sometimes place on standardized tests. If you want to learn more about the pros and cons of such testing, make it the subject of your paper.

Second, you can choose a subject that you know nothing about but would like to investigate. A good place to begin is with terms you encountered once and glossed over, such as "supply-side economics," "circles of work," "big bang," "astral plains," or "cybernetics." Such terms are potential subjects for essays.

Subjects you'd like to learn something about can originate in conversations. A few years ago a student did an essay on what some experts on organizational psychology and management term "theory Z," which is a way of approaching and structuring work that is new to the United States but has been common throughout Japan for decades. When asked how he had decided on such an unusual subject, the student explained that some time earlier he had struck up a conversation with a passenger on a flight from San Francisco to Los Angeles. As it happened, the exchange turned to the subject of work and young people's attitudes toward it. The passenger thought that the Japanese approach to work organization might be more appealing to young American workers and help improve U.S. productivity. The flight ended before the passenger could explain very much about this approach. The student didn't think much more about the encounter until, a few months later, he was asked to write a free-choice essay. Recalling the conversation, he discovered his subject.

Third, you can skim newspapers, magazines, and other periodicals for possible subjects. A good newspaper (and sometimes even a poor one) is a treasure trove of subjects. Daily columns, commentaries, and editorials abound with information about current events, science, medicine, the arts, sports, religion, and education. In fact, brief news reports often inspire a subject. Another enterprising student once chanced upon an item explaining that the Food and Drug Administration had banned for sale in the United States an intrauterine device called the Dalkon Shield. A few weeks later the student came across another item concerning the export of the Dalkon Shield for sale abroad. She found this odd and began to wonder how many other products that were banned in the United States were being shipped overseas for sale. Why not write an essay on this subject? she thought. She did, and was it an eye-popper!

Fourth, you can consult the library for a subject of interest. Because the card catalogs contain information on every subject, merely perusing them should yield a clutch of ideas.

Step 2: Focusing: Identifying Possible Topics

Of course, after you have chosen a subject, you must identify possible topics, then select one and narrow it. Write a 500-word essay on advertising, your English professor might tell you. Faced with such an assignment, you could be confused. What *about* advertising? you wonder. Your instincts rightly tell you that advertising is far too broad and unwieldy a subject to be handled in a mere 500 words. The problem you perceive is analogous to the overabundance of options mentioned just a moment ago. Therefore, before proceeding with your essay you must identify some aspect of advertising that can be managed within the prescribed length.

Your asking "what about" when faced with the assignment can be viewed as a groping for a topic. The topic is some aspect of the subject. Obviously, subjects can spawn countless topics. For example:

Subject	Possible Topics
Football	Salaries of players The strike of 1982 A uniquely American pastime
Education in the United States	The high cost of college education Shortcomings in public education Misplaced priorities
Religion	The Moral Majority The recent rise of fundamentalism The increasing interest in Eastern religions
Advertising	Relationship to the law Deceptive practices Impact on the economy

This step of argumentative writing can be viewed as a brainstorming session in which you identify as many possible aspects of a subject as you can. Here you are in effect generating a range of options, like the range of possible subjects for an essay. This time, though, the options are more narrowly focused so as to be manageable within the framework of an essay of some particular length. Again, you may find the array of options you generate bafflingly large. So don't forget, as we were saying just a moment ago: It's not as if you have to say all there is to say about all of the aspects of your subject area at once.

This problem of focus is one that will continue to crop up again and again. As you focus on a particular subject within the endless array of possible subjects, you begin to see the complexities and the numerous aspects involved in it. As you focus more narrowly on a particular aspect of a subject, you may again come to see further complexities embedded within it.

Step 3: Focusing: Selecting and Limiting the Topic

Having composed a list of possible topics, you should then select one you want to write about and limit it. Note that this step consists of two operations: selection and limitation. The second operation is very important, for failing to limit your topic may mean that you later find it unmanageable. The proper limits of the topic usually are determined by the length of the proposed essay. The possible topics we've listed could be, and have been, the subjects of books. So to tackle any of them in a 500-word essay would prove unwise. They must be narrowed to allow development within 500 words. Here are some possibilities for the subject "Advertising":

Possible Topics	Limited Topic
Relationship to the law	The impact on consumers of three landmark decisions in consumer law
Deceptive practices	The use of ambiguity to sell aspirin, toothpaste, and mouthwash
Impact on the economy	Effects on the retail prices of alcoholic and nonalcoholic beverages

It is worth noting that the limited topics suggested here exhibit a common and effective method of controlling (and organizing) an essay—*dividing it into parts*. Thus, the first limited topic refers to *three* landmark decisions; the second to *three* representative products; the third to *alcoholic and nonalcoholic* beverages. From the writer's viewpoint these divisions reveal precisely what the essay must discuss and even the order to be followed (for example, aspirin, then toothpaste, then mouthwash). From the reader's viewpoint these divisions focus the topic and suggest the order of consideration: The reader knows what you will discuss and roughly when. Using division is enormously helpful because it maximizes the chances of effective communication.

Step 4: Determining Your Attitude Toward the Topic

A thesis consists not only of a topic but also the author's attitude toward it. Determining your attitude will help you decide what it is you're trying to demonstrate. For example, you may be *fearful* of the impact of three landmark decisions; *critical* of the use of ambiguity to sell aspirin, toothpaste, and mouthwash; or *convinced* of the significant effects of advertising costs on the retail prices of alcoholic and nonalcoholic beverages.

It is important to stress at this point that saying anything substantial enough to warrant an essay involves taking risks. To write an entire essay in defense of a thesis that no one would dispute is too safe. It amounts to a waste of your own and your reader's time and attention. "Millions of Americans smoke cigarettes," for example, is an assertion so uncontroversial and so easily verified that the need—and certainly the wisdom—of constructing an essay to demonstrate its truth is precluded.

On the other hand, you should not *confine* yourself in your thesis to assertions about your own attitudes and experience, your own inner life. Suppose that the topic you have selected is the impact on consumers of three landmark decisions in consumer law, and that your attitude is that you are fearful that progress made in consumer protection during the past decade will be undone. Your thesis should of course express your attitude. But it should do more than merely state that you have this attitude.

Suppose someone else has a different attitude. (Indeed, you pretty much have to suppose this. Otherwise, you're not taking enough of a risk.) Having read your thesis, they now challenge you to defend it, and you point out, "My thesis is merely that *I* am fearful that progress made in consumer protection during the past decade will be undone." This is another way of playing it safe. Indeed, it amounts to a retreat from the issue.

Your thesis is determined by your attitude but it is not *about* your attitude. Remember, the aim of an argumentative essay is to be rationally persuasive. You *are* trying to win your reader over. This involves taking risks. One of the risks is the risk of being mistaken. After all, this is precisely why you are looking for good reasons to support your position, isn't it?

Step 5: Writing the Thesis Statement

The next step consists of wedding the topic and your attitude toward it in a single assertion. As for the topics under discussion here, you might write a thesis statement such as the ones in the following diagrams:

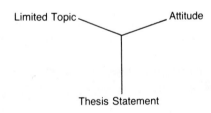

Limited Topic — Attitude

Thesis Statement

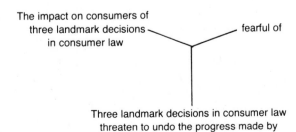

The impact on consumers of three landmark decisions in consumer law — fearful of

Three landmark decisions in consumer law threaten to undo the progress made by consumers in the 1970s.

337

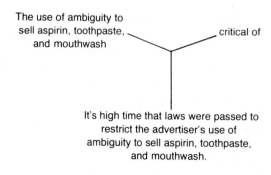

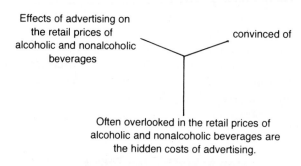

Step 6: Testing the Thesis Statement

After writing the thesis statement it's a good idea to check it for focus. After all, you want to make sure that your topic and viewpoint are crystal clear. A good way to check your statement is to have somebody else read and react to it. Ask the person, "What do you think I'm trying to demonstrate in my essay?" If the reply corresponds with your purpose, you have a well-focused thesis statement. If it doesn't, then back to the drawing board!

Quick Check on Thesis Formulation

By using the six steps just discussed, write a thesis statement for each of the following subjects:

1. job opportunities for women
2. freedom of the press
3. the judicial system in the United States
4. drug use among minors
5. the state of marriage twenty years from now
6. restoring cities
7. gun control
8. premarital sex
9. college curricula
10. defense spending
11. the plight of the handicapped
12. extracurricular activities in college
13. junk foods
14. changing sex roles
15. contemporary music

MAIN POINTS

Every argumentative essay contains main points, that is, principal support as-sertions offered to advance the thesis. Recall the essay opposing voluntary eu-thanasia that we considered in the preceding chapter. In attempting to show why voluntary euthanasia should not be permitted (thesis), the author developed six main points.

1. Euthanasia is wrong.
2. It's impossible to ascertain that the consent is voluntary.
3. Allowing a death decision is unwise.
4. Mistaken diagnoses are possible.
5. Relief or cures can be imminent.
6. Abuses will follow the legislation.

Since any argumentative essay must demonstrate its thesis, writers must look for statements that answer *why* or *how* the thesis is justified. These state-ments are reasons. Thus, *why* should voluntary euthanasia not be legalized? *Why* are stricter regulations needed to restrict the widespread use of ambiguity to sell aspirin, toothpaste, and mouthwash? *How* does even a cursory look at the pricing structure of alcoholic and nonalcoholic beverages reveal the enormous effect of advertising costs? The writer's job is to marshal reasons that answer the *why* or *how* questions.

If the writer assembles enough of the right kinds of reasons, the result will be the basis of a good argument. If the reasons satisfy the audience, then they are persuasive. In writing essays, then, you must (1) select reasons that prove your thesis and (2) limit the essay to the reasons that are likely to be the most persuasive, that is, the reasons that likely will have the greatest impact on your audience. Having discovered and selected your reasons—your main points—you must then support them with evidence.

In collecting reasons and support for them, you can call on several sources. One is *observation*. Observation is awareness of what occurs outside the writer. Usually observations are firsthand studies of scenes, people, objects, and events. Recall that in the euthanasia essay, the author called on observations to make judgments about the effect of drugs and pain on free, rational choice and to indicate the possibility of mistaken diagnoses.

Personal experience is a second source of reasons. As distinguished from observation, personal experience refers to what goes on *inside* the writer. It is one's consciousness of thoughts, ideas, and involvement with incidents, persons, places, and things. Used together with other sources, personal experience can be a rich source of support material. But be careful: Over-reliance on personal experience to make points results in provincialism. This arguably occurred in the euthanasia essay when the author recounted her family's ordeal in attempting to establish main point 3. The author erred not in invoking this touching personal experience but in relying on it exclusively to make the point and ignoring coun-terevidence.

Informed opinion is a third and quite important source for developing reasons and support material. Informed opinion consists of the views of others who have studied the same subject. The euthanasia essay could have been greatly improved had the author made proper use of informed opinion.

Finally, *organized research* is a fourth source of material. Organized research is the systematic sifting of evidence from records, reports, and other printed sources. The author of the euthanasia essay didn't call on this source, but could have, for, as indicated in the overall evaluation, some material is available on alternative approaches to the treatment of the dying.

You can and should use these sources when assembling your main points and support material. Indeed, brainstorm in terms of these sources. Make a list of observations, personal experiences, informed opinion, and organized research relevant to your thesis. From this list select the most effective points; then shore them up with support material by again using these sources.

AUDIENCE AWARENESS

Let's now return to the central aim of the argumentative essay—to be rationally persuasive. The best argumentative essays combine a good argument with a persuasive presentation. And one of the keys to a persuasive presentation is awareness of one's audience.

Have you ever wondered what makes a comic like Robin Williams or Eddie Murphy so funny? Certainly mannerisms, temperament, delivery, timing, and a sense of the tragic and absurd all contribute. But ultimately what makes any comic funny is the audience: without audience response—laughter—a comic "dies."

This is why comics spend much time studying their audiences, learning their age, social and educational backgrounds, sexual and racial makeup, biases, inhibitions, fears, and basic outlook on life. Indeed, audience characteristics influence the comic's choice of words, dialect, and points of reference. Such considerations help the comic draw and then walk that thin line between being funny and being offensive, between good humor and bad taste. When comics overstep the line, chances are it's because they have ignored or misjudged their audience.

There is a lesson in this for you, the would-be argumentative writer. Although you are not trying primarily to entertain or amuse your readers, you are trying to win them over. For the comic, winning over the audience means getting them to laugh often. For the writer it means getting your readers to agree with you, or at least to enter sympathetically into your way of thinking. Whether or not either succeeds depends largely on how well each has shaped the material to suit the audience or readership.

Shaping an argument to suit your readership requires the same kind of audience study that the comic makes. Keep in mind the values, prejudices, and basic assumptions of the people you want to influence. Also be aware of their educational, economic, and social backgrounds; their ages; their occupations;

and their feelings about current issues. Here is an inventory of key areas to think about when analyzing your audience before putting pen to paper.

1. Age: How old are the members of my audience? What effect, if any, will their ages have on their reception of what I'm trying to say?

2. Values: What is important to my audience—family, job, school, neighborhood, religion, country? What are their fundamental ideals—being successful, getting married, realizing their potential, ensuring law and order, guaranteeing civil liberties, establishing international harmony?

3. Economics: Is my audience wealthy, middle class, poor, or a cross-section? Are they currently employed, unemployed, training for employment?

4. Social Status: From which social group does my audience come? What's important to this group? What references will they identify with?

5. Intellectual Background: What does my audience know about my subject? What can I take for granted that they will know? Which words can I expect them to understand; which ones should I make sure to explain?

6. Expectations: What will my audience be expecting of my essay? Why will they be reading it? What will they be looking for?

7. Attitude: What can I assume will be my audience's attitude toward my topic? Will they likely be sympathetic, hostile, or indifferent?

Taking an audience inventory makes your writing job simpler than it otherwise would be. To see why, let's suppose that you're interested in lining up Robin Williams for a show that your college club is sponsoring. You approach Mr. Williams and find him receptive. In short order you work out arrangements and set a performance date. Now, you would certainly think it odd if Mr. Williams didn't ask you at some point, "Who's the audience? Tell me something about them." Even though he improvises most of his standup performance, he needs to know his audience. Indeed, an improvisational performer may rely even more heavily on audience awareness than a performer whose act is scripted. The general point is that knowing that one will be performing for an audience of college students, rather than, say, a general audience of New Yorkers, helps the performer shape the material. And the more one knows about one's audience, the better.

The same applies to writing an argument. The better you know your audience, the better your basis for selecting material, choosing vocabulary, and using persuasive devices. Most important, knowing your audience is the key to knowing how to strike the pose that will win you their respect, sympathy, and approval. Audience consideration thus assists you in deciding what to include, how to express it, and what role to play when preparing an argument. We will return to the concept of role shortly, but first let's examine another example that will further show how crucial audience awareness is.

Suppose that you are a member of a student group that has been selected to meet with a board of professors and administrators to consider giving students academic credit for work experience. You have been chosen to argue the case in favor of such a policy.

In preparing your case you should first identify the characteristics of the members of your audience. First, they will be mostly middle-aged, from thirty-five to fifty-five. Second, they probably never received any such credit when in school and just as likely have never been associated with any institution that gave such credit. Third, they will be intelligent, educated people who see themselves as open-minded, reasonable, and flexible. Fourth, they will be concerned about the institution's academic integrity. Fifth, they will be troubled about the "nuts and bolts" of implementing the policy. (Will *any* kind of work experience count for credit? If not, what conditions should be met to warrant credit?) Sixth, they will be sensitive to the opinions of alumni, the board of trustees, and parents, all of whose financial and moral support the school needs. Armed with this kind of commonsense information about your audience, you can give your argument form and character.

Now to the point about image. We indicated that taking an audience inventory can help you decide which role to project as a writer. In fact, deciding the role that you will play for your audience follows directly from audience analysis.

PERSONA

In rhetoric the term "persona" refers to the role or identity assumed by a writer or speaker.[2] The persona that you select depends largely on audience considerations. For example, in arguing your case before a group of professors and administrators, you will want to appear thoughtful, intelligent, serious, and mature. But suppose you were addressing a student audience. While your argumentative purpose remains the same—to win assent for the granting of academic credit for work experience—you would probably be more effective if you struck the pose of any angry young person who sees elements of elitism and a fundamental injustice in the traditional policy of giving academic credit only for course work. You might heighten this image by projecting yourself as a youthful progressive locked in combat with academic traditionalists out of step with the times. There is nothing in and of itself objectionable about considering your audience and working hard to strike a pose calculated to win them over, assuming of course that there's more to your case than mere posturing—that you have a worthy argument to present.

Quick Check on Audience and Persona

1. Pretend that you are writing a letter to the editor of your local paper protesting the city council's decision to impose a 10 P.M. to

7 A.M. curfew in all city parks. What particularly rankles is that the curfew will prevent you from jogging between 6 A.M and 7 A.M. in a neighborhood park, as is your custom. Identify your audience and persona; that is, list the specific characteristics of the audience and the important characteristics of the role you must play for it.

2. You are asked to write an argumentative essay for some course you are currently taking. Presumably the paper will be read only by your instructor. What specific characteristics of this person must you keep in mind? What important characteristics must you embody in your role? Suppose that the paper was intended more for a student audience. In what ways would the audience and persona characteristics be different?

3. Using the preceding exercises as models, create two situations that call for you to argue some case. Then identify audience and persona characteristics.

In preparing your audience, follow this scheme:

Situation: _____

Specific characteristics of the audience I must keep in mind:

1. _____

2. _____

3. _____

4. _____

Others: _____

Important characteristics to embody in my role:

1. _____

2. _____

3. _____

4. _____

APPRECIATING YOUR OPPONENT'S POSITION

When you argue for a position, you imply that another position exists. After all, if an issue were one-sided, arguing about it would be as pointless as trying to prove a widely known fact. Whether or not you argue effectively for your position depends largely on how well you understand and how deeply and sympathetically you consider the other side or sides to the issue.

But, you might wonder, how do I know for sure that my audience holds an opposing position? True enough. In many cases you don't. But suppose that, like yourself, your readers are critical thinkers. As such, they can be expected to raise challenging questions, just as you would. And chances are that most of the time your readers won't be in complete agreement with the position you're advancing. Inevitably, if you're arguing for an interesting position on an issue of any depth and complexity at all, and you're trying to be rationally persuasive, you'll need to confront the opposition. You'll need to address yourself to readers who presumably disagree with you, and who disagree with you on some point for which they would themselves presumably be prepared to argue. In what spirit should you confront such opposition?

Thomas Aquinas once remarked that when you want to convert someone to your view, you go over to where he is standing, take him by the hand (mentally speaking), and guide him to where you want him to go. You don't stand across the room and shout at him. You don't call him nasty names. You don't order him to come over to where you are. You start where he is, and work from that position.

To put it another way: When you think that someone is wrong, and you disagree, your first task is to determine in what way they are right. This is not as paradoxical as it sounds.

Suppose you're firmly convinced of some particular position on a complex and controversial subject like the death penalty. Are you absolutely certain that you're 100 percent correct? Can you be absolutely certain that someone who disagrees with you is entirely wrong in everything they might have to say? Wouldn't it be wiser to consider thoughtfully what your opponent might have to say, and to concede as much as you honestly can? Then when you go on to offer criticisms of your opponent's position, you can reasonably expect them to be given thoughtful consideration as well. After all, think how you would react as a reader to a criticism of your position. If the criticism starts out by identifying your position as out-to-lunch, you're not likely to be very receptive, are you? You'd be much more open to a criticism that began by stating your position in a way that you would yourself state it, recognizing its intuitive plausibility, or its explanatory power, or the weight of evidence in its favor, or whatever strengths it may have.

Thus, when you oppose a position and undertake to criticize it, you enhance your chances of being persuasive if you can state that position in a way that would fully satisfy someone who holds it—even more so if you can make out a better case for it than the proponent himself can.

ANTICIPATING OBJECTIONS

Just as you should be aware of the possibility that your opponent's position may embody certain strengths, you should be aware of the possibility that your own position may have certain weaknesses—weaknesses that very likely will be more apparent to your opponent than to you. Thus, an additional strategic advantage for the writer of an argumentative essay flows from making a genuine attempt to appreciate the opponent's position. Your opponent's position affords you a much better vantage point from which to troubleshoot your own position and argument—to make yourself aware of points at which your argument stands in need of additional support, or of needed qualifications and refinements of the thesis itself.

For example, suppose you were writing a paper in support of mandatory retirement. You must not ignore the studies which indicate that forced retirement is a threat to workers' physical and mental health. Nor can you overlook the fact that taxpayers incur costs for maintaining people in retirement. Simply acknowledging these objections and proceeding with your argument probably won't settle these matters for your audience. You must try to blunt these potential objections to your thesis. One way to do this would be to find legitimate grounds for challenging the validity of the studies. Another would be to demonstrate that, for example, while society pays for maintaining retirees, it also pays to support the younger workers who cannot find employment because the job ranks are glutted with older workers.

In anticipating counterarguments keep your audience in mind. Their background will largely determine the kind of objections they will raise. For example, in an essay supporting the teaching of creationism in high school biology classes, a general audience likely will raise different objections from those raised by a group of scientists. Anticipating your audience's objections helps you decide which points to emphasize to win them over.

All of this is much more than an academic exercise. These refinements in the arts of argument and persuasion are really of very fundamental practical consequence. When they are forgotten or ignored, disputants have little recourse to anything but violence. The art of argument is learning how to disagree productively.

ORGANIZATIONAL APPROACHES

Organization is the framework that ties together the reasons you assemble to support your thesis. The familiar general essay format—introduction, body, conclusion—is extremely flexible as to length, topical focus, and so on. And it will accommodate a wide variety of more specific organizational strategies or approaches that may prove to be appropriate to a given topic. We will discuss four of the most common of these: (1) the inductive approach, (2) the pro-and-con approach, (3) the cause-and-effect approach, and (4) the analysis-of-alternatives approach. These and other organizational plans can be used individually or in combination with one another depending largely on considerations of your purpose and audience.

Inductive Approach

Suppose you can't validly deduce your thesis from premises so uncontroversial that no one would dispute them. You might structure your main argument as a deduction and then turn to the matter of supporting your main points. Suppose you can't validly deduce *these* from further premises so uncontroversial that no one would dispute them. At some point you might consider proceeding inductively. That is, you might proceed by assembling supporting reasons that, although they leave room for doubt as to the truth of your thesis, do make it more reasonable to believe.

An inductive approach is especially useful when your purpose is to convince the audience of a rather controversial assertion and the evidence you have to present is, although not absolutely conclusive, less controversial than the thesis. Presenting the body of evidence first helps you turn audience attention to the evidence, which is allowed to speak for itself. Ideally, having seen the evidence, members of the audience will change their minds or will at least be more receptive to your controversial conclusion.

For example, suppose your purpose is to convince a skeptical audience that Americans are not as well fed as they think they are. Using the inductive approach, you might structure your essay as follows:

Fact 1: According to the most recent information, 20 to 50 percent of Americans run some risk of not meeting the U.S. recommended daily allowance for at least one or more of the vitamins C, A, B_1 (thiamine), B_2 (riboflavin), and folic acid.

Fact 2: Although the diets of most Americans may be richer in minerals than they were fifty years ago, our intake of such minerals as iron and calcium still is likely to be insufficient.

Fact 3: Many people today, young and old, are dieting and skipping meals. As a result they may be eliminating foods that contain many vitamins, including C, E, and B-complex vitamins.

Conclusion: These facts point to an unmistakable conclusion: There are serious gaps in our national diet, most frequently because of poor eating habits.

Pro-and-Con Approach

Notice that the preceding example presents a "closed case" for your contention. Here is an alternative strategy based on a more dialectical, "balance-of-considerations" approach: The pro-and-con essay attempts to reach a balanced conclusion by treating an issue as an open question worth thinking about. In it the arguer usually begins by discussing the pros and cons of an issue. The discussion serves as a basis for a balanced conclusion to emerge as a compromise position.

This format, then, consists of (1) the confirmation of an idea, (2) the objection to the idea, and (3) the thesis as a compromise arrived at by balancing considerations. This approach has special audience appeal because it flatters their intelligence and sense of fair play and speaks well of the writer's thoughtfulness and impartiality. Here's an example:

Confirmation: Undoubtedly the United States enjoys one of the highest standards of living and is the largest producer of food products in the world. Our agricultural and industrial resources understandably make many Americans and non-Americans alike consider us the best-fed people on earth.

Objection: Current evidence suggests that we are far from realizing the nutritional promise of our bountiful resources. For one thing 20 to 50 percent of us run some risk of not meeting the U.S. recommended daily allowance.

Conclusion: Calling ourselves the best-fed people on earth is misleading. Rather, we appear to be potentially the best-fed people on earth. Whether we realize our potential depends largely on whether we can close the gaps in our national diet by improving our eating habits.

Cause-and-Effect Approach

The cause-and-effect essay, which is especially appropriate for advocating consequential assertions, attempts to ascertain the conditions that have produced some phenomenon. One way to do this is to present the major causes in chronological order, as in treating some historical event. Another is to arrange the causes in order of importance. Often writers of a cause-and-effect essay have in mind some remedy, which they present after they have discussed the causal conditions underlying a problem. In that event the writer's purpose is twofold: (1) to make the audience aware of the causes and (2) to make it accept the proposed solution. The cause-and-effect essay, then, often follows this structure: statement of problem, various causes, proposed solution. Here's an example:

Statement of problem: It is commonly thought that Americans are the best-fed people on earth. Yet current evidence indicates that there are serious gaps in our national diet.

First major cause: The deficiencies in our national diet are attributable to several factors. Perhaps the most important is poor eating habits.

Second major cause: Lack of education is another reason for the deficiencies in our national diet. Although public school curricula inevitably include a "health" component, very little of it is devoted to the study of proper nutrition.

Third major cause: Still another factor that explains our nutritional deficiencies is the medical profession's traditional ignorance of or lack of interest in proper nutrition. Historically, doctors have spent little time impressing on patients the link between poor diet and ill health.

Conclusion proposal: Undoubtedly we Americans have the potential for being the best-fed people on earth. But until we change our eating habits, schools start instructing students in proper nutrition, and health professionals begin reinforcing this instruction, we stand little chance of realizing our potential.

Analysis-of-Alternatives Approach

Often the purpose of an essay is to make the audience accept one of several alternatives. This is accomplished by structuring the presentation according to options. Thus, the essay that analyzes alternatives tries to make the audience accept one option as preferable by examining and eliminating other less desirable options. This strategy is especially useful in making the audience accept the "lesser of the evils" or an untried approach. For example:

Thesis: The eating habits of elementary school children can be improved in many ways.

First Alternative: One way is for the U.S. Department of Health and Welfare to exercise tighter control over the school lunch program. Undoubtedly this approach will invite a full-scale debate about the proper role of government in relation to business and consumers.

Second Alternative: Another approach is for schools to prohibit the sale of junk food on campus. Where this has been tried, it has met widespread opposition from children, parents, and, of course, the junk food industry.

Third alternative: A third alternative is to make nutrition a basic and continuing part of a child's education. This approach has the advantage of being far less controversial than either of the other two. More important, it respects the autonomy of individuals by equipping them to make informed food choices but not restricting their choices. Perhaps most important, this approach stands the best chance of getting students to eat properly outside school and to develop sound eating habits for life.

1. Which organizational format is used in the essay opposing the legalization of voluntary euthanasia (Chapter 12)? How would you describe the author's audience? The author's persona?

2. Identify the organizational patterns evident in the following essay excerpts.

   a. The United States certainly has both the human and material resources to reduce its crime rate. We have enough money and know-how to devise and underwrite innovative ways of dealing with crime and criminals. Indeed, some communities have done just that. Yet a presidential commission recently reported that as a whole the United States is losing its fight against crime.

      What we lack, of course, is the will. We Americans value our creature comforts too much to allow our personal incomes to be taxed for ambitious crime-prevention programs.

      So to say that as a nation we have a serious crime problem really is to admit that we are unwilling to devote more than a minor fraction of our great wealth and human resources to the enterprise of crime prevention.

   b. "There are many different methods of achieving limitation of births.

      "Abortion is undoubtedly preferable to infanticide, though we know too little about the physiological and psychological damage which it may cause to recommend it without serious qualms.

      "Contraception certainly seems preferable to abortion, and indeed the moral objection to contraception in principle seems to be confined to a single major branch of the Christian church. Even there, the difference in practice between this church and the rest of society is much smaller than the difference in precept. Contraception, however, also has its problems, and it is by no means an automatic solution to the problem of population control.

      "The fact that we must recognize is that it is social institutions which are dominant in determining the ability of society to control its population, not the mere physiology of reproduction." (Kenneth E. Boulding, *The Meaning of the Twentieth Century* [New York: Harper & Row, 1979], p. 79.)

   c. "Political pressures in this presidential year have given a militant minority of women powerful leverage for enactment [of the Equal Rights Amendment]. However, the respective states of the Union may come to regret ratification, if the two-thirds majority approves.

". . . legal scholars from the University of Chicago, Yale, and Harvard [have argued] that while the amendment would have no effect upon discrimination, it would 'nullify every existing federal and state law making any distinction whatever between men and women, no matter how reasonable the distinction may be, and rob Congress and the 50 states of the legislative power to enact any future laws making any distinction between men and women, no matter how reasonable the distinction may be.'

"Like the civil rights movement, Women's Lib is seeking, by using the power of the state, to forbid individual discrimination as opposed to discrimination legally enforced.

"But like some elements of the civil rights movement, militant feminists are not really interested in reform, but rather in revolution and destruction of the existing social fabric of the society." (Jeffrey St. John, "Women's Lib Amendment Not Simple Legal Formula," *Columbus Dispatch,* May 9, 1972, p. 23.)

d. "America's young people have found a potent, sometimes addictive, and legal drug. It's called alcohol.

"Why are youngsters rediscovering booze? One reason is pressure from other kids to be one of the gang. Another is the ever-present urge to act grown up. For some, it eases the burden of problems at home or at school. And it's cheaper. You can buy a couple of six-packs of beer for the price of three joints of pot.

"Perhaps the main reason is that parents don't seem to mind. They tolerate drinking—sometimes almost seem to encourage it.

"The Medical Council on Alcoholism warns: The potential teen-age drinking problem should give far more cause for alarm than drug addiction. Many schools have reacted to teenage drinking. They've started alcohol-education programs. But a lot of experts feel that teenagers are not going to stop drinking until parents do." (Carl T. Rowan, "Teenagers and Booze" in *Just Between Us Blacks* [New York: Random House, 1974], pp. 95–96.)

TESTING THE LOGIC OF THE ESSAY

As you build your case you will want to ensure that your argument hangs together and that your thesis is convincingly and legitimately supported. In addition to troubleshooting your own position and argument from the vantage point of an opposing position, an excellent device for testing the web of logical relationships in your essay—as well as for guiding and controlling the work of composition—is an outline.

Most student writers (and nonstudent writers, for that matter) don't fully exploit the outline, a very powerful tool for structuring an essay. Typically, when they do use an outline, they formulate some main and subordinate headings and immediately launch into the writing. Rarely do they pay enough attention to the logic of the relationships connecting their ideas, to their missing premises, or the possibility that informal fallacies are implicit in their outline and may come back to haunt them in the essay. To get the most out of your outline, follow these four steps:

Step 1: *Construct the outline,* using roman numerals to indicate the main points and letters and arabic numerals to indicate support material. (We are assuming that you have learned how to do this elsewhere.)

Step 2: *Indicate on the outline the relationships between the main points and the thesis and between the support material and the main points, with reference to these developmental patterns: fact and opinion, illustration, authority or testimonials, cause and effect, analogy, or statistics (including polls, surveys, and studies).* The reason for identifying these patterns is that they will alert you to potential pitfalls. For example, if you're using an illustration, you must ensure that it's appropriate, that it doesn't depend for its force on a subjective or controversial interpretation of it, and that it is a fair representation of the point it's supposed to make.

Step 3: *Fill in missing premises that are not obvious.* Doing this is as crucial in writing essays as in evaluating them. If you don't fill in your missing premises, you can't be sure that your assertions and inferences have a logical basis.

Step 4: *Examine the outline for possible informal fallacies.* If you expect the audience to agree with you, you must make sure that the force of what you say doesn't rely chiefly on some unreliable inference.

Let's now see how to apply these steps to test the logic of a hypothetical essay that argues for restricting the access of consenting adults to pornographic materials. For illustrative purposes we will repeat the outline in applying each step, although you needn't do this when actually outlining an essay.

Step 1:   Construct an outline.

Thesis: **The state should restrict consenting adults' access to obscene and pornographic materials.**

I.   Pornography leads to crime.
    A.   Newspapers recenty reported the story of an unstable young man who raped a woman after he'd been aroused by lurid scenes in an obscene comic book.

B.   The 1965 Gebhard study confirmed the reports of police officers that sex offenders often have pornographic materials in their possession or admit to having seen them.

II.   Pornography threatens society's moral well-being.
    A.   It makes people preoccupied with sexual gratification.
    B.   It leads to impersonal expressions of sexuality.
    C.   The state has the right and duty to control what threatens society's physical well-being.

III.   People need standards of decency and direction in sexual matters.
    A.   Religious leaders have always said so.
    B.   Polls indicate people desire this.

Step 2:   **Indicate relationships between main points and thesis and between support material and main points.**

Thesis: **The state should restrict consenting adults' access to obscene and pornographic materials.**

Cause and effect	I.	Pornography leads to crime.
Illustration		A. Newspapers recently reported . . .
Study		B. The 1965 Gebhard study . . .
Opinion	II.	Pornography threatens society's moral well-being.
Opinion		A. It makes people preoccupied . . .
Opinion		B. It leads to impersonal . . .
Analogy		C. The state has the right . . .
Opinion	III.	People need standards of decency and direction . . .
Authority		A. Religious leaders have always said so.
Poll		B. Polls indicate people desire this.

Step 3:   **Fill in missing premises.**

Thesis: **The state should restrict consenting adults' access to obscene and pornographic materials.**

Cause and effect	I. Pornography leads to crime.	+<**The state ought to restrict people's access to anything that leads to crime.**>

Illustration	A. Newspapers recently . . .	+<**Viewing the lurid scenes caused the man to commit the rape.**>
Study	B. The 1965 Gebhard study . . .	
Opinion	**II.** Pornography threatens . . .	+<**The state ought to restrict people's access to anything that threatens society's moral well-being.**>
Opinion	A. It makes people preoccupied . . .	+<**Preoccupation with sexual gratification and impersonal expressions of sexuality threaten society's moral well-being.**>
Opinion	B. It leads to impersonal . . .	
Analogy	C. The state has the right . . .	
Opinion	**III.** People need standards . . .	+<**If people need standards of decency and direction, the state should provide them.**>
Authority Poll	A. Religious leaders . . .	+<**If people want standards, the state should provide them.**>
	B. Polls indicate . . .	

Step 4: **Examine the completed outline for possible informal fallacies.**

Thesis: **The state should restrict consenting adults' access to obscene and pornographic materials.**

| Cause and effect | **I.** Pornography leads to crime. **(probably a causal oversimplification)** | +<The state ought to restrict . . .> **(unsupported value judgment)** |
| Illustration | A. Newspapers recently . . . **(Is this typical? If not, it may be a small or biased sample)** | +<Viewing the lurid scenes caused . . .> **(post hoc)** |

Study	B. The 1965 Gebhard study . . . **(Where are the specifics of the study? Did it prove a _causal_ relation?)**	
Opinion	**II.** Pornography threatens . . . **("moral well-being" is undefined; unsupported value judgment)**	+ <The state ought to restrict . . .> **("moral well-being" is undefined; unsupported value judgment)**
Opinion	A. It makes people preoccupied . . .	
Opinion	B. It leads to impersonal . . . **(questionable cause)**	+ <Preoccupation with sexual gratification and impersonal expressions of sexuality . . .> **("moral well-being" is undefined; unsupported value judgment)**
Analogy	C. The state has the right . . . **(questionable analogy: one major relevant difference is that it is easy to agree on what threatens our physical well-being, but not on what threatens our moral well-being.)**	
Opinion	**III.** People need standards . . . **(irrelevant reason: This only shows that _somebody_ should provide them.)**	+ <If people need standards . . .> **(unsupported opinion)**
Authority	A. Religious leaders . . . **(false authority)**	

Poll   B. Polls indicate . . .   + <If people want
                                                             standards . . .>

(Where are   **(unsupported opinion)**
specifics?)

This outline indicates serious problems in the logic of the relationships between thesis and main points and between main points and support material. If the writer wishes to write a compelling argumentative essay advancing this thesis, she must drastically revise the plan.

Here is one additional observation that further points up the value of outlining. Sometimes an outline will suggest a different approach altogether, perhaps even a scrapping of the original thesis. Don't resist this possibility, for it offers you a chance to elevate an issue to a more enlightening level. In any event, it's better to alter a course at the planning stage than midway through the writing of the essay.

WRITING THE ESSAY

Now that you are satisfied with your outline, it's time to start writing the essay. Actually, to be precise, you're already well underway in the writing process. But you will need to compose the results of your work in the form of a finished essay, and in the process, turn fragmentary sketches of your ideas into complete sentences and paragraphs, make smooth transitions, and so on. Essays of any length consist of a beginning, a development, and an ending.

Beginning

Many writers find beginning the most challenging moment in writing. It is helpful to bear in mind what you are doing as a writer in beginning an essay. Your primary tasks at the beginning of an essay are to orient your reader and motivate your reader's interest.

Here are six strategies you can use in beginning your argumentative essay.

1. Clarify your topic. Illustration from a paper linking the media with widespread anxiety: "It is little wonder that many people today show intense anxiety and worry. An uncertain economy makes them wonder whether they will be able to maintain themselves and their families. The deplorable state of the environment makes them question whether the struggle for survival is even worth it. The worsening of international relations leaves them fearful that the world is headed for a nuclear holocaust. In all this, the media play a crucial role in producing anxiety."

2. Indicate your feeling about the topic. Illustration from a paper opposing pornography: "Rarely do we consider it politically interesting whether men and women find pleasure in performing their duties as citizens, parents, and spouses; or, on the other hand, whether they derive pleasure from watching their laws and customs ridiculed on stages, in films, or in books. Nor do we consider it politically relevant whether the relations between men and women are depicted in terms of an eroticism separated from love and calculated to undercut the family. Nevertheless, much of the obscenity from which so many of us derive pleasure today is expressly political."

3. Relate your topic to something current or well known.   Illustration from a paper dealing with the evolution of the term "competition": "In the winter of 1982, two monumental antitrust cases came to an end. In the first, AT&T (American Telephone and Telegraph) agreed to divest itself of a score of subsidiaries; in the second, the Justice Department dropped its suit against IBM (International Business Machines). Some heralded these events as a great victory for the free-enterprise system. Others deplored them as a defeat for free enterprise at the hands of big business. Whether one sees these cases as good or bad for free enterprise depends very much on one's definition of *competition,* a concept whose current meaning does not always parallel its eighteenth-century classical formulation."

4. Challenge a generally held assumption about your topic   Illustration from a paper on the virtues of not voting: "In the last presidential election, at least half of those eligible did not vote. These nonvoters faced the combined scorn of political parties, school teachers, chambers of commerce, Leagues of Women Voters, and sundry high-minded civic groups and individuals. In upcoming elections we can expect to see these same forces again heroically trying to 'get out the vote.' Yet the notion that 'getting out the vote' makes for better election results is not nonpartisan, patriotic, or logical."

5. Show something paradoxical (puzzling) about your topic.   Illustration from a paper on the deficiencies in textbooks: "Textbooks certainly are one of the most influential factors in an individual's intellectual, cultural, and social development. Yet, though they are called 'educational,' textbooks often teach little. Although they are thought 'liberalizing,' they sometimes inculcate narrow-mindedness and intolerance. Though they are viewed as disseminating American values, they sometimes work to undermine them. Yes, textbooks are influential, but not always in a positive way."

6. State some striking facts or statistics related to your topic.   Illustration from a paper dealing with the overconsumption of medical drugs in the United States: "The volume of drug business in the U.S. has grown by a factor of one hundred during the twentieth century. Twenty thousand tons of aspirin are consumed per year, about 225 tablets per person. Central-nervous-system agents are the fastest-growing sector of the pharmaceutical market, now making up 31% of total sales. Dependence on prescribed tranquilizers has risen about 29% since 1962. Medicalized addiction has outpaced all self-chosen forms of creating well-being, such as marijuana or alcohol."

Developing

In developing your essay you will be arguing your thesis, using the material you have gathered to make your points. Your outline contains your whole developmental strategy. Take care, then, that your outline contains a sensible order of ideas. There basically are two ways to ensure this.

1. Let the thesis dictate the order.   If your thesis contains divisions, you should take up points in the order indicated in your thesis. For example, reconsider the two thesis statements we developed earlier:

> It's high time that laws were passed to restrict the advertiser's use of ambiguity to sell aspirin, toothpaste, and mouthwash.

and

> Often overlooked in the retail prices of alcoholic and nonalcoholic beverages are the hidden costs of advertising.

In ordering an essay based on the first thesis, you should take up ambiguity in selling aspirin, then in toothpaste, then in mouthwash. Likewise, in the second take up the hidden costs of advertising in the price structure of alcoholic and then in nonalcoholic beverages.

2. Let the organizational structure determine the order.   In inductive essays the reasons are usually presented in order of importance. In a pro-and-con essay the confirmation of an idea is followed by an objection to that idea, which then is followed by a balanced view. In a cause-and-effect essay causes and effects are arranged either in chronological order or in order of importance. And in an analysis-of-alternatives essay alternatives typically are presented in order of the most common, most popular, or best known first.

Besides an ordering of ideas, developing your paper also calls for an inspection of the kinds of assertions you are making and of the logical relationships among them. So be conscious of the need to support your assertions with facts, illustrations, and examples. Because your paper will include a mix of fact and opinion, you must be careful to distinguish between them and to avoid associated fallacies—false authority or testimonial, popularity, and tradition—and the misuse of statistics, surveys, and polls. If you invoke a comparison or analogy, beware of faulty comparison and false analogies as well as the fallacies of hasty conclusion and half-truth. Should you employ cause-and-effect reasoning, be careful to avoid questionable cause, causal oversimplification, neglect of a common cause, post hoc, and slippery slope.

Always define key terms, or terms that are ambiguous. When you define crucial terms be careful to avoid question-begging definitions, equivocation, and the like.

Finally, since you want to guide the reader through an orderly arrangement of ideas, be sure that your paper is coherent. Helpful here is the use of signal words and phrases (such as "nevertheless," "however," "therefore," and "as a result"). These terms will show readers the logical connections among your ideas and help direct them to the conclusions that you have drawn. Again, the best way to ensure logical relationships is by using an outline as indicated.

Ending

The conclusion of your paper should reinforce your thesis, tie your paper together, and gracefully relinquish your reader's attention. (Think of your essay not as a 'thing' that you hand in, but rather as a communicative interaction, a relational activity between two people, you and your reader. In this context, you play a role rather like leading a dance. Think of your reader as your dancing partner. Your reader has accepted your invitation and now followed you through your arrangement of ideas. Now it is time for you to take your leave. You will want to do so in a way that enhances, rather than detracts from, the experience of your reader.) Here are three strategies for ending the argumentative essay.

1. Put a "new spin" on your thesis.   Rather than merely repeat your thesis, put it into perspective. Draw out some important further implication of it, something for the reader to "take away." Illustration: "In their editorial decisions, communication methods, and marketing devices, the media contribute dramatically to our individual and collective anxiety. For those in print and electronic journalism to ignore or minimize this psychological impact or glibly subordinate it to some lofty mission guaranteed by the Constitution seems irresponsible. To be sure, we need an unfettered press. But we also need a citizenry that is self-confident, optimistic, and panic free.

2. Encapsulate your argument.   Assist your reader in digesting and retaining the substance and complexity of your thesis and its development and demonstration. Illustration: "'Getting out the vote,' then, does not necessarily make for better election results. On the contrary, it is always partisan, for a calm and dignified effort benefits the party in power and a frenetic one benefits the party out of power. It is no more patriotic than the time-honored American attitude of 'a plague on both your houses.' Nor is it logical. Since a successful 'getting out the vote' campaign generates votes from the poorly informed, uninformed, misinformed, and the downright indifferent and ignorant, it undercuts the votes of the intelligent electorate. No, let's not get out the vote; let's get out the *informed* vote."

3. Tie your paper to something further.   Use the occasion of the ending to invite your reader to think on. Indicate an agenda that your paper has helped to determine. Illustration: "When classical capitalists such as Adam Smith talked about competition, they did so in a social and economic atmosphere quite different from today's. Whereas the economy of the Industrial Revolution was characterized by a comparatively free and open market system, the economy of the twentieth century is made up of relatively few enormous holding companies that can secretly fix prices, eliminate smaller companies, and monopolize an industry. Ironically, through intense competition such corporate giants have reached a point at which they can now make a mockery of the classical doctrine of competition. The challenge that lies ahead for society and government is to redefine competition in such a way that the classical notion is integrated into present-day realities. As the AT&T and IBM cases well illustrate, this is no mean undertaking."

Summary

Persuasive discourse is intended to induce readers to accept the opinion of the writer or speaker. Argumentative essays, although they may use narrative, descriptive, and expository discourse, fall into the persuasive category. This is because argument is essentially a persuasive device. It is aimed at *rational* persuasion—persuasion by appeal to reason. The central aim of the argumentative essay is to be rationally persuasive. The best argumentative essays combine a good argument with a persuasive presentation.

The first questions you will need to ask as a writer are, What do I want to write about? and What do I want to say about it? These questions correspond to two essential preliminary steps in the writing process: selecting—and focusing—a subject, and formulating a thesis about it.

Formulating a thesis presents a number of stumbling blocks that can easily add up to a form of mental paralysis known as "writer's block." The following sequence of strategies may help you keep the wheels turning in a productive direction:

1. Select a subject. Remember: It's not as if you have a shortage of interests, or of opinions about interesting and controversial topics. And it's not as if you have to write about all of them at once.
2. Brainstorm possible topics within the general subject area.
3. Having composed a list of possible topics, next select one and limit it. This step consists of two operations: selection and limitation. The second operation is very important, for failing to limit your topic may mean that you later find it unmanageable. The proper limits of the topic usually are determined by the length of the proposed essay.
4. Determine your attitude toward the topic. A thesis consists not only of a topic but also of the author's attitude toward it. It is important to stress that saying

anything substantial enough to warrant an essay involves taking risks. To write an entire essay in defense of a thesis that no one would dispute is too safe. On the other hand, you should not *confine* yourself in your thesis to assertions about your own attitudes and experience, your own inner life. Your thesis is determined by your attitude but it is not *about* your attitude.

5. Write the thesis statement. This step consists of wedding the topic and your attitude toward it in a single assertion.

6. Test the thesis statement. After you write the thesis, it's a good idea to check it for focus. After all, you want to make sure that your topic and viewpoint are crystal clear. A good way to check your statement is to have somebody else read and react to it.

Main points are principal support assertions. In developing your main points and support material, use observations, personal experience, informed opinion, and organized research.

To write effective argumentative essays, you must know your audience. This calls for an audience inventory that isolates key audience characteristics. Armed with this information, you can then give an argument shape and character. Just as important, you must decide on the appropriate persona or role you will play, that is, the characteristics that you must assume in order to gain your audience's respect and approval.

When you argue for a position, you imply that another position exists. Whether or not you argue effectively for your position depends largely on how well you understand and how deeply and sympathetically you consider the other side or sides to the issue. When you oppose a position and undertake to criticize it, you enhance your chances of being persuasive if you can state that position in a way that would fully satisfy someone who holds it, or even make out a better case for it than the proponent herself can.

Similarly, in arguing your case it's crucial to anticipate objections. Taking stock of your audience's background usually will alert you to the kinds of objections they're likely to raise. Your opponent's position affords you a much better vantage point from which to troubleshoot your own position and argument—to make yourself aware of points at which your argument stands in need of additional support, or of needed qualifications and refinements of the thesis itself.

The basic organizational format of the essay will accommodate a wide variety of more specific organizational strategies that may prove to be appropriate to a given topic. For example, you can use an inductive, pro-and-con, cause-and-effect, or analysis-of-alternatives format.

Essential to a good argumentative essay are logical relationships between main points and thesis and between support material and main points. A good test of your essay's logic is an outline. In using an outline follow these four steps: (1) construct the outline; (2) indicate the relationships by reference to developmental patterns: fact and opinion, illustration, authority or testimonial, cause and effect, analogy, or statistics; (3) fill in the missing premises; and (4) examine the outline for possible fallacies.

Applications

1. Write a 500 to 1000 word essay on one of the theses you have worked with in this chapter. Remember to keep in mind your audience and persona.

2. A chairman of the Federal Communications Commission once described television as "a vast wasteland." What he meant was that most network (CBS, NBC, ABC) programming offered nothing of value to adult viewers. Would you agree? Use detailed evidence from shows that you have watched to write an essay (500 to 1000 words) arguing your case. Present your material *inductively.*

3. Write a *pro-and-con* paper in answer to one of the following questions:

   Should the draft be reinstated?
   Should college students be required to take critical thinking?
   Should the United States limit future immigration?
   Should the sale of marijuana be legalized?
   Should federal employees, such as postal workers and air traffic controllers, be permitted to strike?

4. Write an essay in which you analyze the *major causes* of one of the following:

   marital problems and divorce
   cheating on exams
   illiteracy among high school graduates
   incomplete and biased news coverage

5. Write a paper in which you analyze *major alternatives* for achieving one of the following goals:

   a reduction in violent crimes
   a more integrated public school system
   equal job opportunities for women
   avoidance of nuclear war
   a more favorable U.S. image abroad

a fair allocation of the costs of environmental cleanup
a more equitable distribution of the world's wealth and
   resources
energy independence

[1] See V. A. Howard and J. H. Barton, *Thinking on Paper* (New York: William Morrow, 1986).

[2] *Persona* comes from the Latin word for the masks worn by actors in ancient classical drama to immediately delineate their roles for the audience. Accordingly, a smiling mask signaled a comic character, a sorrowful mask a tragic one.

SOLVING PROBLEMS | 14

In our approach to critical thinking so far our primary focus has been on issues and arguments. By now you should be comfortable with recognizing, analyzing and evaluating relatively lengthy arguments about issues, as well as with composing your own in the form of argumentative essays. But this may seem to some readers a too limited focus for critical thinking. After all, not all of us are destined to devote our lives to the study and discussion of controversial issues. Many of us will write nothing other than personal correspondence and shopping lists after we exit college. Yet, each and every one of us will have decisions to make and problems to solve throughout our lives. Does critical thinking have anything to offer outside the limited range of its application to social and political issues? The answer to this question is decidedly yes. In this final chapter we'll take a look at some of the dimensions of everyday decision making and problem solving from the perspective of critical thinking.

Problems come in an extremely wide variety of shapes, sizes, and kinds. And the specific strategies and skills one needs to be an effective problem solver are equally diverse. Solving problems in mathematics requires mathematical skills. Solving writing problems requires verbal skills. The specific strategies and skills you'd need to overcome writer's block probably won't take you very far in balancing the household budget. And budget-balancing skills are not the specific skills you need to resolve a conflict between two sets of in-laws over Thanksgiving dinner plans.

What critical thinking has to offer for making decisions and solving problems generally in everyday situations is quite useful, but it is also very basic and abstract. Accordingly it should not be regarded as sufficient *by itself* for solving particular actual problems. The first basic abstraction of critical thinking for problem solving is that solving any particular problem calls for specific skills, strategies, and insights appropriate to the kind and specific details of the problem one is facing. This is a good example of the kind of knowledge that is important and useful, but not sufficient by itself, for solving problems.

On the other hand, the specific skills and strategies appropriate to a given problem are not sufficient *by themselves* for solving it. In addition, these skills and strategies need to be intelligently and effectively applied. Thus, in general, solving particular problems effectively draws heavily upon the skills, strategies, and dispositions of critical thinking, in addition to whatever more specific skills and strategies may be required. Let's discuss some of these ideas in relation to a typical everyday problem.

An Everyday Problem

Eric is halfway to campus with just enough time to make it to his nine o'clock class, where an important midterm exam is scheduled, when he realizes that he left his essay assignment, due in his ten o'clock class, on his dresser. Should he go back to his room and get it? Should he keep going? If he goes back to his room to get it, he'll be at least fifteen minutes late for the exam in his nine o'clock class, and he can't afford to be late to his ten o'clock class either. The instructor always takes attendance at the beginning of class, and one more absence or tardy will cost Eric a full grade point. Nor can he afford to show up without his assignment. He's scheduled to present the essay orally in today's class.

What a hassle! Eric thinks. Now I'm spending all my energy wrestling with this problem instead of going over the material for the midterm like I planned. My concentration is blown and I'll bomb out on the exam and I still won't be prepared for my ten o'clock class. Maybe I should just quit school!

Then a thought occurs to him. Wait a minute. Today is Tuesday, so my roommate is still at home, and he'll be coming in for his ten o'clock lab. I'll just cut past the gym. There's a pay phone. It'll take two extra minutes to give him a call. Maybe he'll be able to swing by and meet me on his way in and drop the essay off.

CORE SKILLS

Compressed into this small scenario, we can see a number of typical moments in the process of confronting a problem and arriving at a solution—moments that, when viewed in the abstract, will be recognized immediately as core skills basic to all problem solving: Awareness, Analysis, Evaluation, and Generation. No doubt you already recognize these as corresponding to the major sections of this book.

In this context, it is important that these *not* be understood as discreet procedural steps to be followed in serial order in the process of solving problems. Indeed, they are inseparable aspects of what should be understood as an inte-grated—and flexible—process. As we shall see, in actual practice these aspects of problem solving interpenetrate one another. Awareness of a problem involves analysis, analysis in turn involves the evaluation of strategies and options, which involves or presupposes the generation of strategies and options, which involves or presupposes awareness of the problem.

AWARENESS

There is a close connection between awareness and effectiveness at solving problems. It's a truism that awareness is a necessary first step in virtually all problem solving. Problems may occasionally evaporate but they almost never "fix themselves." Problem solving begins with an awareness that a problem exists. For instance, Eric only begins to work on his problem when he realizes that he left his essay assignment on his dresser. Had he not recognized the existence of the problem it would have gone unattended to until eventually he did recognize its existence.

A number of corollaries follow immediately from this. Any of the common blocks to critical thinking, discussed in Chapter 1, that block awareness of the existence of a problem also stand in the way of solving it. Thus, it is of the first importance that one be aware of the common blocks to critical thinking, such as egocentricity, ethnocentricity, self-deception, and so on, and be on guard against them in order to become a more effective problem solver. The old maxim about identifying and tackling small problems early, before they have a chance to grow into larger crises, also deserves mention in this connection.

Moreover, awareness plays an important role in Eric's progress toward a solution to his problem. His awareness of what day it is and of his roommate's routine, his awareness of his own whereabouts and of the locations of campus phones, all help him to identify a course of action that promises a way out of his problem. In general, maximizing awareness of oneself and one's circumstances enhances problem-solving ability.

Sharpening Observation Skills

Recently ABC television produced a program about a blind sports enthusiast, a fan of the Los Angeles Lakers who, in spite of his handicap, is able not only to follow the action of a game in progress but to give accurate and sophisticated play-by-play commentary from courtside. It is worth dwelling on this to appreciate the remarkable difficulty of this individual's accomplishments. Basketball is an extremely complex and fast-moving sport, particularly when played at the professional level. Describing the play-by-play action of the game often strains the abilities of seasoned professional sportscasters who can not only *see* the game, but whose grasp of the action is facilitated by a wide range of visual cues, including the scoreboard, the uniforms of each of the players and officials, the large numerals and names on the players' uniforms to assist in their identification, the painted areas of the court, and so on.

How could a blind person even begin to understand the game, much less appreciate its subtleties and nuances? There is, of course, a courtside announcer, who identifies crucial plays and players over the public address system. But that is the smallest part of the story. The real answer lies in the degree to which this man has cultivated and sharpened observation skills in his other senses. For example, because each player has a distinctive style, gait, and set of moves, he is able to identify players by the squeak of their shoes on the court, the force and frequency with which they dribble the ball, and so on, and to follow the ball as it is dribbled, passed, and shot. He is able to identify, and even determine the mood of, the officials by the sound of their whistles. The crowd's reactions to the game are also full of useful information. In short, he has become acutely aware of the myriad sounds of the game and uses these to construct, if not the actual visual experience of the game, something as rich or even richer in relevant detail.

This is, as is frequently remarked, one of the most profound lessons the handicapped have to teach: the degree to which observation skills can be cultivated, sharpened, and refined. The importance of this for problem solving can't be overemphasized. It's no accident that detectives such as Sherlock Holmes and Lt. Columbo, the essence of whose characters is their problem-solving ability, are portrayed as having remarkable powers of observation. Of course, Holmes and Columbo are fictional characters. But there is a real lesson in the way they are drawn—a lesson for all "real world" problem solvers. They notice what ordinarily goes overlooked, and this is one of the main mechanisms whereby they gather and identify the relevant information that enables them to solve the mystery of the moment.

Problem Finding

Perhaps you've heard the old saying that one shouldn't go looking for trouble—it will find you anyway. There's a common and understandable attitude toward problems associated with this: Problems are to be avoided as far as possible. Nevertheless, there is a very good case to be made for investing energy in *finding* problems. Studies of effective problem solving often focus on the creative and problem-solving efforts of successful thinkers in the arts, the humanities, and the sciences. Such studies have shown that a common factor among the most creative thinkers and successful problem solvers is that they have selected very good problems to devote their energies to: intriguing problems with significant and far-reaching implications, and so on. The great British philosopher Bertrand Russell once remarked on the value of stocking the mind with a store of puzzles. The more difficult, the better. They make great exercise materials for the mind. And working on them often leads to interesting and worthwhile discoveries, valuable ideas that might otherwise never have occurred to anyone. If you can't find any really good problems to work on, you might try making some up.

This too is part of maximizing one's awareness: awareness of life's abundant mystery. Some writers have called this "cultivating a sense of wonder." Good problem solvers are not only keen observers, they are good at wondering and asking questions about what they observe, questions like, Why is a tree trunk round? How come a flag is made of cloth? Why do fish have scales? Why do children ask questions like these? And why do grown-ups react the way they do?

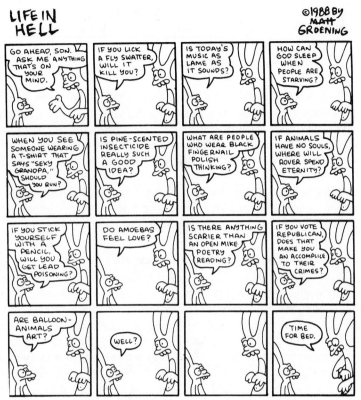

ANALYSIS

Suppose we are aware of the existence of a problem. A second important element in effective problem solving is the analysis of the problem, coming to terms with it. What precisely is the problem? How should we describe or represent it? What precisely does the problem consist of? What sort of problem is it? Is it a calculation problem? A problem involving interpersonal dynamics? A mysterious mechanical problem requiring a diagnosis?

Defining the Problem

In becoming aware of the existence of the problem, we have already begun to come to terms with it, because obviously we have to be able to describe the problem of whose existence we are becoming aware in some way or another. Thus, for example, when Eric realizes that he has a problem, he realizes at the same time a good deal of what the problem consists of. He is immediately aware of a number of the problem's characteristics. He realizes that he left his essay assignment on his dresser, that it is due in his ten o'clock class, that he is already

367

halfway to campus, and that he has just enough time to make it to his nine o'clock class, where an important midterm exam is scheduled.

Clarifying the Problem

But Eric's analysis of his problem doesn't stop there. In fact the analysis of the problem continues throughout the course of solving it. Each of the problem's characteristics has certain further implications. For example, the fact that Eric is halfway to campus entails that returning to his room will triple his remaining travel time. Thus, as Eric proceeds to analyze his problem, he clarifies its various dimensions by drawing inferences. By now you're already quite familiar with the wide range of inferential possibilities. The importance of drawing and assessing inferences in coming to terms with oneself and one's circumstances, in this case with one's problems, should come as no surprise.

Clarifying Available Information

The same applies to observations made in the course of analyzing and solving the problem. Let's return for a moment to the case of the blind sports fan. For most of us, the sound of a basketball game at courtside, were we temporarily deprived of sight, would be an incomprehensible cacophony of squeaks, thumps, grunts, and undifferentiated crowd noise. But a more acute observer can gather from these sounds that Magic Johnson has the ball at the top of the key, has not given up his dribble yet, that Byron Scott has just set a pick for him to the left of the free-throw line, while Kareem is coming around the base line to set a low post on the right side. How is so much information discerned in these sounds? By reasoning about them, by drawing inferences from and about them based on observed patterns and relationships of similarity and difference. For example, if the sound of the bouncing ball and the squeaking shoes is moving from right to left, that means that the Lakers have possession. If the squeaking passes to the left ahead of the bouncing, and the bouncing is heard at a relatively constant rate, that means that one of the guards is advancing the ball deliberately and will be setting up the half-court offense. If the squeaking is faster than normal and we hear only one bounce, that indicates a fast break.

Earlier in this chapter we indicated that the aspects of problem solving interpenetrate one another. This is part of what we meant. Here we can see how the analysis of sensory experience "informs" awareness—literally gives form to it, makes "information" out of it. It also brings into focus an important range of core analytical problem-solving skills: discerning patterns and relationships.

Recognizing Patterns and Relationships

A New Yorker, on first visiting San Francisco, takes a bus tour of Golden Gate Park and immediately thinks of Central Park. A new pop song appears on the radio, and listeners immediately recognize the artist as Sting. An art appraiser examines a canvas and exposes a hitherto undetected forgery of Picasso, and almost as an afterthought, identifies the hand of the forger.

Recognizing patterns and relationships, similarities and differences, is something we each do constantly. Patterns and relationships are present and discernible not only in human artifice but throughout nature. Indeed, pattern is the indispensable guide to the adaptation of any intelligent organism to its environment. Pattern recognition is so basic and central to intelligence and to all intelligent activity that it is impossible to imagine what intelligent life would be like if such "analytical acts of awareness" weren't possible. Accordingly, a pattern which runs throughout all of human inquiry, from the most "primitive" to the most advanced and scientific, is the search for and discovery of pattern.

What you learned in Chapter 7 about making and verifying observations, about formulating and testing hypotheses, and about drawing and assessing deductive and inductive inferences applies here to understanding how intelligent beings seek and discern patterns and relationships. In fact, a very reasonable and insightful way to understand the techniques and standards of reasoning that you've been studying throughout this course would be simply as aspects of intelligence, as ways that intelligence goes about seeking and discerning patterns and relationships.

But although the seeking and discerning of patterns and relationships is as natural for humans as breathing, we don't always do it as effectively as we might. Sometimes this is because we aren't seeking in the appropriate way. This is another area in which awareness of the blocks to critical thinking, discussed in Chapter 1, becomes important.

Let's consider how the limitations of a person's culture and worldview can inhibit the ability to discern patterns. People raised in a technological society sometimes find it hard to understand how so-called primitive peoples could have figured out regularities about the environment that high-tech teams of scientists work on for years, at great expense, and still haven't figured out. And yet, if anything, so-called primitive cultures frequently achieve a more sophisticated and accurate grasp of significant—not to mention "useful"—patterns in nature, particularly the "larger" ones, than do technological cultures like our own. With all of our science and technology, how can this be?

It is highly plausible to suppose that people who are used to and surrounded by technology tend to look for patterns typical of the surrounding technology. For example, they may expect to see regularities at intervals that fall within a certain limited range. They may not expect to wait 150 years for the pattern to emerge. Thus, for example, naturalists schooled in modern scientific methods frequently remark how important is the virtue of *patience* in observation. To gather useful information about the natural environment, we must frequently wait and wait, and watch and wait some more, and watch some more until a pattern eventually becomes evident. Pretechnological peoples would not find this sort of observation of the natural environment extraordinary at all, least of all extraordinarily patient. Indeed, constant, close, and detailed attention to the natural environment has an easily understandable tendency to "tune the observer in" to the environment's natural rhythms, however fast or slow they may be.

EVALUATION AND GENERATION

Let's rejoin Eric on his way to school. You remember that Eric has begun to analyze his problem. He realizes that he left his essay assignment on his dresser, that it is due in his ten o'clock class, that he is already halfway to campus, and that he has just enough time to make it to his nine o'clock class, where an important midterm exam is scheduled. And he has begun to trace the implications of these features of his situation. He knows, for example, that the fact that he's halfway to campus entails that returning to his room will triple his remaining travel time. As Eric's analysis of his problem progresses, it begins more and more apparently to involve evaluation—evaluation of options, evaluation of consequences, evaluation of the analysis itself—and at the same time to generate new information, new options, and even new problem-solving strategies.

Evaluating Options

Returning to his room to retrieve his essay assignment is probably one of the first optional courses of action that occurs to Eric. But following this option would triple his remaining travel time, and that would make him late for his midterm exam, and that would be an unacceptable consequence. This means that returning to his room is not an adequate option. And this is one of the dimensions of the problem, as Eric now understands it.

Evaluating Consequences

Here we can clearly see a number of the aspects typically involved in evaluating optional courses of action. Each optional course of action is going to have associated with it a number of consequences, some of them perhaps certain, some relatively less certain, but probable to one degree or another. Of these consequences some will be more desirable and some less desirable in relation to one's operative goals. So evaluating an optional course of action will involve identifying and determining the relative likelihood and desirability of its consequences. This will involve reasoning inductively about causes and probabilities, and it will also involve being clear about our goals. Again we can see how the various aspects of problem solving interpenetrate one another.

Other optional courses of action are similarly evaluated. One option would be to keep going, take the midterm in the nine o'clock class, and then return to his room for the essay. But this option would make him late for his ten o'clock class, where attendance is taken promptly, and that would cost Eric a full grade point, which would be an unacceptable consequence. This means that returning to his room between classes is not an adequate option.

Another option would be to go to his 10 o'clock class without the essay assignment. But this option would leave Eric unprepared to perform as scheduled, and that would be an unacceptable consequence, which means that this is not an adequate option either.

Evaluating the Analysis

So far Eric's analysis of his problem has led him to a dead end. None of the options he can think of would adequately solve the problem. Now he's becoming frustrated with the problem and with his efforts to solve it, so frustrated that he even begins to consider a relatively self-destructive option: Maybe I should just quit school!

What Eric needs to do is to generate some new options. So far Eric has evaluated only the options that immediately occur to him, as "direct remedies" to the situation, so to speak. But in Eric's frustration we can already see him beginning to evaluate something else. Although he is not fully aware of it, he is beginning to turn his efforts in a creative and constructive direction. He is dissatisfied with his problem-solving process and has begun to evaluate his analysis of the problem so far.

Challenging Assumptions

Consider the following old Chinese puzzle: A man is taking a bushel of apples, a sheep, and a tiger to market when he comes to a wide river. There is a small raft that he can use to cross, so long as he takes only one item with him at a time (otherwise, the raft will sink). The problem is that if he leaves the apples and the sheep alone together, the sheep will eat the apples; but if he leaves the sheep and the tiger alone together, the tiger will eat the sheep. How can he get himself, the apples, the sheep, and the tiger all to the other side of the river?

Let's approach this as methodically as we can. The man cannot begin by taking the bushel of apples, because that would leave the tiger alone with the sheep. Nor can he begin by taking the tiger, because that would leave the sheep alone with the apples. Suppose he takes the sheep, leaving the tiger and the apples. So far, so good. Now he returns for another load.

Suppose he takes the apples on his second trip. He cannot leave the apples alone with the sheep while he returns to get the tiger. Suppose he takes the tiger on his second trip. But neither can he leave the tiger alone with the sheep while he returns for the apples. Hmmm! Now what?

Suppose he takes the sheep back with him on his return trip. Aha! Now we have a solution. It no longer matters whether he takes the tiger or the apples on his second trip, as long as he takes the sheep back with him when he returns for his third trip. Suppose that on his second trip he has taken the apples. Now he returns for the tiger, taking the sheep with him on the return trip. He leaves the sheep and returns across the river with the tiger. He leaves the tiger alone with the apples again, and returns one last time for the sheep.

What stands in the way of a solution to this puzzle is a particular tacit assumption. The assumption is that taking any one of the items back across the river to the point of origin is not an option. This is a perfectly natural assumption. Given that the man's goal is to get all three items across the river, taking any item back in the other direction understandably seems counterproductive. Nevertheless, it is only when this assumption is suspended that a solution to the problem emerges.

This example illustrates a frequent obstacle in solving problems. Quite often, progress toward a solution hinges on identifying and suspending some tacit assumption in terms of which the problem is initially understood or defined. Here is another example.

Try to link up the following arrangement of nine dots using only four straight lines, without raising your pencil from the paper.

Hard, isn't it? A great many people approach this puzzle on the basis of a tacit assumption that the lines may not extend beyond the area defined by the nine dots. As long as this assumption is in effect, it is impossible to link all nine dots using only four straight lines without raising the pencil from the paper. However, as soon as this assumption is identified and suspended, the problem can be reconceptualized, new options become available, and a solution emerges:

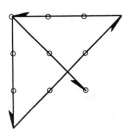

Redefining the Problem

As we have just seen, challenging assumptions facilitates a redefinition or re-conceptualization of the problem, which frequently brings new options into focus. In the example of the Chinese puzzle, the solution depends on a reconceptual-ization of the problem as one of finding a sequence of moves that avoids sac-rificing one of the pieces, rather than as one of moving all of the pieces forward without sacrifice. And this depends on identifying and suspending the assumption that moving any piece backward is not an option. Some writers have called this sort of approach to problem solving "lateral thinking."

Some of the most dramatic examples of successful redefinition of the prob-lem, through the identification and challenge of tacit assumptions, are to be found in the history of science. For example, Copernicus eventually succeeded in explaining the observed motion of the planets, whereas his predecessors had failed, by identifying and challenging the tacit assumption with which his predecessors had begun, and through which they had conceptualized the problem of accounting for planetary motion: that the planets revolved around the earth.

Evaluating Strategies

Redefining a problem can also help us evaluate problem-solving strategies by helping us discover a simpler or more efficient route to the solution. Consider the mathematical problem, What is 3/7 of 1/3? When the problem is represented in this way, the most likely method of calculation would be to multiply the two fractions together, arriving at the result 3/21, then simplifying the result to arrive at 1/7. But suppose the problem had been represented as What is 1/3 of 3/7? A much simpler procedure now suggests itself: Simply divide the numerator.

We can see that Eric also successfully redefines his problem. Initially he conceives of the problem as an impossible time-management dilemma in which his only available options are blocked or unacceptable. He cannot return to his room to get his paper. That will in effect triple his remaining travel time to school, and he cannot afford to be late for his exam. But neither can he afford to be late for his next class, or to appear there without his paper, but there is no time between classes to return home for it. Eventually, however, Eric reconceptualizes the problem as one of coordinating his resources, and thus a new option emerges. He has a potential collaborator, his roommate, and he has a means of quickly reaching his roommate without losing too much time or causing serious inconvenience.

Evaluating and Generating Information

Earlier we remarked how detectives such as Sherlock Holmes and Lt. Columbo are portrayed as having remarkable powers of observation, how they tend to notice what ordinarily goes overlooked, which enables them to solve the mystery of the moment. The inspector arrives at the scene of the crime and orders that nothing be disturbed so that the investigative team can gather information. The room is full of information. Yet, it's not that the investigative team records each and every detail. There are no doubt infinitely many details to be noted. The information is recorded selectively. Some relatively obvious piece of information—the fact that the room, like all the other rooms in the motel, is decorated in loud and tacky floral print wallpaper—may be unimportant, while some seemingly insignificant detail—the position of the hands of the victim's smashed watch—may be crucial. Thus, two of the most important problem-solving skills are evaluating available information and using it to generate new information.

The most important difference between important and unimportant information is relevance. If the tacky wallpaper is an unimportant piece of information, that's because it doesn't help the investigators solve the crime. The position of the hands of the victim's smashed watch is valuable information, however, because it is relevant to solving the crime. It helps establish the time at which the crime was committed. Here the relevance and value of the information as a means of generating new information that is also relevant and valuable.

The tricky thing about relevance, however, as we mentioned in Chapter 9, is that things can seem relevant that aren't, and seemingly irrelevant things can likewise be relevant. In other words, "relevance" is sometimes misleading. Consider, for example, the following puzzle:

> A bus leaves Los Angeles bound for San Francisco. Three hours later a bus leaves San Francisco bound for Los Angeles. The buses are traveling at the same rate of speed. Which of the buses will be nearer to San Francisco when they meet?

What do you make of this? People frequently spend quite a bit of time trying to work out some algebraic formula for the solution to this puzzle: Let's see. . . . Three hours, minus x divided by the same rate of speed equals? But this is all a waste of time. The speed information and the information about the difference in departure time, although they *seem* relevant, are all irrelevant to the problem. The relevant information is contained in the seemingly insignificant words "when they meet." When they meet, the buses will be equidistant from San Francisco.

There are of course reasons why the irrelevant information in the puzzle seems relevant. We naturally tend to assume that any quantitative information given in what looks like a math problem will be relevant to solving that problem. But, however reasonable this is as a general rule, it's not always true. Many mathematical problems contain irrelevant as well as relevant quantitative information. Also, we should not be too quick to assume that what looks like a math problem (because it contains quantitative information) really is one. In other words, we should not be too quick to adopt a problem-solving strategy based on the assumed relevance of certain available information. An appropriate safeguard in this kind of situation is to clarify the problem.

Quick Check on Core Skills

1. Here's an exercise for sharpening your observation skills. For each of the following familiar items (a) identify three properties, including one that you've never noticed before, and (b) using the techniques of functional analysis described in Chapter 3, explain what function(s) each of these properties might serve.

Example:	Item	Properties	Function
	Styrofoam coffee cup	made of Styrofoam	retains heat, does not conduct heat (insulates hand)
		flat bottom	will stand unsupported on flat surface
		conical shape	fits hand, and easy to manufacture

    a. a brick
    b. a nickel
    c. a pencil
    d. a sock
    e. a textbook

2. Identify at least three properties shared by each of the following pairs, and at least one point of difference between the members of each pair.

    a. an orange and a lemon
    b. a family and a nation
    c. a vein and an garden hose
    d. a square and a rectangle
    e. the numbers 7 and 9

3. Identify at least three ways in which the following pairs of things differ, and at least one point of similarity.

    a. verbs and nouns
    b. philosophy and science
    c. philosophy and art
    d. a democracy and a dictatorship
    e. Republicans and Democrats
    f. the numbers 36 and 35

4. Here's an exercise in pattern recognition. See if you can think how the concepts relate to each other. Complete the following analogies, and explain the connection you see in each case.

    Example: Robin is to bird as Chevrolet is to _____.

        To complete the analogy: (1) Think how the first concept (Robin) relates to the second concept (bird). In this case the most plausible answer is that Robin is a species of bird. (2) Try to find a fourth concept that stands in an analogous relationship to the third. In this case Chevrolet would be a "species" of car or *automobile*.

    a. Chinese is to Asian as Protestant is to _____.
    b. Rule is to game as law is to _____.
    c. Artery is to blood as nerve is to _____.
    d. Heat is to energy as push is to _____.

5. Sometimes there's more than one way to complete an analogy. Here are a couple of extra tricky analogies to try. In each case, see how many different ways you can think of to complete the analogy, and explain the various connections.

a. Who would you say is the First Lady of Great Britain?
(i.e., Barbara Bush is to the United States as _____ is to Great Britain.)

b. Who would you say is America's counterpart to Gandhi?
(i.e., _____ is to America as Gandhi was to India.)

6. The following three problems are designed to give you practice in challenging assumptions. If you cannot initially solve them, try to identify, and challenge, your assumptions.

a. You're a gardener. Your employer asks you to plant four olive trees so that each one is exactly the same distance from each of the others. How would you arrange the trees?

b. A man works in a tall office building. Each morning he enters the elevator on the ground floor, presses the button to the ninth floor, exits, and then walks up to the fourteenth floor. At night he enters the elevator on the fourteenth floor and gets out on the ground floor. Account for his behavior.

c. You have two five-gallon cans full of water, and a fifteen-gallon tub. Can you think of a way to put all the water into the tub and still be able to tell which water came from which can?

MORE PROBLEM-SOLVING STRATEGIES

We have just seen how identifying and challenging assumptions can lead to a fruitful redefinition or reconceptualization of a problem, and thus to the generation of new options and strategies in the pursuit of a solution. This constitutes one very effective problem-solving strategy. The most effective problem solvers among us generally have a fairly large repertoire of problem-solving strategies to draw on, and are always open and on the lookout for new such strategies to explore. Here are a few additional problem-solving strategies you can use.

Breaking a Problem Down into Subproblems

Problems that may seem insurmountable because of their size or degree of complexity can often be overcome by breaking them down into more manageable subproblems. Goals whose distance may make them seem unreachable can often be reached by setting a series of intermediate goals. As ancient Chinese wisdom has it, the longest journey begins with the first step. (That's how this book was written, by the way: chapter by chapter, section by section, step by step.)

Here's a simple example of this strategy in application. Suppose you're the student assistant in charge of maintaining the collection in the political science department reading room. For the past year there has been no student assistant. As a result, the collection is all mixed up and a full inventory is in order. The storage capacity of the existing shelf space is already stretched by the collection, but additional shelving for the periodicals has been ordered. You've been assigned the task of conducting the inventory and reorganizing the collection. How do you go about it? You could start by locating all the periodicals in the collection, organizing them chronologically and by title, listing them and arranging them in the new shelving, and then comparing your list with the card catalogue to identify any missing items. This would create a small amount of space on the existing shelves that could be consolidated. Then you could begin working through the collection of books, one shelf at a time.

Working Backward

Some problems are easier to solve if one imaginatively works one's way back from where one wants to wind up to where one is at the moment. This is often an effective way of solving scheduling problems, for instance. Knowing that the deadline is six weeks away, one can often budget the available time more effectively by estimating the time needed to complete the last step, and then the next to last step, and so on back to the beginning. This is often a very good way of avoiding other sorts of problems that would result from inadequate planning.

This strategy comes in handy in other ways, too. Consider, for example, standard reading comprehension tests. Usually these consist of a passage of prose and a set of questions about the passage. One of the best test-taking strategies for this kind of examination is to read the questions first, and then read the passage with the questions in mind.

Analogous Problems

Earlier we mentioned what a wide variety of shapes, sizes, and kinds of problems there are, and that solving any particular problem calls for specific skills, strategies, and insights appropriate to the particular problem one is facing. But few problems are so unique that they are totally unlike every other problem. In fact, often the best way of figuring out what specific skills, strategies, and insights would be appropriate to a particular problem is to try to remember or imagine a similar or related problem.

For example, suppose you are in charge of organizing the annual Ping-Pong tournament. You have a room with four Ping-Pong tables in it, and 208 individual entrants. You are trying to work out the schedule of matches, assuming an hour per match, for a single-elimination tournament (a player is eliminated after losing once). How many hours will the tournament take?

This is not an easy problem, is it? One relatively easy way to approach it, however, would be to ask, how did we schedule the matches in last year's tournament? Are there more or fewer entrants this year, and so on.

Another approach would be to break the problem down into more manageable subproblems, such as: How many matches will be required to determine the winner? And then, how many hours, assuming one hour per match and four simultaneous matches, will it take to complete the required number of matches? Each of these subproblems can be assimilated to a familiar sort of math problem.

Let's take the first subproblem: How many matches will be required to determine the winner? Suppose we had enough tables for all the entrants to play in the first round. That would be 104 matches in the first round (208 entrants, matched one on one). At the end of the first round, the field would be cut in half, to 104 entrants. Round two would then require an additional fifty-two matches (104 entrants, matched one on one). At the end of round two, the field would be cut to twenty-six. In round three, an additional thirteen matches would cut the field to thirteen. In round four an additional six matches would eliminate six more entrants, leaving a field of seven. In round five an additional three matches would eliminate three more entrants, leaving a field of four, which would leave three more matches: two semifinal and one final match. Now we simply add the number of matches in each round, for a total of 207 matches.

Sometimes remembering or imagining analogous problems can be an effective way of discovering or formulating a simple general rule or principle or algorithm for arriving at a solution. Let's take the first subproblem again. How many matches will be required to determine the winner? Let's imagine an analogous, but much simpler problem. Suppose only two people had entered the tournament. Obviously, only one match would be required to determine the winner. Now suppose three people had entered the tournament. In this case two matches would be required to determine the winner. Now suppose four people had entered. In this case we'd need three matches. It's beginning to look like the number of matches required to determine the winner is equal to the number of entrants minus one: in this case 207 matches.

Quick Check on Problem-Solving Strategies

1. Using the preceding problem-solving strategies, or one of your own devising, complete the solution to the tournament scheduling problem. How many hours will be required to complete the tournament? Explain the steps you used to arrive at your solution.
2. Using the preceding problem-solving strategies, or one of your own devising, work out an alternative approach to the reading room inventory problem.

MYTHS ABOUT PROBLEM SOLVING

Before we leave the subject of solving problems, it is worth dwelling briefly on and dispelling a few of the myths or common misconceptions that frequently mystify and obstruct the process.

Problem Solving Is Ineffable

Probably the most common myth about problem solving is that the process is ineffable, that nothing useful or illuminating can be said to facilitate the development of skill at solving problems. As we have seen, solving problems often depends on thinking about them in new and creative ways. It is also true that creativity cannot be fully programmed in terms of procedural steps. But this does not mean that problem solving is a form of magic.

A related myth is that the solution to a problem "emerges automatically" as a result of simply assembling all the "relevant data." One problem with this idea is that frequently we do have all the "relevant data," but we are approaching the problem in such a way that its relevance is obscured. Some psychologists refer to this as the problem of "access to inert knowledge."

For example, consider once again a problem from an earlier Quick Check exercise: You have two five-gallon cans full of water, and a fifteen-gallon tub. How can you put all the water into the tub and still be able to tell which water came from which can? One solution to this problem would be to freeze the water in one of the cans. The knowledge needed to arrive at this solution, namely, that freezing water is easily accomplished and that frozen water can easily be distinguished from water in the liquid state, is already present presumably in most people. But the fact that this solution to the problem does not immediately occur to most people shows that this knowledge is not automatically brought to bear on the problem.

Although we may not always be aware of what it is that "triggered" a particular breakthrough, or be aware of the nature of the mental processes involved, there is nothing "automatic" about problem solving. Nor is problem solving accomplished "passively." Problem solving is an active process. This doesn't mean that it is never a good idea to put a problem aside, or to "sleep on it." But it would be misleading, to say the least, to think that the solution to the problem is produced by *not* working on it. It's much more reasonable to suppose that the mind continues to work on the problem in subconscious ways and that this work is greatly facilitated by the conscious work already invested in the problem.

All Problems Are Soluble

It's tempting for many of us to believe that there are no absolutely insoluble problems, that if we think about a problem long enough, and hard enough, and in the right kind of way, sooner or later we're bound to arrive at a solution to it. There's nothing essentially wrong with maintaining an optimistic attitude in the face of difficulty. No doubt it's better to presume that problems are soluble than to presume that they're insoluble. Nevertheless, on the basis of examples we have already looked at, it is relatively easy to generate truly insoluble problems.

For example: Try to link all nine dots using only four straight lines, which do not extend beyond the area defined by the nine dots, without raising the pencil from the paper.

```
    o       o       o

    o       o       o

    o       o       o
```

There just isn't any solution to *this* problem. The problem is in effect defined in terms of contradictory requirements.

As we learned earlier, the recognition of a problem's insolubility, or that one is approaching it as an insoluble problem, is sometimes very important. Persistent optimism in the face of a problem that is defined in terms of contradictory requirements frequently stands as the main obstacle in the way of any real progress. Recognizing the insolubility of the problem is what leads us toward a fruitful redefinition, toward a reconceptualization of a similar problem that we *can* solve.

Some real-world problems are very much like this. For example, there may be no way to resolve certain disputes so that all parties are completely satisfied. Suppose twin brothers each claim the exclusive right to inherit the family property. The best we can hope for in such a situation is to arrive at some compromise. But any compromise will necessarily fall short of satisfying both parties completely. Recognition of this fact may be necessary before any compromise can be seriously considered.

A related misconception is that there must be some single solution superior to all other alternatives for every problem. On the contrary, there are quite a few problematic situations in which several alternative solutions present themselves, each of which brings certain advantages as well as certain drawbacks.

Suppose you are trying to book air travel home from school for the holidays. There are no nonstop direct flights to your city. Your alternatives are to fly through Denver, changing planes and airlines with a two-hour layover, leaving at 9 A.M. and arriving finally at 6 P.M.; or to take a single flight at a slightly higher fare with stops in St. Louis and Chicago, leaving at 3 P.M. and arriving finally at 9 P.M. Neither of these alternatives is clearly superior overall, although each is clearly superior to the other in certain respects. This, however, is not the sort of problem that can be better resolved by redefinition. Redefining the problem is not going to generate any new travel options.

Summary

Each and every one of us will have decisions to make and problems to solve throughout our lives. What critical thinking has to offer for making decisions and solving problems generally in everyday situations is quite useful, but it is also very basic and abstract. Accordingly, it should not be regarded as sufficient *by itself* for solving particular actual problems.

The first basic abstraction of critical thinking for problem solving is that solving any particular problem calls for specific skills, strategies, and insights appropriate to the kind and specific details of the problem one is facing. This is a good example of the kind of knowledge that is important and useful, but not sufficient by itself, for solving problems.

But neither are the specific skills and strategies appropriate to a given problem sufficient *by themselves* for solving it. In addition, these skills and strategies need to be intelligently and effectively applied. Thus, in general, solving particular problems effectively draws heavily on the skills, strategies, and dispositions of critical thinking, in addition to whatever more specific skills and strategies may be required. Viewed in the abstract, these correspond to the major sections of this book: Awareness, Analysis, Evaluation, and Generation. It is important that these *not* be understood as discreet procedural steps to be followed in serial order in the process of solving problems, but rather as inseparable aspects of what should be understood as an integrated—and flexible—process.

Problem solving begins with an awareness that a problem exists. Thus, it is of the first importance that one be aware of the common blocks to critical thinking, such as egocentricity, ethnocentricity, self-deception, and so on, which might block awareness of the existence of a problem. In general, maximizing awareness of oneself and one's circumstances enhances problem-solving ability. This includes sharpening and refining one's skills as an observer, which includes cultivating a sense of wonder, an ability to ask questions about what one observes.

A second important element in effective problem solving is the analysis of the problem, coming to terms with it. What precisely is the problem? How should we describe or represent it? What precisely does the problem consist of? What sort of problem is it? In becoming aware of the existence of the problem we have already begun to come to terms with it, because obviously we have to be able to describe the problem of whose existence we are becoming aware in some way or another. Specific analytical problem-solving skills include defining and clarifying the problem; clarifying existing information, by drawing and assessing inferences from and about it; and recognizing patterns and relationships.

Analysis of a problem continues throughout the course of solving it. As the analysis of the problem progresses, however, it begins more and more obviously to involve evaluation—evaluation of information and options, evaluation of strategies, evaluation of the analysis itself—and the generation of new information, new options, and even new problem-solving strategies.

Quite often, progress toward a solution hinges on identifying and suspending some tacit assumption in terms of which the problem is initially understood or defined. Challenging assumptions facilitates a redefinition or reconceptualization of the problem, which frequently brings new options into focus. Some writers have called this sort of approach to problem solving "lateral thinking." Redefining a problem can also help us evaluate problem-solving strategies by helping us discover a simpler or more efficient route to the solution.

Effective problem solvers generally have a fairly large repertoire of problem-solving strategies to draw upon, and are always open and on the lookout for new such strategies to explore. Additional problem-solving strategies include breaking a problem down into more manageable subproblems, working backward, and remembering or imagining related or analogous problems.

Applications

Consider the following puzzles and scenarios using the techniques and strategies mentioned above, and any additional strategies you can devise on your own. Can you solve any of the puzzles? Explain how you arrive at your solution. What are the problems involved in each scenario? What possible options can you formulate that would solve these problems? What are the advantages and drawbacks of the options you can devise?

1. Forty years ago, in a certain land, the popular and democratically elected regime was overthrown in a bloody coup and replaced by a tyrannical military oligarchy. Many families were driven into exile, and their land expropriated by the ruling families. In the intervening forty years, peasant families were allowed to work the land in exchange for subsistence wages under increasingly intolerable circumstances until finally they have risen up and overthrown the oligarchy and driven the tyrannical ruling families out of the land. Now, however, members and descendants of families originally driven into exile by the military dictators have returned to claim what they regard as their land.

2. You're a member of a committee that must decide the best place to locate a town dump for burning the town's rubbish. In descending order of importance, list the factors that you would consider in arriving at your decision. Be prepared to account for your priorities.

3. You're placed in charge of interviewing students for the position of tutor in Critical Thinking. If you could ask each applicant no more than three questions, what would those questions be, and why?

4. You have black socks and blue socks in a drawer. You mustn't wake your roommate, and since it is dark, you cannot see the colors of the socks as you take them out of the drawer. But you do know that the ratio of black socks to blue socks is 5/6. How many socks must you

take out in order to be sure that you have a matched pair?

5. You're away from home for your first year at college. You've met the most gorgeous and delightful member of the opposite sex, who has accepted your invitation to join you and your family for Thanksgiving dinner. Meanwhile, your Great Aunt Ethel has sent you one of her usual birthday gifts: a horrible shirt that she thinks you will look cute in but that makes you look like a dwarf. Your parents have just told you that your Great Aunt Ethel will be joining the family for Thanksgiving dinner, and that she asked how much you liked the birthday gift. What should you wear for the occasion?

6. You buy 100 shares of stock in Amalgamated Conglomerates Unlimited (ACU) at $50 per share. A year later you sell the stock at $75 per share. A year later you buy the same shares of ACU back for $8500 and eventually sell them for $90 per share. How much money did you make? Explain two distinct methods of calculating your earnings.

7. The doctor has prescribed thirty pills. The prescription says, Take one every thirty minutes. How long does the prescription last?

8. Scene: the Annual Halloween Exotic/Erotic Masqued Costume Extravaganza for Truth-Tellers and Liars. A man and a woman are dancing. One says to the other, "I'm a man." "That's nice. I'm a woman," replies the other. At least one of the two is lying. Which is the man and which is the woman? Explain.

APPENDIX | 1

ANSWERS TO STARRED* QUICK CHECK EXERCISES

Chapter 2
Quick Check on the Functions of Language (Page 25)

1. Performative
2. Informative: indicates that flat tax rates favor the rich and penalize the poor
   Expressive: evokes feelings of outrage against the flat tax rate
   Persuasive: the outrage is to be understood as a reason to take political action
   Directive: directs you to urge legislators to oppose a flat tax rate
3. Informative
4. Informative: indicates that Democratic administrations have been associated with wars
   Persuasive: this information is intended as a reason not to vote Democratic
   Expressive: evokes fear of the Democrats
5. Informative: O'Neill was the Speaker of the House whose political roots can be traced to Roosevelt
   Persuasive: seems intended to engender an attitude of distrust for O'Neill
6. Informative: indicates that civil wars weaken a nation; foreign wars strengthen it
   Persuasive: the comparison to fever and exercise is intended to convince us that the information is correct
7. Informative: war is destructive
   Persuasive: a number of reasons are offered for avoiding war
   Expressive: evokes antipathy toward war

8. Informative: indicates that unless we stand together, we will all lose our lives
   Persuasive: offers a reason to compromise differences
   Expressive: evokes strong feelings of solidarity
   Directive: proposes that we stand fast together

Quick Check on Logical Definition (P. 33)

1. Too broad
2. Too narrow
3. Too narrow
4. Too broad
5. Incomplete: lacks sufficient conditions
6. Circular
7. Figurative
8. Too broad
9. Too broad
10. Figurative
11. Circular
12. Figurative
13. Negative
14. Figurative
15. Figurative
16. Circular; obscure
17. Figurative

Quick Check on Stipulative and Persuasive Definitions (P. 35)

1. The meanings of "denotation," "connotation," "extension," "intension," "denotative definition," "logical definition," "necessary condition," "sufficient condition," "stipulative definition," and "persuasive definition" were all stipulated in this chapter.
2. a. Persuasive
   b. Persuasive
   c. Persuasive
   d. Stipulative
   e. Persuasive
   f. Persuasive

Quick Check on Disputes (P. 39)

1. Factual: John believes that the Gilsons served a small meal, whereas Joan believes it was big. It is possible, however, that their words don't express a factual dispute about the exact size of the meal but a difference in the amounts of food John and Joan are used to seeing served at a meal.
2. Verbal: If "same car" is taken to mean one that contains all, most, or the most important parts that it contained at some point, then Brad doesn't have the "same car." But if "same car" is taken to mean the project Brad's been working on all this time or perhaps the vehicle designated by a registration certificate or some other constant, then it is the "same car."
3. Evaluative: It wouldn't do any good to define "bad peace" or "disadvantageous peace" here, for the parties disagree about whether it is to be preferred to war. What is now needed is an airing of reasons for each position so that a comparative evaluation can be made.

4. Verbal: Phil did not keep his promise inasmuch as he didn't intend his money to go to Fred. In this sense he broke his promise when he made out his will. But if Phil's intention is not considered, he did keep his promise in that the assurance he gave Fred was, in fact, carried out.

5. Evaluative: In effect Schurz disagrees with Decatur's position that we should support our country even when it is wrong.

6. Factual: In effect James and Jane disagree about whether the majority of Americans favor gun control. They also disagree about the significance of the study, in other words, about whether the evidence supports James's view.

7. Interpretive: Gene and Jean disagree about how to interpret or understand a particular dispute.

Quick Check on False Implication (P. 44)

1. The implication is that London Fog raincoats and jackets are made in London. Actually, they're made in Baltimore, Maryland.

2. The implication is that the pie inside contains that many cherries. But when Consumers Union analyzed cherry pies from McDonald's restaurants in the New York area, it found that they contained an average of five cherries each.

3. The false implication is that doctors recommend <u>Bayer</u> aspirin.

4. False implication of superiority. When asked to substantiate this claim, Armour-Dial company insisted that it was not a claim of superiority at all, but only a claim that Dial soap was "as effective" as any other soap.

Quick Check on Ambiguity and Vagueness in Advertising (P. 47)

1. On the other side of the package on which this claim appears, we read in fine print "Liquid Corn Oil, partially hydrogenated corn oil, water, nonfat dry milk, vegetable mono and diglycerides and lecithin, artificially flavored and colored (carotene), Vitamins A & D added." What then does the front-of-the-package claim mean? That Fleischmann's is made from 100 percent corn oil and nothing else? That the oil that is the main ingredient is 100 percent corn oil, instead of, say, partly soybean oil, as in some other brands?

2. There are two unfinished comparisons here: more body than what? more flavor than what? Then, too, both "flavor" and "body" function as weasels; because it remains unclear what they mean, it's impossible to tell whether the product really delivers what the ad seems to be promising.

3. The false implication here is that the gifts are granted to a depositor without qualification. But typically if the deposit is withdrawn before a minimum period, the gift, or an equivalent amount of money, is taken back. In what sense, then, is this a "free gift"?

4. On the other side of the package, we read in fine print "Blueberry Buds [sugar, vegetable stearine (a release agent), blueberry solids with other

natural flavors], salt, sodium carboxymethyl cellulose (a thickening agent), silicon dioxide (a flow agent), citric acid, modified soy protein, artificial flavor, artificial coloring, maltol.] If we take "Blueberry Buds" to mean what's included in the brackets, then it's true that the box contains real blueberry buds and "other natural flavors" in the blueberry buds. As for the artificial flavors, the package never said it contained none of these. This explanation notwithstanding, the claim is ambiguous and contains false implication and positively charged language ("real" is like "natural"). Many consumers will believe that the product contains whole blueberries or only natural ingredients as opposed to artificial flavors or additives.

5. This claim contains an ambiguous comparison. "Fewer" than whom? (or when?) The ad also contains the false implication that Colgate kids developed fewer cavities than those using other fluoride toothpastes, such as Crest. In fact, the true claim is that Colgate users got fewer cavities on average than they did before using Colgate, when perhaps some of them hadn't been using a fluoride toothpaste or hadn't even been brushing their teeth.

6. False implication. The true guarantee is that you may qualify and that there may be an opening. In fact, there's no guarantee for those who flunk out in training camp, and the Army's personnel needs might warrant your being sent elsewhere than your place of choice.

7. Unfinished comparison: harder than what or whom? Weasel word: "try."

8. Vague: This ad says nothing explicitly, but it suggests any number of things: "If you enjoy it, smoke it!" Or "Maybe smoking *is* bad for you. But if you enjoy smoking, then smoke! Make up your own mind—and make it Viceroy."

9. This one involves a really insidious ambiguity. "Take three" is evidently intended to refer to the pain reliever Anacin Three (Anacin's "extra strength" tablet) by name, but it also effectively encourages the viewer to increase the dosage from the conventional two tablets to three.

Quick Check on Exaggeration (P. 50)

1. The name is intended to suggest that a golfer will get the best performance (longest drives) out of this product.

2. "Super" is a superlative, tantamount to "great" or "fantastic." Thus, Super Shell is far better than other Shell gasolines and of course superior to other gasolines generally.

3. "True" implies that the product is the only real or genuine cigarette— perhaps the only cigarette that gives you a "true" smoking sensation, whatever that means.

4. "Wonder" implies that something special, perhaps unique, and presumably extraordinary benefits await those who eat Wonder Bread.

5. While there are many low-tar cigarettes, supposedly only Raleigh gives you flavor (the road).

6. "Ahhhhhh!" signals not only complete relief for hemorrhoid sufferers, but immediate relief as well.

7. Presumably, low-tar cigarettes don't give smokers pleasure. Barclay is special—a low-tar cigarette with pleasure.
8. "King"—a claim of preeminence. (It makes one wonder which is the "Queen" of beers, but of course that is a naive speculation. Beer, after all, is intended for men.)

Chapter 4
Quick Check on Argument Identification (P. 96)

1, 2, 3, 5, 6, and 8 are arguments.

Quick Check on Argument Analysis (P. 103)

1. TV shows like "Dallas" and "Dynasty" portray marriage in a most unflattering light. <u>First</u>, the partners are always quarreling. <u>Second</u>, they are always lusting after someone they're not married to.
   Conclusion: TV shows like "Dallas" and "Dynasty" portray marriage in a most unflattering light.
   Premises: The partners are always quarreling.
   They are always lusting after someone they're not married to.
2. Two out of three people interviewed preferred Zest to another soap. <u>Therefore</u>, Zest is the best soap available.
   Conclusion: Zest is the best soap available.
   Premise: Two out of three people interviewed preferred Zest to another soap.
3. In the 1980s more and more people will turn to solar heating to heat their homes <u>because</u> the price of gas and oil will become prohibitive for most consumers <u>and</u> the price of installing solar panels will decline.
   Conclusion: In the 1980s more and more people will turn to solar heating to heat their homes.
   Premises: the price of gas and oil will become prohibitive for most consumers and the price of installing solar panels will decline.
4. People who smoke cigarettes should be forced to pay for their own health insurance. They know smoking is bad for their health. They have no right to expect others to pay for their addiction.
   Conclusion: People who smoke cigarettes should be forced to pay for their own health insurance.
   Premises: They know smoking is bad for their health.
   They have no right to expect others to pay for their addiction.
5. This passage is problematic. It's not clear whether it should be read as an argument or as an attempted explanation of what is already taken to be an established fact that government aid to the poor is a failure.
6. Even though spanking has immediate punitive and (for the parent) anger-releasing effects, parents should not spank their children, <u>for</u> spanking gives children the message that inflicting pain on others is an appropriate means of changing their behavior. <u>Furthermore</u>, spanking trains children to submit to the arbitrary rules of authority figures who have the power to

harm them. We ought not to give our children those messages. Rather, we should train them to either make appropriate behavioral choices or to expect to deal with the related natural and logical consequences of their behavior.

Conclusion: Parents should not spank their children.

Premises: Spanking gives children the message that inflicting pain on others is an appropriate means of changing their behavior. Spanking trains children to submit to the arbitrary rules of authority figures who have the power to harm them. We ought not to give our children those messages. Rather, we should train them to either make appropriate behavioral choices or to expect to deal with the related natural and logical consequences of their behavior.

7. In the Dukakis-Bentsen/Bush-Quayle contest, we have <u>the best argument yet in favor of</u> a none-of-the-above category on the ballot. No further justification is necessary.

Conclusion: There should be a none-of-the-above category on the ballot.

Premise: The Dukakis-Bentsen/Bush-Quayle contest justifies adding a none-of-the-above category to the ballot.

8. Public schools generally avoid investigation of debatable issues and instead stress rote recall of isolated facts, which teaches students to unquestioningly absorb given information on demand so that they can regurgitate it in its entirety during testing situations. Although students are generally not allowed to question it, much of what is presented as accurate information is indeed controversial. <u>But</u> citizens need to develop decision-making skills regarding debatable issues in order to truly participate in a democracy. <u>It follows then that</u> public schools ought to change their educational priorities <u>in order to</u> better prepare students to become informed responsible members of our democracy.

Conclusion: Public schools ought to change their educational priorities.

Premises: This would better prepare students to become informed responsible members of our democracy. Citizens need to develop decision-making skills regarding debatable issues in order to truly participate in a democracy. Public schools generally avoid investigation of debatable issues. Instead they stress rote recall of isolated facts. This teaches students to unquestioningly absorb given information on demand so that they can regurgitate it in its entirety during testing situations. Although students are generally not allowed to question it, much of what is presented as accurate information is indeed controversial.

9. "In policy debates one party sometimes charges that his or her opponents are embracing a Nazi-like position. . . . Meanwhile, sympathizers nod in agreement with the charge, seeing it as the ultimate blow to their opponents. . . . The problem with using the Nazi analogy in public policy debates is that in the Western world there is a form of anti-Nazi 'bigotry'

that sees Nazis as almost mythically evil beings. . . . Firsthand knowledge of our own culture makes it virtually impossible to equate Nazi society with our own. The official racism of Germany, its military mentality, the stresses of war, and the presence of a dictator instead of a democratic system make Nazi Germany in the 1940s obviously different from America in the 1980s. . . ." (Gary E. Crum, "Disputed Territory," *Hastings Center Report* August/September 1988, p. 31)

Conclusion: It is virtually impossible to equate Nazi society with our own.

Premises: Nazi Germany in the 1940s, unlike America in the 1980s, had an official policy of racism.

Nazi Germany in the 1940s, unlike America in the 1980s, had a military mentality.

Nazi Germany in the 1940s, unlike America in the 1980s, was stressed by war.

Nazi Germany in the 1940s, unlike America in the 1980s, had a dictator instead of a democratic system.

Chapter 5

Quick Check on Argument Organization (P. 120)

1. Chain
2. Series
3. Series
4. Series
5. Chain

Quick Check on Casting (P. 125)

1. <u>Since</u> [it is only a matter of time before space-based missile defense technology becomes obsolete,]^1 <u>and since</u> [the funds earmarked for the development of such technology are sorely needed elsewhere,]^2 [we should abandon the Star Wars program.]^3

2. ["The diet works]^1 <u>because</u> [it specifically mobilizes fat.]^2 [It <u>also</u> stimulates the release of ketones and fat mobilizers.]^3 [It causes a disproportionately greater loss of fat.]^4 [It helps eliminate excess water.]^5 [It stabilizes blood sugar.]^6 [It lowers insulin levels and cortisol levels.]^7 [And it delivers a metabolic advantage."]^8

3. [President Reagan promised to balance the federal budget by 1984.][1] [But in his first term of office he succeeded in multiplying the budget deficit by[2] more than 250 percent.] [And he refused to seriously address the issue of the budget deficit throughout the 1984 reelection campaign.][3] [Such behavior clearly amounts to a betrayal of the public trust.][4]

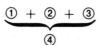

4. [The Star Wars program is our only realistic option for national defense in[1] the nuclear age.] [Any defense program that relies on deterrence raises the[2] risk of nuclear war,] and [that is not a realistic option for national[3] defense.] [The Star Wars program is the only option yet proposed that does[4] not rely on nuclear deterrence.]

$$\underbrace{② + ③ + ④}_{①}$$

Quick Check on Casting Premise Support (P. 131)

1. ["A recent five years study at a major electronics company indicates that[1] getting fired may have a lot to do with overreaching.] [Among 2,000 technical, sales and managerial employees who were followed during their first five years with the company, the 173 people who eventually were fired[2] started out with much higher expectations of advancement than either the 200 people who left voluntarily or the people who remained.] [On a questionnaire given during their first week on the job, more than half the people who were fired within the first two years ranked themselves among[3] the top 5% of typical people in their job category.] [Only 38% of those who stayed with the company ranked themselves that highly.][4]

Comments: We're inclined to see 3 and 4 as interdependent reasons for 2, because neither is statistically meaningful without the other. It's not unreasonable to view them as independent reasons, nor will this interpretive difference affect later evaluation of the argument. But we should agree that 3 and 4 are supporting 2.

2. [We must stop treating juveniles differently from adult offenders.]¹ [Justice demands it.]² [Justice implies that people should be treated equally.]³ Besides, [the social effects of pampering juvenile offenders have sinister social consequences.]⁴ [The record shows that juveniles who have been treated leniently for offenses have subsequently committed serious crimes.]⁵

3. ["The development of the human being from conception through birth into childhood is continuous.]¹ Then it is said [to draw a line, to choose a point in this development and say 'before this point the thing is not a person, after this point it is a person' is to make an arbitrary choice.]² It is further said that [this is a choice for which in the nature of things no good reason can be given.]³ It is concluded that [the fetus is . . . a person from the moment of conception.]⁴

4. [It's high time we seriously investigated the impact of television on children.]¹ [Children spend most of their time watching television.]² [The average American child by age eighteen has watched thousands of hours of

television.] [The same average viewer has watched[4] thousands of hours of inane situation comedy, fantasy, soap operas, and acts of violence.]

5. ["The tax cuts will result in higher deficits than would[1] have occurred had the Democrats stayed in office.] [The result will be blistering[2] inflation.] [The federal deficits for the last half of[3] the 1970's totalled $310 billion.] [Without the tax cuts, they would have totalled at least[4] twice that amount for the first half of the 1980's.] [With the tax cuts, they will probably[5] total $800 billion for that period."]

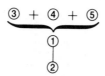

6. [Such crises [of employees departing[1] with a firm's trade secrets] are not surprising. . . .] [The highly educated employees of R&D [research and development] organizations[2] place primary emphasis on their own development, interests and satisfaction.] [Graduates of major scientific and technological institutions readily[3] admit that they accept their first jobs primarily for money.] [They <u>also</u> want the early and brief experience they feel is a prerequisite[4] for seeking more satisfying futures with smaller companies. . . .] [Employee mobility and high personnel turnover rates are <u>also</u>[5] due to the placement of new large federal contracts and the termination of others.] [One need only look to the Sunday newspaper employment advertisements for evidence as to[6] the manner in which such programs are used to attract highly educated R&D personnel."]

7. "To the extent that it is working at all, [the press is always a participant.]¹ [Our decisions on where (and where not) to be and what (and what not) to report have enormous impact on the political and governmental life we cover.]² [We are obliged to be selective.]³ [We cannot publish the Daily Everything.]⁴ And so long as this is true—so long as [we are making choices that 1) affect what people see concerning their leaders]⁵ and 2) [inevitably cause those leaders to behave in particular ways]⁶—we cannot pretend we are not participants."

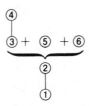

Quick Check on Casting Unexpressed Premises and Conclusions (P. 134)

1. Missing premise: Whatever animal chews the cud is a ruminant.ᵃ
   [Cows are ruminants]¹ because [they chew the cud.]²

$$\frac{② + ⓐ}{①}$$

2. Missing premise: Most men dread responsibility.ᵃ
   [Liberty means responsibility.]¹ That is why [most men dread it.]²

$$\frac{① + ⓐ}{②}$$

3. Missing conclusion: Wealth must be a good.ᵃ
   [Whatever isn't evil must be a good.]¹ [Wealth isn't an evil.]²

$$\frac{① + ②}{ⓐ}$$

4. Missing conclusion: The American ᵃgovernment is a laissez-faire
   government.
   [The American government leaves business on its own.]¹ [A government that
   lets business alone is said to be a laissez-faire government.]²

5. Missing premise: Being a pragmatist is incompatible with having strong
   philosophical bents.ᵃ
   [There are no strong philosophical bents on the Supreme Court.]¹ [Each of
   the justices is a pragmatist who takes each case as it comes.]² [The
   philosophical inconsistencies in their rulings are proof of this.]³ Besides
   [most of the justices themselves have said that they must judge each case
   on its own merits.]⁴

Quick Check on Casting Rhetorical Features (P. 141)

1. ["Evolution is a scientific fairy-tale]¹ just as the 'flat earth theory' was in the
   12th century. [Evolution directly contradicts the Second Law of
   Thermodynamics,]² which states that unless an intelligent planner is
   directing a system, it will always go in the direction of disorder and
   deterioration. . . . Evolution requires a faith that is incomprehensible!"

2. "Contrary to popular assumption, [volcanoes are anything but rare.]¹ [The
   Smithsonian Scientific Event Alert Network often reports several dozen
   [volcanic eruptions] per quarter.]² [America's slice of the volcanic 'ring of

fire' includes the Cascades,³ a mountain range that arcs across the Pacific Northwest.] When peaceful, shimmering Mt. St. Helens exploded this past spring, blasting 1.3 billion cubic yards of rock into powder, the people of Washington state received a rude lesson about nature's penchant for change. Bathed in ash every few weeks over the summer, the Washingtonians queasily came to the realization that the mountain might stay belligerent for years, that they had, in a sense, been living on borrowed time between inevitable eruptions. ['There are potential volcanoes all over the Cascades Range⁴ where Mt. St. Helens stands,'] says geologist Alfred Anderson of the University of Washington. "There's still a lot of change, a lot of formations, going on in that area of the world.' "

3. "A scientific colleague of mine, who holds a professorial post in the department of sociology and anthropology at one of our leading universities, recently asked me about my stand on the question of human beings having sex relations without love. Although I have taken something of a position on this issue in my book, *The American Sexual Tragedy,* I have never quite considered the problem in sufficient detail. So here goes. . . . In general I feel that [affectional, as against nonaffectional, sex relations are *desirable*. . . .]¹ It is usually desirable that an association between coitus and affection exist—particularly in marriage <u>because</u> [it is often difficult for two individuals to keep finely tuned to each other over a period of years."]²

4. "Scientists are human beings with their full complement of emotions and prejudices, and [their emotions and prejudices often influence the way they do their science.]¹ [This was first clearly brought out in a study by Professor Nicholas Pastore . . . in 1949.]² <u>In this study</u> [Professor Pastore showed that the scientist's political beliefs were highly correlated with what he³ believed about the roles played by nature and nurture in the development

of the person.] [Those holding conservative political views strongly tended[4] to believe in the power of genes over environment.] [Those subscribing to more liberal views tended to believe in the power of environment over[5] genes.] One distinguished scientist (who happened to be a teacher of mine) when young was a socialist and environmentalist, but toward middle age he became politically conservative and a firm believer in the supremacy of genes!"

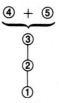

Comment: You may not have cast assertions 4 and 5. We did because in assertion 2 the author states that Pastore's study "clearly brought out" the point that emotions and prejudices often influence the way scientists do science. In order to evaluate that claim, we need as much pertinent information about the study as possible. Assertions 4 and 5 provide at least some of it. If this information is inadequate to support assertion 3 (which we think is the case, given the absence of data that establish a causal and not just a statistical correlation between scientists' political beliefs and their scientific beliefs), then the author has no basis for inferring assertion 2 and therefore none for inferring assertion 1. As for the last sentence, while amusing, it says no more than was previously said in assertions 4 and 5. Also, you may have interpreted the first clause in the first sentence as an independent reason for the clause we cast as assertion 1.

Chapter 6
Quick Check on "What If" Strategy (P. 155)

1. Incomplete: Suppose it's true that prisons fail to rehabilitate. Must it therefore be true that they are an ineffective form of criminal punishment? Not necessarily. It may still be the case that prisons effectively remove from the streets threats to society. They may also help deter crime.
2. Incomplete: Suppose it is imperative that the United States become energy independent. Does it follow from this alone that the United States should develop solar energy? Not necessarily. There are those, for example, who would advocate nuclear power and coal as preferable means to energy independence.
3. Incomplete: Suppose it is true that abortion involves taking a life. Does it follow from this alone that abortion should be discouraged? Not

necessarily. The use of pesticides also involves taking lives. So does killing in self-defense. Yet these are not discouraged.

4. Incomplete: Suppose Jane is wearing a wedding ring. Is there no other possible explanation for this other than that she is married?

5. Complete: Suppose it is true that if men weren't innately superior to women they wouldn't establish and work hard to maintain caste systems to ensure their preferred positions. Suppose also that they do both of these things. Now try to deny the conclusion of this argument.

Quick Check on Plausibility (P. 157)

1 and 4 seem open to discussion

2. We think *a* is clearly more plausible than *b* given the complexity and fallibility of computers and other relevant technology.

3. We think *a* is more plausible than *b* because those who hold high office in Washington constitute such a tiny subset of those alive.

Quick Check on Relevance and Topic Coverage Strategy (P. 158)

1. Reconstruction *b*
2. Reconstruction *c*

Quick Check on Filling in Missing Premises (P. 161)

1. a. Rehabilitation is a necessary part of any effective form of punishment for criminal behavior.
   b. Only the development of solar energy on a widespread basis can make the United States energy independent.
   c. Probably the arguer is committed to the premise that "any life-taking action should be discouraged," although the implausibility of this position is probably as serious a problem for the argument as its original incompleteness.
   d. "Women who wear wedding rings probably are married" would be a good choice. So would "Most women who wear wedding rings are married." So would "A wedding ring usually indicates that the wearer is married." The qualification in the argument's conclusion indicates that the arguer would not commit to anything stronger than a "most" or a "probably." An unqualified generalization would also be less plausible. However, the last of the three is slightly preferable. Because it does not restrict itself to the category of women, it has a broader scope and is consequently a slightly stronger premise than either of the others. Yet it is no less plausible.

2. a. Comment: Reconstruction 3. Reconstruction 1 is too weak. Reconstruction 2 provides no basis for drawing the conclusion, for simply because everyone carrying clubs is a golfer doesn't exclude the possibility that those not carrying clubs are also golfers.

399

b. Comment: Reconstruction 2. Reconstruction 1 merely repeats what's already stated. Reconstruction 3 is too weak, given its use of "usually."

c. Comment: Reconstruction 2. Reconstruction 1 is far too strong. Reconstruction 3 does not cite the reason why a tax bill originating in the Senate should not be made law, whereas reconstruction 2 does.

3. a. Missing premise: All ambitious people are self-serving. ^a

[All successful politicians are self-serving.]¹ for [only ambitious people² succeed in politics.]

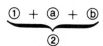

$$\frac{② + ⓐ}{①}$$

b. Missing premises: Whatever threatens justice is serious. ^a
Subjecting people to polygraph tests as a condition of employment^b invades privacy.
[Whatever invades privacy threatens justice.]¹ That's why [subjecting people to polygraph tests as a precondition of employment is so² serious.]

$$\frac{① + ⓐ + ⓑ}{②}$$

c. Missing premise: To alter the usual location of a mobile home park is^a unthinkable.
["I have nothing against mobile homes as a way of living,]¹ but [it's unthinkable to put a mobile home park right in the middle of a² residential area.] After all, [they're usually in outlying areas."]³

$$\frac{③ + ⓐ - ①}{②}$$

d. Missing premise: Doctors generally welcome any hedge against^a malpractice suits.

Because [they see it as a hedge against malpractice suits,]¹ [doctors typically welcome a patient's informed consent.]²

e. Missing premise: A country that gives millions of dollars to help the starving and dying people of another country can't be imperialist.^a
   "Imperialist is a dirty word, all right, but [it hardly fits a nation like the U.S.]¹ [which, (with all our faults,) is ready to give millions of dollars to help the starving and dying Cambodians."]²

f. Missing premise: Violating what is divinely ordained is a moral perversion.^a
   ["Surely this resolution and its supporting statements are designed to legitimize sex and social relationships other than those that form the basis of divinely ordained marriage, parenthood and home.]¹ From which it follows that [this resolution is a moral perversion.]²

$$
\underbrace{①\ +\ ⓐ}_{②}
$$

Comment: The speaker makes other assumptions that we have not made explicit; for example, that a God exists and that God ordains certain institutions and prescribes human behavior. You could examine these other assumptions when evaluating the argument. Also, we have expressed the conclusion as if it were a part of the argument. You might prefer to treat it as unexpressed, in which case you would make it explicit and signify it with a letter.

Chapter 7
Quick Check on the Concept of Deductive Validity (P. 179)

1. True. Remember: <u>If</u> the premises of a deductively valid argument are true, then the conclusion must also be true. But a deductively valid argument may have false premises, and in that case nothing is guaranteed regarding the conclusion.
2. True. For example: "Snakes can fly, and some birds are snakes, therefore some birds can fly" has false premises, but is deductively valid.
3. False. Remember: <u>If</u> the premises of a deductively valid argument are true, then the conclusion must also be true. But a deductively valid argument may have false premises. Therefore, there must be a way to tell whether a deductive argument is valid independent of verifying its premises.
4. True. For example: "Snakes can fly, and some birds are snakes, therefore some birds can fly" has false premises, a true conclusion, and is deductively valid.
5. False. A cogent argument is valid and has true premises.

Quick Check on Testing for Deductive Validity (P. 182)

1. Invalid. Some cars are made by General Motors, and all Ford Mustangs are cars. So it stands to reason that some Ford Mustangs are made by General Motors.
2. Valid.
3. Valid.
4. Invalid. Some women are college professors, and some college professors are men. So at least some women are men.

Quick Check on Valid Deductive Arguments (P. 186)

2. a. Valid: <u>Since</u> [All birds eat worms]^1 <u>and</u> [(all) chickens are birds,]^2 [chickens must eat worms.]^3

$$\frac{① + ②}{③}$$

b. Incomplete (as it stands): Unless you add as a missing premise: [All athletes are male chauvinists.]^a (In that case, it's valid, and can be cast as follows):

[Marty must be a real male chauvinist.]^1 <u>After all,</u> [he's an athlete,]^2 isn't he?

402

$$\frac{②+ⓐ}{①}$$

   c. Invalid. Some women are fathers, for all fathers are parents, and some women are parents.

   d. Invalid. Most of today's movies are worthless, but some of today's movies are real masterpieces. So, some real masterpieces are worthless.

Quick Check on Valid Inductive Arguments (P. 188)

  2. Arguments a, c, d, and e are deductive. Argument b is inductive.

Quick Check on Inductive Strength (P. 191)

     Argument 1 is the strongest of the three. The sample size appears to be quite large and representative in terms of ethnic, socioeconomic, regional, and international diversity. Argument 2 is the weakest of the three. The sample is small and it is impossible to determine how representative it is. We can safely assume, however, that with such a small sample, adequate representativeness is unlikely. Argument 3 falls in the middle. Although the sample is apparently fairly large, the group from which the sample was taken is not representative of the target population as a whole. Presumably, all members of the sample were readers of the magazine, thus they all had to have decent reading skills themselves as well as an interest in reading for information. Thus, their children would have had literate role models as parents. This is not necessarily typical of families in the population at large, and may be atypical of those in especially low income groups.

Quick Check on Verification and Cogency (P. 194)

  1. In *a*, the first premise is problematic. Depending on what is meant by "eat worms," the premise may be either true or false. There are species of bird whose natural diet does not include worms (penguins, pelicans), although they may yet be capable of digesting worms.
     In *b*, the unexpressed premise "All athletes are male chauvinists" is patently false.
     In *c*, the premises are true.
     In *d*, the first premise is suspect. Without supporting evidence, we'd reserve judgment as to its truth. Reserving judgment isn't the same as judging it to be false. In fact, the assertion may be true. But until its truth is no longer in reasonable doubt, it must be considered as *possibly* false. (Note: Be sure to test for truth the premises of the arguments you constructed.)
  2. When an argument's conclusion does not follow validly from its premises or if any of its premises is false or in doubt, the argument is not cogent. Thus

none of the arguments—*a*, *b*, *c*, or *d*—is cogent. Notice, however, why they fail the test of cogency. Arguments *a*, *b*, and *d* are not cogent because of faulty premises, even though *a* and *b* (with the added premise) are valid. Arguments *c* and *d* are not cogent because they are invalid, even though *c*'s premises (and conclusion) are true.

Quick Check on Value Judgments (P. 198)

1. Value judgments: *a*, *b*, *e*, *g*, *h*, *i*, *j*, *l*, *m*, *n*, *q*, *r*

Quick Check on Clarifying Language (P. 202)

1. "wrong"
2. "evil"
3. "ought never"
4. "highest"
5. "immoral"
6. "best"
7. "greatest"
8. "should not"
9. "morally justifiable"
10. "should never"
11. "godless"
12. "threatens"

All these words can be interpreted in ter is of personal preference, social preference, and conformity to principle, standard, or law. Once the interpretation is ascertained and translated into empirical form, the justification of each assertion can be assessed. For example, "Needlessly inflicting pain is wrong" may mean "*I disapprove* of needlessly inflicting pain"; or "*society disapproves* of needlessly inflicting pain"; or "needlessly inflicting pain is inconsistent with how people should treat each other." Regarding the autobiographical interpretation, you could ask: "On what grounds do you base your disapproval?" Regarding the sociological: "What makes society's view correct?" Regarding conformity to principle: "On what grounds can you state how people ought to treat each other?"

Chapter 8
Quick Check on Fallacies of Ambiguity (P. 215)

1. a. An amphiboly. Has the preliminary OK been extended to 50,000 undocumented immigrants during the first month of the amnesty, or does the preliminary OK cover only the first month of the amnesty?
   b. This involves an ambiguity of accent. Willy Sutton is answering the question why he robs <u>banks</u>, rather than why he is a robber.
   c. An example of amphiboly. This could be read as "He gave biscuits to her dog" or "He gave dog biscuits to her."
2. a. Amphiboly. Do all such subsidies and laws promote unemployment (and therefore should they all be dismantled)? Or should only those that promote unemployment be dismantled?
   b. Fallacy of division. Even if the Steelers, as a team, were the best, that doesn't necessarily mean that Ham or any other individual Steeler was the best at a given position.
   c. Equivocation. The equivocal terms are "disabled" and "disability."

    d. Division again. From the fact that the fortunes of Federalists as a group decayed it does not follow that the fortunes of any particular Federalist decayed. There is also an equivocation here. Do we mean financial or political fortunes?

    e. Ted is equivocating on the term "neighbor," which, in its proverbial sense, is not restricted to those living near one.

Chapter 9
Quick Check on Ad Hominem Appeals (P. 232)

1. "Fascist flunkey," "reactionary guts," "petty bourgeois," "disease," "lost the last remnants of common sense," and "fanatical" are all instances of abusive ad hominem.

2. Although Davis is surely right to object to such ad hominem attacks as "crackpot," "faddist," and "quack," she herself makes an ad hominem attack when she insinuates crass conspiracy and conflict of interest in her opposition.

3. Aside from the obvious abusive ad hominem pervasive throughout this statement, there is the suggestion that anyone who stands in opposition to the Klan is guilty by association of some form of moral degeneracy.

4. Guilt by association. Not all minors (not all who would be subject to the 100% fare increase proposed here) are responsible for graffiti. Not all minors watch, and not all who watch do so with approval.

5. This can be criticized as an instance of circumstantial ad hominem. Senator Rudman's Republican affiliation is the primary reason appealed to here in support of the criticism of his conduct in the Iran-contra hearings. (Also notice the appeal to loyalty.)

Quick Check on Appeals to Authority (P. 238)

1. Provincialism. (Also notice the appeal to pity.)

2. Appeal to tradition.

3. This is a legitimate appeal to the authority of someone with relevant expertise.

4. Popularity.

5. In addition to pandering to provincialism, this exemplifies positioning. Reagan is effectively linking himself with one of America's most well-regarded presidents. In addition, he thus effectively links himself with a tradition of statesmanship, and also with popular German tradition, in his invocation of the line from the song. Thus we also have appeal to popularity and appeal to tradition.

6. "High technology," "new," and "here today" are appeals to novelty. (Also notice the abuse of vagueness in "you know it's going to do what you bought it to do.")

7. Positioning. The Sabena ad forges a link in order to make a favorable comparison with more widely recognized TWA (whose slogan is "the world's most experienced airline").

8. Viewed as an inductive argument this is probably not an unreasonable one. However, if it is intended as more than an inductive argument, it commits the fallacy of appeal to tradition or popularity.

Quick Check on Emotional Appeals (P. 241)

1. Appeal to fear.
2. Senator Inouye's reference to the tragedy is an appeal to pity. (Also notice the implicit appeal to tradition in the invocation of the values of fatherhood and family.)
3. This is both a mob appeal and an appeal to fear in that it is evidently designed to arouse fear of official enemies in the population en masse.

Chapter 10
Quick Check on Fallacies of Statistical Inference (P. 257)

1. This assumes that the sample (those readers who write letters to the opinion page editor) are representative of the community at large.
2. An obviously slanted study, because the selection of the sample predictably influences the study's findings in a way favorable to the interests of the study's sponsors.
3. The target population is the student body at large. The polling technique is not well designed to generate a random sample because it is limited to students who happen to be in the cafeteria on Tuesday mornings.
4. In spite of the merits of the questionnaire as a polling instrument, Professor Smith compromises the study, by conducting the study in his office on individual students currently subject to his authority and power as an instructor. Because these circumstances are likely to influence the student's responses, the study may be said to be slanted.
5. A vague question slants the study.
6. This question slants the study by eliminating from consideration at least two significant policy alternatives: neither and both equally.
7. Suppressed evidence and bad base line.
8. Gambler's fallacy.

Quick Check on Fallacies of Comparison (P. 261)

1. Questionable classification (paper tiger?!).
2. Questionable analogy.
3. Questionable analogy. The period used as the basis of the analogy (1945–1949) is unlike subsequent periods of history, in which nuclear weapons have become available more widely and to a wider variety of political entities, some of them subject to quite centralized and authoritarian forms of government, some of which demonstrate the propensity for willful and erratic conduct.

Quick Check on Fallacies of Questionable Cause (P. 264)

1. Causal oversimplification. The second premise implicitly attributes full causal responsibility to the Reagan administration for the budget deficit, which is arguably the result of a more complex interplay of economic forces. It should be added, however, that a reasonably strong case can be made for identifying a number of Reagan administration policies as among the central causal factors in the rise of the deficit.
2. Might there not be some further common cause of both drug use and low productivity?
3. Post hoc.
4. Slippery slope and causal oversimplification. Even if it is true that a new tax in effect gives rise to a new form of profitable and illegal activity, the tax itself is not to be held accountable for criminal activity that takes that form.

Quick Check on Unwarranted Assumptions (P. 267)

1. A circular explanation. Begs the question.
2. Arguing from ignorance.
3. Begging the question.
4. Invincible ignorance. In the face of what must amount to prima facie evidence to the contrary, Lagomarsino refuses to doubt the credibility of the witness.
5. More circular reasoning. Begs the question.

Chapter 12
Quick Check on Thesis Identification (P. 300)

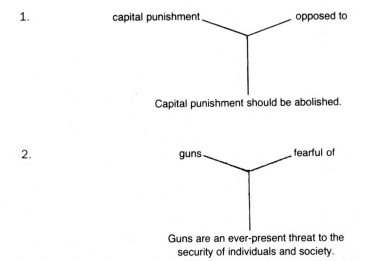

1. capital punishment — opposed to

   Capital punishment should be abolished.

2. guns — fearful of

   Guns are an ever-present threat to the security of individuals and society.

3.

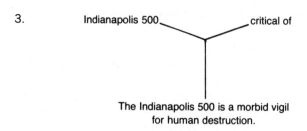

Indianapolis 500   critical of

The Indianapolis 500 is a morbid vigil
for human destruction.

4.

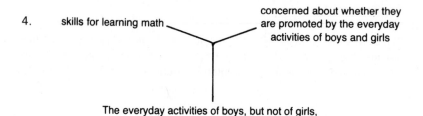

skills for learning math   concerned about whether they
are promoted by the everyday
activities of boys and girls

The everyday activities of boys, but not of girls,
teach them basic concepts in math.

Chapter 13
Quick Check on Organization (P. 349)

1. Inductive.
2. a. This could be viewed as either an analysis-of-alternatives (alternative causal hypotheses) or a cause-and-effect essay.
   b. Analysis of alternatives. Pro-and-con organization is also used in evaluating the alternatives.
   c. Inductive
   d. Cause and effect

SUGGESTIONS FOR FURTHER READING

CHAPTER 1
Critical Thinking: What It Is and What It Is Not

To further orient yourself to the subject of critical thinking and at the same time get a sense of the level of consensus about what critical thinking is in essence you might look at alternative texts, particularly at their introductory sections and their tables of contents. Here is a fairly representative sample of good texts in the field.

Beardsley, Monroe C. *Thinking Straight: Principles of Reasoning for Readers and Writers* 4th ed. (Englewood Cliffs, N.J.: Prentice-Hall, 1975).

Browne, M. Neil, and Stuart Keeley. *Asking the Right Questions: A Guide to Critical Thinking* 2nd ed. (Englewood Cliffs, N.J.: Prentice-Hall, 1986).

Chaffee, John. *Critical Thinking* 2nd ed. (Boston: Houghton Mifflin, 1988).

Johnson, Ralph, and J. Anthony Blair. *Logical Self-Defense* 2nd ed. (Toronto: McGraw-Hill Ryerson, 1983).

Kahane, Howard. *Logic and Contemporary Rhetoric* 5th ed. (Belmont, Calif.: Wadsworth, 1988).

Nosich, Gerald. *Reasons and Arguments* (Belmont, Calif.: Wadsworth, 1985).

Scriven, Michael. *Reasoning* (New York: McGraw-Hill, 1976).

Sternberg, Robert J. *Intelligence Applied* (New York: Harcourt Brace Jovanovich, 1987).

Weddle, Perry. *Argument: A Guide to Critical Thinking* (New York: McGraw-Hill, 1978).

Blocks to Critical Thinking

Gardner, Martin. *Science: Good, Bad, and Bogus* (Buffalo, N.Y.: Prometheus, 1981).

Paul, Richard. "Teaching Critical Thinking in the 'Strong' Sense: A Focus on Self-Deception, World Views, and a Dialectical Mode of Analysis," *Informal Logic* (May 1982).

CHAPTER 2
Functions of Language, Meaning in Language, Issues and Disputes

Alston, William P. *Philosophy of Language* (Englewood Cliffs, N.J.: Prentice-Hall, 1964).

Austin, J. L. *How to Do Things with Words* 2nd ed. (Cambridge: Harvard University Press, 1975).

Bennett, Jonathan. *Linguistic Behavior* (Cambridge: Cambridge University Press, 1976).

Govier, Trudy. *Selected Topics in Logic and Communication* (Belmont, Calif.: Wadsworth, 1987).

The Information Environment: Advertising

Baker, Samm Sinclair. *The Permissible Lie* (Cleveland: World, 1968).

Ogilvie, David. *Confessions of an Advertising Man* (New York: Atheneum, 1963).

Preston, Ivan. *The Great American Blowup: Puffery in Advertising and Selling* (Madison: University of Wisconsin Press, 1975).

Schrank, Jeffrey. *Snap, Crackle and Popular Taste* (New York: Delacorte, 1977).

CHAPTER 3

Fink, Conrad C. *Media Ethics: In the Newsroom and Beyond* (New York: McGraw-Hill, 1988).

Gerbner, George, et al. "Television Violence, Victimization, and Power," *American Behavioral Scientist* 23 (1980).

Herman, Edward S., and Noam Chomsky. *Manufacturing Consent: The Political Economy of the Mass Media* (New York: Pantheon, 1989).

Hertsgaard, Mark. *On Bended Knee: The Press and the Reagan Presidency* (New York: Farrar Straus Giroux, 1988).

Mander, Jerry. *Four Arguments for the Elimination of Television* (New York: Quill, 1978).

MacLean, Eleanor. *Between the Lines: How to Detect Bias and Propaganda in the News and Everyday Life* (Montreal: Black Rose, 1981).

Postman, Neil. *Amusing Ourselves to Death: Public Discourse in the Age of Show Business* (New York: Viking, 1985).

Rodman, George. *Mass Media Issues: Analysis and Debate* 2nd ed. (New York: Science Research Associates, 1984).

CHAPTER 4

Fogelin, Robert J. *Understanding Arguments: An Introduction to Informal Logic* 3rd ed. (New York: Harcourt Brace Jovanovich, 1987).

Govier, Trudy. *A Practical Study of Argument* 2nd ed. (Belmont, Calif.: Wadsworth, 1987).

CHAPTER 5

Freeman, James B. *Thinking Logically: Basic Concepts for Reasoning* (Englewood Cliffs, N.J.: Prentice Hall, 1988) Part II.

Govier, Trudy. *A Practical Study of Argument* 2nd ed. (Belmont, Calif.: Wadsworth, 1987).

Scriven, Michael. *Reasoning* (New York: McGraw-Hill, 1976).

CHAPTER 6

Govier, Trudy. *A Practical Study of Argument* 2nd ed. (Belmont, Calif.: Wadsworth, 1987).

CHAPTER 7
Cogency, Argument Form, Deduction and Induction

Copi, Irving. *Introduction to Logic* 6th ed. (New York: Macmillan, 1982).

Moore, Kathleen Dean. *A Field Guide to Inductive Arguments* (Dubuque, Iowa: Kendall Hunt, 1986).

Truth and Verification

Moore, Brooke Noel, and Richard Parker. *Critical Thinking: Evaluating Claims and Arguments in Everyday Life* 2nd ed. (Palo Alto, Calif.: Mayfield, 1989).

CHAPTERS 8, 9, and 10

Bentham, Jeremy. *The Handbook of Political Fallacies* (New York: Harper, 1962).

Damer, T. Edward. *Attacking Faulty Reasoning* 2nd ed. (Belmont, Calif.: Wadsworth, 1987).

Green, Mark, and Gail MacColl. *Reagan's Reign of Error: The Instant Nostalgia Edition* (New York: Pantheon, 1987).

Michalos, Alex. *Improving Your Reasoning* 2nd ed. (Englewood Cliffs, N.J.: Prentice-Hall, 1986).

CHAPTER 12

The best supplementary exercise for the material in Chapter 12 is to apply the format to arguments on a range of issues. There are quite a number of excellent anthologies organized as collections of opposing arguments on controversial issues. Here are several.

Miller, Robert K., ed. *The Informed Argument: A Multidisciplinary Reader and Guide* (New York: Harcourt Brace Jovanovich, 1986).

Rottenberg, Annette. *Elements of Argument: A Text and Reader* 2nd ed. (New York: St. Martin's Press, 1987).

Sterba, James. *Morality in Practice* 2nd ed. (Belmont, Calif.: Wadsworth, 1987).

CHAPTER 13

Howard, Vernon, and J. H. Barton. *Thinking on Paper* (New York: William Morrow, 1987).

CHAPTER 14

Perkins, David. *The Mind's Best Work* (Cambridge: Harvard University Press, 1981).

Shushan, Ronnie, ed. *Games Magazine Big Book of Games* (New York: Workman, 1984).

_____. *Games Magazine Book of Sense and Nonsense Puzzles* (New York: Workman, 1985).

Smullyan, Raymond. *This Book Needs No Title* (Englewood Cliffs, N.J.: Prentice-Hall, 1980).

_____. *What Is the Name of This Book?* (Englewood Cliffs, N.J.: Prentice-Hall, 1978).

_____. *Alice in Puzzle Land* (New York: Penguin, 1982).

Sternberg, Robert J. *Intelligence Applied* (New York: Harcourt Brace Jovanovich, 1987).

Periodicals Worth Knowing About

American Heritage Interesting for historical detail.

Amnesty Action Published by Amnesty International to document government abuses of human rights around the world.

Atlantic Monthly General interest.

Columbia Journalism Review Journalism's professional journal of record.

Commentary Conservative establishment orientation.

Consumer Reports Published by Consumers Union, the model of public interest research; good source of consumer product information.

Covert Action Quarterly A good example of watchdog journalism; covers the secretive intelligence activities of government.

The Economist British news weekly with a special interest in business.

Environmental Ethics Quarterly journal for discussion of environmental issues.

Ethics Well-established academic quarterly for discussion of legal, political, and ethical issues.

Foreign Affairs Establishment quarterly; defines the official position or the range of officially acceptable debate on foreign policy.

Harper's General interest.

Hastings Center Report The bimonthly publication of the Hastings Center; the forum of record for biomedical and health care policy issues.

Inquiry Libertarian orientation.

In These Times Radical left perspective on current affairs.

Media & Values Thoughtful, balanced, accessible critiques of values projected in contemporary media; each issue is thematically focused.

Ms. A mainstream feminist perspective.

The Nation The (?) definitive left-wing perspective on current affairs.

National Review The (?) definitive right-wing perspective on current affairs.

The New Republic The (?) definitive liberal perspective on current affairs.

The New Yorker Urbane lengthy articles, witty cartoons, thoughtful editorials.

New York Review of Books Liberal intellectual orientation.

Nucleus Quarterly report of the Union of Concerned Scientists.

Philosophy and Public Affairs Well-established academic quarterly for philosophical discussion of a wide range of social issues.

The Progressive Left-wing perspective on current affairs.

QQ: Philosophy and Public Policy The journal of the Maryland Center for Philosophy and Public Policy; publishes sophisticated but very accessible pieces on a wide range of public policy issues.

Quarterly Review of Doublespeak Excellent and entertaining review of the most ingenious Orwellian innovations and abuses of the day.

Reason Libertarian; "Free Minds and Free Markets" is the official editorial stance.

Rolling Stone Magazine Once devoted entirely to rock'n'roll journalism; now evolved into trendy pop-culture coverage, but continues to include significant investigative and opinion journalism.

Scientific American The science monthly; can be somewhat technical.

Skeptical Inquirer The antidote to the *National Enquirer*.

Utne Reader A digest. The best of the "alternative press."

The Village Voice Once an "underground" paper; now has more lofty pretensions as a barometer of in-the-know Big Apple taste.

Zeta New; the cutting edge of left-wing political analysis.

GLOSSARY

Ad hominem: An informal fallacy consisting of an irrelevant attack on the person rather than on the person's position or argument.

Ambiguous: Can be legitimately interpreted in more than one way.

Analogy: An elaborate comparison; a comparison involving multiple points of similarity.

Antecedent: The "if" part of a hypothetical statement. *See also* Hypothetical statement.

Argument: (Functional definition): A persuasive device that appeals to reason. (Structural definition): A connected series of claims, one of which [the thesis or conclusion] is supposed to be supported by the rest [the premise(s)].

Assumption: A claim accepted or supposed to be true without proof or demonstration.

Begging the question: An informal fallacy consisting of assuming what is at issue.

Conclusion: The part of an argument supported by the premise(s). *See also* Thesis.

Connotation: The set of characteristics that define a term's denotation [*see* Denotation] plus the emotional associations of the term.

Consequent: The "then" part of a hypothetical statement. *See also* Hypothetical statement.

Contingent: A statement that is neither true by definition nor self-contradictory.

Deductive: Reasoning or an argument that is supposed to provide absolutely conclusive proof of a thesis. *See also* Valid.

Denotation: The set of objects designated or referred to by a term.

Egocentricity: The tendency to view everything in relation to oneself.

Ethnocentricity: The tendency to view everything in relation to one's group.

Evidence: Information relevant to an inference.

Fallacy: An unreliable inference.

Formal fallacy: A fallacy whose unreliability may be traced to its formal structure.

Hypothesis: Thesis supposed to be true for purposes of testing its implications.

Hypothetical statement: A statement that asserts the truth functional relationship between two component statements: namely, that if the one [the antecedent] is true, so is the other [the consequent].

Hypothetical syllogism: A valid argument form composed of three hypothetical statements, where the consequent of the first premise and the antecedent of the second are identical, and the antecedent and consequent of the conclusion are identical with the antecedent of the first premise and the consequent of the second, respectively.

Implication: What may legitimately be inferred from a claim.

Inductive: Reasoning or an argument that is supposed to provide something less than absolutely conclusive proof of a thesis. *See also* Validity.

Inference: The move or transition from premise(s) to conclusion of an argument.

Informal fallacy: A fallacy whose unreliability may be traced to some factor other than its formal structure.

Invalid: Reasoning or an argument that fails to provide the sort of proof it is supposed to provide. *See* Deductive, Inductive, and Valid.

Irrelevant: Something that does not count one way or another in an issue.

Issue: A disputed or disputable topic.

Modus ponens: A valid argument form consisting of a hypothetical statement and the separate assertion of its antecedent as premises, leading to the assertion of its consequent as a conclusion.

Modus tollens: A valid argument form consisting of a hypothetical statement and the denial of its consequent as premises, leading to the denial of its antecedent as a conclusion.

Necessary truth: A statement whose negation is self-contradictory.

Plausible: An idea likely to survive strenuous attempts to falsify it.

Premise: The part(s) of an argument supporting the thesis or conclusion.

Relevant: Something that counts one way or another in a given issue.

Syllogism: A deductive argument with more than one premise.

Thesis: Originally meant "proposed idea." In argument analysis: the part of an argument supported by the premise(s). *See also* Conclusion. In composition: the main idea presented in an essay.

Vague: Terminology whose range of application is unclear or ill-defined.

Valid: Reasoning or an argument that does provide the sort of proof it is supposed to provide. *See* Deductive, Inductive, and Invalid.

INDEX

Accent, fallacy of, 214
Ad hominem, 228
  abusive, 229
  circumstantial, 230
Advertising, 42
  ambiguity in, 44–47
  and parity products, 43
  exaggeration in, 47
  false implication in, 43
  hidden facts in, 52
  hyperbole in, 48
  psychological appeals in, 50
  purposes of, 42
  puffery in, 49
  sex in, 51
  subliminal, 51
  vagueness in, 44–47
  weasel words in, 46
Age, 66, 74, 340–342
  of audience, 340–342
  in news reporting, 74
  reality warp on, 66
Allport, Gordon, 20n
Ambiguity, 35–36
  argument signal words and, 100
  in advertising, 44
Amphiboly, 213
  fallacy of, 213
Analogy, 258–260
  argument from, 258–259
  fallacy of questionable, 259
Analysis, 2, 97–173, 364,
  367–369
Analysis-of-alternatives approach in
  argumentative essay, 348
Antecedent, 182
  fallacy of denying the, 185
Argument, 93–329
  analysis, 97–173
  casting, 117–173
  defined functionally, 96
  defined structurally, 95

distinguished from explanation,
  95–96
  evaluation, 174–329
  forms, 176–180, 182–186
  identification, 95–96, 98–103
  organizational structure, series
  and chain, 119
  signals, 98–102
Argumentative essay, 297–361
  anticipation of objections in, 345
  argument and persuasion in, 332
  audience and, 340
  main points of, 298, 302, 339
  organization of, 297, 345–348
  testing logic of, 350, 355
  thesis of, 298–300, 332–338
  writing, 331–361
Aristotle, 234
Asch, S. E., 20n
Asides, casting, 136
Assertions, 98
  arguable, in essay, 339
  casting of, separately, 135, 140
  justification of, 195–205
  types of, 194–197
Association, fallacy of guilt by, 230
Assumption, 265
  challenging, in problem solving,
  371
  loaded labels, 15, 217
  unwarranted, 265–270
Audience, for argumentative essay,
  340
Authority, 13–15, 82–87, 233–238
  reliance on, 13–15
  fallacious appeal to, 233–238
  in news reporting, 82–87

Bagdikian, Ben H., 91n
Background information, casting,
  137

Background knowledge, observation and, 196
Baker, Russell, 83, 91n
Begging the question, fallacy of, 266
Behavior, impact of television on, 63–69
Beliefs, 7–12, 192
Bennett, Jonathan, 20n, 61n
Bias, 29, 75, 77–79, 83
Burden of proof, 267

Carroll, Lewis, 61n
Casting arguments, 117–144
Cause, 261–264
    common, 262
    and effect approach in argumentative essay, 347–348
    false, see also Post hoc, 262
Causal oversimplification, 262–263
Chain structure, 119
Change, resistance to, 10
Circular
    definition, 32
    reasoning, 266
Clarifying
    information, 368
    meaning, 29–36, 200–202, 278, 304
    problems, 368
Class (social) as factor in news reporting, 73–74
Classification, fallacy of questionable, 260
Cogency, 175–176
Comparison, 258–260
Complex question, 221
Composition, fallacy of, 214
Conclusion, 97
    signals, 98
    jumping to, 251
    hasty, 251
    unexpressed, 104–107, 133–134
Conformity to principle, standard or law, value assertions and, 202
Connotation, 28–29

Consequences, 204
Consequent, 182
    Fallacy of Asserting the, 184
Consistency, 268
Contingent statements, 194–195
Convention, meaning in language as, 25–28
Conventional meaning, 27–28
Copernicus, N., 11
Creativity in critical thinking, 5–7, 366, 371–373
Crime, reality warp on, 67–68
Critical thinking, 2–16
    blocks to, 8–16
    nature of, 2–8
Criticizing arguments, 175–321
Cultural conditioning, 12

Deductive, 179
    argument, 179–187
    signal words, 188
    validity, 179–182
Definition, 29–36
    denotative, 30, 33
    logical, 30–33
    persuasive, 34
    stipulative, 33–34
Denotation, 28–29
Denotative definition, 30, 33
Directive function of language, 23
Disagreement, critical thinking and, 3, 36–39
Disjunction, 185–186
Disjunctive syllogism, 186
Disinformation, 71, 85
Dispute, 36–39
    factual, 37–38, 195–197
    verbal, 37, 194
    evaluative, 38, 197–205
    interpretive, 38–39, 194–197
Diversion, 242–244
Division, fallacy of, 215
Division of expert opinion, 235–236
Donaldson, Sam, 85
Double standard, 269
Dramatic and visual values in news reporting, 79–80

Economics, 80–82
Economy, 80–82
Efficiency, 80–82
Egocentricity, 10–11
Empirical justification, 195–197
Equivocation, fallacy of, 212–213
Ethnocentricity, 12, 82
Euphemism, 217–219
Evaluating
　arguments, 175–329
　consequences, in problem solving,
　　370
　information, in problem solving,
　　373
　options, in problem solving, 370
　strategies, in problem solving,
　　373
Evidence, 37–38, 251–267
　empirical, 37–38
　evaluating, 195–197
　suppressed, 255
Exaggeration, 47–50
Examples, casting, 138–139
Expectations of audience, 341
Expert opinion, division of, 235–236
Explanation, distinguished from ar-
　gument, 95–96
Expressive function of language,
　22–23
Extended argument, 109, 297–359
　anticipation of objections in, 345
　argument and persuasion in, 332
　audience and, 340
　critique of, 297–320
　main points of, 298, 302, 339
　organization of, 297, 345–348
　testing logic of, 350, 355
　thesis of, 298–300, 332–338
　writing, 331–361
Extension, 28–29

Fact
　and opinion, 192–193
　justifying assertions of, 195–197
　hidden, 52–53
Fallacy, 179–181, 184–185,
　209–272

False analogy, 258–260
False dilemma, fallacy of, 265
False implication, 43–44
Faulty comparison, 258–261
Fear, fallacy of appeal to, 240
Federal Trade Commission, 45, 48,
　53
Fink, Conrad, 91n
Food and Drug Administration, 48,
　53
Force, fallacy of appeal to, 240
Foreign news, reporting of, 75–76
Form, argument, 176–180,
　182–186
Formal fallacy, 180–185
Format for analysis and evaluation,
　277–290
Frame of reference, 9, 196,
　344–345
Functions of language, 22–25

Galileo, 10–11, 233–234
Gamblers' fallacy, 256–257
Gans, Herbert, 73–76, 82, 91n
Gender
　in news, 74
　reality warp on, 66
General area premise signals,
　99–100
Genetic appeal, fallacy of, 231
Gerbner, George, 65–69, 91n
Good, triumph of, on television,
　68–69
Guilt by association, fallacy of,
　230–231

Halevy, David, 85
Half-truth, 255
Harwood, Robert, 83–84, 91n
Health, reality warp on, 67
Hidden facts in advertising, 52
Humiliation, and critical thinking,
　3–4
Humor, fallacy of diversion through,
　242
Hype, in advertising, 47–49

Hyperbole, 47–49
Hypotheses, 39
  evaluating, 196–197
Hypothetical reasoning, 39
Hypothetical statements, 182

Ideology, 68–69, 75
Ignorance, fallacy of appeal to,
    266–267
  fallacy of invincible, 266
Illustrations, casting, 138–139
Images and symbols, ideology con-
    veyed through, 68–69
Implication, 269
Inconsistency, 268–269
  checking for, 268–269
Indirect proof, method of, 269
Inductive, 187–191
  approach in argumentative essay,
    346
  arguments, 187–191
  signal words, 188
  strength in, 189–191
Information, 9, 368, 373–374
  age, 9
  background, casting, 137–138
  environment, 40–42
  in problem solving, 373
Informative function of language, 22
Innuendo, 220–221
Intensifiers, 219
Intension, 28–29
Invincible ignorance, fallacy of, 266
Issues
  and disputes, 36–39
  evaluative, 38, 197–205
  factual, 37–38, 195–197
  genuine, 37–194
  interpretive, 38–39, 117–118,
    194–197
  verbal, 37, 194

James, William, 36–37, 78, 192
Jensen, Carl, 70–72
Judgment, 12
  moral, 12
  value, 38, 194, 197–205

Jumping to conclusions, 12, 251
Justification, 175
  and observations, 195
  and types of assertions, 193–194
  of main points in argumentative
    essay, 307
  of value assertions, 194,
    197–205

Kaddafi, Muammar, 84–86
Kalb, Bernard, 85–86
Kepler, J., 11
Key, Wilson Bryan, 61n

Labels, 15–16, 25–26, 217
  as blocks to critical thinking,
    15–16
  as basis for meaning in language,
    25–26
  assumption loaded, 15, 217
Language, 21
  clarifying, of value assertions,
    197–200
  convention in, 25–28
  definition in, 29–34
  functions of, 22–25
  rule of common usage in, 27–28
Lee, Irvin, 15
Lewis, Anthony, 72
Lippman, Walter, 78, 91n
Logic, formal, 176–186
  testing of argumentative essay,
    350–355
Logical definition, 30–33

MacNeil, Robert, 70
Main points
  of argumentative essay, 302, 304,
    307, 339
  of extended argument, 298, 304,
    307
  testing logic of relationship be-
    tween thesis and, 350–355
Meaning
  in language, 25–28
  assertions about, 29
  usage as guide to, 25–28

Milgram, Stanley, 13
Missing premises, 105, 133–134, 149–168, 279
  analyzing and evaluating for, 154–155
  in critique of essay, 307, 314–315
  difficulty of filling in, 152–154
  filling in, 133–134, 149–168
  guidelines for filling in, 155–161
  importance of filling in, 149–152
  in longer arguments, 163–168, 307, 314–315
  testing logic of essay by filling in, 288
  topic coverage strategy for, 158
  "what-if" strategy for, 154–155
Mob appeal, fallacy of, 239
Modus Ponens, 183
Modus Tollens, 184
Moral judgment, hasty, 12
Multiple functions of language, 22–25
Myths, ideology and television and, 68–69

National Aeronautics and Space Administration, 86–87
Necessary
  conditions, 31
  truth, 194
News
  reality judgments in, 72–76
  sources of, 82–87
  values in, 77–82
Newsworthiness, 70–82
Novelty, fallacy of appeal to, 237–238

Objections, anticipation of, in argumentative essay, 345
Objectivity
  and observation, 196
  as news value, 77
Observation
  conditions, 195
  in verification of hypotheses, 196–197
  skills, 365–366
  to support main points, 339
Organization
  of argumentative essay, 297, 302, 345–348, 357
  in arguments, series or chain, 119
  of extended arguments, 297, 302
Outline of argumentative essay, 320–321, 351–355

Patterns, discerning in problem solving, 368–369
Perception, 365
Performative function of language, 23–24
Perkins, David, 61n
Persona of writer or speaker, 342–343
Personal attacks, 228–232
Personal experience, 339
Persuasion in argumentative essay, 332
Persuasive
  function of language, 23
  definition, 34
Plausibility, 156
Poisoning the well, fallacy of, 231
Polls, 252–255
Popularity, fallacy of appeal to, 236
Positioning, fallacy of, 236
Positive emotional charge, ambiguity and, 45–46
Post hoc argument, fallacy of, 262
Postman, Neil, 70
Premise support, 107–109
Premises, 97–109
  casting support, 126–131
  specific signals, 101
  general area signals, 99–101
  support for, 107–109
  missing, 104–106, 133–134
  unexpressed, 104–106, 133–134
Preston, Ivan L., 49, 61n
Pro-and-con approach in argumentative essay, 346

Problem
  finding, 366
  solving, 363–380
Project Censored, 70–71
Provincialism, fallacy of, 238
Psychological appeals in advertising, 50
Ptolemy, 10
Puffery in advertising, 49

Quantifiers, extreme, 219
Questionable analogy, fallacy of, 258–260
Questionable cause, fallacy of, 261–264
Questionable classification, fallacy of, 260

Race
  in news, 73
  reality warp on, 66
Randomness, poll or survey, 253
Reality
  judgments in news, 72–76
  warp on television, 65–69
Red herring, fallacy of, 244
Reductio ad absurdum, 269
Reedy, George, 82–83, 91n
Relativity
  of truth, 193
  of value, 199–200
Relevance, 157–158, 227–244, 251, 374
Repetitions, casting, 135–136
Rhetoric, 332
Rhetorical features, casting, 135–140
Rhetorical fallacy, 211, 216–222
Rhetorical questions, 220
Ridicule, fallacy of diversion through, 242
Roscho, Bernard, 91n
Rorchler, Richard, 91n
Russell, Bertrand, 366

Schrank, Jeffrey, 43
Scriven, Michael, 121

Self-deception, 11
Sensory acuity, observations and, 195–196
Series structure, 119
Seven-step format, 277–289
Sexual pitches in advertising, 51
Signal words, 98–102, 188, 278
  conclusion, 98
  deductive, 188
  general area premise, 99–100
  inductive, 188
  specific premise, 101
  arguments with no, 102
Singer, Dorothy and Jerome, 91n
Slippery slope, fallacy of, 263–264
Smith, Jack, 211
Soundness, 176
Sources in news, 82–87
Specific premise signals, 101
Statistics, 190–191, 252–257
Strategies, in problem solving, 373, 376–378
Straw person, fallacy of, 243–244
Stipulative definition, 33–34
Subliminal advertising, 51–52
Sufficient conditions, 31
Surveys, 252–255
Syntax, 26

Television, 63–70
Testimonials, 234
Thesis, 298–300, 304, 332–338
Thought, 63
Topic coverage strategy, 158
Topics, 36, 299–300, 333–338, 355–356
Tradition, fallacy of appeal to, 237
Truth, 78, 175, 192–193
  necessary, 194
  verification and, 193–205
Two wrongs, fallacy of, 242–243
Tu Quoque fallacy, 243

Unexpressed conclusions, 104–107, 133–134
Unexpressed premises, 105, 133–134, 149–168

Unexpressed premises and conclusions, casting, 104–107,
   133–134, 149–168
Unwarranted assumptions, 265–270
Urban VIII (Pope), 11

Validity of arguments, 175–190
   deductive, 179–188
   inductive, 187–190
Vagueness, 36
   abuse of, 216
   in advertising, 44–47

Value judgments, 197–205
Verification, 193–205
   of factual assertions, 195–197
   of value judgments, 194,
      197–205

Weasel words, 46–47
"What if" strategy, 154–155
Wishful thinking, 11
Words, 21, 25–26, 28
Wordsworth, William, 23–24
Writing, 355–359